Basic Income - From Vision to Creeping Transformation of the Welfare State

Rolf G. Heinze • Jürgen Schupp

Basic Income - From Vision to Creeping Transformation of the Welfare State

Springer VS

Rolf G. Heinze
Fakultät für Sozialwissenschaft
Ruhr Universität Bochum
Bochum, Germany

Jürgen Schupp
SOEP
Deutsches Institut für Wirtschaftsforschung
& Freie Universität
Berlin, Germany

ISBN 978-3-658-40268-6 ISBN 978-3-658-40269-3 (eBook)
https://doi.org/10.1007/978-3-658-40269-3

This book is a translation of the original German edition „Grundeinkommen – Von der Vision zur schleichenden sozialstaatlichen Transformation" by Heinze, Rolf G., published by Springer Fachmedien Wiesbaden GmbH in 2022. The translation was done with the help of artificial intelligence (machine translation by the service DeepL.com). A subsequent human revision was done primarily in terms of content, so that the book will read stylistically differently from a conventional translation. Springer Nature works continuously to further the development of tools for the production of books and on the related technologies to support the authors.

This Springer VS imprint is published by the registered company Springer Fachmedien Wiesbaden GmbH, part of Springer Nature.
The registered company address is: Abraham-Lincoln-Str. 46, 65189 Wiesbaden, Germany

Foreword

In recent years, a number of books and articles have been published on the subject of unconditional basic income (UBI – in this book we refer to the German abbreviation BGE), and the topic has also been discussed in political parties, trade unions, and economic and social associations. In terms of content, it has been examined both interdisciplinarily and in international comparison. For the most part, the debates were bipolar: people were either against or in favour, and normative and emotional lines of argument were put forward. But even in the balanced argumentative (often social science) publications, the question of implementation or the conditions for success and the identification of possible blockages were only dealt with marginally. Recent publications on a BGE, which have been widely received in the media, also display this political-institutional "blindness", for example by calling for simply abolishing the institutional structure of the welfare state. "This also eliminates social contributions. There is no longer a parallel welfare state structure fed by wage contributions alongside the basic income financed by taxes. This eliminates the anachronism that nowadays only a part of the population up to a capped contribution assessment ceiling is subject to compulsory social insurance – namely, dependent employees – while everyone else is not" (Straubhaar 2021, p. 45). If there is no transfer strategy, the idea will fail with this implementation naivety, even if many facts about basic security are aptly analysed. In the following, the state of the debate on basic income will therefore be developed further, if not overcome, by integrating it into welfare state development processes and current challenges for "securing social security".

In addition, the reasons for the *failure* so far of such far-reaching welfare state restructuring strategies are discussed. Despite a large front of rejection, elements of a basic income have nevertheless increasingly seeped into the reality of the welfare state. The historical localisation shows this "silent" change towards a socially investing welfare state, which has been going on for some time, and points to current alliances for the expansion of a *universalistic basic income*. In the autumn of 2021, during the last phase of the Bundestag election campaign, a broad alliance of 22 civil society organisations, associations and trade unions went public with a joint demand for the introduction of a basic child allowance in order to eradicate child poverty, which has been high in Germany for years, during the next legislative period. Such a tax-financed basic security for the equal financial treatment of *all* children would be a further concrete step towards a fundamental transformation of the welfare state in Germany.

The fact that so much attention is currently being paid to the basic income narrative is also due to the Corona pandemic that has been rampant since spring 2020, which has highlighted existing weaknesses in the welfare state architecture and brought about systemic changes in the social security system that had been delayed for some time. Thus, in the Corona crisis, a *low-condition basic income* was established in the field of social policy, which *at* least temporarily overcomes the functional deficits of traditional social policy measures. An unconditional basic income offers the chance to alleviate energy-sapping existential fears and to give people confidence, especially in times of necessary comprehensive changes, such as digitalisation and the decarbonisation of the economy. In other socio-political fields, too, discussion forums and networks have proliferated – driven by the new social media – calling for social experiments, similar to those in comparable countries, to find out more about how an unconditional basic income would work in real terms and perhaps also provide a superior alternative to the status quo. Even if the groups of people can certainly not be representative, they are an indication of the *states of exhaustion of* the classic welfare state, which is suffering from a loss of legitimacy, especially among the younger generation.

But it is not only the professionally staged campaigns on basic income that point to the increased interest in a *transformation of* the traditional system of social security. This also applies to old-age provision, the future viability of which has been repeatedly invoked by a number of commissions on the part of the government, but which nevertheless raises considerable doubts, particularly from the scientific side, as to whether this can be solved with the conventional measures. In the early summer of 2021, an expert opinion on pension reform caused a stir, which once again pointedly summarised data that had also been available for some time and referred to the need for a fundamental reform. Like other reform proposals, these fell flat, giving the impression that the responsible actors in this political-institutional arena have no interest in a public debate on complex issues (non-decision-making).

There are thus many reasons to treat the basic income issue beyond the well-worn and often ideologically coloured strands of argumentation as an answer to welfare state problems, especially as the challenges are becoming rather greater, and not only due to external effects such as the Corona pandemic. Here, one should think of the demographic change that has been taking place for several decades now, and in particular the ageing of the population, as well as the digitalisation processes with all their effects on the German model of social security, which is centred on gainful employment. It is not only the proliferation of home-offices triggered by the Corona crisis and spreading abruptly that point to a *transformation of work*, but overall digitalisation and the flexibilisation and individualisation that has grown with it in individual sectors of the economy are accelerating the erosion of traditional collective protection for employees that have been observed for many years. According to estimates, this affects almost half of current jobs and requires new institutional labour and social policy safeguards. The usual *time lag*, for example in the political handling of demographic challenges, is no longer likely to be an adequate response, because, as in climate policy, time is pressing and civil society counter-movements are forming.

The losses in collective security are offset by gains in freedom through the digitisation processes, which have so far only been used by the privileged groups of workers. These ambivalences make it difficult to reach a collective consensus, which is also evident from the fact that the trade unions' power to shape policy has been considerably weakened in recent years. When considering these broadly publicised questions, it is striking why, despite the developments that have been foreseeable for some time and the associated risks that now appear in crisis mode as if in a *burning glass*, socio-political actors cling to the fiction of a sustainable model. One reason for this may be that for years now they have failed to make the emerging undesirable developments the subject of political debate and to put forward fundamental proposals for reform. Admitting these failures could lead to further losses of legitimacy for the governing parties and is therefore not only avoided, but the (previous) functioning of the welfare state is used to raise their own profile. However, increasing *scepticism* is also spreading in Germany on this issue, so that this strand of legitimacy is in danger of fading.

We have therefore included political science research on the rationality limits and performance of politics in our consideration and used the multiple streams approach to classify the delays and appeasements of normality analytically. It became clear – and this applies not only to the arena of social and labour market policy, but also strikingly to climate and energy policy – that several "streams" have to come together in order to initiate systemic reforms that affect existing organisational cultures and structures and thus existing interests. And since social security is a *sensitive issue* in Germany in particular, touching many people quickly, especially in times of crisis, party-political actors tend to focus more on continuation of the status quo and thus on meeting expectations of continuity. If corrections are unavoidable in some areas (such as pensions), they are made in small doses. With regard to working life, for example, such corrections have been introduced, and these in themselves have caused considerable unrest. Due to such experiences with negative effects on the election results of the responsible parties, when major systemic changes are made (such as with the "Agenda 2010" under Chancellor Gerhard Schröder), a defensive policy aimed at reliability continues to be preferred. However, the short-term political advantages of *suppressing reality* or the reaction that sets in with a time lag – be it in the case of the climate challenges or the lack of sustainability of the traditional security systems – tend to intensify the constraints on action in the medium term, and there is no time to implement the risks of a transformation in a democratically legitimized manner and in conformity with the constitution by means of checks and balances and without emergency decrees. For the most part, government policy was only corrected in its basic direction by external effects such as nuclear accidents or pandemics. However, no implementation consensus can yet be derived from the treatment of the issue and also in the case of a consensus on action, which can currently be studied in a sustainable manner in German energy and climate policy.

Even if from a political science perspective an interpretative foil is offered for the insufficient responsiveness of the political-administrative system and the limits of political control with regard to basic income demands, there are nevertheless options for policy change. On the one hand, there is a *creeping transformation*, and on the other hand, policy can be put under pressure by external actors and actions. Against the backdrop of the declining binding power of the major popular parties, political issues are also making it onto the agenda through new forms of protest and social media, which have been neglected by established political actors. In this way, politicians are driven to react in ways that can be boosted by new government constellations. However, it is impossible to predict when such a window ("window of opportunity") will open. From a social science perspective, we attempt not only to reconstruct the hesitant course of systemic reforms and to sketch the silent change, but also to point out perspectives for a new welfare state project.

But here, too, it is important to overcome bipolar strands of argumentation. It is *not a question* of the alternative between an unconditional basic income versus a socio-ecological and democratic infrastructure state; rather, a sustainable social security system must include both elements of a basic income and a non-profit provision of general interest at the local level. Such a change of path will, according to all experience, be gradual and follow the creeping change of welfare state control logics in the direction of a *universalistic welfare state.* However, since the welfare state also represents a cultural good and enjoys high recognition, a new model will slowly spread and gradually shape the signature of society.

Whether an unconditional basic income will be introduced in the medium or long term, or whether at least lower-condition forms of basic security or even elements of a partial basic income for individual population groups will be introduced in the individual branches of the social system, has not yet been decided. This open question prompted the authors of this book to undertake an up-to-date, social-science motivated classification of the current state of the debate on an unconditional basic income and to "survey" the political landscape with regard to this topic. In doing so, we focus on the current *interfaces of* a BGE and the institutionalized socio-political overlaps and extensions. Nevertheless, the vision of an unconditional basic income reaches further than pure social policy. It also poses challenges and possible new responses in the areas of labour market, family and social policy. In addition, it is our common conviction that the current – often very passionately presented – front positions of proponents of a BGE on the one hand and opponents on the other hand should be overcome in order not to prematurely reject possible future development paths due to thought blockades.

Although the authors are united in their high regard for the current system of social security in Germany, they are no less sceptical about the medium- and long-term sustainability of this system. Against this background, we are therefore committed to *exploring* possible new guarantee elements of social security, but link this option to the socially comparative promotion of a public infrastructure and activating social spaces that support the existing potential for engagement. The normative conflicts of values that are already smouldering in the foundations of social theory require a broad social debate on future social structures to be striven for or prevented.

However, there is a lack of convincing political actors (political entrepreneurs) on the political stage so far, who aggressively promote a structural reorientation of social security linked to more local enabling spaces. Instead of an offensive debate on a strategy of restructuring, new, non-systemic elements are being added to the existing system rather silently (e.g. the current demands for a basic child benefit, the fundamental *need for reform in* the area of contribution-financed old-age provision that flared up once again in the summer of 2021 (and had been suppressed for some time), and also the current accentuation of labour market policy such as the low-condition basic benefit in the wake of the Corona pandemic). These various pieces of the mosaic are evidence of *the* continuing *topicality of* social and labour market policy restructuring strategies, which must, however, go beyond the classic pro- and con-debate on an unconditional basic income and should also take up the desire in the population for trials on this subject without lapsing into morally discrediting defensive reflexes.

Bochum, Germany
Berlin, Germany
September 2021

Rolf G. Heinze
Jürgen Schupp

Contents

About the Authors

Rolf G. Heinze, Ruhr University Bochum, Faculty of Social Science, Germany

Jürgen Schupp, Senior Research Fellow at the German Institute for Economic Research (DIW Berlin) and Freie Universität Berlin, Germany

List of Figures

1 Crises as a Focal Point for Socio-Economic Problems

1.1 The Corona Pandemic as a Catalyst for Welfare State Transformation

The topic of basic income has gained popularity and media attention not only in Germany with the outbreak of the Covid 19 pandemic. In his current book, economist Thomas Straubhaar (2021) even invokes the "rescue of the market economy" through the introduction of an unconditional basic income (UBI) – in this book we refer to the German abbreviation BGE). In mid-March 2020, a petition for the introduction of a basic income was submitted to the Petitions Committee of the German Bundestag, which was supported by around 176,000 people (Deutscher Bundestag 2020a, b), making it one of the most successful petitions in a long time. It called for the introduction of an unconditional basic income of around €1000 per month for all citizens in the short term and for a limited period of time, due to the economic impact of the Corona pandemic and the associated loss of income for many citizens. Admittedly, the debate in the Petitions Committee did not take place until after the summer break at the end of October 2020, while the Federal Government pushed the Social Pact I through the debate in the Bundestag at parliamentary record speed and was able to bring it into force as early as May 2020. Attempts were made to cushion the social and economic consequences of the Corona pandemic for citizens by expanding the short-time working regulations and simplifying access to basic social security benefits.

In March 2021, a large number of additional social policy benefits were agreed as part of the Social Pact III and the previous time limits were generally extended until the end of 2021. The combined 353 billion in aid programmes and 819 billion

R. G. Heinze, J. Schupp, *Basic Income - From Vision to Creeping Transformation of the Welfare State*,
https://doi.org/10.1007/978-3-658-40269-3_1

in guarantees[1] provide a protective shield for employees, the self-employed and companies. It serves to provide social security for those who are existentially affected and is carried out both within the framework of existing social law options and, in addition, new population groups with negative tax payments are included. In addition, emergency aid for the self-employed and cultural workers has provided a temporary net of tax-financed social security. This is because the restrictions imposed by the pandemic suddenly meant that people who had previously been able to secure their livelihoods themselves through gainful employment were suddenly dependent on benefits from the basic security systems on a large scale. In total, the federal government borrowed around €130 billion for its budget in 2020 and another €240 billion in 2021 as part of a supplementary budget[2] . As a result, the debt ceiling of the Basic Law was also significantly exceeded and a reduction of the debt is currently not expected before 2023.

In a simulation study presented in spring 2021, the Institut der Deutschen Wirtschaft (IW) even assumes that federal, state and local government debt will rise to €650 billion by 2022, of which around €480 billion is classified as corona-related (Beznoska et al. 2021). Thus, even more than the Corona-related economic slumps, a large number of fiscal policy measures (support for the healthcare system, companies or private households) taken by the federal, state and local governments to cope with and overcome the pandemic have had an impact since spring 2020. As these Corona measures are generally temporary, they only have a temporary impact on the national budget. Nevertheless, the Deutsche Bundesbank[3] assumes that these measures taken together will have increased the government deficit by an estimated three percent of GDP in 2020 alone. Or to put it another way: according to calculations by the Federal Ministry of Finance, the government deficit in 2021 has increased to nine percent of GDP, which would be more than twice as much as in 2020 (Fig. 1.1).

According to the IW's April 2021 estimates, and based on modelling an intact economy without Corona and a comparison with real development, GDP losses from January 2020 to June 2021 will total around €300 billion.

[1] Bundesfinanzministerium – Fight against Corona: Largest aid package in Germany's history

[2] https://www.bundesfinanzministerium.de/Content/DE/Standardartikel/Themen/Oeffentliche_Finanzen/Bundeshaushalt/2020-09-23-bundeshaushalt-2021-und-finanzplan-bis-2024.html

[3] Deutsche Bundesbank (2021). Public Finance. Monthly Bulletin, February 2021, pp. 70–84.

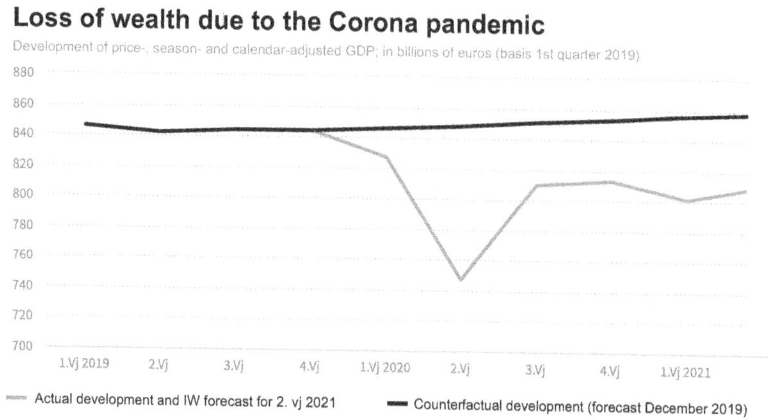

Fig. 1.1 Development of price-, season- and calendar-adjusted gross domestic product (GDP) – in billions of euros (basis first quarter 2019). (Source: IW 2021)

Against this backdrop, it can be assumed that it will take several years for the economy to overcome the economic setbacks. In view of these current developments and the aid packages worth billions in public spending, which were also described as a "bazooka"[4] by the responsible Federal Finance Minister Olaf Scholz, even the main argument usually put forward against a BGE, namely that it simply "cannot be financed", has been put into perspective.[5] In labour market policy and the employment service, the existing processes of administrative action and regulations that were regarded as indispensable were adapted and in some cases completely redesigned within a few days of the start of the lockdown in March 2020, with the new regulations clearly moving in the direction of a lower-condition security system. The social protection package with far-reaching procedural changes in Book II of the Social Code (in the following SGB II), the short-time working allowance, emergency aid for companies amounting to billions and much more was passed within a few days by the German Bundestag, the Bundesrat and the state parliaments with large political majorities. The players in public administration, but also chambers and associations, found themselves in a state of emergency in which many habits, rituals and procedures and necessities that had been established

[4] https://www.bundesfinanzministerium.de/Content/DE/Interviews/2020/2020-05-10-Tagesspiegel.html

[5] https://www.fr.de/meinung/corona-coronavirus-wirtschaftskrise-bedingungsloses-grundeinkommen-olaf-scholz-13601317.html

as virtually irrevocable were discarded within hours and corresponding decisions had to be implemented.

It is difficult to imagine that after the temporary legislation within labour market and social policy, which in many cases will expire at the end of 2021, all actors will return to familiar bureaucratic routines and procedures as they applied before Corona. In autumn 2021, it is more likely that the topic of social policy in the form of "social justice" will be given a dominantly important role within the election campaign for the Bundestag elections, especially in its hot phase[6] . However, it is still unclear whether a future coalition government – not least to initiate a debt limit – intends to save substantial funds in social policy, return to the level before the Corona crisis or perhaps also use the *momentum* to tackle more far-reaching welfare state reforms combined with public infrastructure investment. "Unconditional basic income offers more than a utopian response to the dystopian experience of the Corona pandemic. It is a timely modernisation of old tried and tested principles of the social market economy that made Germany, Austria and Switzerland so successful in the post-war period. It allows for a rebalanced interplay of 'freedom', 'security' and 'justice'. It is non-partisan and equally liberal and social. This makes it capable of winning a majority for socially broad-based movements beyond old party structures" (Straubhaar 2021, p. 238). The societal problematic situations shine more clearly under the burning glass of the Corona pandemic, defining multiple tasks for government actors and policy management. "We need to talk about the development of a new resilient infrastructure, about the entrepreneurial state, the investing state, but also about what a culture of public goods actually means and what the meaning of subsidiarity is in such a culture" (Bude 2021, p. 55).

Even before the Corona pandemic, increasing attention was being drawn to the challenges of a fragmented society with growing social polarisation and ecological threats, which in the medium term probably cannot be solved by the established institutions of welfare state security. For example, in the context of the sixth Poverty and Wealth Report of the Federal Government, a longitudinal study found that there has been a systematic *decline in* upward mobility from lower social strata of poverty or precariousness in Germany over the last 30 years (cf. Groh-Samberg et al. 2020). Whether and to what extent a complete transfer of the predominantly contribution-financed system of social security into a purely tax-financed system of an unconditional basic income could already represent a superior future alternative is assessed with marked scepticism in the current debate, even if critical voices are

[6] Cf. https://www.zdf.de/nachrichten/politik/politbarometer-bundestagswahl-spd-union-100.html?slide=1615298015943 and https://civey.com/umfragen/3013/welches-politische-thema-ist-ihnen-aktuell-am-wichtigsten

increasing. For example, in their recent book on the *fundamental need for reform of* social policy, the two 2019 Nobel laureates in economics state, "The goal of social policy in these times of change and adjustment should be to help people cope with the upheavals without damaging their sense of self-worth. Unfortunately, the existing system does not provide for that. Our social security is still dominated by Victorian notions, and all too many politicians don't even try to hide their contempt for the poor and disadvantaged. And even with a change in attitude, social policy needs a fundamental rethink and is in desperate need of creative new ideas and approaches" (Banerjee and Duflo 2020, p. 482 f.).

Against the background of the pandemic, this assessment is currently finding a fertile resonance and in the next few years will also stimulate the debate in Germany on the future viability of the classical welfare state. According to our thesis, the abrupt turnaround in labour market and social policy initiated by the Corona crisis policy has led to a (partial) erosion of traditional administrative procedures and close-meshed regulations both in the field of social security and in labour administration, which will have long-term effects on the micro-level and on the macro-level of administrative action. These lasting consequences will take effect in the discourse on a basic income or on a social investment content aimed at promoting socially productive activities, and will complement and probably sharpen the previous narratives, since new experiences are now being made with a *low-condition basic* income – even if not yet with a basic income.

A current referendum on the immediate introduction of a basic income in Germany, similar to the 2016 referendum in Switzerland and the 2019 referendum in Austria, where the quorum for a referendum failed, would be completely hopeless. However, there is a growing number of initiatives, especially from civil society, that are seriously addressing the issue and, without ideological blinkers, are also carrying out scientifically accompanied practical trials of basic income payments. On the one hand, there is the association Sanktionsfrei (Sanctions-Free), which is primarily committed to abolishing the practice of sanctions in the basic income scheme for the long-term unemployed. But also the initiative Expedition Grundeinkommen (Expedition Basic Income) is attempting to bring about a limited, scientifically accompanied field trial lasting several years by means of referendums in individual federal states and local referendums. Currently, a widely discussed experiment with the basic income is being added. For example, the project cooperation presented in mid-August 2020 by the association Mein Grundeinkommen and the DIW Berlin in the form of a three-year field trial with a grant of €1200 per month (pilot project basic income) was followed both by very broad media (even international) coverage (SPIEGEL 2020) with expected sceptical comments and by an unexpectedly high level of willingness among the population to participate in the long-term study. This broad media attention of the topic of basic income, possibly also due to the "summer slump", also provoked at least a number of spontaneous, negative comments by politicians with government responsibility.

In this social debate, *sociology* has the task of closely observing the current special situation empirically, recording and critically reflecting on both intended and unintended positive and negative developments and dynamics, and drawing attention to signs of changing institutional policy arrangements. In addition, it should bring on board related disciplines such as economics or political science as well as psychology in a multi- and interdisciplinary treatment of issues and social debates. The premise should be that, contrary to expectations, situations that are unfamiliar in principle can also have positive effects and that trust can also represent the superior, more effective alternative to control in many individual as well as institutional moments. Hartmut Rosa has distinguished himself in the direction of a BGE, seeing in it the most plausible welfare state correlate to the post-growth society: "It gains its attractiveness precisely not from a promise of increase and increment, as materialized, for example, in the lockable sequence of wage struggles, but from the fact that it would be able to switch the basic mode of being-in-the-world from *struggle* to *security* and thus take existential *fear* (of social death, which I have identified as a comprehensive loss of resonance) out of play, without undermining a positive economic incentive structure or the possibility of rediscovering libidinous labor relations, as outlined by Marcuse. On the contrary, it is only on the basis of a basic income that the horizontal and diagonal resonance quality of work could really be developed and put to use. Productivity and innovative capacity would possibly even increase as a result, but this increase would not be mechanically enforced" (Rosa 2016, p. 730).

In this sense, there is currently a great *opportunity for* the actors involved, for example, to view the current situation in the employment service as a laboratory for incremental reforms in SGB II and in doing so to tie in with the concept of experimental rooms or innovation laboratories developed in the BMAS. In general, experienced administrative experts such as the chairman of the National Standards Control Council (based in the Federal Chancellery), Johannes Ludewig, see the current crisis as an opportunity for fundamental reforms of state administration, after the state revealed considerable deficits in administrative action during the Corona pandemic. Precisely because the administration is the central "tool" for policy implementation, opportunities for sweeping reforms – also coupled with digitisation options – should now be sought. "An efficient, customer-oriented administration is nowadays a digital administration" (in: Bernau 2021). The maxim should apply: "The fact that something is formally done correctly is the necessary prerequisite for good action, but not a sufficient one. What is sufficient is that citizens and businesses are satisfied. Many administrative lawyers do not have an eye and a feeling for this" (loc. Cit.; cf. on administrative reforms also Bogumil and Jann 2020, p. 290ff.).

Therefore, the experiments started in the employment service should be broadened, although the period of a trial is of limited duration and the outcome is open. However, before returning to the usual agenda, it is important to scientifically evaluate or accompany the experiences of even new *innovative ideas* and to discuss findings in an open-ended manner. Thus, after more than 15 years after the introduction of the Hartz reforms, there is still no study on the fundamental effectiveness of sanctions – also in the light of the concealed criticism of the legislator by the BVerfG – and it seems high time that more experimental studies on the effectiveness of regulations with fewer sanctions were carried out on this controversial instrument of current welfare state practice. A recently presented register-based study by the IAB, in which the integration of sanctioned SGB II recipients into the labour market was examined in comparison to a statistical control group, does little to change this. Nevertheless, the ambivalent effect of sanctions imposed by the welfare state is once again empirically proven: "Sanctions can have a negative effect both on the employment history of those sanctioned and on their sustainable integration into the labour market. This in turn can make it more difficult to strengthen the personal responsibility of benefit recipients and their long-term integration into the labour market, as called for in Section 1 of Book II of the Social Code. When sanctions are applied, there thus tends to be a conflict of objectives between rapid and sustainable employment integration" (Wolf 2021). However, sanctions are still presumed to be more effective than a regime without sanctions. "Whether imposed sanctions increase the willingness to cooperate by intensifying the job search has not been empirically proven so far. Likewise, it has not yet been investigated and, due to the ubiquitous effect, it is also hardly verifiable how high the so-called ex ante effect of sanctions is" (BVerfG 2019, para. 61).

The court objected to paternalistic interpretations of the duties to cooperate enshrined in SGB II. "In contrast, a legitimate aim of such duties to cooperate cannot be seen in promoting the development of one's own personality. Such paternalism is alien to the Basic Law. There is no "sovereignty of reason" of state bodies over those entitled to fundamental rights; rather, the Basic Law demands respect for the autonomous self-determination of individuals" (BVerfG 2019, para. 12). The mandate given by the BVerfG to the legislator to present a constitutional reform in the Social Code for the practice of sanctions will also provide a broad public stage for the topic of "unconditional granting of basic security benefits" at the latest during the associated parliamentary debate. By analysing the social experiment of a simplified and less conditional basic income in the field of labour market policy triggered by the Corona pandemic, one of the essential questions regarding the effects of a more broadly based basic income could also be answered far better than in the experiments with a sanction-free basic income which have been regionally and socially limited so far.

With a view to fundamental reforms, however, there is also a *need for* further *action* that goes beyond the Corona crisis and has been discussed for decades (for example, the demographic challenges in old-age provision, which are being accentuated anew by the accelerated digitisation processes). Some time ago, the unconditional basic income was discussed as a promising answer to the ever-increasing deficits in the traditional employment-centred security system. As we will show, this discussion has increasingly moved out of the ivory tower and into a broader public sphere, and is getting new impetus, especially through digital social media as well as the Corona crisis. "Society now needs a positive blueprint of a successful, happy future – precisely as a counter-world to the dystopia of the Corona era. Basic income meets that very need. It is the heart of a New Deal for the twenty-first century – a true generational contract of today's society with its children's children. It provides a framework that meets a truly sustainable aspiration of our time: to hand over a better world to future generations" (Straubhaar 2021, p. 227).

This also raises structural questions about basic income. Kovce and Priddat see three basic strands of argumentation with regard to an unconditional basic income, which its advocates must confront: "Firstly, how could it be financed? Secondly, who would then still be working? Third, how could it be experimented with?" (this. 2019, p. 17). Related to an implementation and dovetailing with our existing welfare state model, a pressing fourth question would therefore be: *"How do we transfer the current subordination of the community of need as a claimant for benefits in our Social Code into a purely individual citizen's right to a basic income?"*, which would also require a further development of our tax system into a strictly individual-oriented taxation model. Undoubtedly, while such more guaranteed benefits of citizenship would come at a high cost, unconditional entitlements make it easier to include *all* citizens in the provision of benefits, as non-claiming due to social shame, stigma and uninformedness would be virtually eliminated.

1.2 Narratives and Conjunctures of the Public and Academic Debate on Basic Income

The year of the outbreak of the Corona pandemic in Germany probably marks a preliminary historical peak in public awareness of the topic of basic income. In his most recent book, Robert J. Shiller, winner of the Nobel Prize for Economics in 2013, deals with economic narratives (ibid. 2020) and their recurrence and mutations. If one assigns the topic of unconditional basic income to recurring narratives, then three recurring topics and, due to Corona, a fourth topic can be assigned:

- Changes in the *world of work* and the fear of mass unemployment (from automation, digitalisation, artificial intelligence and the elimination of activities/jobs to support in the care and alternative economy)
- *Demographic change* and the increasing burdens of a "contribution-financed" social security system as well as the declining belief of young cohorts in long-term contribution equivalence (especially with regard to old-age provision) – (argument of reducing social bureaucracy)
- *Socio-political arguments (autonomy)* with the demand for subsistence and minimum security *as an individual civil right* as well as the *decoupling* of *gainful employment and income* – end of "hidden poverty" as well as sanctions as well as external determination of work – "motivating instead of punishing" – further development or even transformation of the "conservative welfare state regime" (Esping-Andersen 1990) into a guaranteeist model of participation
- *Reduction of (existential) fears* in the event of external shocks (e.g. Corona pandemic or also the ecological restructuring with decarbonisation to achieve the climate targets in 2030)

However, the current substantive debate on basic income so far still resembles a philosophical salon in good moments, while in bad moments it is still mainly a religious war of personal opinions or assumptions and is rarely based on sound and evidence-based knowledge. The debate is dominated – on both sides – by *clichés* as well as *stereotypes:* Opponents claim that with a basic income, people would stop working or become socially isolated, driving the division of the population into those who continue to work and those who rely solely on basic income. Proponents argue that people would not make mass use of their future choice to refuse bad work and would continue to pursue fulfilling work, become more creative and charitable, strengthen social cohesion and save democracy.

First of all, a *definition of the term:* What is a basic income and which central prerequisites would remain in place even if a basic income were to be implemented politically? A BGE grants every citizen of a country a permanent and unlimited (from the individual's point of view, lifelong) individual basic income that secures his or her existence, prevents poverty and enables social participation. Such a legal entitlement would exist without a priority obligation to pursue gainful employment or other obligations, as well as without drawing on existing own or family income or asset resources of the spouse or other dependants.

The principle of unconditionality thus implies empowering individuals *ex-ante,* rather than supporting *ex-post* those whose own resources or reserves are no longer sufficient. This is seen as the innovative emancipatory potential of a BGE and the gained individual freedom "to be able to say no" (Widerquist 2013, p. 187). This delimitation, which is propagated in Germany by the Basic Income Network, is based more on the claim of securing a livelihood and enabling social participation, on the welfare state requirement of the German constitution and on securing the socio-cultural subsistence minimum of every citizen, and is therefore also more comprehensive than the approach advocated by the Basic Income Earth Network (BIEN)[7] or by the World Bank, which also speaks of a basic income even if it is only partially able to secure subsistence (cf. Gentilini et al. 2020).

A BGE also remains linked to necessary fulfilled preconditions; these include that a nation state remains in a position to generate sufficient financial resources on a sustainable basis by means of tax revenues in order to continue to meet its other state obligations in areas such as education, justice, internal and external security, road construction and regional mobility, energy, communications infrastructure, health, etc. to a sufficient extent in addition to the usually monthly payment of a BGE to citizens, and that the polity continues to be organised democratically, freely and on the basis of solidarity. Nevertheless, there are differences depending on the design of the various existing basic income models, to what extent benefits currently paid out by the welfare state should continue to be paid to people with special needs (e.g. health restrictions), or whether the welfare state should be completely replaced by the model of a basic income. As a result, there are also many very different ideas in the debate on basic income in Germany, especially since the history of basic income has both liberal roots and a number of origins critical of capitalism to overcome distributional problems (cf. on this Kovce and Priddat 2019).

Topics of basic security as well as the BGE have not only been in the public discussion since the outbreak of the Corona pandemic. This can be shown visually

[7] https://basicincome.org/

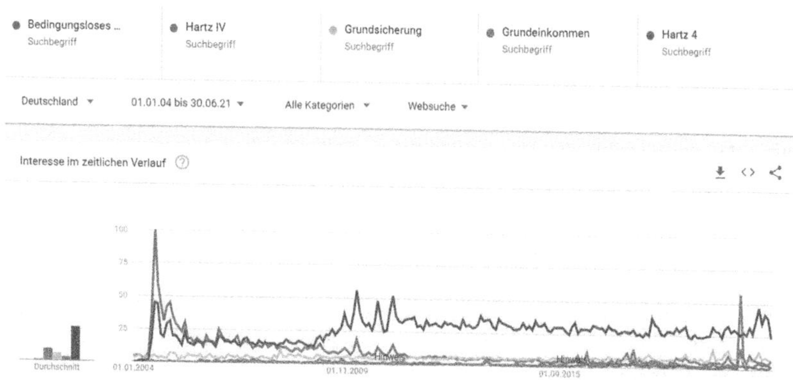

Fig. 1.2 Development of the frequency of search queries to Google from 1.1.2004 to 1.07.2021. (Source: https://trends.google.de/trends/explore?date= -01-01%202021-06-30&geo=DE&q=Bedingungsloses%20Grundeinkommen,Hartz%20IV,Grundsicherung,Grundeinkommen,Hartz%204)

with the help of Fig. 1.2, which documents the development of selected terms over time on the basis of Google searches. Thus, in economics as well as in the social sciences, thanks to the growing access to large amounts of data and to more powerful IT resources, data from Internet search queries have been used for some time to determine conjunctures of moods or topics in public debates. Data from Google Trends (Choi and Varian 2012) are distinguished by the fact that, unlike expensive surveys, they are publicly available and also easily reproducible as well as updatable. Even though each Google search is done for very different reasons, conclusions about the public's interests, concerns, or intentions on particular topics can be drawn from a large amount of aggregated search data.

The values of the Y-axis indicate the search interest relative to the highest point in the diagram for the selected region (Germany) in the specified period (1.1.2004–30.06.2021). The value 100 represents the highest popularity of this search term. The value 50 means that the term is half as popular and the value 0 means that there was not enough data for this term.

Figure 1.2 now shows the development of the frequency of search queries from the field of the debate up to the middle of the year 2021 since the last major welfare state debate with the introduction of the Hartz IV basic security as well as the reform of social assistance in 2005. The following five terms were used as search terms: Unconditional Basic Income/Basic Income, Hartz 4/IV and the search term Basic Security.

While the search term Hartz IV dominated over the entire period and only the spelling of the Roman numeral IV used by the Federal Agency on its homepage has been replaced by the Arabic numeral 4 since around 2008, the search terms unconditional basic income/basic income first appeared somewhat more frequently in 2009. This is probably due above all to the model of the "solidary citizen's income" propagated by the then Thuringian Minister President Dieter Althaus, but also to the liberal citizen's income model favoured by the FDP. The topic first began to receive really noticeable attention in autumn 2013, when a first popular initiative for an unconditional basic income was initiated in Switzerland. When a referendum was held in all cantons in Switzerland in June 2016, the popular initiative failed with an approval rate of only 23% and a participation rate of 46% of all eligible Swiss voters.

The activists of the popular initiative also explained that, despite the rejection by the Swiss population, the basic income had won in any case, as one of the aims of the vote had been to promote the issue of basic income and the necessary change in awareness by means of an internationally perceptible debate. A second initiative on the subject of basic income is currently being prepared in Switzerland (cf. Sect. 6.6).

Since then, the topic of (unconditional) basic income has also regularly featured in the public debate, with comparatively low search frequency. In Finland, for example, a government-funded pilot project on basic income for the long-term unemployed was launched in 2017, with interim results of the experimental study being presented in early 2019, which also attracted widespread international attention. In 2020, the aforementioned pandemic-related calls for the introduction of a temporary basic income led to a steady increase in search queries on the topic of basic income. The peak index value of over 50 in the month of August 2020 is probably due above all to the great attention paid to the announcement of the basic income pilot project, as a result of which more than one million interested people registered on an Internet portal of the non-profit association My Basic Income within three days[8] (cf. Sect. 1.7). At the same time, this led for the first time to a higher rate for the search term basic income than Hartz 4. The second public announcement of the start of payments for the pilot project in June 2021, on the other hand, also led to a slight increase in search frequency, but significantly lower than the call for recruitment to the study.

However, to what extent is the topic of BGE also a topic of increased and growing attention within the academic debate? For this purpose, a so-called "culturomics"

[8] https://www.spiegel.de/wirtschaft/soziales/grundeinkommen-studie-erreicht-eine-million--bewerber-binnen-70-stunden-a-380d1b7a-419f-4139-bad1-8f794dd80783

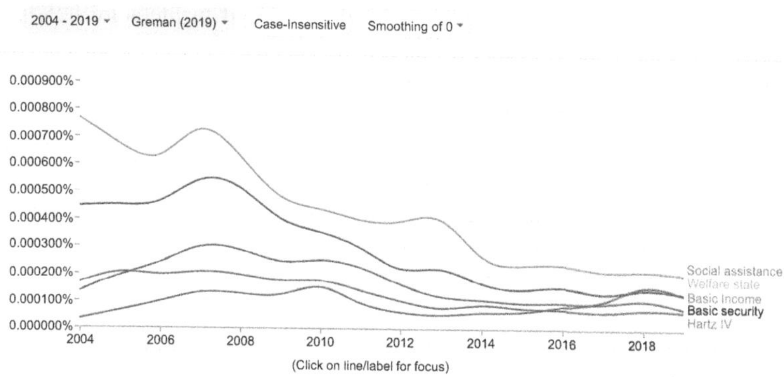

Fig. 1.3 Development of the frequency of terms of the book stocks recorded in German from 1.1.2004 to 31.12.2019. (Source: https://books.google.com/ngrams/graph?content=Grundeinkommen%2CHartz+IV%2CGrundsicherung%2CSozialhilfe%2CSozialstaat&year_start=2004&year_end=2019&corpus=31&smoothing=0). Note: The y-axis shows the percentage of searched terms in relation to all terms within the available literature for the searched criteria. In this case, the searched criteria were the terms from 2004 to 2019 with the search term "Hartz-IV, basic security, basic income, welfare state as well as social assistance". The x-axis shows the years

approach as well as the library holdings that have been made by Google for years are used (cf. Younes and Reips 2017).

Figure 1.3 shows, based on a corresponding query, that for almost the same[9] period and the same terms Hartz-IV, Grundsicherung, Grundeinkommen, Sozialstaat as well as Sozialhilfe, that in the German-language literature recorded by Google, the term Grundeinkommen rose continuously from a lower level and showed a first peak of increased index values for the first time in 2010 and then the frequency dropped in the following three years. This initial boom was probably also due to the debate on the citizen's income at the time. At the same time, however, it is clear that in this first phase of the growing relevance of the concept of basic income, terms such as Hartz IV and basic income support appeared with noticeably greater frequency in library collections.

Since 2013, the frequency of the term basic income has been rising steadily, while the terms Hartz IV and Grundsicherung are already appearing less frequently than basic income in library collections. The term welfare state, which was still used much more frequently in 2004, has also fallen significantly in frequency since 2008 and is on a par with the term basic income in 2019. Only the term social wel-

[9]The current value for 2020 is currently not available, so the time series ends in 2019.

fare is used most frequently of the five words examined in literature holdings throughout the entire observation period; however, the use of this term also halved over time compared to the initial year. This empirical evidence, which is certainly only superficial, nevertheless documents that the topic of unconditional basic income has gained in popularity in recent years and that curiosity about the topic has obviously increased. It is, of course, quite another question whether this increased attention to basic income will already be in a position to increasingly influence or even dominate the debate on social security reform.

1.3 Main Forms and Alternatives of a Basic Security System

The concept of a basic income has thus been enjoying a boom in the public and academic debate on the welfare state for some time now, although very different forms can be associated with it within the debate on basic security. In accordance with the welfare state requirement of the German Basic Law[10] and in conjunction with the protection of human rights enshrined in Article 1, every citizen in Germany is guaranteed the socio-cultural minimum subsistence level. This principle and connection was also confirmed by the Federal Constitutional Court (BVerfG) in its ruling on the legality of sanctions in social law.[11] In its ruling, the court confirmed on the one hand the legality of obligations to cooperate on the part of the long-term unemployed and, on the other hand, defined the maximum amount of reductions in the level of basic welfare benefits. Accordingly, since the promulgation of the law, sanctions exceeding 30% of the basic income support may no longer be imposed in the future, as this is *not* seen as compatible with Article 1 of the Basic Law. According to the court, the reductions in the basic income support are not intended to "regressively punish misconduct", but to provide incentives to co-operate so that existential neediness is avoided, shortened and, in the best case, completely overcome. In addition, the general principle is confirmed that state benefits to secure a dignified existence are only to be granted on a *"subordinate" basis* and that they can therefore also be tied to duties to cooperate insofar as they are aimed at overcoming the need for assistance, provided that they are proportionate when measured against this objective.

[10] Justified in articles 20 and 28 of the Basic Law.

[11] See the BVerfG ruling of 5 November 2019. https://www.bundesverfassungsgericht.de/e/ls20191105_1bvl000716.html

On the other hand, the principle of action and value "whoever does not work, should not eat", which was often expressed at the time of the introduction of the Hartz IV laws, has been unequivocally prohibited by state institutions with the ruling of the BVerfG. Also, the previously applicable rigid sanction period of three months for benefit reductions is no longer considered proportionate and can since then be shortened by increased examination of exceptional cases of hardship. The amendments to the relevant paragraphs of the Social Code imposed by the court have since been complied with by ministerial instructions and regulations.

It should be remembered that "social politicians" and "exit propagandists" were equally involved in the debate on guaranteed minimum income in the 1980s: the "social politicians" were mainly concerned with the goal of protection against impoverishment for excluded problem groups and risks. For the "exit propagandists", protection from impoverishment was also on the list, but at least as important was "liberation from false work" (Schmid 1984). In concrete terms, this meant creating the material conditions for individuals to reject inhumane gainful employment, guaranteeing a financial basis for unconventional or alternative gainful employment, and providing economic and social security for self-help and communal forms of working and helping. Likewise, as early as the 1980s, the strategic consideration emerged that a guaranteed basic income could be used to promote the "emergence of a new, alternative entrepreneurship that practices the non-technological overcoming of the Fordist mode of production" (Schmid 1984, p. 16). To sum up, it can be stated that the "social politicians" favoured the base income models, while the "exit propagandists" sympathised with the negative income tax or the citizen's salary.

In the negative income tax model, a distinction is made between earned income, negative and positive tax and disposable income: earned income is the remuneration for wage labour, negative tax means transfer payments from the state and positive tax the payments to the treasury. In the case of low salaries, wages or salaries, disposable income results from earned income plus negative tax payments from the state; those earning higher incomes, on the other hand, still pay positive taxes. If earned income is zero, the maximum negative tax, i.e. the guaranteed minimum, is paid out. The amount of government payments decreases steadily as earned income increases. Normally, the negative income tax works with a fixed proportional tax rate, through which the transfer withdrawal rate (or tax rate for income above the guaranteed minimum) is determined. However, models in which lower incomes are taxed less than higher incomes are also conceivable. A *negative income tax* represents an integration of the tax and transfer system. At the same time, this would eliminate those parts of the current social administration that currently check and pay out welfare state benefit entitlements, or they would have to be transferred to tax authorities to increase staffing. Lower income earners could be subsidised with it via tax credits, which would have huge social policy effects and highlights the need for a joined up view of the tax and benefits system. "The effect of a negative income tax is effectively equivalent to an unconditional basic income" (Wagschal 2019, p. 823).

In a similar vein, the Citizen's Income (Bürgergeld) would also provide for an income-independent tax-financed payment from the state for all registered citizens in Germany. Like the current tax-free allowance, this would be tax-free, but taxes would have to be paid on all additional income earned. In contrast to the negative income tax, most German advocates of the *Citizen*'s Income do not consider the abolition of other social benefits. This is unlike the American economist Milton Friedman, who many "left-wing" basic income critics like to cite as a witness to neoliberal "ghosts" in the basic income community. In the basic income concepts, which are certainly regarded as worthy of discussion by the socio-political elites, the guaranteed minimum is to be achieved by raising all existing transfer payments in the existing social security system to a level measured by the socio-economic subsistence minimum through the introduction of means-tested foundations. The central sub-sectors of social security (pension and unemployment insurance, social assistance) should be harmonised with existing universal benefits such as child benefit and supplemented with further means-tested entitlements (e.g. in the case of severe health impairments).

A first courageous step towards such harmonisation was most recently implemented when unemployment assistance and social assistance were merged in 2005 in the newly created and synchronised Social Codes II and XII. Since the mid-1980s, proposals of this kind have appeared in trade union and social democratic concepts. In general, this would leave the social insurance systems responsible for their respective areas of risk, but would ensure a level of protection based on the level of social assistance according to uniform but means-tested and, above all, continuously means-tested criteria. The basic social security system in Germany currently follows precisely the administration-intensive principle of means-testing after receipt of a corresponding application for basic security benefits and the subordination of benefits granted.

In the case of means-tested basic income support, poverty traps and underprovision can generally no longer occur, but for people of working age the focus is still on gainful employment. A socketed social security system continues to be constructed around gainful employment and, after any contribution-financed benefit entitlements to Unemployment Benefit I expire after 12 months as a rule, allows further "voluntary" unemployment only as an exceptional condition. In addition, the means tests remain in place and, for the most part, there was no provision for an independent minimum benefit for inactive spouses, independent of the spouse's income. On the positive side, a means-tested basic income support would reduce the burden on social assistance enormously. Traditionally, the federal budget has been the guarantor for deficits in the social security system, which also led to a new regulation within the framework of the Hartz IV legislation and, in particular, relieved the municipalities financially.

Systematic deficits in the existing social security system were seen by a large number of otherwise very differently oriented social policy makers and social policy researchers. However, considerable differences of opinion can already be identified at that time (in the 1980s) in the proposals on how a benefit assessment independent of gainful employment, or a guaranteed minimum income, should look: Differences can be found, for example, in the size of the target group. For example, some proposals only envisage basic security in the pension system, while others advocate a guaranteed minimum as a perspective for the social security of the entire population. Another important criterion for differentiation is the relationship of the respective basic security mechanisms to the traditional, work-centred benefit assessment basis. Here, reference can be made, on the one hand, to concepts that seek to guarantee a minimum or basic income in place of all other social policy insurance benefits (with the exception of health, accident and long-term care insurance). On the other hand, it has been proposed to guarantee basic security in the form of top-up contributions to existing insurance entitlements in such cases where equivalence-oriented insurance benefits do not reach in. This is always the case if the social insurance schemes provide a level of security below or close to the level of social assistance, which is often the case in families with several children and only one working person.

Despite the different forms, the central idea of the basic security models is the same; however, in one aspect it breaks with the German welfare state model by supplementing the system of social security, which is centred on working hours and linked to the normal employment relationship, with a guaranteed minimum security. In the first wave of the welfare state restructuring debate, the arguments for such a reform were strongly related to the unemployment and poverty issue as well as the crisis of the labour society, which had already been discussed in the 1980s. If there is no return to full employment, social policy will produce more and more structural selectivities due to its design principles and will get into a legitimatory downward spiral. "The core idea of such citizens' rights to income is that the entitlement to sufficient income is decoupled from gainful employment (or from previous inactivity, from the willingness to work, from the demonstrable existence of exempting circumstances, etc.). In concrete terms, this would then mean that the proposals of the type 'negative income tax', 'citizen's income' or degressive income subsidies, which are now appearing on a broad front in the socio-political debate, would not take effect only when a person plays his role in the labour market (or formally prepares to do so, cf. Bafög), but already when he is merely in possession of civil rights" (Offe 1994, p. 804 f.).

Since the beginning of the debates, it has been argued against the different variants of a basic income independent of earned income that they run the risk of becoming a permanent subsidy for precarious and poorly paid employment and of accelerating the growth of a low-wage sector. A low-paid part-time job would then become financially acceptable as long as the minimum income and (low) earnings together amounted to a total disposable income that was just above the subsistence level. However, this objection was countered by the argument that subsidising or indirectly promoting work in the lower income range also offers a wealth of opportunities in terms of social, labour market and even economic policy. They could offer the prospect of creating many and, above all, secure (part-time) jobs in the area of alternative forms of organisation or provide financial backing for the establishment of micro-enterprises. Innovations in the economic and labour system could thus be promoted by means of a basic social security system, which is once again being emphasised in many discussions today.

In addition, it has been stressed from various sides that in the "protected" sectors (above all in human services) employment opportunities in the area of low-skilled work lie fallow. With a regulated income subsidy through the negative income tax, wage settlements below the previously applicable low rates would also be possible without privately disposable income melting away. In addition to the technical dimension, the legitimacy of such a system is equally significant. In particular, if it becomes obvious that minimum income recipients would be supported by the state without prior input and without the willingness to work in the future, a loss of legitimacy of such a social security system may have to be expected. "If a minority receives a citizen's income independent of gainful employment, then the (positive) tax-paying structural majority will be politically disposed to push down the level of this citizen's income in such a way that the supply-relieving effect approaches zero and only the alternative-free compulsion to work remains, which the market-liberal originators of the idea of the negative income tax have in mind anyway" (Offe 1994, p. 805).

In summary, the fundamental or systemic difference between an unconditional basic income and the forms of a basic income guaranteeing the socio-cultural minimum subsistence level that apply in Germany lies in the *order of priority in* which benefits are granted, as also emphasised by the BVerfG (2019). A "subordinate" granting, as in the Social Code in Germany, has the consequence that first of all an income- and asset-dependent needs test is carried out. With the exception of single-person households, basic security benefits are granted to so-called "needs groups" and thus do not constitute an individual entitlement. This expresses the fundamental idea of subsidiarity in the German welfare state system. Accordingly, the state gives priority to smaller social units, such as marriage or a community of need, before the state itself becomes active in providing assistance to the individuals of this social unit.

In addition, a corresponding application for the granting of basic security benefits must be submitted in due time and in an appropriate manner and must also be approved as an administrative act by the case workers for the granting of benefits after appropriate examination. Social law requires the authorities to investigate, advise and check the eligibility criteria for basic security benefits, even if they are based on information provided by the applicants themselves. Applicants and those in need of assistance then have legal recourse to defend themselves against such a decision. This is initially done by filing an objection. In its annual statistics for 2019, the Federal Employment Agency reports 660,179 decided appeals (disposals) against a benefit decision under SGB II (BA 2020). Of these, more than a third had their appeal upheld and more than half had their appeal rejected. The claimant can also take legal action against such a negative decision. If we then add the decisions upheld by appeal in 2019, the total proportion of appeals was around 41%. If one takes the approximately 20 million Hartz IV decisions in 2019 as a reference figure, this results in an *objection rate of* 3% and a *complaint rate* of 0.5%, or an *overall refund rate of* 1.2% for improper benefit decisions. Such a subordinate granting of minimum income benefits is therefore not error-free and also requires considerable bureaucratic expenditure both for the examination of claims and the provision of a social jurisdiction for appeal and legal action under the rule of law.

This implies that basic security benefits are only granted in a community of need if the applicant or other members of the community of need have no or too little income of their own and any "substantial" assets have already been used up. The level of benefits for the socio-cultural subsistence minimum is set uniformly throughout Germany[12], while any costs of accommodation, which are also granted in case of need, are based on the regional level of rents.

The first line of Fig. 1.4, prepared by Hauser (2007), describes the "design of the current institutional arrangements for granting a socio-cultural subsistence minimum" that coexist. These include:

[12] The standard needs are determined annually on the basis of the national average price development for goods and services relevant to standard needs and the national average development of net wages and salaries per employed worker according to the national accounts as a (mixed index) (cf. Bäcker et al. 2020, p. 257).

Designation of the basic security	Coverage	Contributions to other social insurances cial insurances	Eligibility requirements	Ranking	Inclusion in income taxation
1. income- and asset-dependent basic income of communities in need	All residents	Sickness and long-term care insurance; old-age insurance (credited periods) too low	Residence and low income of the community of need	subordinate	No
2. unconditional and universal (unconditional) basic income	All residents citizens	At least health and long-term care insurance necessary	Birth certificate and residence permit	priority	no
3. unconditional restricted (partial) basic income	Old, children, disabled	At least health and long-term care insurance necessary	Birth certificate, residence permit, medical disability certificate	priority	No
4. negative income tax	All residents	At least health and long-term care insurance necessary	Residence and low family income	subordinate	combined
5. income-dependent individual basic income	All residents	At least health and long-term care insurance necessary	Residence and low income	priority	No

Fig. 1.4 Main forms of a basic income guaranteeing the socio-cultural subsistence minimum. (Source: Hauser 2007, p. 63)

- Basic income support for job-seekers (SGB II), which is granted as a "top-up" to both long-term unemployed persons capable of gainful employment between the age of 15 and the standard age limit and to employed persons with a low income from gainful employment. Furthermore, social benefit is paid to non-employable family members and the costs of accommodation are reimbursed. The prerequisites for the granting of benefits include the ability to work for more than 3 h a day.
- Social assistance (SGB XII), which is granted to persons who are unable to work – unless they live together with a recipient of SGB II – below the standard age limit in the form of assistance towards subsistence. The second full reduction in earning capacity counts as a prerequisite for benefits.
- Basic income support in old age and in the event of reduced earning capacity (SGB XII), which is granted to persons in old age above the standard age limit and to persons with reduced earning capacity.
- Benefits under the Asylum Seekers' Benefits Act (Asylbewerberleistungsgesetz), which are granted as a basic benefit to asylum seekers and to tolerated foreigners and foreigners who are under an enforceable obligation to leave the country.

In addition to the payment of basic security benefits, the contributions to health and long-term care insurance are fully covered for beneficiaries. Contributions to statutory pension insurance, on the other hand, are extremely low and are based on the amount of income from marginal employment.

Taken together, these four systems represent an almost universal tax-financed basic security need, although "the subsystems [] are differentiated according to population groups and [are] socially hierarchised with regard to the levels, the conditions of eligibility as well as the legal status of those concerned: At the upper end of the hierarchy is basic security for the elderly, at the lower end are benefits under the Asylum Seekers' Benefits Act." (Bäcker et al. 2020, p. 247). This basic state security is available to all residents in Germany in case of need and is also supplemented by charitable and altruistically motivated services provided by civil society and non-profit aid organisations, which, for example, distribute food that is no longer used in the economic cycle and would otherwise be destroyed to the needy or give it away for a small fee. If all persons on minimum income are added together, *7.4 million of* the population are currently living for a shorter or longer period of time on the level of a basic income dependent on income and assets for communities in need in 2018. This equates to around *9% of* the population. This does not rule out the possibility that there is a currently not precisely quantifiable, but certainly appreciably large group of people who also live in Germany and have not applied for the benefits to which they are entitled (cf. Bäcker et al. 2020, p. 248).

One consequence of the need to apply for basic security benefits and their subsequent subordination in the granting of benefits, which is not unique to Germany, is that in many cases these benefits are not claimed at all, even though the requirements for payment of benefits are met. Both in the case of basic security in old age and when applying for benefits under Book II of the Social Code (Hartz IV), a high proportion currently do not apply for state benefits due to shame or insufficient information, even though they would be entitled to them. For example, an empirical study by the DIW Berlin found that around 60% of senior citizens eligible for basic old-age benefits do not claim them, even though they could. The result is hidden poverty, which could be avoided by receiving basic benefits. If this social benefit were claimed in full, senior citizens' incomes would increase by an average of 30% or €220 per month (cf. Buslei et al. 2019).

The granting of a basic income would at least put an end to such non-claims, just as child benefit is currently granted and paid out for every child in Germany, even if the tax credit and the transfer-reducing offset of this income for children is currently asymmetrical. Thus, the sixth Poverty and Wealth Report of the Federal Government also states in summary: "In total, around 6.9 million persons or 8.3%

of the population received benefits from the minimum security systems in 2019. This is the lowest value of the minimum income rate since the beginning of the calculations" (BMAS 2021a, b, p. 96). In the current system, a reduction in the minimum income rate is usually considered a social policy success. However, whether a reduction in this rate may have increased the proportion of those who avoid the welfare state institutions is not usually the focus of attention and remains ignored. In this context, it would be desirable if a seventh Poverty and Wealth Report would again address the issue of "non-take-up of basic security benefits", as it did last time in 2003, and commission a current dark field study.

Instead, an unconditional basic income would be granted with *priority* over other market incomes, but also possible continuing social benefits such as possible family maintenance obligations. The only prerequisite for entitlement would be existence and residence in Germany, and would therefore be paid irrespective of the amount of assets and own earned income or other income. Since an unconditional basic income would also not be included in income taxation, with an amount of around €1000 or even €1200 currently widely discussed in the public debate, a BGE would also already have to significantly raise the current tax allowance of €9984 in 2022, since the tax allowance is based on the amount of an income that may not be reduced by taxes in order to meet a subsistence minimum. It must be taken into account that the current subsistence level is made up of the standard rate for basic security benefits and (flat-rate) accommodation and heating costs.

The determination of the amount of a BGE would thus have to be closely interlinked with such current tax allowances. The current state of the discussion is less clear as to whether voluntary contributions to health and long-term care insurance would then also have to be paid from such an amount. In a BGE system, a number of family benefits (child benefit, education allowance, child benefit supplement, BAföG) could be dropped, as could the minimum income benefits discussed above. It is unclear whether Unemployment Benefit I, which is financed by contributions from employers and employees, could also be abolished in a BGE system of social security, because the current level of Unemployment Benefit I, in contrast to basic security benefits, is based on the net income previously received and secures – at least for twelve months – the standard of living roughly achieved before becoming unemployed. If the general obligation to pay unemployment benefit were to be abolished after the introduction of a BGE, this could have the consequence that a large number of employees could leave this previous "solidarity system" and the insurance contributions would then presumably increase many times over for those employees subject to social insurance who remained in the system. Since the pension entitlements acquired by employees over the course of their working lives are subject to property-like protection, our current system of old-age provision, which is predominantly financed by contributions, would have to be gradually restructured from a certain age cohort onwards, and the benefit level of existing pensioners would then have to be financed entirely by taxes in future.

At this point, we would like to refer to the current proposal of the election manifesto of the CDU and CSU (2021) and the introduction of a fourth pillar of pension insurance, which is to be established for each child – tax-financed and guarantee-based. We interpret this as a creeping departure as well as withdrawal from the purely contribution-financed system of social security: "We want to develop a concept to establish a new form of funded old-age provision in Germany. A generational pension for old-age provision from birth can be a good building block for this. We will examine how the generation pension can be designed with a state monthly contribution to be invested in a pension fund – with protection against state access. Our aim is to use an attractive mix of instruments to effectively prevent old-age poverty" (CDU and CSU 2021, p. 61). The CDU politician Friedrich Merz (who so far has not become known for his social policy theses) concretised this idea in a newspaper interview: "If we were to start with, say, €50 a month for each child, then in the first year that would be about €400 million that the state would have to contribute. After 18 years you would then be somewhere between €8 and €9 billion out of the state budget. For that, every pensioner would then have a capital of more than €200,000 at their disposal, given a normal interest rate trend, even if they had not made any more payments of their own in their working lives."[13]

However, this new and innovative sounding idea is historically rather "old hat", which is not to say that such a concept (already more than 200 years old) should *not* be revitalised, as it touches on fundamental issues. In 1797, one of the intellectual fathers of the basic income debate put it this way, "It is proposed that payments be made, as already stated, to everyone, rich or poor. It is best to do it this way to prevent envious distinctions. It is further right that it should be so, because it represents the place of natural inheritance, which belongs to every man as a right above and apart from the property which he has acquired or inherited from people who have acquired it. Those who do not wish to accept it may throw it into the common fund" (Paine 2019, p. 86). Kovce/Priddat classify the proposal of the English-born and French honorary citizen as an alternative to the poor relief known up to that time as well as to the social insurance that developed only 100 years later as a basic security, which provided for "endowing everyone with a basic capital once on entering adulthood and later regularly with a basic pension" (this. 2019, p. 29).

[13] Friedrich Merz defends the Union's expensive plans in an interview (faz.net)

With regard to the criteria of *target efficiency*, i.e. ensuring the currently intended protection target of guaranteeing the availability of a socio-cultural subsistence minimum with the lowest possible – publicly financed – expenditure of resources, the current system of contribution-financed social security is more likely to be achieved than in a guarantee-based system of a BGE. This applies exclusively to the aspect of the cost efficiency of the socio-political measure, because a comprehensive welfare-economic cost-benefit-efficiency analysis could in principle also come to other results of an increase in social welfare. Besides the comparatively low cost-effectiveness of a BGE, other main fundamental problems are listed. "First, the coordination with the other elements of the social security system; second, the high financial outlay required, which has to be used up by cutting other social benefits and by raising taxes; third, the effects on the willingness to work of those capable of working and on the economy as a whole; fourth, the pull effects on citizens of the EU and other countries; fifth, the redistribution effects" (Hauser 2007, p. 68).

Of course, it would also be possible, as shown in line 3 of Fig. 1.4, not to grant a BGE to all citizens at the same time, but to introduce it step by step for individual population groups to be prioritized. In this case, some of the main problems of a BGE would be significantly mitigated and the phased plan would have to be prioritized by politicians and could be implemented in supplementary chapters of the Social Code with legal force.

As a further alternative to the current system, line 4 of Fig. 1.4 lists the negative income tax. The basic idea was tested in the 1960s in the US and also on the basis of model experiments in the 1970s (see Hoynes and Rothstein 2019). The idea behind it is that both tax- and contribution-funded social benefits are replaced by a single transfer and that the payment of benefits is to be made as a negative tax. Such a model implies that both tax and transfer subject are identical and would also have to be made according to uniform criteria, which, at least in Germany, would entail a number of open questions not only with regard to joint tax assessment for couples and would also require the transfer of the Bedarfsgemeinschaft construct to the respective tax subjects. A central aspect of the system of a negative income tax is that the payment would not be granted to all persons, but would be paid out *subordinate* to market income as well as to transfer payments financed by contributions. A central question here would be the determination and communication of a so-called "break-even point", from which the integrated tax and transfer payments made would be equal to the negative income tax amount or, in other words, the net transfer would be zero and how high this proportion of the population would then be.

With regard to the main arguments against a negative income tax, the costs would be significantly lower than for a BGE and a significantly smaller financial mass would have to be moved. The cost efficiency of a negative income tax would presumably be higher compared to a BGE. In terms of cost efficiency, the existing basic income support system in Germany would presumably be the *clearly* superior alternative overall compared with the design alternatives described in Fig. 1.4.

At present, there are many different models of the BGE, ranging from purely philosophical basic concepts to alternative sociological, economic and political science concepts of the welfare state. The spectrum ranges from more market-liberal approaches, whose future welfare state conception would then be less differentiated and less bureaucratised in a BGE world (cf. Straubhaar 2017), to so-called emancipatory or solidarity-based approaches[14], which, in addition to a basic income, also want to maintain a social benefit system in future – then oriented towards "needs". Only a concrete design will ultimately decide whether a BGE could be financed at all and what the net economic costs of implementation would be. The "rule of thumb" that is repeatedly put forward in connection with questions about the financing of a BGE, namely that if around €1000 were paid to around 82.5 million people in Germany if it were introduced, this would lead to annual costs of €1 trillion, must first be countered by the fact that this amount would be the *gross cost of* public budgets. On the one hand, the already existing budget titles (e.g. child benefit, basic security benefits, etc.) would have to be deducted and offset, and on the other hand, possible cost savings in bureaucracy and administration, not to be excluded additional tax revenues due to increased propensity to consume, as well as other possible financially effective consequences. How high the estimated annual *net costs of* a BGE would ultimately turn out to be, and the question of whether a BGE would ultimately also be sustainably financeable, is by no means an easy question to answer (cf. on this Opielka 2004, p. 253ff.; Osterkamp 2015; Krämer 2018; Werner et al. 2013 and Straubhaar 2018).

A recently submitted expert report prepared by the Scientific Advisory Council to the Federal Ministry of Finance, in which four different variants of a BGE were presented with the aid of microsimulation studies, concludes that "in an open society, an individual, unconditional BGE whose amount ensures a livelihood is therefore not feasible in the view of the Advisory Council" (Wiss. Beirat 2021, p. 40). The report does not make any statements on the possible financing of a BGE from other possible tax sources. Moreover, in the underlying simulation studies (Blömer

[14] Cf. the proposal for an emancipatory basic income by the Federal Working Group on Basic Income of the Left https://www.die-linke-grundeinkommen.de/fileadmin/lcmsbaggrundeinkommen/PDF/NeufassungBGE_dinA5_ohneNES.pdf

and Peichl 2021), dynamic behavioural adjustments of people, e.g. triggered by potential increases in productive potentials of the population receiving basic income, cost reductions in the health sector that cannot be ruled out, adjustments in the demand for goods and labour or also quality improvements in social cohesion are usually left out of such purely microeconomic simulation studies and partial models of the national economy. The question of financing the net costs of a BGE as well as the corresponding necessary changes in tax policy determine the question of how a BGE will affect the income situation of individual population groups and which groups would ultimately – at least in the short term – be net gainers or net payers.

One question that has been raised too rarely in the BGE debate so far relates to a "transfer" of the current system of granting state benefits on the basis of applications and means-testing, which now comprises more than 170 individual regulations, and of enabling equal participation in society into a system of a general civil right that would be granted to all citizens. The more market-liberal conceptions would link a BGE with a residual welfare state, which in the end would in many cases be precisely not a central element of a BGE, namely to abolish the compulsion to wage labour as well as a decoupling of gainful employment and income.

If one roughly sifts through the published articles on this topic in the German-language social science and economics literature (cf. Figure 1.5), there is an increasing number of authors – especially from the social sciences – who agree with a BGE and do not want to link it at all with a market-liberal, dismantled welfare state model in Germany.

On the other hand, there is a whole series of – mainly economic – authors of contributions who are by no means advocating a dismantling of the welfare state, but are striving for necessary reforms of the existing system. Some of the proponents also link their preference with an overcoming of the current capitalist economic system preceding the introduction of a BGE. Nevertheless, such detailed proposals usually lack public attention; an emancipatory utopia like a BGE has it much easier here.

This is also stated by Bäcker et al. 2020 in their comprehensive appraisal and presentation of the current welfare state concepts as well as possible reform options in the direction of a so-called citizen's insurance: "A counter-model would be a forward-looking reform policy that starts at several concrete points and fits into an overall concept for a modern welfare state. There is no doubt that it is not easy to find sufficient support or even to arouse enthusiasm for such *"level-headed efforts"* as a better alternative to basic income. For inevitably such reforms are both small-scale and complex. They would have to provide for improvements in basic security – especially with regard to the level of benefits and the rules on

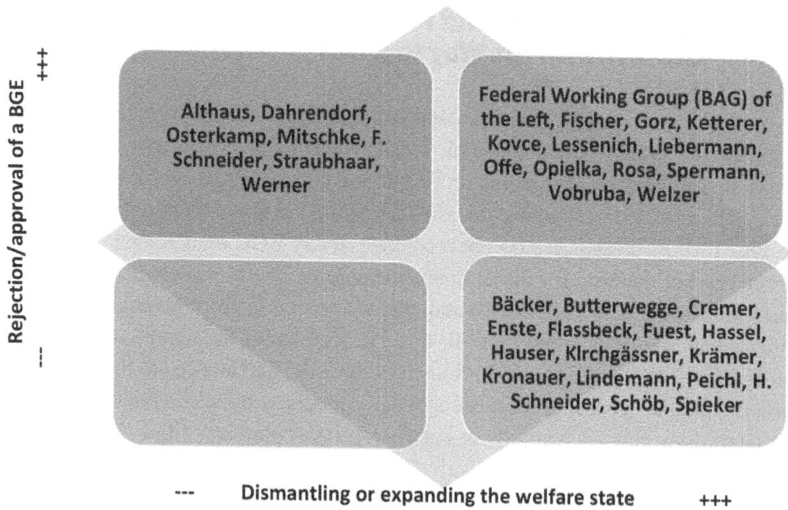

Fig. 1.5 German-speaking – *exemplary* – supporters as well as opponents of a UBI according to their attitude towards the development of the welfare state

reasonableness and sanctions – as well as an upgrading of social security. The position of strengthening social insurance aims to secure and improve the level of benefits provided by social insurance and to extend insurance cover beyond the current group of those liable to insurance and entitled to benefits to the entire population. In the sense of an insurance for the gainfully employed, civil servants and the self-employed would be included in the benefit system and at the same time in the obligation to pay contributions, in addition to workers and employees. In the case of a citizens' insurance scheme, the entire population, including the non-employed, would be covered" (Bäcker et al. 2020, p. 311).

In the following, we have formulated a series of different questions, primarily addressed to the proponents of a BGE, whose clear and precise answers we believe are still pending, but which nevertheless appear necessary in order to be able to make a fair weighing of arguments in the sense of the quoted "troubles of the level" at the end, whether – supposedly intended or unintended – consequences of a welfare state transformation would on balance be superior or inferior to the current system in the welfare economic sense. For it is precisely the high public popularity of a BGE that harbours the great danger that too high and, on closer examination, possibly also (currently) unrealisable expectations will be attached to it among the population.

1.4 Open Questions and Probable or at Least Possible Obstacles on the Way to a UBI

In the following, a series of smaller and larger, partly solvable or partly unsolvable open questions are listed in nine topic areas, which in most cases have already been expressed in principle by critics of a basic income (cf. for example Butterwegge 2018; Cremer 2019b; Flassbeck et al. 2012 as well as the authors rejecting a BGE in Fig. 1.5). At present, we do not recognize in any BGE model under discussion the necessary maturity for discussion to be able to clearly answer the majority of questions in an empirically robust and evidence-based manner. Lessenich has classified open questions around a BGE as a "pessimism of the mind", which on the other hand is countered by an "optimism of the will" and attested to the concept in general that the "charm of the basic income is inherent in the combination of revolutionary idea and – potentially at least – reformist practice" (ibid., 2009, p. 32). The "revolutionary element" is likely to lie in the fact that a BGE is supposed to open up access to a basic material security benefit to practically every member of society, and thus there is more than a purely socio-political dimension hidden in it. "The basic income is supposed to put the 'social democracy' of the welfare state on stable feet of basic social rights" (Opielka 2008, p. 91). It is above all this *unconditionality of* the granting of regular cash benefits as a legal entitlement in a world of a BGE, which would ultimately also result in a changed basic understanding of social justice and would have to lead to a new or fundamentally expanded understanding of values. The unconditionality of the basic income, which entails that market events are not only corrected ex post by the welfare state, but already unfold ex ante under completely different conditions, is the most difficult to justify and the easiest to doubt, because with its unconditionality the basic income loses, as it were, the social problems for which it could be a fitting solution. Indeed, it is above all its (reference) conditions that predestine a social benefit to solve a particular social problem" (Kovce and Priddat 2019, p. 23). The break with the previous value principle of an *obligation to help oneself,* which finds its counterpart in the principle of subordination of the granting of state benefits, is therefore also mentioned first by critics of a BGE: "The basic problem of the unconditional basic income is: it undermines the idea of the solidarity community. It only defines rights vis-à-vis society. The duty to help oneself is abolished. The principle of solidarity is thus unilaterally abandoned in favour of an unconditional claim of the individual against society. It remains open who in society will then still be prepared to fulfil these claims. If there are too few of them, even vested rights can no longer be enforced" (Schöb 2020, p. 123).

The multitude of detailed questions listed below will presumably not trigger any fundamental scepticism or uncertainty among convinced supporters of a BGE, since it is "precisely the missing problems that free the unconditional basic income from having to be a solution merely for or in favour of this, and give it a fundamental legal radiance beyond the welfare state's need to solve problems" (loc. cit., p. 24). The Belgian social philosopher Philippe van Parijs and founder of the Basic Income European Network (BIEN) (cf. Sect. 1.7) sees as "the" decisive objection against a BGE, which would be put forward by social theorists such as Jon Elster or also John Rawls, that a BGE *supposedly* contradicts "a widely accepted notion of justice" (ibid. 2019 [1991], p. 375). Van Parijs uses the example of wave surfers at the Californian coastal resort of Malibu to try to justify why this group, which is committed only to its own private pleasure and without any reciprocity for other members of society, is also "entitled to such a high income – without questioning, without conditions – that they can support themselves" (op. cit., p. 410). However, he also qualifies that this liberal understanding of the autonomy of the free choice of the use of time only applies to a society "which is so prosperous that it can afford an unconditional basic income in the corresponding amount" (op. cit., p. 410).

Against this background, with the introduction of a BGE, such a liberal understanding of justice enters into competition with current concepts of social justice. A fundamental challenge would be to readjust the current balance of the partial goals of social justice, which already contain "partly complementary, partly competing aspects of justice" (Becker and Hauser 2009, p. 47). The four partial goals of justice of opportunity, justice of achievement, justice of need, and intergenerational justice are related to each other as if in a magic square and require politicians to bring these four principles of justice into balance. Already at present, especially the principle of performance justice, which implies "inequality in the distribution of material goods" (loc. cit., p. 47), is in a conflict of aims with the principle of need, which assumes "tendential equality in the same recognized needs". "The more pronounced the merit principle is, leading to high inequality of market incomes, the greater the violations of the goal of justice of needs are likely to be, unless compensatory state transfer payments are made. Conversely, a far-reaching redistribution to equalise the possibilities of satisfying needs tends to impair the justice of performance" (loc. cit., p. 47 f.). In contrast, the aspect of justice of opportunity, namely the "equality of opportunities for a self-determined life" (loc. cit., p. 27), is more in a *complementary* and less competitive relationship to the other principles of justice, whereby the principle of equality in accordance with Article 3 of the Basic Law does, after all, enjoy constitutional status and thus also gives politics a clear mandate to protect citizens from violations of the principle of equality, for example in the form of discrimination. More than ten years ago, the aspect of intergenerational justice in the sense of an intergenerational understanding of justice was still said to be "subordinate to other aspects of justice" (loc. cit., p. 50).

However, at the latest after the most recent ruling of the Federal Constitutional Court on the Climate Protection Act (cf. Sect. 6.7), intergenerational justice is likely to be given a higher weighting also by our constitutional norms, and its significance is likely to increase in the future with regard to possible conflict relationships, especially in the area of statutory pension insurance and the question of pension increases or also pension reductions. A BGE could certainly also come into conflict with regard to the discussed partial goal of performance justice as well as needs justice, but from the perspective of the philosophy of justice it is nevertheless basically attested to possess positive spillover effects on opportunity and performance justice that cannot be excluded: "From a liberal point of view ... the unconditional basic income can be described as just. It would increase the equality of opportunity and the real freedom of the individual and thus give real validity to the rights of freedom. In addition, the BGE would achieve a moderate compensation of the unearned – and without decisively violating the liberal principle of neutrality or the principle of reciprocity. Moreover, there is enough room in the concept of the BGE for the liberal requirements of responsibility, the reward of performance and private property; indeed, the basic income could possibly contribute to a strengthening of responsibility and performance. In addition, the BGE would make it possible to achieve a fairer justice of performance because, thanks to better equality of opportunity, the principle of one's own effort would be more likely to be reflected in earnings and disadvantages due to one's own origins could be mitigated" (Reuter 2016, p. 169).

With regard to the principles of social justice, Opielka et al. assign the basic income to a value type of recognition as a guaranteeist concept of participatory justice, which primarily aims to strengthen people's abilities; an approach that is not far removed from Amartya Sen's so-called capability approach. They arrive at a similar assessment regarding the fundamental compatibility of different principles of justice: "Participatory justice is the intellectual basis of basic income – even if the idea of basic income is compatible with all four types of justice" (Opielka et al. 2010, p. 24 f.).

Even if there are no fundamental contradictions to existing principles with regard to the justice dimension, attention should be drawn to the necessary immense change processes in the population's perception of justice and values, which are also raised, for example, by the economist and inequality researcher Branko Milanovic: "With the introduction of a universal unconditional basic income, the principle on which the current welfare state is based would be abandoned. The unconditional basic income doesn't insure citizens against risks; it ignores risks altogether. It distributes money equally to all people, with the wealthy giving back the basic income received through taxes. This is not necessarily a decisive argument against the BGE. The philosophy on which a welfare system is based can be changed, and in some circumstances that may be advisable. However, it must and clear that moving away from the current social security system and towards an unconditional basic income would not be a simple technical and financial change, but would require a comprehensive reformulation of the philosophy that has shaped the welfare state for more than a century" (Milanovic 2020, p. 287 f.).

In addition, it is important to warn – despite all fundamental optimism – that in a world of a BGE with corresponding institutional conditions, *socially comparative* phenomena such as resentment, a thirst for recognition, arrogance, envy or other socially comparative orientations would suddenly dissolve and disappear: "It is not to be expected that solidarity, striving for cooperation, altruism or egoism will prevail as consistently dominant or even exclusively occurring motivations for action. Socially comparative orientations will always be added as motivations for action" (Nullmeier 2016, p. 65). This skepticism of a complete dissolution of socially comparative phenomena is also shared on the part of moral philosophy, even in a "good society": "Envy (and not only its good relative, emulation) should also continue to exist, because competition and the interest in goods that are competed for is something that a good society cannot put shackles on without losing positive energy. The institutions of a good society keep fear and envy in check and protect citizens from humiliation" (Nussbaum 2014, p. 566). In current sociological debates on *post-growth societies* and the "Great Transformation" (Dörre et al. 2019), the guaranteed basic income is also seen by some authors as the most convincing socio-political proposal for future social development: "Now there is a reform proposal that makes such a pacification of existence conceivable under late-modern conditions. It lies well within the horizon of what is politically possible, but its implementation would have far-reaching, even revolutionary cultural consequences. I am referring to the idea of a *guaranteed, unconditional basic income.* This seems to me the most plausible welfare state correlate to an economic post-growth society." (Rosa 2016, p. 729).

Incidentally, the *open questions* formulated in the following also extend far beyond those individual consequences of action for which empirical and generalizable answers could be obtained, for example, with the help of field experiments, and even in the following sections of the book by no means all questions are taken up again and possible answers elaborated. So far, the state of research on the effects of a BGE is comparatively *sparse,* but *it is* nevertheless growing steadily thanks to a series of field experiments that have also been scientifically accompanied. In the past, a number of "microsimulation studies" have been carried out (cf. e.g. Osterkamp 2015), which mainly refer to the financial aspects of a possible introduction and whose results are supposed to inform policy-makers and the public about possible redistributive effects of a transfer of the current system into a BGE world. Methodologically, however, such simulation studies assume only very short-term effects in the form of the so-called "morning after" effect. Moreover, due to the scarcity of resources, one of the behavioural assumptions of the central actors of the model (individuals, households) is that they pursue clearly defined goals (utility maximisation). In our view, this is the point at which the following questions, which are currently open or have not been discussed publicly to a sufficient extent, would arise at the latest – if possibly not too late. We would hope that the future debate on a BGE would take these up and develop (preliminary) answers.

Open Questions and Possible as Well As Not to Be Excluded Consequences of a BGE

Costs and Financing

1. What monetary or fiscal policy instruments would be available in the event of inflationary threats, e.g. triggered by employers in certain sectors having to increase wages drastically or because growing demand could lead to sudden price increases in the short to medium term?
2. What monetary or fiscal policy instruments would continue to be available to the economy in the event of austerity and deflation traps?
3. In the worst case, national bankruptcy could also be imminent if the concept was not soundly and sustainably financed – what would a plan for a possible successful return to the status quo or a superior plan B for this look like?
4. How can populist policies to secure the majority but without qualms about national debt and endangering economic performance be stopped (e.g. in the form of a "debt taboo" for BGE costs?).
5. Will the introduction of a BGE possibly promote investments in predominantly "speculative investments" with high price risks and possible losses?
6. With a possible contentious introduction of a BGE, what would be the response to a widening "tax strike" to fund a BGE?

Investment Infrastructure and Institutional Reforms

7. How is it avoided that the means of a BGE do not neglect the financing of public goods as well as investment infrastructure?
8. A BGE requires comprehensive reforms with many simultaneous changes in the tax and welfare system as well as in the institutional structure of the traditional welfare state. The overall effect of these reforms is difficult to predict. What would be possible "checks and balances" on an institutional path of implementation?
9. What are the implications of the point that in a BGE world, the Minister of Finance – and no longer the Minister of Labour and Social Affairs – becomes the main actor for the concerns of BGE recipients?
10. The trade unions are very difficult to win over as allies, especially in countries with contribution-financed social security systems; after all, they represent the insiders – whereas in a BGE it is presumably above all the outsiders who would tend to be the winners. So how does one go about convincing the trade unions in Germany that a BGE is also institutionally the superior alternative to the welfare state principle?
11. Wouldn't the best way be to start with a small basic income (which does not fully cover needs) in order to gradually (phasing in) move from a partial to a living wage level of a BGE?
12. Who pays out a BGE at all – the (central) tax administration (tax file) or the local municipality where one is registered (residents' registration office file?) or mixed jurisdictions, but which would then have to operate corresponding data exchange?

Nation State Implementation in Europe and a Globalised World

13. In the case of a purely national introduction, how will it be prevented from fuelling immigration or stimulating mass abuse in a Europe of open borders? (cf. Agersnap et al. 2020)
14. How is it to be prevented that the number of "seasonal workers" or "temporary workers from abroad", "Eastern European domestic and care workers" does not grow (commuting migration), as non-attractive jobs are then presumably not further offered by the domestic population?

15. What instruments would be available to counter a "capital strike" that cannot be ruled out in order to politically destabilise a BGE implementation? (cf. Benanav 2020, p. 84)

(Unintended) Side-Effects of Action and Their Possible Solutions

16. It cannot be ruled out that small (homogeneous/heterogeneous?) groups will increasingly lose their motivation to engage in gainful employment and that "social parasitism", laziness and sloth will increasingly grow in certain groups? What plans exist to counteract this and which state institutions (federal, state, local) have a responsibility to prevent such developments?
17. How can we counteract possible growing tendencies towards inactivity when money alone does not solve people's problems and it can be observed how growing parts of the population no longer engage in socially necessary and required activities?
18. The political and moral willingness to make permanent payments also to those not in need will be more than difficult to achieve. What strategies would there be to counteract a correspondingly growing "anti-BGE movement"?
19. If "weaker" members of society "learn" that they will always be helped, the risk of losing "self-confidence" may increase; here too: which state institutions (federal, state, local) are responsible for preventing such possible developments?
20. Without the possibility of sanctions and the suspension of payments of a BGE, how can repeated egoistic exploitation of public resources for activities endangering democracy be combated?
21. How can growing avoidance (e.g. in the form of undeclared work) of tax payments and social security contributions be effectively countered?
22. The BGE promises a fairer, simpler, more efficient welfare state that preserves the dignity of each individual, protects them from poverty and enables them to participate in society. Which poverty prevention measures (e.g. can a BGE be seized?) would be necessary and are there minimum expectations of social participation in a BGE society (participation in voluntary services, voluntary work, etc.)?
23. Doesn't a BGE conception of man ultimately assume completely responsible and rational or reason-based citizens? Which motivational

strategies are available (by whom?) after an introduction to transform also "unreasonable" ways of acting back into citizen activities?

24. The proponents of the BGE have a vision of a different society. In doing so, they assume a certain image of man, namely that of (at least in a vast majority) intrinsically motivated people. This image of man is an important prerequisite for the functioning of the idea. The question of what percentage of "free riders" a BGE society can survive with in the medium term remains unanswered.
25. One must be prepared for the influence of powerful lobby groups and (trade unions, social bureaucracy, employers' associations) counterarguments that will be asserted, which will undermine and torpedo the political efforts to introduce a BGE. Which instruments as well as communication formats should be used for this purpose?

Establishment of Thresholds of Higher Burdens

26. At what level of earned income should employees be taxed more to finance a BGE than under the status quo? How should a tax scale (threshold values) be designed, especially in the lower income deciles?
27. Does social policy and the state have to "protect" some of its citizens from themselves (e.g. because of the dangers of addiction) even in a world of an unconditional basic income payment – which institution would be responsible for this?

Open Implementation Arrangements

28. Is it still conceivable in a world of unconditional monetary payment that citizens can also have their payment "withdrawn" or "reduced" (e.g. due to criminal offences)?
29. How much should a BGE be for legally convicted persons? To an individual blocked account for the time of a resocialization?
30. Who would *not be* eligible for a BGE? (e.g. refugees, Germans abroad, persons without registered residence in Germany, homeless persons, persons living illegally in the country).
31. In which amount and on which basis should a BGE for children/youth be set? Does one follow the current practice analogous to the determination of the amount of the tax allowance/living minimum?

32. The current practice of child allowances staggers the amount according to the number of children. How can it be prevented that a BGE sets negative incentives for child-rich families in terms of labour supply?
33. In a BGE world, would the subsidiary responsibility of a family support within a family household be reduced to zero on complete individualisation (e.g. without maintenance obligations)?

Potential Consequences on the Labour Market

34. Do unintended side effects occur when leaving the primacy of primary income growth (gross wages and salaries)?
35. Will minimum wages remain and what will happen if, after the introduction of a BGE, a number of workers are also prepared to work at lower wages than the minimum wage?
36. What will happen to the current employers' social security contributions? Also in the future per employee, or as a lump sum payroll tax?

Interaction with the Current Contributory Welfare State

37. Do those groups in our society that currently receive cumulative means-tested benefits fare at least as well after the introduction of a BGE as they do under the current social security system?
38. By whom and in what amount should the financing of the current level of statutory/private health/care insurance be provided?
39. Which instruments of the current welfare state can be used to prevent a "levelling down" of those currently in need in the most difficult life situations (e.g. severely disabled persons with high extra costs)?
40. How high will the BGE amount remain in the case of inpatient care dependency – with an "allowance" of €120 as is currently the case for social assistance recipients?
41. Will the current competition between statutory and private health insurers continue?
42. Offsetting the BGE against existing social benefits may not be feasible in practice, since not all current social benefits are transfer payments or maintenance payments. Instead, they also consist of services (e.g. work of nursing staff in hospitals and old people's homes). Which social benefits are non-negotiable/non-substitutable even in a BGE world?

43. With which birth cohort at the earliest should the statutory obligation to contribute to an old-age insurance scheme with property-like entitlements at retirement age be terminated or converted?
44. Would the current taxation shares of statutory pension payments remain frozen in the case of a BGE, or would this also have to be increased to refinance a BGE?

Normative Social Questions

45. How can it be ensured that even in a BGE world normative principles of a utilitarian welfare state principle as well as that of an "optimal" tax theory (welfare maximization) are maintained?
46. How should society deal with it if, for example, 10% of the population would refuse to receive a BGE for fundamental reasons?
47. Since, in comparison to current recipients of welfare state payments, new groups in particular (childless persons, persons without impairments) will in future also be able to enjoy state benefits for the first time, would higher tax burdens then also have to be demanded from these groups, or are special demand effects expected from these groups?
48. How can it be ensured in the future that, especially for women from migrant families, labour market integration after the introduction of a BGE would not become even more remote than it already is?
49. On which levels (outside of Twitter, Facebook, Instagram, etc.) will it be necessary to intensify future debates, especially with the protagonists of a BGE, in order to also address necessary questions on factually relevant points in detail and to develop approaches to solutions so that the discussion does not move beyond the real economic, social, financial and political world?
50. Will it be possible in a BGE world to preserve and ensure the core elements of modernity, such as democracy, the rule of law, the separation of powers, public freedom of opinion, and to let possible tendencies of neo-nationalism run into the void?

It would be desirable for possible risks in a reform or transformation process towards a BGE to be openly discussed and for an understanding to be found on which questions there is already sufficient empirical evidence to provide a clear answer. At this point, it is also worth recalling economist Branko Milanovic's call for caution: "We must examine these questions before deciding for or against an unconditional basic income. None of the previously mentioned objections is sufficient in itself to dismiss the idea; these issues could all be resolved, circumvented, or perhaps ruled out as unlikely. But taken as a whole, they should lead us to think hard about whether it is advisable to introduce unconditional basic income" (ibid., 2020, p. 288 f.). Certainly, by initiating scientifically accompanied field experiments, only a few of the listed open questions will be able to be answered in an evidence-based manner in a few years. Nevertheless, despite all our sympathy for experimental research in this field, we agree with Georg Vobruba's sceptical assessment: "All in all, you can compare test groups equipped with different versions of a basic income with each other, but you cannot extrapolate from the test results to society. It doesn't help: if you want to know whether and how a basic income changes society, you have to introduce it. That is a difficult obstacle to overcome" (ibid. 2019, p. 212).

The comprehensive list of small and large open questions is intended to draw attention to the fact that – despite all the need for reform of the status quo model of our welfare state – there are good reasons to significantly dampen *overly high expectations of* an early transition to a BGE world. More likely, however, we see a gradual adoption and integration of a number of guarantee elements as individual civil rights that will transform the contributory conservative welfare state model into a more individualized – and emancipated – future model. The introduction of a BGE through the back door (Back Door) discussed by Parijs/Vanderborght (ibid. 2017, p. 210) as well as the beginning of a transition with an implementation of the "participation income" proposed by Anthony Atkinson (1996 as well as 2015, p. 219) also goes in this direction and Lee also proposes a very similar concept (ibid. 2019, p. 284). A participation income is a kind of *priority citizen's income* for all those who are in *some form of* gainful employment either full or part-time, are in education or training, are actively seeking employment, are engaged in care work for children, the elderly or disabled, or are engaged in voluntary or honorary work in civil society. Such approaches are, of course, also rejected by some proponents of a BGE as "progressive paternalism" (Liebermann 2015, p. 15).

1.5 Legitimacy Problems of Contribution Financed Welfare State Models and Grown Consent to a UBI

Even though we have been able to show that interest in a BGE has risen significantly in recent years and that there is also strong support for the idea in principle among the population, we should not be too quick to believe that a concrete implementation and realisation of the basic income idea and a replacement of the current welfare state with all its institutions is within reach. Thus, both the phases of defence and further development with regard to the conditions of access as well as the scope of benefits of welfare state measures have always been the subject of political conflicts and foreign negotiation processes. From the perspective of the empirical dimension of democratic legitimacy, several representative surveys identified evidence for the popularity of a BGE (Schupp 2020c).

Thus, the survey results show that for the period from the turn of the year 2016/17 to autumn 2018, the approval rate for the introduction of a BGE was largely stable as well as tending to increase and was at a value between 45 and 55% and in autumn 2019, the approval rate for a BGE was a few percentage points lower at now 48%. In East Germany, the level of approval is 58%, in West Germany 46% of the adult population. Differentiated analyses according to socio-demographic characteristics show (Fig. 1.6) that support for a BGE often goes hand in hand with young age, high education and also a low income as well as politically rather left-wing attitudes.

Nevertheless, caution should be exercised when interpreting the approval rates with regard to a concrete willingness to reform towards a BGE. This is because the explanations of the internationally comparable survey question (cf. Soomi 2018) generally do not explicitly state whether respondents would be financially better or worse off after the introduction of a BGE.

Thus, in surveys – as in the European Social Survey (ESS) – the BGE is often presented to respondents in the following way and the respective degree of approval or rejection is then determined:

- The state pays everyone a monthly income that covers all basic living expenses.
- This will replace many existing social benefits.
- The goal is to guarantee everyone a minimum standard of living.
- Everyone receives the same amount, regardless of whether or not work is done.
- One can also keep the income from employment or other sources.
- The basic income is financed through taxes.

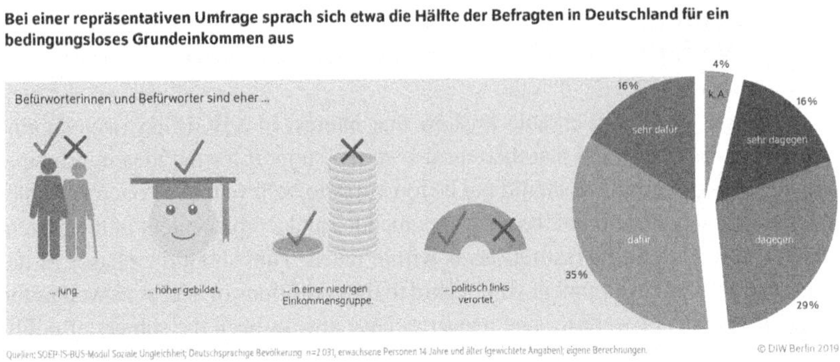

Fig. 1.6 Degree of approval for an unconditional basic income in Germany. (Source: Adriaans et al. 2019)

These explanations of a BGE, which are mainly used in international comparative surveys, do not make it explicit, on the one hand, what concrete level of a basic income would be associated with it, which social benefits would be cut in future and which would be retained, how much of gross earnings one would still be allowed to keep net after the introduction of a BGE and, of course, the most important question, which taxes would presumably have to be increased to finance a BGE. Thus, for the majority of respondents, it is likely to be rather unclear whether they personally would be in a better or worse financial position after the introduction of a BGE.

In the SOEP-IS survey of autumn 2019, following the less concrete question on approval or rejection of a BGE, the question was asked whether one personally assumed that after the introduction of such a BGE one would probably have less money net, would have about the same amount of money or would probably have more money net at one's disposal (Fig. 1.7).

Around 40% of all respondents stated that they would probably have more money at their disposal, while 26% tended to assume that they would have less money at their disposal and a good third stated that a basic income would not make them financially better off. Unsurprisingly, more than half of those in favour of a basic income believe that they would have more money at their disposal after the introduction of a basic income. But even among those who reject a BGE, around 26% expect that they would have more money at their disposal, while 45% of those who reject a BGE assume that they would have less money at their disposal net with a BGE. The results make it clear that by no means all those who oppose a basic income do so solely because they expect to be in a worse economic position,

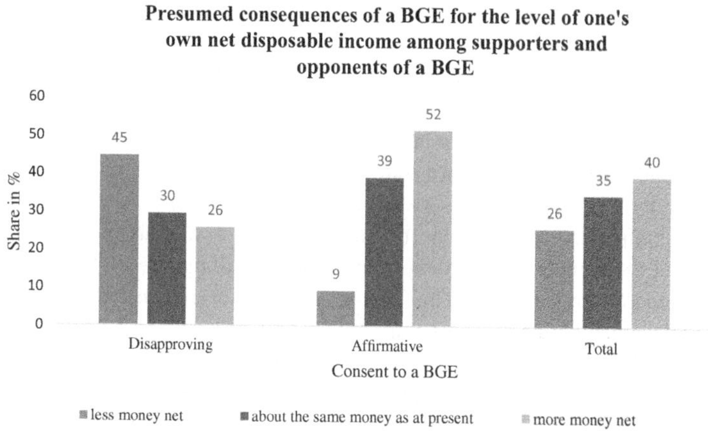

Fig. 1.7 Presumed consequences of a UBI on the level of one's own net disposable income. (Source: *SOEP-IS – BUS – Module BGE 2019; German-speaking population n = 1930 adults 14 years and older (weighted data)*)

just as, conversely, in the group of those in favour, one in eleven assumes that they are in a better economic position under the current system and still agree.

In addition to questions of the economic consequences for the individual, the debate on the introduction of a BGE is also directly linked to the question of the justice of a changed welfare state principle. While critics see above all the principle of meritocracy in danger through the unconditionality of the basic income, the empirical analyses (Adriaans et al. 2019 as well as already Lee 2018) show that the widely shared principle of needs-based justice is quite in line with the introduction of a BGE. Thus, for *both* preferences, a high correlation with the rejection or approval of a basic income can be found. Those who value needs-based justice very highly are quite sympathetic to basic income, but those who place a high value on performance based justice tend to have a negative attitude towards basic income.

Based on surveys and the questioning of possible consequences of one's own actions or even assumed consequences of actions in the case of a BGE, it can also be shown that the assessment of how people would generally react to a basic income and how one would act oneself differ significantly. "Compared to the 56% of respondents who assume that other people would work less, for example, only 22% of respondents assume that they themselves would work less" (Oostendorp and Paulus 2021).

Obviously, there is a strong interest among the population to think about fundamental alternatives to the existing system of social security, although in recent years the financial means in Germany for the further development of the welfare state have continuously increased.

The proportion of adults who agree with the statement "I am satisfied with the services provided by the welfare state in Germany" is around 42%. But a good third are dissatisfied with the current benefits of the welfare state and, together with the comparatively high proportion of people (23%) who are indifferent to the benefits of the welfare state, a rather critical attitude dominates in the population (Lüders and Schröder 2020). The Democracy Monitor also asked about a complete replacement of the previous contribution-financed welfare state structures by a BGE.

In this study, too, the result is quite clear, as shown in Fig. 1.8. More than half support a BGE to varying degrees, while in this survey less than a third of respondents argue *against* a system change in social security.

If the findings identified by political scientists are correct that an independent socio-political influence also emanates from the empirical legitimacy of the democratic system, one cannot avoid the worrying classification of the BGE approval by Lüders and Schroeder (2020): "In any case, this result must be understood on the one hand as an indication of a lack of trust and a certain dissatisfaction with the existing system, but on the other hand it may also have been taken out of ignorance.

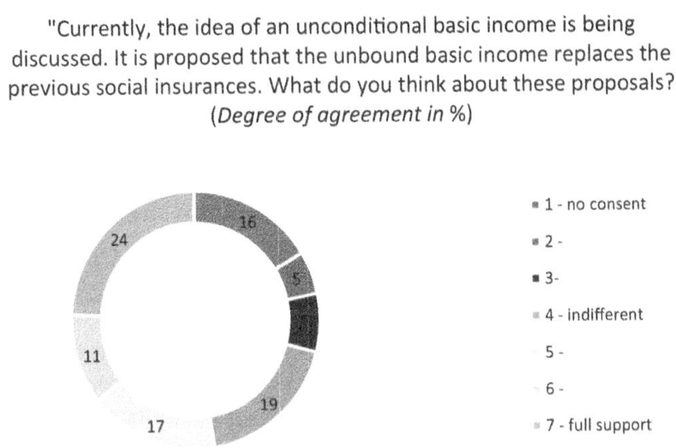

Fig. 1.8 Attitude towards basic income. (Source: *Demokratiemonitor (2019), data weighted, N = 6719; cited in Lüders and* Schroeder 2021, *p. 359*)

However, the high approval rates for the basic income could also indicate an erosion of the consensus on the social security principle" (Sirovátka et al. 2019, p. 359 f.).

1.6 The Relationship of the Parties Represented in the Bundestag to the BGE

For the election campaign taking place in the summer of 2021, the fundamental continuation of the contribution-financed social security system was not up for discussion for the parties represented in the Bundestag. In the case of the Bündnis 90/Die Grünen party, the sentence "We welcome and support model projects to research the effect of an unconditional basic income" can be found in their election programme adopted at the beginning of June 2021[15] . In addition, this party was the first to commit itself, at least in its basic programme adopted in autumn 2020, to the medium and long-term further development of the welfare state in perspective, that "subsistence-securing social benefits [should] be merged step by step and in the long term the payment should be integrated into the tax system. [...] Concealed poverty is to be overcome. In doing so, we are guided by the central idea of an unconditional basic income."[16]

The Left Party also opens up to the idea of a BGE in its draft election manifesto "We are conducting the social discussions about an unconditional basic income controversially and will decide next year with a membership vote whether we will change our stance on this."[17]

In its manifesto, the FDP advocates a so-called liberal citizen's income[18] . Thus, tax-financed social benefits, such as the standard benefit and the accommodation costs of the unemployment benefit II, the basic security in old age, the social assistance for living, the child supplement and the housing allowance, should be combined in one benefit and at one state agency. But the FDP makes it clear at the same time that a liberal citizen's income would not be paid unconditionally and would therefore be subordinate.

In its draft election manifesto for the Bundestag elections, the SPD has left Hartz-IV behind and intends: "We will fundamentally develop basic security into a

[15] Cf. p. 46, Wahlprogramm_DIE_GRUENEN_Bundestagswahl_2021.pdf

[16] 20200125_Grundsatzprogramm.pdf (gruene.de)

[17] Social security for all: DIE LINKE (the-left) (die-linke.de)

[18] 20.170.807-wahlprogramm-wp-2017-v16.pdf (fdp.de)

citizen's income. Our citizen's income stands for a new understanding of a welfare state that provides support and is close to the people.[19]

More than ten years ago, the CDU/CSU engaged in a relatively broad discussion about the so-called solidary citizen's income, which was favoured by Thuringia's then Prime Minister Dieter Althaus (CDU). This reform concept would have entailed the introduction of a partial unconditional basic income, combined with a reform of income tax, the reorganisation of the financing of social insurance and the amalgamation of most transfer payments. The model envisaged that all citizens in the traditional Bismarckian welfare state would in any case receive an average of around €9200 a year, thus exceeding the limits of what they could bear. In addition it is pointed out that apart from the contributions of the insured ones the federal budget with over 80 billion € for the old age pension insurance participates substantially in the social security. As alternative the concept of the solidary citizen money is suggested, which 600? per month citizen money as unconditional basic income for all plans. Other leading CDU politicians at the federal level, such as the then Federal President Köhler in 2005, also suggested at the time to "think about a kind of basic income", especially to curb the splitting tendencies on the labour market and the exclusion of the long-term unemployed. The first version of the Solidarisches Bürgergeld was presented in 2006 (Althaus 2006). In 2007, the commission "solidarisches Bürgergeld" was founded, which further developed the concept. The second version was presented in 2010, but was quickly forgotten again after Dieter Althaus withdrew from politics, both within the party and the general debate on a BGE, after the German Council of Economic Experts had looked at the reform proposal in 2007, but pointed to considerable additional financial resources of an introduction (SVR 2007, p. 222ff.). Thus, in the entire government era of Chancellor Merkel this topic was not explicitly addressed any more, although in view of the increased challenges for the traditional system of social security (especially in the area of pensions) such a problematisation would have been quite appropriate (cf. Sect. 1.3).

There are also supporters of the concept of an unconditional basic income within the AfD. Nevertheless, at the AfD's federal party conference in November 2020, it was not possible to pass a corresponding motion to test a citizenship income[20] with the majority of delegates. This concept is a (conditional) basic income that would be linked primarily to the condition of German citizenship and would be paid directly to citizens in the form of a negative income tax.

[19] This is in the draft for the election program of the SPD [forward (vorwaerts.de)

[20] 20201029_Application_Trial_State_Citizen_Money_Basic_Income.pdf.

1.7 Civil Society Movements and Organisations to Test a UBI

Despite the fact that the topic of BGE was not dealt with in the parliamentary debates of the German Bundestag, Petition 1422 "Reform Proposals in Social Security – Unconditional Basic Income"[21] was presented in a public discussion in the Petitions Committee in November 2010 and in June 2013 the result of the discussion was finally presented that the request would not be met.[22]

Outside the parliaments, however, the Basic Income European Network (BIEN) had already been formed in 1986 to serve as a link and institutionalised stabilisation between the growing number of individuals and groups from civil society, politics and academia interested in the topic of basic income and to promote an informed discussion on this topic throughout the world. In 2006, BIEN became the Basic Income Earth Network. In Germany, the Basic Income Network was founded in 2004. Its self-conception is that it is "a pluralistic forum for academics and political activists who are committed to the introduction of a basic income". The network also joined the internationally active BIEN and in 2020 had over 5000 members and 130 organisational memberships[23].

But above all, one association in Germany has made a substantial contribution to increasing the public debate and perception of a basic income, which was launched by the social entrepreneur (cf. also Chap. 3) Michael Bohmeyer in 2014 and has since experienced enormous growth as a non-profit association.

The idea for the association started with the question of whether people are willing to finance someone else's livelihood – unconditionally. For the first raffle in 2014, Michael Bohmeyer called for a simple video on the website www.mein-Grundeinkommen.de, which quickly spread via social media channels. Since then, basic incomes of €1000 per month have been raffled off monthly on this page for a period of one year. Free of charge. Registration by e-mail and the declaration of the presumed plans of use in the case that one is selected, are sufficient thereby. The basic income winners are financed and made possible by people who are willing to support this idea financially through their money payments. Via crowdfunding, donations are collected on an internet platform and as soon as 12,000 € have been collected, this amount is raffled off as a one-year Unconditional Basic Income of 1000 € per month. The popularity is enormous; in the first year after the foundation

[21] https://epetitionen.bundestag.de/epet/petition/pdfdownload?petition=1422

[22] https://epetitionen.bundestag.de/petitionen/_2008/_12/_10/Petition_1422.abschlussbegruendungpdf.pdf

[23] https://www.grundeinkommen.de/netzwerk/mitglieder

just under 5000 so-called Crowdhörnchen made possible that at that time 15 BGE winners got a basic income financed for one year, so until today more than 200,000 such Crowdhörnen made possible that from the beginning to summer 2021 approximately 900 persons the possibility was created to receive one year, without any obligations, monthly payments at a value of 1000 €. In other words, close to ten million euros have been "redistributed" within civil society and around three million people have now registered on the platform to win a basic income for one year by drawing lots. Although the association is non-profit and donations to the association can also be deducted for tax purposes, the allocations for the granting of a basic income are made without tax deductibility.

When asked about the motives of the crowdfunders, Mein.BGE states: "It varies greatly. Quite a few of them are not in such an extremely good financial position themselves, so they know from their own experience how it feels to have existential fears. Among them are single parents, artists or self-employed people with small businesses. They get involved in the form of a donation because they want the idea to grow and perhaps one day be implemented on a larger scale. On average, people donate €6."[24] In the meantime, the team of the association Mein.Grundeinkommen consists of more than 30 employees, whose tasks include answering daily media inquiries and – if winners are willing – putting them in contact with journalists[25] . With its regular raffles of basic incomes as well as its professionally designed and regular presence on social media, the association ensures that the debate on a BGE is also kept up to date in the media. At the end of January 2019, a book about the experiences of people who were granted a basic income for a year with the help of a Berlin crowd-funding initiative shot up the bestseller lists within a week of its publication, and the book (Bohmeyer and Cornelsen 2019) was featured in many media outlets to great acclaim.[26]

Although the slightly more than 20 profiles of the random winners described in the book provided a wealth of "anecdotal" evidence on the supposed effects of a BGE, Michael Bohmeyer aspired, following the book project, to accompany his BGE winners through a scientific research project as part of a field experiment.

---

[24] See "Basic income puts people in a better bargaining position" (xing.com).

[25] If one believes the results of the survey institute Civey, which are described as representative, more than half of adult Germans *"have already heard of the association „Mein Grundeinkommen e. V.", which raffles off basic incomes financed by crowdfunding*. https://civey.com/umfragen/5635/haben-sie-schon-einmal-vom-verein-mein-grundeinkommen-e-v-gehort-der-per-crowdfunding-finanzierte-grundeinkommen-verlost3

[26] E.g. https://www.zeit.de/2019/04/grundeinkommen-verlosung-verein-michael-bohmeyer

Thus, in 2019, the idea matured for a pilot project Basic Income[27], in which 122 people would be randomly selected to determine the effects of unconditional cash payments on behavior as well as subjective well-being with the help of a comparison group (Schupp 2020b, d). The necessary financial resources of more than €five million in cash payments are also raised here by civil society and the "crowd-funders" of the association Mein.Grundeinkommen, and the researchers designing and carrying out the project conduct the analysis independently and without being paid by the association (Schupp 2020a).

The study was publicly launched with a press conference[28] on 18.8.2020, which was reported on with high media resonance and a public call to register for participation in the study (see also Sect. 1.2). More than one million adults responded to this call within the first two days, and by the end of the recruitment phase more than two million people had completed a short questionnaire and applied to take part in the study.

The researchers selected a sample of 20,000 individuals who were invited to respond to an online-based baseline survey in March 2021 to answer key socio-demographic questions such as subjective characteristics of well-being, personality, and preferences of the study group. Within a field period of two weeks, 14,420 (72%) individuals provided comprehensive information about their current work and life situation. From this group, the actual target group of 1500 study participants was identified in April 2021, which was then randomly assigned into 122 individuals who will receive a monetary payment of €1200 for three years and 1378 individuals who will then also participate in semi-annual surveys as a comparison group (Fig. 1.9).

Whether the certainly manifold observable behavioural changes within the study period can really be attributed exclusively to the effect of the basic income grant or to other circumstances is attempted to be tested by always comparing the group of basic income recipients with a group of persons who are – if you like – statistical twins of the basic income recipients. In other words, they are very similar and ideally differ only in that they do not receive cash benefits. In this way, statistical procedures can be used to determine the supposed causal effect of basic income for the large number of hypotheses that have been put forward. 107 basic income recipients will participate exclusively in the quantitative study; in the case of 14 persons in the measure group, an additional threefold qualitative survey of the study participants is also planned. This group has also agreed to be available as

[27] https://www.pilotprojekt-grundeinkommen.de/

[28] DIW Berlin: Livestream_PK_Pilot_Basic_Income

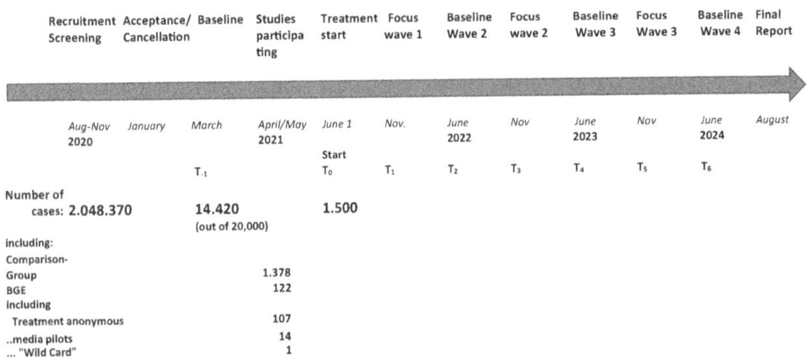

Fig. 1.9 Timetable and survey plan of the long-term study Pilot Project Basic Income. (Source: https: //www.pilotprojekt-grundeinkommen.de/www.pilotprojekt-grundeinkommen.de/)

so-called "media pilots" and to answer questions from journalists about their personal experiences of unconditional monthly cash payments[29] .

The central methodological constraint for such a design is that the selection of whether a person receives basic income or not is made at *random* and that the initial survey was also conducted before this random classification of whether one receives basic income or not. On 1 June 2021, the first payment of €1200 was then made to the so-called treatment group of the study, and in November 2021 the first survey *after* the payment of the regular unconditional basic income was carried out. At the start of payment, it was then also publicly communicated[30], on which target group a restriction and focus was quite deliberately made. Namely, only single-person households were selected[31], persons between 21 and 40 years of age and who normally have between 1200 and 2600 € net monthly at their disposal. For this group, the best possible approximation of the socio-demographic structural characteristics, in terms of gender, level of education, as well as regional distribution, was made in the baseline survey in accordance with the structure of the microcensus. In addition, the selection was made under the secondary condition that around half of

[29] Similarly, in the Finnish basic income experiment, a few participants were brought into contact with the press on request. For first reports on the experiences of the "media pilots" see https://taz.de/Bedingungsloses-Grundeinkommen/!5794276/

[30] Cf. https://taz.de/Bedingungsloses-Grundeinkommen/!5771713/

[31] In addition, one study participant who did not fall under these restrictions was also selected to receive the three-year basic income payment ("wild card").

the study participants tended to support the idea of an unconditional basic income and the other half tended to reject it.

Since in such a field experiment initiated by civil society it is not possible – as would be the case with state-mandated trials – to temporarily suspend the validity of state regulations within the framework of a statutory experimentation clause (Maaß 2001), but the scientific claim in the pilot project is to identify the individual causal effects of unconditional regular cash payments of € 1200, multi-person households were excluded and the level of income group chosen also excludes transfer recipients at the beginning of the study. In this way, the *maximum possible* individual behavioural changes of a BGE are to be identified – if you will – especially in the middle class.

The specific research questions of the pilot project thus include the following:

- How much of the basic income is actually consumed?
- Do BGE recipients participate more in society?
- Is the incentive to continue working diminishing, growing or remaining the same?
- Are more people choosing to become self-employed?
- In addition to effects on the labour market, the psychological and health effects as well as the impact on attitudes and behaviour should also be determined?

However, the pilot project will *not be* able to answer most of the open questions about a BGE raised in Sect. 1.4 for design reasons and methodological limitations. The final report of the study will be presented after the completion of the last data collection in 2024.

Another movement initiated by civil society is taking the route of citizens' petitions and referendums at the state level. The Berlin Senate, for example, has dealt with the application to initiate the referendum *"Expedition Grundeinkommen: Testing an unconditional basic income in the state of Berlin"* and forwarded its result of the admissibility check to the House of Representatives in April 2021[32]. The examination on the part of the Senate showed that the petition for a referendum was admissible and the House of Representatives now had to decide whether or not to adopt the petition for a referendum or the draft bill unchanged. The application for the initiation of a referendum was accompanied by the required written support of at least 20,000 persons. The subject of the referendum petition is a "trial of an unconditional basic income in the Land of Berlin", which would oblige the Land

[32] Admissibility check on the application to initiate the petition for a referendum „Expedition Grundeinkommen: Testing an unconditional basic income in the state of Berlin" – Berlin.de

of Berlin – in the event of a successful majority endorsement by the Berlin population – in the context of a referendum to commission research for a model trial on an unconditional basic income and to carry it out. In the pilot project, the effect, acceptance and feasibility of different variants of a basic income, which would be granted without further preconditions and basically independent of other income, would be scientifically investigated over a period of three years. According to the draft law of the popular initiative a spatially delimited, representative area with at least 3500 inhabitants is to be selected for the experiment. All inhabitants of this area are to be offered participation in the experiment and thus the receipt of the experimental basic income, whereby the amount of the payment is to be arranged in several variants. Participation should be voluntary, but subject to the obligation to take part in scientific surveys. The definition of the experimental area, the modelling of the variants, the survey of the participants and the evaluation should be prepared or carried out by a "research partner" to be selected by the competent Senate administration. The Senate is to issue implementing regulations as a legal ordinance. The total costs of the experiment are to be limited by law to €70 million. After completion and evaluation of the model experiment, a decision is to be made as to whether an extension and/or expansion of the model experiment is to be carried out and/or whether a nationwide, permanent introduction of an unconditional basic income is feasible on the basis of the knowledge gained. The sponsor of the referendum is an association of persons founded from civil society.

The application to initiate a petition for a referendum, together with the position of the Senate, was initially referred by the Berlin House of Representatives to the Committee for Integration, Labour and Social Affairs in May 2021, and then voted on in the House of Representatives. At the hearing in the committee, the Senator responsible for the subject, Elke Breitenbach, stated on record: "I too confess that I have many reservations about an unconditional basic income. But there was a debate. There was a debate about it for many years, in which the question was also asked: What is work? Does only gainful employment count? What women do, i.e. care work, is not so important? What about the voluntary work that we want? – There's always been the argument: people who have basic funding, as it were, can decide exactly how they want to live their lives because of that basic funding, and they have a lot more freedom to do so. That can all be considered. I still have my reservations about that, but, as I said, this is a model project that is being evaluated. Yes, it is expensive. – But I can't get involved in the political debate here. I will learn that too." (Berlin House of Representatives – see Abgeordnetenhaus Berlin 2021, p. 42 f.)

Although the majority of the committee recommended an urgent treatment and rejection of the petition in the House of Representatives, which would have shortened the four-month waiting period until the start of the second phase of the referendum and would have given the opportunity to start the signature campaign already in the summer of 2021, the House of Representatives nevertheless took the corresponding negative vote on the proposed resolution of the committee meeting only *after* the summer break at the end of August 2021. After the final rejection by the House of Representatives, the initiators have the opportunity to obtain the approval of at least 7% of those eligible to vote for the House of Representatives within four months. This would currently be a little more than 170,000 people who would have to agree to the proposal of Expedition Grundeinkommen, in order to then obtain a referendum from all eligible voters in Berlin to vote.

It is noteworthy that for the election of the Berlin House of Representatives in September 2021, the Greens have decided on a pilot project for an unconditional basic income in their election program. Should the party succeed in taking over government responsibility in the Red City Hall in autumn 2021, the aim of the referendum could possibly also already be overtaken by a parliamentary decision to implement such a trial in the state of Berlin.

In a second federal state – Hamburg – sufficient votes were also collected to carry out such a petition for a referendum. However, the Hamburg Senate has not yet reached a final decision on the admissibility of the petition and is currently having the matter examined by the courts. In Berlin, one is thus already one step further, however, it is also important to point out here that on the part of the senate it was not to be examined whether the law is expedient. A high administrative burden, additional costs, possible adverse effects on administrative activity or doubts about feasibility do not lead to violations of the constitution; such questions are to be evaluated and decided by the legislator – in this case the people.

Bloomberg, a financial news service in New York that is by no means suspected of being a mouthpiece for BGE advocates, ventured the prediction "2021 will be the Year of Guaranteed Income Experiments" at the beginning of January this year[33]. So, on the one hand, guaranteed income has gained a lot of popularity in recent years, also in the United States, and a first round of pilot projects was spearheaded by Stockton's SEED program in 2017 (SEED 2018). Also engaged in this effort is the Jain Family Institute (JFI), a nonpartisan applied research organization in the social sciences that promotes the path of a guaranteed basic income from conception in theory to implementation in society. This New York-based NGO has developed a toolkit to provide a concrete starting point for anyone interested in starting a guaranteed income for their community by launching an income pilot and what to consider when creating a local pilot (Jain Family Institute 2021). Their

[33] https://www.bloomberg.com/news/articles/2021-01-04/guaranteed-income-gains-popularity-after-covid-19

briefing provided an overview of the cities implementing guaranteed income pilots and their relative differences in design and goal setting. In addition, a unique feature is that there is an association and web presence[34] of "Mayors for Guaranteed Income". A BGE has also been not only discussed in the US and other countries as an instrument to cope with and alleviate the social consequences of the Covid 19 pandemic, but also tested in many cities, in many cases with accompanying scientific research. The new administration of US President Joe Biden also passed a billion-dollar Corona aid package shortly after taking office in the US Congress[35] . This includes cash payments for millions of citizens amounting to 400 billion US dollars in the form of cheques for 1400 US dollars each.

All these initiatives prove that Bloomberg's forecast is not likely to be so wrong. For Germany, on the other hand, the SPIEGEL cover story (24/2021) published in June could prove to be true, which, with the headline "Bloß keine Experimente" ("No experiments"), tried to highlight the Germans' willingness to change as a myth.

All the examples listed show that in 2021 a number of initiatives and experiments will be launched in Germany which, in the best case, can make a constructive contribution to objectifying the debate on the effects of a basic income.

For some time now, mobilization for both petitions and citizens' petitions has been taking place primarily via online petitions, which have become a new form of participation in digital civil society. For example, a whole series of petitions have been launched on the subject of basic income, which have been signed by thousands of people and sometimes also attract a great deal of public attention. In the case of basic income, too, the initiators of petitions only indirectly intend to prevent a particular policy, but rather to gather committed citizens with the intention of shaping politics and society.

Despite the high popularity of the topic of basic income, a corresponding BGE initiative nevertheless failed in the spring of 2021 as part of a joint initiative in a nationwide petition competition of over 500 petitions, in which just under half a million people took part within eight weeks, in the effort and mobilization that the topic of basic income is one of the four topics with the most votes. Thus, it is planned to mobilize at least one million participants among four possible topics in autumn 2021 with a "first self-organized, nationwide referendum"[36].

Efforts to push for nationwide referendums and more opportunities for direct democratic forms of participation as a means of addressing progressive concerns have also long been called for within the Green Party. Nevertheless, a correspond-

[34] https://www.mayorsforagi.org/

[35] https://www.tagesschau.de/ausland/amerika/usa-hilfspaket-107.html

[36] https://abstimmung21.de/aktuelles/die-vier-abstimmungsthemen-stehen-fest/

ing motion to anchor this demand in the party's new basic programme failed. During the debate on a corresponding amendment, Robert Habeck in particular had pointed out the danger of strengthening populism, as referendums often do not promote discourse in society, but rather the division of society. Instead, the Greens will in future rely on so-called citizens' councils, selected by *lot*, to ensure that the everyday expertise of citizens can be incorporated into legislation on selected issues. Within political science, potential dangers of direct democratic political influence are pointed out: "On the one hand, increased citizen participation should not simply repeat or even exacerbate the political selectivity of parliaments. Participation should therefore be based on lottery or similar procedures. This encourages participation by those who would not otherwise participate. The logic of mini-publics can serve as a model in this regard" (Schäfer and Zürn 2021, p. 210). Other political scientists warn against too high expectations of a more direct-democratic system: "The hope that direct democracy could act as a remedy for deficits in representative democracy must also be viewed with some scepticism, given the sometimes low participation rates in direct-democratic referendums and the resulting lack of representativeness and input legitimacy" (Vatter et al. 2020, p. 370). Moreover, there are warnings of possible disadvantages of growing direct democratic elements, which may run the risk that plebiscites articulate less the will of the people and more only the opinion of a group of activists. Thus Manfred G. Schmidt counts among the *disadvantages* of direct democracy: "It is a sharp majority-democratic instrument. It is susceptible to "passions" and "interests", to passions and egoistic interests" (ibid. 2019, p. 367).

In his book, Andrew Stern, former president of the US trade union Service Employees International, describes how and with what activities civil society organisations can gain influence outside political parties for the issue of basic income. He vividly describes how in a world where change is vastly accelerated by the proliferation of smartphones, tablets, instant information and 24 h news cycles, that even what one day seemed impossible could become mainstream: "Build a significant social media presence by setting a goal of reaching ten million 'likes' on Facebook or one million followers on Twitter …Engage a charismatic leader, actor, athlete, businessperson, or several of them to the cause, especially to help us crystallize the jobs problem and communicate the importance of Unconditional Basic Income as a solution." (Stern 2016, p. 220).

2 Conjunctures of the Welfare State Crisis: The Cracks Are Deepening

2.1 Basic Architecture of the Welfare State

The "safeguarding of social security" has been a central topic in public discourse not only since the financial crisis of 2008/2009 and the Corona pandemic. The *tension* between the functional logic of the existing social security systems and the demographic, labour market and social challenges and changes was explicitly analysed in various academic studies as early as the mid-1980s. In the following, we will examine the *waves of* discussion that have risen again and again since then, indicating that the challenges to social security systems are not recent but have been accompanying the "long-term project" of the welfare state for several decades. The topic is currently gaining new topicality both during the Corona crisis and for the phase of the subsequent repayment of the immense public debt as well as possible neoliberal instruments that want to restrict or even dismantle the welfare state because of Corona debt. The need for welfare state services, as well as its relative share of GDP, has been *growing* steadily even before the onset of the Corona pandemic. In parallel, alternative and complementary social policy architectures have also been presented, but these have not found their way from theory into practice. The complex welfare state and nationally oriented regulatory system has largely preserved its basic architecture (despite additions and individual reforms), leaving well-known historians to ask "why this structure has not changed more" (Kocka 2020, p. 9).

Table 2.1 clearly shows that the so-called *social benefit ratio* – measured as a proportion of gross domestic product – increased significantly in the Corona year 2020 and, at 33.6%, was considerably higher than in the year before the outbreak

R. G. Heinze, J. Schupp, *Basic Income - From Vision to Creeping Transformation of the Welfare State*,
https://doi.org/10.1007/978-3-658-40269-3_2

Table 2.1 Indicators of Germany's economic performance, tax revenue and social benefits

	1991	2000	2010	2018	2019	2020
Gross domestic product (GDP) in EUR billion	1586	2109	2564	3344	3449	3332
Total tax revenue (EUR million)	338.434	467.252	530.587	776.263	799.308	739.700
Total social benefits (in million)	395.601	608.510	771.408	995.168	1.040.323	1.119.400
Public debt (in millions)	538.000	1.211.000	2.113.000	2.069.000	2.053.000	2.333.000
Benefit ratio (social benefits as a percentage of GDP)	24,95	28,85	30,08	29,76	30,16	33,59
Tax share of GDP (in %)	21,34	22,15	20,69	23,21	23,17	22,20
Government debt to GDP ratio (in %)	33,9	57,4	82,4	61,9	59,5	70,0

Sources: BMAS, Social Budget 2021; Deutsche Bundesbank, Destatis 2020

of the pandemic. According to the report, social spending grew to about €1.1 trillion in 2020 and will continue to rise, according to federal government estimates. Shortly after reunification, social benefits still accounted for around a quarter of economic output. According to the Social Report, the year 2020 and the pandemic have led to enormous challenges for social security systems and public finances: "In addition, lower revenues and higher expenditures in the wake of the COVID-19 pandemic will place a heavy financial burden on social security systems. In order to prevent a pandemic-related increase in non-wage labour costs during the crisis, the federal government has stabilised social security contributions at a maximum of 40% as part of a 'Social Guarantee 21' by covering any financial needs above this from the federal budget until 2021 at any rate" (BMAS 2021b, p. 20f.). The fact that the social benefit ratio remained at a level of around 30% even during the sustained economic upswing after 2009 is also due to the expansion of benefits in health, long-term care and pension insurance. Their increase in 2020 (by 3.3 percentage points compared to the previous year) is assessed as "probably the highest increase since the reunification of Germany" (ibid., p. 249), although the pandemic-related nominal decline in gross domestic product also contributed to an increase in the social benefit ratio. The most recent Social Report assumes that in the event of a new economic upswing after the pandemic, a decline in the *social benefit ratio* "to then 32.1%" will again be apparent by 2025 (ibid., p. 250).

Traditional social policy in Germany has so far been concerned with social risks, which were essentially addressed as employee risks. It saw itself primarily as a social insurance policy, and indeed there are separate social insurance schemes for all the classic social risks: pension insurance for old-age risk, health insurance against the risk of illness, occupational accident insurance against accidents at work and invalidity caused by gainful employment, long-term care insurance against the risk of long-term care, and unemployment insurance against unemployment. But there are also elements of provision and welfare in German social policy (for example, traditional social assistance, now known as basic security, or civil servants' pensions, and war victims' pensions through benefits under the Federal Pensions Act). "Cash benefits in social insurance are calculated according to the (modified) equivalence principle. According to this principle, the (relative) amount of entitlements from pension, health, accident and unemployment insurance depends directly on the amount of the individual's earnings subject to insurance and contributions or on the contributions previously paid. There is a relationship of correspondence between the amount paid and the amount of income or contributions, i.e. between performance and counter-performance. A high salary leads to relatively high, a low salary to relatively low insurance benefits. It is not taken into account in which working time the income level has been reached. The level of household income or measures of need and indigence play no role in the calculation of benefits. There is no minimum benefit" (Bäcker et al. 2020, p. 231).

The German conception of the welfare state can therefore be described in summary as a *wage-based equivalence principle* enriched by solidarity-based elements, so-called non-insurance benefits and tax-financed subsidies that provide a certain social compensation. The functioning of a social security system based on equivalence of this kind therefore depends on a number of socio-economic preconditions. If, for example, adequate provision in old age can only be achieved through lifelong full-time employment, it is implicitly assumed that each person will also find employment in a "normal employment relationship" for around 35–40 years. If the financial resources for the acquired pension entitlements are raised from the contributions of the currently employed (pay-as-you-go system), this can only work if the ratio of regular employees and pension recipients is more or less balanced over several generations.

Accordingly, the understanding of the welfare state as well as the concept of social justice in Germany refers to the balance between capital and labour, the safeguarding of the achieved status as well as the stabilisation of the "normal family". At the same time, the understanding of the welfare state is characterised by the principle of subsidiarity, according to which state tax-financed basic security benefits are only granted if no own or family resources are available. However, this guiding principle has been increasingly undermined in recent decades by processes of social and economic change, which are often sweepingly labelled as neoliberalism. "The revolution of the self" characterizes the neoliberalism that has now been with us for nearly 50 years. Not only do collective forces animate, not only do the cast-iron structures of society guide us, but individuals can make a difference. Individuals can change the world, garage entrepreneurship, the virtuosos of civic awakenings, the grassroots movements. So a revolution of the self that basically culminates in the idea that a good society is a society of strong individuals. And that politics should do nothing but enable individuals to develop their strength. That was the idea. Through education, through granting rights of participation" (Bude 2021, p. 28).

The trends towards more *flexible work* as well as globalisation and individualisation tendencies created new risks for a growing number of employed people, which were initially given little consideration in the welfare state systems as well as in the traditional concept of justice. The general public was slow to recognise that social policy safeguards only work in the long term if there is positive economic development. This insight could already be gained almost 100 years ago and could also be observed in more recent historical phases: "At the latest during the Great Depression, it became depressingly clear that the most beautiful welfare state is of no use if it overstretches the economic and social resources that make it possible. The late GDR was to have a similar experience; its collapse was partly caused by the increasing discrepancy between generous social policy benefits and very limited economic capacity. It cannot be overlooked that the welfare state also depends on preconditions that it itself creates only to a small extent" (Kocka 2020, p. 8).

These conditions had been in place in the "old" Federal Republic for almost three decades. The international successes of the "Model Germany" in locational competition had established themselves in the mentalities of the population and created trust in the system; people had become accustomed to the expanded welfare state and the prosperity it had achieved. This acceptance has a real background, for social benefits have risen steadily since their introduction at the end of the nineteenth century and have built up a high level of social security by international standards. In the context of the (from today's point of view relatively "mild") employment crisis in the 1970s, however, the first questions about "safeguarding social security" came into focus – albeit more among the "problem analysts" than the "problem solvers" in social policy.

Whereas during the development phase of a "social market economy" in the Federal Republic of Germany the main focus was still on monetary redistribution within and between different groups of employed persons, the relationship between the employed and the inactive as well as the marginally employed gradually crystallised as a social tension. Social justice was defined more strongly as participatory justice or even start-up justice, and the conflicts between in's and out's were problematised (for example, the segmentation processes on the labour market and the debates about the "new social question"). Alongside the intensification of social fragmentation, however, traditional injustices, for example in the area of gender equality, did not become obsolete, with the result that complex problem situations piled up, putting pressure on government policies that emphasised stability and constancy. Parallel to the erosion of the traditional "Model Germany", which for decades had seen itself as an upwardly mobile affluent society with extensive social security, the problem-solving potential of the political actors relevant to governance had not grown to the same extent. On the basis of socio-political discourses, social science studies have noted "a low propensity for policy change" (Köppe et al. 2007, p. 227; cf. also Heinze and Streeck 2000; Trampusch 2009).

Even though sociologists were already talking about the "short dream of perpetual prosperity" (Lutz 1984) at the beginning of the 1980s, the fact that economic crises are part of the normality of a socio-politically flanked market economy was lost in society's self-descriptions. Added to this was the fact that in Germany in particular there was (and still is) a "deep, historically grown longing for harmony, economically speaking for a disturbance-free equilibrium of development" (Plumpe 2012, p. 67) and therefore people react sensitively to crisis phenomena. Flaring conflicts about the aggravation of social problem situations and socio-political course-setting could also be pacified for the most part with the on-board means of economic growth on the part of politics. The consequences of the disintegration of the "full employment society" (such as the exclusion of the long-term unemployed and the spread of precarious zones) have led to an increase in collective social protests in most Western European societies only in isolated cases, because unemployment was on the one hand more socially structured and for a long time also much more dynamic than many crisis theorists believed. For many of those affected, it was only a biographical phase and, on the other hand, the permanently unemployed – apart from the unemployment initiatives in East Germany and their Monday demonstrations against Hartz IV – were unable to develop any sustainable organisational capacity.

Against this background, both the adherence to and the pride that builds up in the proven architecture of social security and only small steps towards reform in German social policy can be explained. This diagnosis regarding the *hesitant implementation of* reforms is anything but a new insight, but was formulated decades ago by Graf von Krockow. Referring to interest groups and their veto positions, he uses the image of the dinosaur. "The mechanism of the dinosaur reaction can be determined quite simply: Every social institution creates leadership positions and solidifies leadership groups to whom power within the institution, power exercised through the institution to the outside world, and the prestige, self-esteem, and top income associated with power primarily accrue. They are on the sunny side of the existing; they develop conservative interests and ideologies of self-justification; they react – subjectively completely understandably – to threatening changes with defensive or aggressive resistance. They function all the more successfully as veto groups the more they succeed in passing off their judgement as the 'insiders' – which they are – as those who are the only experts, and to devalue any criticism pressing in from outside or 'below' as the irresponsible, merely emotionally determined talk of laymen, if not of malicious people, of 'subversive forces' who are seduced and directed as 'useful idiots' by power-hungry conspirators, backers, wire-pullers. The suspicion of ideology is thus diverted from the existing to the critique or cynically dismissed" (von Krockow 1976, p. 20f.).

Even if confidence in the social security systems crumbled among some groups and at the same time the socio-economic turbulence led to further uncertainty, the pillars of the model remained relatively untouched until the end of the 1990s, even though the financing principles increasingly focused on relieving the burden on the labour factor and the steadily growing social budget was secured with the help of increasing tax-financed shares in the branches of social security. As a result of the growing individualisation processes and the selective social concerns, the consequences of the upheavals could in many cases be gradually shifted to the individual's own responsibility and thus defused in socio-political terms. Nevertheless, a growing social insecurity was unmistakable, which was increasingly able to affect even the social centre and thus extended questions of social inclusion from the traditional "victims" of the labour market to the "normal workers" (cf. among others Lengfeld and Hirschle 2009). Permanent full-time employment continued to shrink (albeit interrupted by primarily cyclical phases with upward trends in employment subject to social security contributions) and atypical forms of employment spread.

A look at other developed welfare states shows, however, that in Germany the spread of low-wage sectors and atypical employment was rather hesitant for a long time. As with the passivisation of large parts of the population through social policy, e.g. in the form of early retirement programmes, the cause of this is seen in the welfare theory literature in the one-sided fixation of the traditional model of Germany on high-tech sectors. "The low-wage debate in Germany is the consequence of neglecting low-productivity jobs that contribute to a country's prosperity and standard of living just as much as a highly productive export sector, because they ensure, for example, that public infrastructure is kept in good shape, school classes and university seminars remain small and care-intensive, trains and subways are safe, service offerings are of high quality and food is healthy, or customers receive competent advice. A poor state of maintenance of the sewage supply, irresponsible care ratios in schools and universities, the rationalisation away of service personnel and a loss of quality in many labour-intensive and skill-intensive fields of activity are the result of a conservative welfare state focused on highly productive sectors and a corresponding economic and social policy" (Czada 2008, p. 203f.).

Overall, the hesitant orientation of modernisation policy described above increased the *heterogenisation of* socio-structural situations, firmly established schemes of social inequality became more differentiated and, at the same time, traditional social polarisations were stabilised and social closure processes took effect in the absence of increasing intergenerational mobility. Those employed in the core sectors were also affected by corporate flexibilisation measures, which undermined traditional employment security and produced fears of discontinuities. Stable life planning, which was still possible for the post-war generation, thus also became increasingly difficult in the middle of society (for example, among skilled workers), because the global acceleration dynamics with shortened production cycles ensured an increasingly rapid devaluation of seemingly secure qualifications. Digitalisation has accelerated these polarisation processes on the labour market since the beginning of the 2000s: the number of highly qualified and unskilled workers (e.g. security guards, parcel delivery staff, etc.) is growing, while the number of skilled workers in industry is *shrinking*.

The fact that the structural change in gainful employment is leading to an erosion of compulsory insurance and gaps in security has also been noted by pension experts for years and a general "citizens' insurance" has been proposed as one answer: "What is needed first of all is comprehensive compulsory insurance for all adults. On the one hand, this is necessary to counteract the erosion of the system as it has happened in the last 15 years. On the other hand – and this is the central point of view – this is the only way to avoid gaps in security, which have to be financed in any case, in case of doubt by the public hands" (Krupp 2007, p. 28). But even this rational conclusion got stuck in the undergrowth of the complex welfare state institutional system or new compulsory systems (example Riester pension) were prevented with the reference to constitutional concerns already in the discourse or at the latest in the process of the legislative procedure. It is impressive to study the stability of the architecture of the welfare state and how much criticism and concrete proposals for improvement bounce off it, or how much solutions developed in commissions are pulverised in the subsequent legislative process.

The crisis discourse reached a first preliminary climax with the financial market crash of 2008/2009, when not only many illusions about the strengths of the German production model tended to collapse, but also about the supposed stability of social security in Germany. Although the welfare state was able to fulfil its basic social security functions, system confidence was nevertheless shaken and new social problem zones grew with all their negative effects on the social foundations of democracy. "Ironically, it is the welfare state that has further reinforced this impotence. The flip side of the German economic miracle and welfare state model is the dissolution of the remnants of pre-capitalist modes of production, the imposition of the market and the state as the sole guarantors of socialization, and thus the complete dependence of households on market and state benefits for subsistence and to secure their social position. If the market fails in its socializing function, the state must intervene in a regulatory way. However, the state itself then comes under pressure from the economic side. The implementation of capitalist-welfare state socialization after the war thus in turn generates new social risks" (Andress and Kronauer 2006, p. 51). Precisely because the traditional welfare state had built up a level of social security never before achieved in history and was thus a successful model, even in comparison with other countries, many people felt they were in good hands in this social model – despite all the criticism of individual components such as Hartz IV or the gradual increase in the retirement age to 67. However, in an increasingly globalised world, many people felt that the wind had become rougher around Germany as an economic and social location and was putting more and more components of the traditional welfare state culture under pressure, because social security is centrally dependent on the stability of financial market institutions. "For although the cause of the financial market crisis is not to be found in a crisis of confidence, it has brought about one. Overcoming it requires institutional reforms. The basis for the political enforceability of such reforms is also a loss of confidence: the loss of confidence in markets that are as unbridled as possible" (Beckert 2010, p. 40).

When it comes to the *future viability of* social security systems, trust and acceptance play an important role alongside economic performance, which is why the financial market crisis of 2008/2009 can be seen as a further turning point in the development of the welfare state. There is no lack of clear evidence from the academic world that trust in the system is continuing to shrink and that, overall, the legitimacy of traditional security in Germany is being undermined. The recurring financing problems of the social insurance institutions and the experience of contribution rate increases accompanied by benefit cuts have shaken confidence in the social security systems. Nevertheless, the institutional robustness as well as the ability to overcome crises of the social security system should not be underestimated either. "The system is cognitively and morally undemanding in an almost ideal way: it makes it easy for every participant to cherish the subjective certainty that he will get what he is entitled to – just as it nourishes the certainty that no one will get something that he is not entitled to. It is precisely to this double lack of entitlement that it owes its remarkable historical robustness, which can be seen in the fact that the German social security system (essentially unchanged in most of the basic institutional features mentioned!) has survived a whole century and no less than four fundamentally different state constitutional systems and has continued to develop in unbroken continuity on the basis of these features" (Offe 2019 [1990], p. 128).

Nevertheless, *doubts* about the reliability of social policy continue to grow. The thesis vehemently advocated by critics of the welfare state and taken up in the media that pay-as-you-go solidarity systems are not sustainable and financially viable in the long term is gaining support. "The fear is spreading that pension insurance will no longer provide an equivalent value for the contributions paid in. Particularly among the younger generation, the mood is growing that, in view of the demographic upheaval, an exit from social insurance is the only rational answer to being able to take social security into one's own hands through individual provision. Individual provision instead of solidarity compensation, private insurance instead of social insurance is the conclusion, which may be in line with the interests of the private banking and insurance industry, but in view of the turbulence on the international capital and financial markets, anything but social security can be expected" (Bäcker et al. 2020, p. 50f.).

The now widely shared growing risk of vulnerability to crisis was already an issue in social science discourses from the 1980s. Pierre Rosanvallon saw relatively early the welfare state, developed since the late 1940s with its correction of the effects of the market and thus balancing function, in a structural crisis. "The slowdown of growth and new economic conditions challenge, first of all, the previous progressive tendency of the welfare state. Collective bargaining is also changing its character with the segmentation of the labour market and the signs of disintegration in the working class (diversity of status, delocalisation of production separation between legal and real enterprise, etc.). They were only meaningful in the context of a relatively homogeneous, globally comprehensible social structure. Today, it is precisely the dissolution of this social fabric that has become the main means of economic regulation of social costs for companies" (Rosanvallon 1982, p. 72; see also Obinger and Petersen 2019).

This description of the end of the "golden age" of the welfare state is still apt today and perhaps even more meaningful at present with regard to the rapidly expanding and globally active *internet companies* such as Amazon, Google, Apple,

Microsoft, IBM, Facebook in the United States or Baidu, Alibaba and Tencent in China. With a view to the labour market and social security, *digitalised capitalism* intensifies the processes of division, which overall lead to social fragmentation (cf. inter alia Staab 2019, p. 282ff.). In this context, challenges that have existed for some time have not yet been adequately addressed by government actors (such as the demographic problem with regard to old-age provision). Whereas in the period from the 1950s to the early 1980s the ratio of those in work to those receiving pensions was 2 to 1, it has now swung to almost 1 to 1. The existing social security system was therefore already regarded in the 1980s as being *inadequately* equipped to meet the expected challenges of economic, demographic and social change, and the principle of equivalence was put to the test for the material side of social security. In the next few years, the German economy is expected to lose two to three million employees when the baby boomer generation retires. For those paying contributions, this implies further increases in contributions combined with future cuts in benefits and, at the macroeconomic level, *lower tax revenues* and *rising social security contributions.* Both demographic change and the consequences of digitalised capitalism have on the one hand increased the pressure to reform the contribution-financed social security system and at the same time increasingly shattered confidence in the future validity of the equivalence principle if, for example, statutory pension entitlements are not higher than tax-financed basic security benefit entitlements in old age.

In particular, the increasingly obvious deficits of this principle were addressed with terms such as "new poverty" or "poverty traps" and the demand was raised to grant claims to social security to a greater extent than before independent of previous gainful employment subject to social insurance contributions. Added to this were the *rigidities of* welfare state regulations that had become visible. "The mechanisms that generate solidarity have become abstract, formal, indecipherable. The excesses of bureaucracy and the increasing cumbersomeness of social legislation are due to this abstraction and in turn reinforce it. The consequence of this is a relative reduction in efficiency' (Rosanvallon 1982, p. 67; cf. also ders. 2004). Against this background, it is not surprising if design alternatives for an upcoming reform of social policy have been publicly debated. The tendency has been to discuss a switch from the insurance principle to a principle of participation in sociocultural standards, based on the idea of solidarity. And this is where the guaranteed minimum income comes into view as an answer to poverty traps and gaps in security. Interestingly, leading social democratic politicians in particular already saw this as an imminent danger at this time; for example, the former federal director of the Social Democratic Party (SPD), Peter Glotz: "A spectre is haunting Europe: the 'system-disrupting' idea of a guaranteed basic income" (cf. 1986).

To this day, these ideological reservations about basic security models outside of social assistance or basic security are firmly anchored above all in the ranks of the social democratic party and the trade unions. Contribution-financed compulsory insurance – at least within income thresholds of contribution assessment limits of statutory health and pension insurance that have only moderately increased over time – has been the foundation and also the basic consensus against life risks since Bismarck's reforms. "What all systems of state-regulated provision for life's risks have in common in Germany is that they are based on the *employment relationship*. Entitlements are acquired through work and (with the exception of civil servants' pensions) income-related contributions. Analogous to the insurance thinking in private insurance, the principle of *equivalence of contributions and benefits* is also widely accepted: Sickness benefits, unemployment benefits, disability pensions and old-age pensions are in principle based on insurable income" (Kaufmann 2003, p. 284; cf. also ders. 2015; Bäcker et al. 2020, esp. Chapters I and II).

Due to the deep grammar and cultural roots of the German welfare state, it is also not surprising that the reservations expressed as early as the 1980s against universalistic basic security models that overcome the strict employment-relatedness, such as the proposal of the Kronberg Circle at that time (cf. Mitschke 1985), met with almost unanimous resistance from the established social policy actors. In the end, adherence to the national tradition of the welfare state led politicians and the widely ramified social administration, with equal representation of employer and employee representatives and politicians, to continue to strongly emphasise the insurance principle in order to secure legitimacy, financial viability and efficiency, and to allow corrections only in individual questions inherent in the system. However, new models that see themselves as a supplement to social security systems, especially social insurance, and not as an alternative, were certainly stimulated by the first "boom in the basic income debate" that took place at that time at the level of economic and social policy. In this respect, it would be wrong to speak of general blockades; rather, a "dynamic immobilism" is to be found in the social policy of the 1980s and 1990s (cf. Lessenich 2009; Vobruba 2019).

One lesson should be drawn from these debates: The *interest of* socio-political institutions in themselves and the maintenance of the institutional logic of the social security idea cannot be fundamentally shaken or even changed within a short time by normative policy designs (and may they be morally or tax systematically "superior"). "The goal of social inclusion, meanwhile, still lies at cross-purposes with that of status preservation as institutionally embedded in the conservative German welfare model" (Czada 2008, p. 204). However, they have triggered discussions that have resulted in social-philosophical debates in the feuilleton rather than social or labour market policy discussions in the business section of newspapers and media articles. However, the self-image, the future viability due to demographic change as well as technological change in the work process and also the value basis, were problematized by parts. However, the irritations were not yet so great that they triggered fundamental reforms of the welfare state, even if, in view of the increasingly serious gaps in security and financing in various branches of social insurance, the need for tax-financed readjustment in the form of an increase in federal subsidies increased. This phenomenon of increasing federal subsidies contradicts the actual design principles of exclusive contribution financing, which is supposedly thereby also able to escape the grasp of politics. "Contribution financing, in contrast to tax financing, has the function of withdrawing the disposition of the use of social insurance budgets from state sovereignty and the legislative process, at least to the extent that use of the funds for purposes other than those of the insured is excluded. In this way, the collection and use of contributions is secured against "non-insurance" redistribution ambitions and attempts and reliably depoliticized" (Offe 2019 [1990], p. 127).

2.2 Excursus: A Look Back to the Future

Building blocks for concrete reform projects in the field of social security were already available in the 1980s. Both in view of the foreseeable demographic challenges and the effects of the new technologies, the risks of the welfare state apparatuses that still functioned well and were appreciated in the 1960s and 1970s were pointed out. Due to the wage-based nature of the social security systems, technological developments (today one would speak of digitalisation) could undermine the financing foundations, so that it was questionable whether the contribution-financed revenue would still be sufficient in the future to compensate for the acquired pension entitlements. In addition, the question was increasingly asked whether it is desirable in principle at all to organise the provision of social security on the basis of wages. The indications of a "new poverty" as a result of the wage-based calculation of social security entitlements were also problematised and not only called for detailed theoretical and empirical reviews of the underlying relationships, but also pointed to necessary changes.

Against this background, the project "New Technologies and Social Security" (for the Ministry of Labour, Health and Social Affairs in North Rhine-Westphalia/project management: Gretschmann/Heinze) was launched in the mid-1980s and will be briefly summarised below. On the one hand, it can be made clear that a vital socio-political debate not only existed in scientific as well as political circles, but that the central concepts were also passionately discussed (sometimes with different terminology). Even then, the demographic trend, a period of precarious economic situations and the strongly diffusing new technologies confronted us with a situation in which it was necessary to think about setting a course. This also applied to the already then visible marginal employment relationships, quasi-employment relationships based on contracts for work, etc. The fragmentation of the labour market was already evident, and so one should be cautious today about discovering entirely new phenomena in mini-jobs or solo self-employment. Moreover, precisely in order to bring lasting security and trust to the welfare state institutions, it was already important at that time to critically question the problem-solving capacity and to discuss alternatives. In the summary of the study (quoted from the book version), the following conclusions are drawn:

"If we summarize the main findings of the present study, we come to the following conclusions:

* A characteristic feature of the existing, historically developed system of social security is that the consideration and calculation of individual benefit entitlements are linked back to (previous) wage employment. Only wage earners and persons identified as contributors (and their family members) acquire entitlement to benefits; in the event of risk, the others are left with only subordinate social assistance. This labour-centredness of social security results in several points of incursion through which the New Technologies – by means of their quantitative and qualitative effects on the labour market – also have an impact on social security. To the extent that the New Technologies bring about changes in the use of the factor labour, they also influence the nature and scope of the social security system. This applies both to the financing (revenue side) and to the quantity and quality of social benefits (expenditure side).

* An evaluation of the available studies on the effects of New Technologies on the employment level and the employment structure does not provide a clear picture: The release or compensation ultimately depends on a series of boundary conditions, the empirical existence of which could not be examined within the framework of this study. Just as the changes in the labour market caused by the use of new technologies cannot be determined precisely and with certainty for the future, the consequential effects on social security cannot be forecast precisely and with certainty either.

The technology factor – one explanatory variable among others – cannot be separated from the financing and performance gaps of social security: it is and remains a component of a complex bundle of influencing factors that also – according to our hypothesis – correspond to each other, i.e. are interdependent. In particular, the demographic and technological components are not independent of each other as causes of strain on social security. On the contrary, if the structure of social security remains unchanged, the demographic upheavals will drive up wage-related social security contributions in the coming decades to such an extent that this alone will increase the business incentive to use the New Technologies to reduce the number of jobs and to make the use of labour more flexible in order to save costs.

The problem potential of the New Technologies is thus considerably increased by the demographic framework conditions. In order to create the basis for an examination of the question of whether and to what extent the various reform proposals addressed in this study are suitable for countering the technologically given risk to the stability of social security systems, a coherent picture of the probable economic development and the resulting changes in the situation of social security was drawn up using and further developing current forecast scenarios, with different development assumptions leading to a pessimistic release scenario and an optimistic compensation scenario. These two scenarios mark out a probable development corridor, a bandwidth with upper and lower limits.

This forms the analytical framework for the model calculations carried out, which clarify the economic consequences of the individual reform proposals and thus their suitability and any problematic side-effects.

As far as alternative financing models are concerned, the following are being examined: (a) the conversion of employer contributions to a value-added-based assessment basis, (b) the financing of the foreseeable additional expenditure of the social insurance system by means of an additional value-added-based assessment basis, (c) an increase in the federal subsidy to cover the additional expenditure, and finally (d) the financing of the additional expenditure by means of an energy levy.

We arrive at the following results: A revenue-neutral rebasing of employers' contributions to social insurance would, albeit to a quantitatively unsatisfactory extent, be able to relieve the labour market at least temporarily. Demographic development and economic structural change can thus be synchronised to a limited extent by this reform proposal. However, the price, namely the loss of growth in the national economy, is not insignificant. In contrast, the negative effects of an additional value-added-based tax base are much smaller. The shifts in the sectoral burden are less drastic in the case of an additive value-added contribution. The reform model of financing demographically and technologically induced additional expenditure via a "third pillar", which brings value-added-based levies into social security, is therefore to be preferred to rebasing. In order to cover the expected shortfalls in social security by 2015 completely by increasing the federal subsidy, the latter would have to be multiplied in volume. The federal subsidy is therefore at best suitable for flanking other financing strategies, but not as an independent financing model.

Compared to the value added contribution, its distributional and allocative effects can be regarded as comparatively harmless. As far as the proposal to tackle the financing problems of old-age provision via an energy tax is concerned, our model calculations show that the assessment base for the sums to be covered would be narrow and the necessary tax rates correspondingly high. Moreover, the tax base for an energy tax is variable and therefore not very stable. There would also be sectoral shifts in the burden to the disadvantage of those industries that suffer particularly from labour market problems. Weighing up all the advantages and disadvantages, we come to the conclusion that the supplementary value-added levy is probably the most viable reform model for the financing side to date. Of course, a mixed solution would also be conceivable, but this could not be pursued further in the context of this paper.

* In addition to analysing the advantages and disadvantages of different financing alternatives, various reform ideas were also examined for the benefits side. First of all, different variants of a minimum benefit system were examined, which are supported by socio-political and modernisation considerations. The conceptually coherent models fail because of the costs. Our calculations show that the additional costs of a means-tested social dividend for everyone are beyond the limit that can realistically be set as a target point. But the costs of a means-tested "base" in the various social security systems are also likely to be higher than is currently being claimed by their advocates.

In essence, every variant of a guaranteed minimum income involves a departure from the equivalence principle. However, not every reform that is designed to overcome the wage-labour-centredness of social security has to throw the equivalence principle overboard at the same time. The reform proposal we finally examined therefore adheres in principle to the equivalence principle, but opens up the opportunity for individuals to build up benefit entitlements vis-à-vis the social security system beyond wage labour. This model works with social vouchers, which are granted as a social policy counterpart for socially useful activities outside formal gainful employment. Such social vouchers can be used to build up benefit claims against the social security system without the need for a codified employment relationship. Such a reform takes account of the fact that, as a result of structural change in the labour market, not least due to technological developments, more and more people have larger time quotas but fewer monetary resources at their disposal. In our opinion, this change in resources requires a redefined equivalence principle. In our model, the groups of people with a lot of time and little money are given the opportunity to build up their own social security for the future through recognised services in the areas of care and education, for example.

If our analysis is correct that wage-relatedness as a core element of our welfare state security is historically outdated in view of demographic and technological problems, then the question arises as to the appropriate reform strategy – after all, the traditional instruments of the welfare state are no longer adequate. In view of the diversity of problems and the corresponding breadth of reform proposals, and taking into account the fact that the individual improvement projects are only ever capable of solving partial problems, a combination of reform models seems most promising – an optimal mix, so to speak.

Which combination will turn out to be the optimal one, or at least an appropriate one, which one is most likely to be implemented politically, and whether the two are congruent, must be left open at this point. For it is true for social policy, as for other fields, that people make their history under the circumstances and conditions they find themselves in, but that they still have enough room for manoeuvre to allow the scientist to speak of 'indeterminacy'. However this may be, if the massive social, economic and technological challenges of the future are to be met, then the above considerations, however realutopian they may seem, must not remain characterized by that resounding ineffectiveness which scientifically ambitious expert reports and policy advice generally have to experience" (Gretschmann et al. 1989, p. 231ff.; cf. also the contributions in Heinze et al. 1988).

This *retrospective* can exemplarily illustrate what has been worked out in policy research: that a problem stream (here the challenges for the social security system due to demography, new technologies and segmentations of the employment system) is not (yet) sufficient for the start of a structural policy change. Despite the objective challenges, no appropriate political decision-making options were discussed because new priorities, such as the reunification phase in the 1990s, also forced full attention from the political actors and, with the monetary, economic and social union that came into force on July 1, 1990, there was a determination to establish "without experimentation" these institutional structures now also in East Germany the West German welfare state model. In order to finance the unification-related burdens, social contributions were increased in addition to taxes. "Thus, the contribution rates to unemployment insurance were raised as early as 1991 and, step by step *until 1997*, the contributions to pension insurance; on balance, an unification-related increase of about five percentage points is calculated. This formidable increase was a consequence of the fact that, as a result of the transformation crisis, a high unemployment rate had to be financed and relatively more persons in East Germany had independent claims to support payments, because more working people were employed in the GDR (with lower productivity)" (Vesper 2020, p. 14).

Gerhard A. Ritter put the amount of the transfer from West Germany to the new federal states at more than 2 trillion euros, more than 40% of which was financed from the West German social security systems. This form of financing in particular gave rise to discussions even at that time as to whether financing via the social security funds instead of via taxes was not a "wrong" way to go (Meinhardt and Zwiener 1997). Within a very short time, a large number of new institutions were set up in the new Länder with corresponding administrative sponsorships from the old Länder in order to mitigate the transformation shock of a transition from a centrally planned economy to a social market economy. With regard to the structural problems of the German welfare state already identified in the 1980s, as a consequence of coping with mass unemployment in East Germany, these problems were if anything further exacerbated and the restructuring already due was *delayed* rather than tackled. "It is to be hoped that the urgency of the problems to be solved in the welfare state, which is now seen in ever wider circles, will lead politicians, experts, the functionaries of the major associations, and also the voters to jump over their shadows and find the strength to support comprehensive reforms of the welfare state. But these reforms cannot be achieved in one fell swoop. Since it is not just a matter of short-term corrections, but above all of long-term solutions, they require politicians to have staying power, innovative strength, a sense of proportion, expertise and political skill in presenting reform plans in the media, winning majorities and balancing conflict and cooperation" (Ritter 2006, p. 406).

In addition, there are the well-known "shifting stations" in social and labour market policy between the political-administrative levels (federal government, Länder, municipalities) and the social administrations as well as political-organisational priorities (e.g. leadership personalities). Consequently, there are many reasons to "live with" the problems for the time being and to turn the existing "screws" only when individual areas of conflict come to a head. The problem backlog was only spectacularly addressed at the highest political level in the mid-1990s, when the then Federal President Herzog openly denounced the blockades in government policy in a much-noticed public speech in the spring of 1997 and spoke of the need for "a jolt" to go through Germany. The then Red-Green federal government then announced a modernisation of labour market and social policy at the outset and introduced various measures that actually led to a policy change in the first decade of this millennium. "In the mid-nineties, radical reform forces both in the parties and on the side of the business community question the social consensus. In the parties, the business wing is increasingly critical of Kohl's and Blüm's course of cooperation; in the business associations, the industrial middle classes are demanding a reduction in non-wage labour costs. Attempts at group consensus on social reform fail due to the dynamics of party conflicts and dissonance between the state, business and the unions over the need for social policy change. As a result of the discrediting of a trilaterally agreed structural reform of the welfare state, a change of course decided on bypassing the trade unions is already being implemented under the Kohl government. This was continued by the Schröder government after the renewed failure of an attempt at an alliance with the Agenda 2010 and the Hartz reforms" (Trampusch 2009, p. 123; cf. also Heinze and Streeck 2000).

The states of exhaustion in the socio-political institutions were – and this becomes clear in the following longer quotation – already present for a long time and therapy offers were also on offer in the scientific field. But a political current gaining momentum is not enough on its own to seriously affect an institutional system that has become so entrenched historically and to trigger a gradual change. In addition, there must be effective internal shifts in political priorities. From the point of view of *policy research*, one could say that although individual "streams", such as the growing social problems, the costs of German unification, which were also cross-subsidised via the social systems and placed a particular burden on the labour factor, and also socio-political discourses were already pushing for new decisions, these tended to run alongside each other and were not sufficient to implement such a fundamental change in strategy in social policy. "What is decisive is not the factual need to solve the problem, but the context of the decision-making process, i.e. which and how many decision-making opportunities present themselves, which problems the organization is currently dealing with, which solutions present themselves at the moment, how the participants distribute their attention and time among different decisions, and how much time is available. The coupling of the elements of the decision-making process can thus rather be described as a random confluence of relatively independent streams" (Schmid 2011, p. 329; cf. also Rüb 2009).

The fundamental conclusion from this is that there is no systematic or quasi-natural historical link between a problem (a policy stream) and a particular policy decision, and therefore analyses need to look much more intensively at the reasons why certain policy concepts cannot be changed overnight, although the challenges are plausible and immediately obvious. We will show later (in Chap. 4) that the "multiple streams approach", which assumes relatively autonomous streams with their own dynamics and driving forces, can be used to explain both the persistence in the national social security context and the linkages necessary for policy change through political entrepreneurs and new forms of political participation and civic engagement. In almost all fields, policy decisions are not as rational as is often believed by the public and assumed by many classical political science theories.

The decision-making processes take place against the backdrop of different thematic conjunctures on several levels with different participants and solution options and are usually no longer in a firmly structured context. For this reason, special attention must be paid to the linking of the flows, and it is therefore a matter of actors and actor alliances that link the different flows in real terms and carry them onto the stage of public debate. If one has these contingencies of action in mind, then it is no longer surprising why, despite many factually appropriate lines of argument and evidence-based results, the socio-political turnaround has so far failed to materialize and fundamental reform efforts have been averted. It will only succeed if, based on a problem pressure, an opportunity space is available and political entrepreneurs have prepared the decisions wisely. A *policy window* that opens either because of significant shifts in indicators in the issue area or because of a change of government or personnel at the decision-making level relevant to the issue area can then bring about a constellation that is also capable of initiating a system change.

In summary, therefore, from a real socio-political perspective, the first episode of the debates on a new architecture for the German welfare state was no more than *agenda-setting* without any further-reaching consequences. Although some of the debates at the time were rather polemical, the debate about a minimum or basic income did make waves in the academic discussion and was discursively stimulating from a social science perspective. As early as the mid-1980s, the guaranteed minimum income was one of the most frequently and controversially discussed topics, and the subsequent waves of economic activity demonstrate the prominence of this debate, which is by no means coincidental, since it touches on the central construction principles of social security in Germany. Benefits from the current social security system are largely dependent on prior contributions in the employment system, but a growing part of the population is either unable to make these prior contributions at all or can no longer make them in sufficient amounts. This development has been emerging for quite some time, which is why the debate on a basic income periodically returns (cf. from different perspectives the contributions in Kovce and Priddat 2019; Osterkamp 2015).

The causes of the return are, apart from unemployment (especially long-term unemployment), a change in the nature of employment relationships (increase in part-time and precarious work, etc.) as well as social changes in forms of cohabitation in civil partnerships, marriage and family. For women in particular, it became increasingly 'risky' to rely only on husband-derived entitlements for social security, a theme raised in the women's movement from the 1970s onwards. "Women are often only 'one man away' from poverty" (Beck 1986, p. 183; see also the contributions in Opielka and Ostner 1987; Heinze et al. 1988). With regard to women's participation in the labour market, there has been a steady change in recent decades, which has brought considerable progress in terms of independent social security, which has also found expression in reforms of the social security system towards increasing individualisation of contribution-related entitlements and decreasing derived family security entitlements by contributors. However, this does not exclude the fact that today's poverty is still female-dominated in many cases (especially in old age) and thus refers to the systematic security gaps in the traditional social security system. Above all, the expansion of childcare facilities initiated by federal funding made a decisive contribution to the growth of social services and thus also created the necessary infrastructural conditions for the possibility of gainful employment in parallel with the fulfilment of family upbringing and care obligations.

However, the fragmentation processes on the labour market, which were already discussed in the 1980s, have deepened further as a result of years of disregard or only symbolic discussion in politics and have taken on new dimensions as a result of digitalisation in production processes and consumer behaviour. Here, the constantly recurring theme of precarious forms of employment with inadequate social security is evident, without, however, structural reforms in labour market and social policy having been implemented. An often cited example of the systematic disadvantages of flexible forms of work in the German welfare state are *mini-jobs, which* are mostly performed by women (as well as by pensioners and students) and may appear rational in the short term as "more net from the gross wage", but accept poor social security as the price in the long term.

This form of employment has expanded over the last 20 years (at the end of 2019, there were almost eight million employees in the mini-job segment, which represents an increase of 43% compared to 2003) and repeatedly provides grounds for fundamental criticism of the system (cf. on this also Grabka et al. 2020). "A main point of criticism is the lack of possibility for independent social security for employees. Although employers pay flat-rate contributions of currently 13% of pay to health insurance, mini-jobbers are not registered with a health insurance fund and have to take out health insurance on their own, unless they have derived insurance coverage. Likewise, neither the employer nor the employee pays contributions to unemployment insurance. In cases of unemployment, marginally employed persons are only entitled to unemployment benefit II. A special feature is the pension insurance, to which employers contribute a reduced flat-rate contribution of 15%. Since 2013, marginally employed persons have had to top up their pension insurance contributions to the regular rate. However, in practice, an overwhelming majority use the opt-out option because they want a favourable gross-to-net ratio of income, expect only marginal entitlements, or are encouraged by their employer to opt out. Overall, the opt-out reform has not had the desired effect" (Beckmann 2020, p. 103; cf. also ed. 2019).

The security gaps could be counteracted if mini-jobs were to act as a stepping stone into employment subject to social security contributions. However, direct transitions are rare and most remain in this employment status for several years, which does not necessarily result in direct social disadvantages, as many mini-jobbers have derived (e.g. as wives) or otherwise acquired entitlements (as pensioners or students). In an empirical study on the motivation of those working in this segment of the labour market, it was found that many people employed in this form "paradoxically do not wish to move up into 'regular' and thus better paid and more secure forms of employment, despite the deficits in social security and the obvious risks" (Beckmann 2020, p. 119). Against this background, the question arises whether this form of employment should either be limited in amount with a significantly lower maximum amount such as €200, thus making it less attractive (cf. Grabka et al. 2020), or whether the normal-labour-centred security system should not be enriched to reflect these processes of differentiation on the labour market by establishing an all-encompassing employment or labour insurance scheme (cf. also Schmid and Schröder 2020). Another answer would be a universalistic basic income that would provide basic security irrespective of the respective forms and scope of employment, although the question of (monetary) incentives to take up gainful employment would also have to be resolved in such a system. The fact that there is nevertheless hardly any movement in the political treatment of this obvious social problem area is due, among other things, to the separation of workers' and poor people's welfare, which has historically shaped the German welfare state, and the continuity of socio-political regulations, as well as a basic consensus among the organisations concerned not to question these institutional arrangements at their core. "It is impressive how much the structures of social insurance laid down in Bismarck's social reforms have survived and yet continued to develop through all political conjunctures" (Kaufmann 2003, p. 304; cf. also the contributions in Leibfried and Tennstedt 1985).

2.3 Constancy and Dynamics: Concepts of Restructuring and Reform for Social Security

If the classical welfare state is coming under increasing pressure to keep up with the forms of work and lifestyles of the post-war period and the ongoing rapid changes in the economy and living conditions, the idea and concrete proposal of decoupling social security benefits from prior contribution payments cannot and must not be left out of the debates. Conceptually, this represents a switch from a causal – i.e. dependent on the accumulation of entitlements in gainful employment – granting of benefits to a payment of social transfers in the form of negative tax payments oriented towards the avoidance of poverty. Somewhat pompously, there is occasionally talk of a "decoupling of work and food"; in essence, such a reorientation would be tantamount to a guaranteed minimum income based on a legal entitlement as a citizen that is independent of gainful employment. Social policy was thus finalised to a certain extent in monetary terms. In this way, "on the one hand, clearly objectifiable performance standards can be formulated, which make unjustified accumulation of benefits and blatant underprovision avoidable. On the other hand, finalisation means – according to its idea – the possibility of establishing pure socio-political objectives and thus a principle that corresponds to the idea of a guaranteed basic income. Participation instead of ownership as a legal leitmotif and purpose (finalization) instead of causality as a socio-political orientation" (Vobruba 2019, p. 26f. [1986]; cf. also Opielka 2019 [1984]).

Demands for a strategic reorientation of social security, as currently reflected in the various public campaigns for an unconditional basic income, are therefore not at all original, but have been discussed in socio-political discourses and expert debates for over 30 years. Since then, a general criticism of the guaranteed minimum income in all its variants has mainly referred to the fact that, for financial reasons, it would ultimately be impossible to avoid placing a heavier burden on large sections of the working population in particular. In particular, if it becomes obvious that minimum income recipients who are capable of working are supported by the state "unconditionally" without any prior contributions and without the supposed willingness *to* work in the future, a loss of legitimacy of such a social security system must be expected. Almost all the major players in the social policy institutional system have subscribed to this line of argument, presumably not least because they see a fundamental reform as endangering their institutionalised interests in maintaining power.

The *decoupling* of work and income could, for example, from the point of view of trade union representatives, become a serious threat to the organisational and conflict capacity of trade unions, which have already been struggling for years with declining membership figures and which are not succeeding in winning new members in technology-driven growth sectors. Their most important pillars are strongly work- and performance-oriented groups of the population, among whom, according to their own organisational interpretation, there is little understanding of non-work-centred lifestyles and ways of life. In addition, the trade unions themselves are strongly anchored in the self-governing bodies of the social security systems and can thus participate in shaping and preventing reforms of the social security system and have also made active use of these opportunities to exert influence. This general characterisation of trade unions does not, of course, rule out the possibility that individual personalities may have had divergent views, such as Detlef Hensche, the former chairman of the industrial trade union for the media: "A civilised society with an eye to emancipation would do well to dispense with systems of compulsory work and not to hand the unemployed over to collective denunciation as work-shy. In a free, rich society at the highest level of productivity, it must be possible to leave the labour market without having to justify oneself and without being forced to work. The unconditionality of social income therefore deserves applause" (Hensche 2009, p. 213).

The adherence of the trade unions and their management levels to the traditional welfare state can be understood from the point of view of organisational sociology, but in view of the loss of power and the necessary new strategic options, orientation towards a social investment model is an interesting option for the future. "In political terms, we conclude that unions and their members are not hostile to the transformation of European welfare states from the traditional towards the social investment model, but they are unlikely to be at the spearhead of this development. Potentially, however, putting a strong emphasis on SI policies could be a winning strategy for unions to recruit new members, in particular among the educated middle classes as other research has shown that SI policies are broadly popular across different classes" (Bledow and Busemeyer 2021, p. 279).

Incidentally, the same applies to employers' associations, which also know how to assert their institutional influence in the social security system by paying employer contributions as a component of wage costs. This stabilising function has certainly helped to uphold the traditional model or, at times, to exaggerate it ideologically, but it must also be repeatedly legitimised within the organisation. "Integration into the welfare state institutional system generates – in addition to the primary interests of members – its own secondary interests in the existence of the organisation and its employees. On the one hand, participation in self-government brings with it opportunities for personnel influence – and at the same time it promoted the trade union development towards centralised large organisations. On the other hand, through their incorporation into the cross-class institutions of the social security state, they are bound to compromises that in individual cases can also run counter to the direct interests of their members" (Schroeder 2019, p. 230).

If one roughly reviews the individual proposals and their criticism, one is left with the impression that, due to the 150-year institutional dependence of social security, *the* ideal path to a guaranteed basic income simply cannot exist in Germany. What a basic income solution with the fewest disadvantages and as a fundamentally superior alternative could and should look like can probably only be judged once evidence-based research is available and also after an intensive and open-ended debate on principles. This also includes satisfactory clarification of a host of design issues (as outlined in Sect. 1.4). The knowledge currently available on the actual effects and consequences, which are not based solely on simulation studies, is far too limited, and this is one of the reasons why it was relatively easy until a few years ago to defend the status quo and reject fundamental debates on reform.

In view of the increasingly serious security gaps in various branches of social insurance, which are appearing in the Corona crisis as if in a *burning glass*, the topic of fundamental changes to the social security system can no longer be permanently pushed off the political agenda. Rather, individual elements are flowing into social policy practice, and new political actors have also established themselves who no longer share the concerns and clichés against basic security models that have been voiced for decades. Despite this softening, the majority of politically responsible actors (not to mention the social administrations concerned) have so far tended to continue to strongly emphasise the insurance principle and the principle of means-tested basic security benefits and their review in order to secure the legitimacy, financial viability and efficiency of the welfare state. But also in the "camp" of the trade unions and in the circle of the social democratic party, voices were raised that productively took up the restructuring debate and called for radical or system-hybrid reforms, albeit within the existing welfare state development path:

"The cornerstones of a new, investment and infrastructure-based welfare state would be, in our view, as follows:

- Universalism
- Citizenship principle
- New mix between contributions and taxes as basis for financing
- Development of a quality social infrastructure that supports families and individuals, especially in the areas of education, training and care.
- Participation: inclusion instead of exclusion
- Strengthening the individual in a society based on solidarity (personal responsibility)
- Social security as the basis for performance

In these associative and solidarity-based forms of governance and structural elements, civil society actors, including the trade unions and employers' associations, on which the concept is all too quick to sound the death knell, should be increasingly involved. What we need in Germany is a strong reform of the welfare state that is capable of tackling the deficits of the established welfare state in a manner that is, as it were, path-dependent, without getting lost in hopeless transformation problems and leaving the population behind. A stronger accentuation of the existing welfare state in favour of an investment and infrastructural restructuring would correspond to these goals" (Schroeder and Weinert 2006, p. 205f.).

2.4 Ways Out of the Employment Crisis: Reform Approaches since the Red-Green Government Era

Starting from an employment deficit of the German economy that had grown considerably in the 1980s and 1990s, coupled with low labour force participation rates (compared to neighbouring countries), the newly elected red-green federal government under Chancellor Gerhard Schröder was faced in autumn 1998 with the problem of overcoming the traditional path of German labour market policy, which had long been pursued more or less amicably by government, opposition, employers and trade unions. This consisted in passivising growing parts of the labour supply (in early retirement, i.e. old-age provision, the family – indicated by low female employment rates – or the education system). Changing values, however, no longer allowed this exclusion of *women* from the labour force (which was also reflected in the fact that in West Germany the share of women in employment increased from 47% in 1960 to almost 70% in 2016). Since paid gainful employment is for more and more women the most important access to both personal autonomy and social ties, women in Germany demanded the same access to gainful employment as men. The defensive instruments developed over many years in the Federal Republic to balance supply and demand in the labour market had become part of the problem it was once intended to solve. This made a redefinition of the goals of German labour market and employment policy inevitable.

It became explicitly apparent in the establishment of the benchmarking group at the "Alliance for Jobs" in the first legislative period of the Red-Green federal government that one can no longer assume a universally accepted and action-guiding "model Germany" that is considered a model for other countries. Instead, a systematic comparison was made with other countries in order to gain ideas for Germany as an economic and social location. The benchmarking group drew up a comprehensive report on Germany as a business and social location which was explicitly intended to look at reforms in the field of labour market and social policy in other comparable countries (cf. Eichhorst et al. 2001; Heinze and Streeck 2000, 2003). An important finding in this context was that, parallel to a paradigm shift in policy, the far better managed structural change to a flexible service society played a central role in overcoming the labour market crisis. The fact that the service sector in the Federal Republic of Germany did not develop in the same way as in the aforementioned country examples was largely due to the comparatively high welfare state levies on low-paid work, which made it difficult for weaker workers in particular to enter regular employment. One particular segment of the low-wage sector that already existed at that time (and which has continued to expand in recent years) was, in addition to undeclared work, the 630-DM jobs (from 2002: 325-Euro jobs), in which around 4 million people were employed. These so-called mini-jobs are still under discussion today (cf. Beckmann 2019 and Grabka et al. 2020, as well as the discussion on this in Sect. 2.2) and calls regularly emerge from academia and politics to ban these forms of gainful employment without contributions such as entitlements to social security protection – but so far without success.

A core dilemma of the German welfare state has been seen to lie not only in the unemployment-related revenue crises of the social insurance funds but also, and above all, in the cost burden placed on labour by rising rates of social insurance contributions. Although the unit labour costs in Germany, which are decisive in industry, have developed favourably, this measure is less meaningful for the service sectors, which are continuing to grow in all western countries. At the end of the 1990s, Germany's complete non-wage labour costs, including taxes, ranked high in an international comparison; only in France, Italy, the Netherlands, Belgium and Austria was the labour factor even more heavily burdened (cf. Eichhorst et al. 2001, esp., p. 313ff.).

The benchmarking examples show that socially embedded development of low-skilled work was and is an obvious part of government policy in a number of countries. In particular, the labour market opportunities of low-skilled workers could be improved by relieving low incomes from social security contributions. The Benchmarking Working Group of the "Alliance for Jobs" had therefore decided to devote special attention to this possible solution. Almost all of the many proposals and measures implemented abroad to reduce social security contributions for low incomes provided for a progressively graduated contribution structure. This involves defining an income zone at the lower end of which all contributions are waived for those involved and at the upper end of which the obligation for employers and employees to pay the full contribution rate begins. Within the progression zone, the contribution rate to be paid increases gradually from zero to the normal level, while the subsidy paid by the state decreases accordingly. The concrete design is a political decision on which, among other things, the amount of the total relief and thus the compensation to be paid out of tax revenues depend. The gradual build-up of the full contribution burden along a progression zone is intended to avoid the kind of misguided incentives that occur in the case of sudden increases in contributions, for example above the low-income threshold or the level of social assistance. The purpose of graduating the contribution is to make work more rewarding than non-work at any point along the progression curve.

This is also the starting point of a current reform proposal by the two economists Krebs and Scheffel (2021), which they developed for the Bertelsmann Foundation. According to this proposal, *mini-jobs* should be abolished as a form of employment except for students, pupils and pensioners, while other employees in the low-income bracket should pay less social security contributions in future up to a level of €1800, with contributions rising slowly from zero euros in income. In doing so, the authors argue that these additional tax-financed costs in the field financed by contributions from employers and employees could be offset by possible additional revenues in the medium term. "The initial cost of the reform to the public budget, consisting of foregone social security contributions, amounts to €0.57 billion. This amount is offset in the medium term by additional fiscal revenues resulting from the employment effects, the associated additional revenues in the form of taxes and social security contributions, and the savings from the reduction in transfer payments" (Krebs and Scheffel 2021, p. 30). It should be recalled at this point that the proposal to subsidize social security contributions was already discussed some 30 years ago (Scharpf 1993). At the beginning of the Red-Green government coalition in 1989/99, it was also taken up in the benchmarking group at the then Alliance for Jobs and classified by academics (cf. Streeck and Heinze 1999 and, critically, Schupp et al. 1999).

In order to close the estimated employment gap of about four million jobs in the services sector and at the same time achieve an improvement in the employment opportunities of the low-skilled, the Benchmarking Working Group proposed a structural change strategy to promote the expansion of those sub-sectors of the services sector in which jobs are typically created for low-skilled workers. Accompanying measures of active labour market policy as well as programmes to support selected problem groups among the low-skilled would probably be indispensable as flanking measures. Furthermore, appropriate support for the creation of small businesses in particular would be useful, because the necessary structural change cannot be achieved without a considerable number of start-ups. The demand for simple personal and household services, and hence the level of employment generated by their production, depends to a large extent on their price. If the price is too high, potential customers will produce the offered services themselves or do without them. Since personal services are produced in a labour-intensive manner, their price is determined primarily by labour costs. This means that demand for simple services is particularly sensitive to price changes.

As an *alternative* to lowering low wages and their neighbouring social security benefits, the possibility of reducing unemployment in low-productivity employment by relieving state-induced non-wage labour costs rather than by lowering gross wages was already discussed in the 1990s and increasingly used in one form or another. In this context, the entitlements of the beneficiary employees to social security benefits are in principle fully preserved, since the waived contributions are reimbursed to the social security funds by the state from tax revenues. To the extent that such employment relief from social security contributions benefits employers, there is a chance that it will lower the price of low-wage labor and widen the spread, not of wages, but of labor costs incurred by employers. To the extent that it benefits workers, it brings their net income closer to their gross income and increases it. By contrast, at the time there was (still) no political majority against the introduction of a minimum wage to prevent a further downward slide in wages, since both employers' associations and the majority of trade unions were opposed to a uniformly fixed minimum wage and saw in it an undermining of the autonomy of collective bargaining.

The idea of improving employment opportunities for the low-skilled by expanding employment in the private service sector and promoting the latter by reducing the state-induced non-wage costs of low-paid work, was and is found both in various resolutions at EU level and in member countries. Various countries have used this strategy in recent decades to achieve what Germany has struggled to do: establish itself in innovative growth markets and grow dynamically. "The Scandinavian countries were pioneers in the field of active labour market policies and they also ensured a comprehensive expansion of social service offers in the areas of care and family at the local level at an early stage. This expansion pushed high female employment, while at the same time the state service sector became an important employer for women" (Obinger and Petersen 2019, p. 24).

Despite existing differences to the German social model, there were points of contact which could have been combined to form a socially investing and thus sustainable welfare state project, if the view of learning from one's neighbours had not only been shared rhetorically. However, the "Alliance for Jobs" failed and in the early 2000s there was probably the biggest break in German labour market policy, the so-called Hartz reforms: "The acute cause was the so-called "placement scandal" at the Federal Labour Office. In a 2002 audit report, the Federal Court of Auditors found serious errors in the placement statistics of the Federal Labour Office, so that the federal government appointed a 'Commission for Modern Services on the Labour Market' headed by Peter Hartz, in addition to a series of personnel consequences. The Hartz reforms departed from the tradition of the Employment Promotion Act by focusing on an activating labour market policy in which a faster integration of jobseekers into gainful employment gained in importance over a labour market policy that was in part more passive and geared towards long-term qualification measures" (Eichhorst and Schroeder 2019, p. 212).

Whereas in the 1980s and 1990s there was still lively discussion about the "second labour market" or combi-wages, a similar discussion is currently taking place within the framework of the *Participation Opportunities Act for* the group of long-term unemployed who have not been able to be placed in employment for 6 years or more. Here, an answer is being sought to the long-term unemployment that has been rampant and entrenched in Germany for decades, and the legislature responded to the persistent problem of entrenched long-term unemployment and a hodgepodge of largely failed measures to combat it at the beginning of 2019 with the Participation Opportunities Act (§16e and §16i SGB II). There was a need for political action not least because the labour market upswing of the past decade up to the start of the Corona pandemic, with a significant increase in employment subject to social security contributions and a continuous decline in unemployment, had not contributed sufficiently to a sustainable thinning out of long-term unemployed benefit recipients. Especially for "problem groups" with multiple placement obstacles who are far from the labour market, employment opportunities on the primary labour market remain low and are often exhausted in short-term integration measures without the sustainable success of permanent employment subject to social security contributions. Now, since January 2019, the Participation Opportunities Act (Teilhabechancengesetz) aims to place people who are particularly distant from the labour market and who have been in receipt of basic social security benefits for at least six of the past 7 years in a targeted manner in tax-financed employment (the *social labour market) that is* subsidised in the form of wage subsidies for employers (with wages that are not set below the minimum wage). The terms of the subsidy are: For a maximum period of 5 years, a degressive wage subsidy of 100% in the first 2 years and ten percentage points less each year from the third to the fifth year.

The primary objective is to improve the employability and social participation of those supported. The socio-political character of §16i should be emphasised, because even if the goal of reintegrating the assisted persons into the primary labour market, and thus at best into unsubsidised employment, is not abandoned in principle, the risk of social disintegration and exclusion from participation should be counteracted first and foremost, and only then should sustainable integration into the "primary labour market" be sought. This socially integrative character, accompanied by concrete support from coaches, is certainly also due to the fact that the socio-political debates of recent years on long-term unemployment have led to a consensus in large parts of the economy, science, politics and administration. Accordingly, the establishment of a permanent social labour market for (groups of) people whose reintegration into the primary labour market is almost impossible in the short and medium term can be a sensible approach to mitigate the numerous negative consequences of a permanent exclusion from the labour market.

Analyses from recent decades on the individual reintegration probabilities of the long-term unemployed into the primary labour market show a thoroughly *heterogeneous picture, which* is why the differentiation of the Participation Opportunities Act according to different target groups appears to make sense in principle. One common feature of both instruments is that both §16e and §16i subsidise part-time or full-time employment subject to social security contributions – but without contributions to statutory unemployment insurance – and are intended to appeal to public as well as private employers and independent providers. In contrast, there are clear differences in terms of target groups and objectives. For example, §16e SGB II is aimed at benefit recipients who are capable of working and have been unemployed for 2 years or more, with a maximum subsidy period of 2 years and a degressive wage subsidy of 75% in the first year and 50% in the second. In line with the basic logic of publicly funded employment, the aim is to improve employment opportunities and reintegration into the primary labour market. In contrast, §16i is aimed at a different target group and thus at more than primary integration into the primary labour market. The focus of this funding instrument in SGB II is primarily on social participation and inclusion.

However, for the group of §16e recipients, this should not mean giving up the right to reintegration into the primary labour market. There are good reasons for this. First and foremost, the prospect of finding regular, unsubsidised employment on the primary labour market may be subjectively important for those receiving support. This does not necessarily exclude comparatively long bridging periods in subsidised employment. The importance of an unsubsidised employment perspective applies in particular because a sustainable, independent reintegration into the primary labour market can break through the unsatisfactory logic of project cycles and/or (simultaneous) remaining in basic benefits. Many people in publicly funded employment have already experienced a lack of follow-up prospects in the past (cf. Bruckmeier and Hohmeyer 2018). However, alternating episodes of exclusively receiving benefits and publicly funded employment have a demotivating effect in an employment-oriented society, as every hopeful high is followed by disillusionment and employment opportunities exclusively follow project cycles and do not open up sustainable future prospects free of worries and fears.

The establishment and permanent maintenance of a *social labour market* is nevertheless cost-intensive, and a continuous expansion of the group of people supported is only possible and can be financed without further increases in the budget for basic security benefits if entry is also linked to the possibility of upward mobility into regular employment, i.e. the funds are not cumulatively tied up in the long term for a selective group of people. Such a *dynamic* is also necessary for reasons of fairness, since it is not plausible to justify to unsubsidised benefit recipients why they do not benefit from subsidised employment. A social labour market is thus an important building block of an inclusive labour market and a labour market policy based on solidarity (cf. Knuth 2018), but faces the challenge of being selective in the absence of upward mobility and closure processes and thus – despite good intentions – exclusionary to a certain extent.

This is also associated with a new form of tradition of the interrelationship between reintegration into the primary labour market and social participation. Originally, the credo was to establish social participation through the most "regular" possible integration into the primary labour market – at least as a central component of social participation. Following the logic of the funding instrument §16i, the aim could therefore be to create social participation within the framework of publicly funded employment in the social labour market – at least in the medium term – to enable either regular integration into the labour market or, in the case of the group of older long-term unemployed, at least an employment-based transition to old-age pension. It is obvious that, in view of the multiple obstacles and challenges of the group of people addressed, such dynamisation will not succeed in all cases. This should not mean, however, that the social labour market should be regarded as the only alternative for long-term unemployed benefit recipients. At the same time, solutions are also needed for the group of recipients who cannot be placed and for whom, despite all efforts at dynamisation, realistic follow-up prospects are needed, i.e. prospects that correspond to individual possibilities, including on a permanent social labour market, which could then presumably be more closely oriented to the model of inclusive enterprises or workshops for people with disabilities, in which gainful employment with a primarily inclusive claim is promoted in the legal sphere of Social Code IX. Initial experience with the social labour market gives grounds for confidence with regard to acceptance, although integration effects cannot yet be proven due to the length of time involved, especially as the Corona pandemic, 1 year after the start of the limited statutory funding option, is posing additional challenges for the evaluation commission in identifying original effects of the measures (cf. Bauer et al. 2021).

The desired decentralised implementation of the instrument by the local job centres generates different support strategies, which are determined by the acting actors and the regional labour markets. Empirical findings from a regional labour market study (in the district of Recklinghausen/NRW) so far show a good uptake on the part of public and private employers and low drop-out rates. Among the assisted groups, as expected, the share of young assignees under 30 years of age is low, while the share of persons over 55 years of age is relatively high. On the one hand, this points to the high demand for this group of persons; on the other hand, only a few from this group are likely to find permanent employment in the primary labour market. However, the authors of the empirical study also draw attention to the fact that the Corona pandemic has limited the dynamics of labour market policy with regard to this instrument and may itself rule out negative consequences. "Such a development could lead to problems of acceptance and legitimacy, especially in view of a pandemic-induced tightening of the labour market and new competitive situations, and specifically if this instrument is (mis)understood as alimentation for a few. This danger is real, because empirical studies show that welfare chauvinist attitudes towards unemployed people are powerful and the willingness to support them is correspondingly fragile. In the course of the labour market consequences of the pandemic, debates on justice and acceptance could flare up and questions could be asked as to whether publicly subsidised employment, which materially places the subsidised just as well as unsubsidised persons at the lower end of the general labour market, can be legitimised. This is all the more true in times of costly and historically unique economic, cyclical and social policy programmes that will restrict the state's financial room for manoeuvre in the coming years. Political debates about necessary cuts in public spending will not stop at the social labour market" (Beckmann and Schad 2021, p. 8).

The Berlin model with the promising name "solidarity-based basic income" (cf. Bach and Schupp 2018) aims in a similar direction to these social labour market programmes. Here, too, the underlying motivation of the model project is to offer people subsidised employment instead of paying basic welfare benefits for the long-term unemployed. This job offer is aimed at people who, after 2 years of unemployment, are on the threshold of receiving basic welfare benefits and are voluntarily willing to take up the offer to take up a publicly funded auxiliary and support activity. The job had to meet the criterion of "additionality", which proved to be a tough search process. The employees finally hired are then paid in a lower pay scale group as employees subject to social security contributions, also with the acquisition of entitlements to later unemployment benefit payments. The public employers of the Land of Berlin, welfare associations or the municipal housing industry receive wage cost reimbursements for the de-funded new hires for a period of up to 5 years. The costs of the measure must be covered by the Berlin state budget, but no evaluation studies have been conducted to date, although an evaluation has been commissioned and is currently being carried out. It remains to be seen, however, whether the model project, which was initiated by the then governing mayor Michael Müller, will be continued after the red-red-green coalition government in Berlin ends in autumn 2021.

On the basis of the new *social participation projects it* can be seen that the debates of the past years on permanent long-term unemployment have led to a consensus in large parts of the economy, science, politics and administration. According to this, the establishment of a permanent social labour market for (groups of) people whose reintegration into the primary labour market is virtually impossible can be a sensible approach to alleviating the numerous negative consequences of permanent exclusion from the labour market, promoting (meaningful) activities and thereby strengthening self-efficacy and self-confidence. This reorientation can also be interpreted as a paradigm shift in dealing with long-term unemployment, which, at least in tendency, involves a shift in emphasis from fiscal policy concerns of publicly funded employment to the problematisation of the disintegrative social consequences of a segment of the "superfluous". Nevertheless, it remains the central task and major challenge of job placement services and the other actors involved, both in the selection of persons and in the monitoring of the support process, to master the balancing act between reintegration into unsupported employment on the one hand and the use of the social labour market as a socio-political safety net on the other. Although unexpected transitions of long-term benefit recipients into work that meets their needs are always successful, it seems to be enormously important to create low-threshold meeting places on site in order to reduce reservations and prejudices. This is also derived from the fact that in 2017, around 50% of the companies surveyed as part of the IAB job survey stated that, in principle, they would not consider applicants with an unemployment period of 1 year or more to fill a job (cf. Kubis and Rebien 2019). These reservations are powerful, but the examples confirm the possibility of using relationships of trust and experimental approaches to convince at least some companies to be more open. On a more positive note, a not insignificant 42% of firms also say they will consider applicants even if they have been unemployed for more than a year. It depends very much on regional implementation practices whether such model projects can be successfully established.

Labour market policy investments in human capital can not only have positive individual effects, but can also be efficient for the economy as a whole and even contribute to reducing the trend of growing polarising social inequalities. "Transfer payments that guarantee basic security with regard to the most important dimensions of individual life situations may influence not only the employment or pension behaviour, but also the risk behaviour of individuals: if there is no threat of complete economic and social collapse in the event of failure, they may take greater risks. Insofar as higher risks are accompanied by higher expected returns, risk can be regarded as a factor of production. Inducing individuals to take greater risks with the help of socio-political measures is then productive in the aggregate, even if not in every individual case, and leads to efficiency in the sense of a better position for all in principle. In this context, it is even possible that the inequality of the outcomes of the market process (e.g. gross incomes) increases to such an extent because of the insurance character of redistribution that it remains higher after redistribution (i.e. in net incomes) than without redistribution and without incentives to assume risk" (Eichhorst and Marx 2019, p. 504).

The new labour market policy programmes outlined in outline prove that in recent years there has certainly been *movement in* the labour market and social policy institutional system in Germany. However, the path dependency has not been structurally changed; rather, more and more elements of a different logic, which relies on universal social participation, have seeped into the institutional setting. This also gives the debate on a basic income a different strategic orientation. At the same time, the projects motivated by labour market policy are by no means concerned with decoupling work, income and social security in order to promote the transition from a working society to an active society. Rather, the focus is on the networking of labour market actors and on the empowerment and activation of those affected, which also includes targeted counselling in order to emerge from the passive status of unemployment. If a cross-connection is drawn with the debates on a basic income, then the social labour market nevertheless represents a further development of earlier instruments and programmes of publicly subsidised employment with the primary aim of social and societal participation, but which also includes finding opportunities for permanent unsubsidised employment. Although this turn may seem marginal, it can be interpreted as a step towards a "participation society" (cf. on the comprehensive welfare state model of the participation society Grözinger et al. 2006).

This *creeping change in* labour market policy programmes and models, also in comparable Western countries, is interpreted from a welfare state macro perspective as the overcoming and transformation of outdated security arrangements. "In line with developments that have taken place throughout the OECD area, the departure from the protecting and caring to the enabling and guaranteeing welfare state has taken place. The 'activating welfare state' is no longer intended merely to provide protection against the unpredictable developments of markets, but to enable individuals to secure their 'employability' even under dynamic conditions in labour markets. There is a growing understanding that people's individual abilities should be strengthened in such a way that they are able to reverse changes caused by external influences in the future, even under their own steam. This personal characteristic, which is often paired with the term "resilient", thus represents a psychological power of resistance to overcome even personally difficult phases with tenacity and stamina and to overcome risks. Thus a shift has taken place from a policy of collective guarantees of social situations to one of individual promotion and nurturing of individually differentiated working capacity" (Bude 2010, p. 192).

In 2021, such activation practices, even if accompanied by advisory processes and networking on the ground, will still be difficult to implement due to the Corona pandemic and the associated knock-on effects on the labour market. Social security forms will also only be able to be maintained if a socially and ecologically balanced innovation and growth dynamic is fanned. This cannot be achieved solely by improving the placement of the unemployed, but must be directed centrally towards both the creation of employment and the restructuring of social security systems. Without the opening of new fields of employment (for example in the area of ecological modernisation and the necessary decarbonisation of industry, as well as in the social and health economy), neither the traditional nor a modernised welfare state is likely to survive. For this to happen, however, the heart of the architecture of our welfare state must be renewed, for it is tending to prove anti-employment by overburdening the factor of gainful employment with constantly rising contributions and levies. In view of the changed framework conditions, on the one hand the necessary political competences are increasingly demanded, on the other hand the limits of the traditional welfare state are becoming massively apparent. These were already clearly pointed out in the 1990s, and not only by economists or economic representatives: "Under conditions of political competition between popular parties, the development dynamics of the welfare state are leading to a situation in which constantly expanding categories of people are being protected against a growing spectrum of risk situations while benefit claims are rising. If all the signs are not mistaken, this expansive dynamic of the inclusion tendency has come to a permanent standstill. All proposals to include even further categories of need, further groups of people with further rising levels in social security systems, have clearly lost their persuasive power and, above all, their chances of being implemented in electoral politics" (Offe 2019, p. 131/zuerst 1990).

The state interventions during the Corona pandemic emphatically pointed out how *variable* the limits of public tasks and margins are and therefore there are no automatic stopping points for an expansion of welfare state services, although the urgently needed expansion in the area of care as well as the improvement of the working conditions prevailing there have not only gained in importance since the outbreak of the pandemic. Welfare state security systems, regardless of whether this means basic security in the form of a citizen's income or in modified social security systems centred on gainful employment, are, however, ultimately always dependent on dynamic economic development and can only maintain an appropriate level in this way. A policy to "secure social security" must therefore be reoriented from the principle of status preservation in the direction of a more investment-oriented welfare state, which both contributes to a dynamisation of the economy and employment and establishes social justice by providing and securing public goods. Promises of social policy can only be fulfilled if the reciprocal links between social and economic policy are not only recognised, but a new complementarity between economic performance and social security is established.

There is no lack of proposals for more justice and social balance; they range from basic security models to the development of new alliances within the framework of an active civil society (cf. Heinze 2020b; for classification also Schmidt 2021). So far, however, no fundamental change in defensive policy is (yet) discernible and the potentials of civil or civic society are currently instrumentalized by politics rather than secured and promoted with an expansion of local infrastructure. The basic pattern of German politics, especially in the field of labour market and social policy, is an extreme obsession with detail and extensive regulation. However, the dynamic in labour market and social policy that began in the 1990s has continued in the first decade of the new century, and the traditional tendencies towards inertia have dissipated to some extent (one need only think of the Riester pension reform or the Hartz laws). Against the background of the historical stability of social policy, these processes of change initially appeared fundamental to some observers; from today's perspective, no profound change towards a new architecture of the welfare state has developed from this, but certain *transformation processes* have been triggered. "The mechanism of this transformation is the "exhaustion" of the welfare state as a consequence of the former relative autonomy of the policy field, which entails the de-autonomisation of social policy. The relative autonomy of the policy field allowed it to be consolidated and constantly adapted to changing conditions until the mid-nineties. However, because resources were consumed and conflicts generated during this heyday of social policy, tensions developed subliminally that are now radically altering the policy field. The causes of change are thus identified in the policy field itself. The policy field is not being reformed, but is being transformed in a planned way. It transforms itself through its own momentum" (Trampusch 2009, p. 17).

This is accompanied by a creeping erosion of the independent social policy subsystem, and the closed decision-making arenas of social policy self-administration, in which the experts (with equal representation from political parties, associations, trade unions and institutions) remained among themselves, are losing their significance. Due to pluralisation processes, the corporative system, which had given the "community of social politicians" a certain special position, is opening up. In the opened field, which now partly defines itself as a market with "products", further actors gain influence who historically have only been partially identified with social policy (e.g. solo self-employed, but also private companies from the social economy, such as commercial providers of state-paid social services or private insurance companies). This general objective clearly emerged at the international level and there were various efforts to use instruments of an investment-oriented social policy in order to improve the competitiveness of the locations.

From a sociological perspective, Anthony Giddens already saw the general goal of a policy to restructure the traditional welfare state model as being "to dynamise the economy, create jobs and, at the same time, establish social justice" (ders., 2005, p. 50). Based on this guiding principle, political reform concepts – as described – were also at least considered during the Red-Green phase of German government policy. In retrospect, from a political science perspective, these are not considered to have been particularly successful. In a review of the first phase of Red-Green government policy in the area of labour market/social policy, it is stated that the old development path of "a persistently rigid, employment-hostile labour law protection of job owners" was not only accepted, but was brought about by the tendency of the Federal Ministry of Economics in particular, which "destroyed economic livelihoods" and made the repeatedly propagated "labour market-politically sensible path to economic independence more difficult in the long term" (Schmidt 2003, p. 6). And the second red-green coalition government is also praised for its entry into a "realistic social policy", although it is conceded with regard to the now even greater need for restructuring that this "has been somewhat reduced with all kinds of corrections" (ders., 2007, p. 308).

2.5 Basic Income Reaches the Governing Parties

In the context of the modernisation of labour market and social policy, the corridor for more far-reaching reform ideas also remained open and a further stage towards a fundamental reform of social security systems began just over 10 years ago. The spread of the financial market crisis in 2008/2009 and the associated economic recession, which led to widespread uncertainty among many sections of society, also made basic security models attractive again. They would offer social safeguards that could prevent a fall into impoverishment. If the socio-political option could be implemented of using a basic income as a "civil rights reinsurance" to make the now insecure classical welfare state security more reliable, there would also be scope for useful activities that could increase social inclusion. However, this will only succeed if the sector of basic income recipients does not become an economy of poverty, where primarily the losers of the labour society cavort.

In the government era of Chancellor Merkel, however, this issue was no longer explicitly addressed, although the need for structural reforms became increasingly clear in view of the increased challenges to the traditional social security system (especially in the area of old-age provision). At the same time, government subsidies to social security systems have increased significantly in recent years. "The financing of non-insurance benefits in the social security systems through tax revenues is most evident in federal subsidies for pension and health insurance. In the 2017 federal budget, over €91 billion in subsidies and reimbursements were paid for pension measures alone, more than 27.7% of the total federal budget. In 1993, this share was still 15.7%. Widows' and widowers' pensions account for by far the largest share of non-insurance benefits. The crediting of child-raising periods ("maternity pension") or periods of training at university are also included here" (Wagschal 2019, p. 821 f.).

Despite this progressive tax financing of social security systems, universal guarantee-based social security combined with a fundamental reform of income taxation was not able to gain political acceptance, which will be explained in more detail below (cf. Chap. 4). It should be noted that the circles of advocates have expanded and are increasingly supported by individual business personalities – who by no means act as spokespersons for employers' associations (cf. e.g. Werner 2017). There is a consensus among the proponents of the basic income or the solidarity-based citizen's income that the traditional welfare state has reached its limits. In addition, they advocate a *radical simplification of* the social benefit system by providing a tax-financed "unconditional" basic income (without means-testing and reciprocity) for all from tax revenues. This would allow welfare state security benefits to be de-bureaucratised, because many previous social benefits (unemployment benefit, child benefit, BAföG, etc.) would be replaced. "A flexible social network that guarantees at least the subsistence level in all circumstances is just as indispensable for a sustainable economic and social order as free citizens who live, decide and work in a self-determined manner. For responsible action towards fellow human beings and the environment can only flourish free from existential fear. In order to be able to meet the need for social security even in times of changing living and working conditions, both individual entitlement and a decoupling of social benefits from gainful employment are of fundamental importance. It must be ensured that children no longer represent a risk of poverty, irrespective of their parents' way of life" (Straubhaar 2008, p. 6).

This is where the counter-criticism of Cremer comes in, who is committed to the preservation and further development of the German welfare state model: "Perhaps the most problematic aspect of the debate on an unconditional basic income is the discrediting of the current welfare state. Anyone who thinks that all problems can be solved with a basic income is saying goodbye to the dialogue on practical social policy. However, social policy will have to address some of the issues driving the yearning for a basic income" (Cremer 2019a, p. 25).

Even if nothing fundamental has changed in this direction in recent years, a *creeping trend* towards more individual entitlements is unmistakable. For example, independent child protection is currently being discussed in the election manifestos of the established parties and is likely to become part of government policy in the next legislative period (cf. Sect. 6.5). However, even the defenders of the status quo never tire of pointing out that Germany already has a quite presentable social security concept in the form of social assistance, or the merged unemployment and social assistance, and that a significant increase and universalisation is not possible in view of the permanent financial bottlenecks in public budgets.

Even after the various "minor" reforms in the last two decades, however, the structural dilemma for the long-term security of social security remains: While regular employment grows only slowly even in times of economic upswing (and now, against the background of the Corona pandemic, an employment crisis may even loom again), various branches of marginal employment are expanding, further eroding the social security system, and at the same time, demographic change is increasing the number of people to be provided for. The *gap* between growing entitlements and thus expenditure on social security and the trend towards shrinking income (also due to the digitalisation processes on the labour market) is widening even without the negative employment effects brought about by the Corona crisis. Moreover, despite all the labour market policy reform measures, long-term unemployment has not been significantly reduced and is even threatening to rise again. This also threatens to exacerbate the social disintegration processes that have been deplored for some time anyway.

Thus, it can now be considered confirmed that people are affected to *different degrees* depending on their socio-economic position (cf. Wachtler et al. 2020). Low income often also leads to immune deficiency. A recently published RKI study shows that "the increase in COVID-19 deaths [was] greatest in socially disadvantaged regions of Germany – in both men and women. In December and January, COVID-19 mortality in highly socially disadvantaged regions was about 50 to 70% higher than in regions with low social disadvantage" (RKI 2021). Regarding the consequences on income inequality in Germany, the draft of the Sixth Poverty and Wealth Report of the Federal Government states: "It becomes apparent […] that the income risks associated with the pandemic are greater in the lower income ranges. In this context, the higher vulnerability of the lower income groups is also due to the fact that they have few reserves or other financial leeway" (BMAS 2021a, p. 48 f.).

A basic income could certainly also reduce social tensions and develop a new self-confidence in some insecure population groups. Such a revitalisation of the political culture was highlighted in a study on the spread of extreme right-wing attitudes. "The example of a basic income for all people in this country makes it clear what the fundamental change would also be in the social climate: from the state side, unconditional participation in society would become the yardstick for the functioning of democracy instead of a repressive distribution of handouts that can be granted but also withdrawn. New structures of appreciation are needed in society, and these must not stop at considerations of honorary office. Ultimately, it must also be about strengthening individuals vis-à-vis social and state institutions" (Decker et al. 2010, p. 154).

A bindingly guaranteed basic income could also open up or expand scope for useful activities in civil society that increase social inclusion and strengthen cohesion – but only if the sector of exclusively basic income recipients does not become an economy of poverty, where primarily the less able-bodied people of labour society cavort. If this is ensured, there is a chance that it will "allow people to secure a position in the non-market economy. It allows them to volunteer, start co-ops, write articles for Wikipedia, operate software for 3-D design, or simply exist. It allows them to spread out their work hours, to join us at a later point in their working lives or to leave earlier, and to make a commitment to demanding, stressful jobs dependent on their needs" (Mason 2016, p. 363). The introduction of such a universal, state-guaranteed basic income is seen by Mason as the central prerequisite for 'post-capitalism' and, accordingly, its political implementation is also seen as the greatest obstacle, as his expectations of a basic income would be directly linked to an overcoming of the current system of a social market economy. A key point again emerges in the argument: The extraordinarily high burden on the state budget, which makes it seem realistic only in the context of a comprehensive transformation project. This explicitly reiterates the common thread in all the debates of the last four decades: financing. Simple calculations quickly show that an annual basic income (e.g. in the UK of £6000 a year) would double current welfare state costs. However – and this too has been repeated for years – the other effects must be included. It would be financeable "if various tax exemptions were abolished and at the same time other public tasks were reduced" (loc. cit.).

However, the issue of comprehensive tax reform has been at a standstill for decades. This is probably also due to the fact that (so far) no elections have been won in Germany with radically simplifying reform proposals for income taxation, as the constitutional and tax law expert Paul Kirchhof had to experience painfully in the 2005 Bundestag election campaign as a short-term CDU shadow finance minister. People do not trust the calculations and promises about such a fundamental restructuring of public budgets and radical promises of tax simplification and instead suspect social cuts and a continuation or even acceleration of the redistribution from the bottom to the top.

In addition, it is pointed out that a basic social security already exists in Germany in the form of the merged unemployment and social assistance. A significant increase in the level of basic security has been demanded by social associations as well as the Left Party and Bündnis90/Die GRÜNEN for years, but has so far been prevented by the grand coalition. "The majority of the proposals are completely half-baked in terms of social policy and definitely not financeable. The decisive factor, after all, is that a universally granted, unconditional basic income weakens employment and performance incentives of all kinds, both for recipients and for those who finance it. To date, there has been no experiment or practical experience with such an instrument on the basis of which these effects could be reliably assessed. However, the aim of some proposals for a citizen's income is explicitly stated as being to remove the constraint on living wage employment in favour of a broader range of ostensibly more self-determined forms of activity and social engagement. It is completely disregarded that the free space for such activities must also be worked out – if not by those who want to pursue them, then by others. Ultimately, gainful employment is thus downgraded in perspective, without any real alternative being offered for it" (Werding 2009, p. 44; cf. also Schöb 2020, p. 111ff.).

In view of the huge sums spent on short-time allowances, compensation for loss of earnings etc. in the context of the Corona pandemic, however, these arguments have *recently* come to appear in a somewhat different light. They fail to recognise that such a realignment of the existing tax and welfare system has considerable political enforcement problems and that considerable resistance must be taken into account, but economists also point out that "for realistically set amounts, budget-neutral financing of a BGE can in principle be achieved" (Osterkamp 2015, p. 241). What is assumed in the models of the time for an unconditional basic income (BGE) of around €600 per month – if there is social acceptance – should apply all the more strongly to a gradual introduction of a basic income either for initially selected population groups or with an initially partial amount of a basic income. For this reason, the financing side of the basic income should not be turned into a "killer argument" against serious debates and differentiated forms of basic income, as often happens in both economic and political debates.

Against the backdrop of demographic change processes and the consequences of digitalisation and globalisation processes on the labour market, the traditional welfare state in Germany is also facing both far-reaching and fundamental challenges. Without dynamic employment development and, in view of demographic ageing, without a further extension of the active employment phase, social finances cannot be stabilised (see, among others, Werding and Läpple 2019 and Werding 2020). The German Council of Economic Experts argues along the same lines, stating unequivocally with regard to future generations of pensioners: "Moreover, the equivalence principle is suspended for specific groups. Individual pension entitlements are fully offset against the basic old-age pension. Thus, for employed persons who know or fear that they will access basic security, there is no income-generating effect from their pension insurance contributions. The situation is similar for unemployment insurance and for employed persons who do not fulfil the qualifying period, i.e. were employed for less than 12 of the past 24 months subject to social insurance contributions" (SVR 2019; para. 660). Nevertheless, the assessment still prevails that in the field of statutory pension insurance "the chances for real system reforms are low, at least in the short term" (Ebert 2020, p. 33).

Even if it is possible, for example, to give the old-age security systems new tax-based financing impulses through decisive reform steps such as an extension of the working life, an expansion of employment subject to social security contributions through the abolition of mini-jobs, etc., there still remains a growing proportion of people who need a *safety net* not only in old age. Here, a lower-condition basic income security would be a first step within the logic of the needs principle to ensure social protection. Moreover, a new basic security architecture could also increase acceptance for a reform of the traditional security systems, which have increasingly lost acceptance in the eyes of many citizens. This argument thus aims at reconciling the "camps" that have become strongly polarised in recent years, not only on the political stage, but also in social policy and welfare state research.

A certain caution with regard to the possibilities of implementation is also to be recommended to the representatives of a rapid political realisation of an unconditional basic income or a solidary citizen's income. Even in the case that questions of the financing of the basic income and a restructuring of the existing tax and social systems would be answered positively, the freely chosen activity society does not automatically arise. On the contrary, it is necessary to point out the "modernisation trap" of modern societies, according to which, for many working people, market work is much more rewarding than informal and self-supporting forms of activity. "Basic income assumes a world in which laid-off workers see their layoff as a liberation because then they don't have to work. One imagines young retirees living on their basic income finding new meaning in their lives, working at home, engaging in community service, learning a craft, or exploring the world. But unfortunately, evidence suggests that people struggle to find meaning outside of work and its associated structure" (Banerjee and Duflo 2020, p. 452).

However, there are also much more optimistic assumptions about the potential that lies in growing free time and the individual freedom to decide autonomously for oneself: "Personal work, free activity, education and further training, sport, play and leisure, conviviality and contemplation – with growing free time, people are offered so many opportunities for enjoyable and meaningful activity that we should not be misled by culturally pessimistic prophecies of doom. In the end, everyone will have to answer the question "What is freedom for? A society that does not trust its members to answer this question and therefore thinks it has to "keep them busy" at all costs cannot be a free society" (Strasser 1999, p. 80).

Nevertheless, it is important not to lose sight of the social disintegration processes that have become more apparent in recent years, which have led to a "savaging" of social conflicts and a decline in self-esteem in the lower strata of the social structure. These socially "disconnected" groups are more and more "excluded" from the established spheres of recognition (Bude 2008) and therefore it remains questionable whether an unconditional basic income is really able to promote and vitalise social integration. Although the semantics of a basic income suggest a reduction in social fragmentation and an increased potential for individual freedom and self-efficacy, it is nevertheless not capable on its *own* of automatically having an equalising effect after payment and of re-establishing mutual recognition in the form of social obligations. In addition, there must be structural investments in *social infrastructures* that can trigger a meaningful use of time. Without this "nudging" for activities that create a sense of community, financial transfers alone will probably not bring about social integration, even if there is no shortage of more optimistic speculations in this field: "All those who – as the case may be – hope or fear that, as leisure time continues to grow, people will give themselves over ever more restlessly to consumption are overlooking the fact that one of the most reliable sources of human happiness is freely chosen activity, self-imposed effort, self-determined achievement. And because this is so, we can confidently assume that people will generally make only limited use of their right to laziness" (Strasser 1999, p. 75).

Against this background, the question arises from a sociological point of view how the time available to a growing number of individuals could be converted into welfare gains without this time first having to be converted into monetary income as paid working time or as self-employed economic activity (cf. for theoretical elaboration and an international comparison Offe and Heinze 1990 and the contributions in Heinze and Offe 1990). What is sought, then, are "social technologies" that allow the use of hitherto neglected activity potentials and a contribution to the improvement of supply situations outside the state, the market and the household or family (e.g. the "cooperation ring" model or other forms of an economy based on solidarity). Some social scientists even speak of the threshold of a new age – especially through the Corona pandemic and climate change (cf. with regard to an unconditional basic income the contributions in Kovce 2019 and on the Corona crisis Rosa 2020). However, as correct as the references to an expansion of narrowly defined gainful employment to include cooperatively organized forms of interaction are, they are currently of little help to the groups that have been "left behind" or "excluded" from the employment system. The social centrifugal forces are hardly banished by this, rather a political economy of insecurity has established itself in the meantime, which lets ideas of a local culture of trust run into the void as long as they are not accompanied by the establishment of an appropriate universal basic social security and freely selectable civil society participation possibilities.

In contrast to these rather sceptical attitudes towards an almost inevitable expansion of self-organised spaces, voices are being raised that see precisely in the new social technologies the reason for overcoming capitalism – for example in the form of the growing sharing economy or *collaborative commons production* (such as Wikipedia). "Basic income, circular economy, platform cooperatives, and turning information into a public good: most of these ideas have been around for some time. Some are being put into practice by local governments or, in niche areas, by large corporations. But as their opponents admit, the most likely carriers of the post-capitalist solution to the current crisis are the radical left and green parties, or the radical left factions within social democratic parties. The first concrete step they could take, if they agree with my analysis, is to make this four-part approach a reflex – in parties, unions, communities and social organisations: Try to make things cheaper or free, decouple work from income, make data a public good, and fight certain corporations' attempts to monopolize information" (Mason 2019, p. 318). Recent considerations from sociological transformation research, which aim to *link* the basic income idea with civil society concepts, also aim in this direction. A basic income would increase the autonomy of action of individuals and civil society initiatives. An "unconditional and participation-securing basic income [can] serve as a material and symbolic enabling structure for practices beyond a market-conforming orientation towards consumption and gainful employment, which are of fundamental importance for a fundamental transformation of the present way of life in its material, institutional and habitual dimension. However, a successful social transformation, as envisioned by Eric Olin Wright, towards a way of life for which the preservation of its natural and human reproductive foundations would be central, is very preconditional. In the article, a possible mutual transformation process was outlined, which could reduce the material and energetic throughput of the economy and way of life through individual and collective counter-hegemonic practices and have a structure-building effect, especially through cooperation between state and civil society actors" (Ketterer 2019b, p. 345; cf. also this 2019a).

However, it is not to be expected that self-organised networks and exchange rings would spontaneously form on a broad basis solely on the basis of regular cash payments and, above all, that they would be able to keep themselves alive for a longer period of time – especially not in the currently socially underprivileged population groups. Even if a basic income provides security against life risks and maintains a certain social level (without having to fear sanctions or having to work in unpopular jobs), this does not automatically mean an upgrading and growing appreciation of work carried out in the household, civil society commitments or care activities. Self-determined forms of living and working can only develop if there is a supportive political framework, and they must be supported by a public infrastructure and lived out in social spaces. The gain in time made possible by a basic income in the case of self-imposed or involuntary unemployment otherwise threatens not to be used "productively" for one's own way of life, but threatens to lead to inactivity or even psychological isolation.

In current international political debates, explicitly alternative models of "social security" play a significant role (cf. with regard to European discussions on a basic income Haagh 2019). Chinese authors such as Lee, one of the leading figures in the internet economy and platform economy, also constructively address the demands for an unconditional basic income as well as, alternatively, a *social investment salary*. This would be "a proper government remuneration given to those who invested their time and energy in such activities that promote the building of a lovable, compassionate, and creative society. These activities would include three broadly defined areas: Care work, community service, and continuing education. They would form the cornerstones of a new social contract that rewarded socially useful activities in the same way that we now reward economically productive activities. Remuneration would not be a substitute for the social safety net that covers basic needs with welfare or unemployment benefits and government health care, but would provide a respectable income to those who engage in these socially productive activities" (Lee 2019, p. 284 f.; see also the contributions in Grözinger et al. 2006). Even if caution is fundamentally called for with regard to social concepts from the Internet economy, especially since they are not formulated on the basis of expanded welfare state security systems as in Germany, he points out that universal basic income has become the focus of socio-political and economic policy debates worldwide. Lee also distances himself from the corresponding advocates of various multi-billionaires in Silicon Valley (such as Mark Zuckerberg or Elon Musk).

As realistic as the introduction of this concept is in some economically much less developed countries as a more effective instrument for combating poverty than traditional forms of development aid, it still seems utopian for Western welfare states, even though a thorough restructuring is abstractly advocated or urged by a large number of experts. Whether the increasing wave-like thematizations with the latest climax in the Corona pandemic point to an imminent entry into the promotion and development of new basic social security elements as a supplement to the traditional welfare state system is something we will discuss later. From an international comparative perspective, however, it is already clear that "in recent years the rationale for global social policy has shifted from a worker-centered social insurance approach to a universalist basic income approach" (Nullmeier 2019, p. 61). However, discussions about a basic income can no longer be contained and are currently taking place in all EU countries. However, a sober ideology-free view is needed in order not to lose sight of the problems (e.g. the granting of a basic income in combination with a reduction of welfare state benefits, as is practiced in the context of austerity policies in some countries) in addition to the new welfare state options. "Therefore, sustainable steps towards basic income today involve a battle on two fronts, with two different time-horizons: in the short-term, focusing on benefit reform moving in the direction of unconditionality and universality; and – in the medium and longer term – securing wider conditions for public funding and governance" (Haagh 2019, p. 259).

2.6 Lessons from the "Low-Condition" Basic Income Scheme

As part of the Social Protection Package I adopted at the end of March 2020, the Federal Government not only launched emergency aid for companies worth billions, but also far-reaching procedural changes to the Social Code Book II (SGB II). By §67 the way was paved into a hurdle or condition-poorer basic safety device. The changes are primarily aimed at enabling rapid and unbureaucratic access to social security as well as the speedy provision of cash payments for subsistence. This was necessary because the pandemic in spring 2020 exposed, as if under a burning glass, the weaknesses of a wage- and normal-work-centred and contribution-financed social security system. Especially for marginally employed and (solo) self-employed persons, its architecture systematically (re)produces social security gaps, because while employees subject to social insurance in the core of the labour market can count on both unemployment insurance and the short-time allowance derived from it, mini-jobbers and solo self-employed persons fall through this security grid due to the lack of contributions to social insurance and especially unemployment insurance in many cases.

An overarching challenge for reform efforts in the area of SGB II will be how to deal with *solo self-employed persons*. Their pandemic-related gaps in security were not cushioned by the emergency aid in spring 2020, which is why many of those affected were dependent on basic security benefits, as their personal reserves were quickly exhausted in the sense of "self-insurance" and the de facto ban on carrying out certain activities. However, basic benefits for jobseekers are only partly conceived as an institutional contact point for this group of employed persons and this specific pandemic-related variant of "unemployment", because from the perspective of labour market policy in particular, this group of persons was (and is) rarely concerned with placement in a new (dependent) employment relationship, but primarily with material security. In the course of the Corona pandemic, a largely "non-systemic" element is thus introduced – at least for a limited period – into the basic security system, for which the established processes and instruments of demanding and promoting can only be applied to a limited extent.

From the point of view of labour market and social policy, the "new" (as things stand at present, for the time being temporary) *low-condition basic income support* is remarkable: largely under the radar of public attention, a temporary social policy readjustment was undertaken. The Corona pandemic brought about a "natural experiment", in the course of which new accentuations in basic security are being subjected to a practical test and formative guidelines of recent labour market and social policy – above all activation and means testing – are being weakened, while universalistic basic security aspects are becoming more prominent. For some time now, there has been a controversial debate about the relationship between demands and support. In this context, the now temporary increase in the "sheltered assets" and the delayed introduction of cost reduction procedures have been at the centre of these debates for years. The increase is also seen by many supporters of the existing system as a possible reform option, which would give greater recognition than before to life-time achievements, especially for those who have been working for many years, and would increase the feeling of social security, presumably without entailing negative labour market effects in the process. Moreover, the current assessment and detailed and comprehensible determination of the amount of existing realisable assets is highly complex in practice and time-consuming to examine. Since the introduction of basic benefits for jobseekers in 2005, the Code has so far undergone ten amendments, some of them far-reaching. An eleventh amendment law had already been announced for 2020 and has now been postponed until 2021. Consequently, it will be up to the next government coalition to be elected in autumn 2021 to concretise and implement social policy aspects of their respective government programmes in an eleventh amending act in 2022 and, in doing so, also to reform the sanctions practice of SGB II, which will be in force until then, as decided by the Federal Constitutional Court on 5 November 2019.

The amendments to labour market policy that have been carried out for decades are exemplary for the corpus of programmes and measures that has grown so large and complex in the meantime that even the most competent attempts at adaptation and restructuring run the risk of going largely unnoticed by the public. Corrections to the existing instruments are of course necessary, but they are not enough on their own. However, the readily accepted demand for bundling, lumping together and perhaps even streamlining various measures remains within the framework of a technocratic fine-tuning of current programmes or a pluralistic consideration of the special interests attached to them, or on the basis of steadily growing rulings by the social courts in favour of "clients". The problem, however, is that beyond a certain level of problem and complexity, small changes are not noticed or taken seriously either in policy implementation or by policy addressees. The fate of the countless pilot projects and new forms of integration measures implemented by job centres, which in the best case have led to nothing more than evaluation reports that fade away in the files or are sometimes discovered by chance in long-term digital memories, speaks for itself.

The fact that the Corona pandemic has given new momentum to the discussions on reforming the basic benefits for jobseekers is also due to the fact that the controversies about the normative orientation of this institution have once again become the subject of debate. The fundamental reform discourse is also receiving growing public attention from a normative perspective. For a long time there has been controversy about the extent to which the legally stipulated activating and "demanding" administrative practice sets the wrong priorities, overtaxes people with weak resources and often mentally unstable people, has an authoritarian-disciplining effect through sanctions, and the extent to which the desired activation and participation actually works at all, especially for problem groups far removed from the labour market. The advocates of a sanction-free system, on the other hand, see it as offering more opportunities through increased autonomy and less coercion. A system that relies more on positive incentives should generate more individual motivation, creativity and initiative and stimulate more sustainable personal development, thereby also increasing acceptance of and trust in the welfare state.

With regard to the socio-political reform discussion on SGB II, the experiences of the first half of 2020 show that fundamental changes could be made very quickly and implemented in an organised manner. The implementation was empirically examined in more detail in a job centre in Recklinghausen (NRW) (Beckmann et al. 2021b). The standardised survey was aimed at 1055 Jobcentre employees in a total of 15 departments and was conducted in June/July 2020. Of a total of 1055 employees, 602 took part in the survey (response rate: 57.1%). The core topics of the survey included the work situation during the pandemic, professional insights and an assessment of the changed procedures as well as the evaluation of the pandemic-related special regulations according to §67 SGB II. The explorative study does not allow a final statement on the effects of a low-condition basic income support. However, it can provide suggestions for aspects that should be taken into account in the scientific and political discussion.

This includes firstly the need for a holistic perspective. This must take into account both the fiscal policy effects and also illuminate which organisational changes in the job centres and which effects can be observed at the individual level of the benefit recipients. In doing so, it will be necessary to weigh up the relationship between costs and benefits. As an example, it can be shown for the area of housing costs (KdU) in the Recklinghausen district job centre that the low-condition regulations can very well be associated with additional costs. However, as long as these additional costs are only in the low single-digit percentage range and at the same time a reduction in bureaucracy is achieved organisationally through procedural simplifications (e.g. fewer inspection costs) and the pressure on benefit recipients is reduced at the individual level, thus releasing potential for successful job placement, a well-balanced low-condition basic benefit can represent the superior alternative to the existing system.

By streamlining or abolishing sanctions, constitutional concerns could be addressed and the financial as well as normative pressure on benefit recipients reduced. Here, the current more generous regulations on the crediting of assets (in particular planned private reserves for old-age provision) and the reimbursement of accommodation costs would also make a contribution. In the best case, an efficient authority would be opposed to a more "customer-friendly" culture of job placement. However, according to our survey, such a reorientation may meet with organisational resistance in the job centres in the short term, because a continuation of the individual pandemic-related special regulations is viewed critically by the majority of employees in the job centres. These findings should be taken seriously, because they show that path-dependent organisational cultures can favour sticking to the familiar and that a continuation of the reform cannot hope without doubt for acceptance in the employment services.

However, it is already apparent that many of the arguments against a reduction of bureaucratic regulations in labour and social law should be regarded as invalidated by the *unforeseen large-scale experiment.* The assertions that low-condition basic security is out of touch with reality are no longer regarded as absolute truth even by a large part of the staff. The new ways that were put into effect beyond previously conceivable patterns of action can therefore potentially also be seen as a catalyst for developments towards a low-condition basic security. Whether this snapshot in crisis mode will ultimately be remembered more as an accelerating stage, or whether empirical evidence of a preponderance of disadvantages will be remembered on the basis of new experiences of abuse, is currently still open. The results can act as "nudging" to stimulate the discussion for an eleventh amendment law SGB II and to initiate concerted course corrections in the SGB II – Hartz IV practice. The results of the survey indicate that cultural changes are not only necessary on the part of the benefit recipients, but must also be systematically introduced in the mediation and benefit provision of the job centres.

The external shock of this pandemic-related crisis thus offers an opportunity to explore suitable means and also new instruments (such as the "social labour market" or low-condition basic benefits) in order to couple needs-based, more tailored and more efficient procedures with a new culture of trust in labour market and social policy. Against the background of the economic consequences of the Corona pandemic, labour market policy offensives may soon be necessary again. The number of *long-term unemployed* has already exceeded one million again since spring 2021 and there are many indications that unemployment will worsen (cf. Klös and Schäfer 2021). Moreover, the increase in employment prior to the pandemic was also due to the expansion of a *low-wage segment* and atypical employment, although the share of low-wage earners in all dependent employees has decreased significantly in recent years (especially in eastern Germany). In a European comparison, Germany has one of the largest low-wage sectors, for which several factors interacted. In addition to a service sector dominated by small businesses, these economic sectors are characterised by low collective bargaining coverage and a decline in the enforcement power of trade unions and works councils. While the low-wage share was over 20% in West Germany and over 30% in East Germany 10 years ago, it decreased to 18, 9% in West Germany and 25, 3% in East Germany in 2019 (cf. Kalina and Weinkopf 2021).

Thus, despite the increase in employment, *income inequalities* in Germany have therefore increased in recent years. Nevertheless, the second government coalition of CDU/CSU and SPD cannot be denied to have taken up several social policy projects that were more social democratic and oriented towards traditional clientele structures, in distinction to the social policy pursued in the first decade (which was mostly superficially called liberalization policy). "However, for the most part, the Union and the SPD adopted very popular and generous social policy reforms. The government parties did not use the large political leeway – and the possibility of blame-sharing – to push through unpopular reforms. In summary, needed structural social-policy reforms have failed to materialize in this legislative period. What the parties did use for their numerous social policy measures, however, were the favourable socio-economic conditions: be it the great social support for the measures or for a generous social policy in general, or be it the good economic situation in the form of falling unemployment figures, growing GDP and rising numbers of contributors. And be it the favourable political framework conditions in the form of a majority in the Bundestag vis-à-vis a weak, but also welfare state-savvy opposition without a liberal corrective" (Voigt 2019, p. 437; see also Schulze Buschoff and Hassel 2019 and further contributions in Zohlnhöfer and Seebacher 2019).

However, there was hardly any sign of a fundamental reform of the labour market constitution and a targeted dismantling of the segmentation processes in the legislative period of the Federal Government ending in autumn 2021 (if one excludes the regulations on the Participation Act or the Social Labour Market as well as the decided gradual increase of the minimum wage, which, however, hardly make a quantitative impact), although a grand coalition would actually have had the political-institutional prerequisites for a "major" reform of the labour market and the social security systems, although the massive loss of both mainstream parties in the 2017 federal election and the entry of the AfD as the largest opposition party into the German Bundestag probably slowed down the courage and will for comprehensive reform steps. Even a glance at the historical development of the German social policy institutional system points to a highly complex structure of nested partial responsibilities and interdependent levels of control, as well as self-governments and non-profit institutions, which suggest that the prospects for structural reforms are only given if a broad political majority of political parties and associations (including the trade unions) are behind them. This historic opportunity was not seized, but the Corona pandemic opened a new "window" and created quasi-laboratory enabling spaces, which will be analysed below in terms of real implementation.

Although the trend towards state income guarantees and social investment policies has been observed for some time, public discourses are now also discussing building blocks of a new welfare state model. So far, it could be assumed that the established welfare state institutions and actors were able to maintain their status and that the path dependency often described dominated. However, due to the experienced positive effects of lower-condition basic benefits, path-breaking feedback effects could now result from the special character of these projects. "Access to universalistic programs is more open and less stigmatizing, which is why public support for expanding these programs is greater than for means-tested programs" (Busemeyer and Neimanns 2019, p. 284). As in the first round of the debate on basic income, there is also today a cross-party circle of supporters from all political camps and scientific schools of thought, which has recently broadened considerably and has been able to mobilise new groups of supporters, such as the German Cultural Council, which has brought a basic income for artists into the discussion (cf. currently Ash 2021).

However, the *exogenous shock* caused by the Corona pandemic could also lead to a break-up of the social and labour market policy consensus cultivated in recent decades by the two traditional welfare state parties (SPD and CDU/CSU), which, although conflictual on individual issues (such as care policy or the basic pension introduced in 2021 as well as minimum wages), never seriously called into question the traditional basic consensus of the German welfare state. The now enormously increased socio-political burdens on public budgets, which will drive social spending to new record highs in parallel with shrinking tax revenues and presumably lead to rising social security contributions, could lead to conflicts both in the current governing parties and in new coalitions after the Bundestag elections in autumn 2021. At the end of December 2020, the Economic Council of the CDU already warned publicly of the enormous increase in social security contributions, which would be to the detriment of the younger generation and the competitiveness of the location. While, on the one hand, the Union parties refer to the limits of the welfare state, on the other hand, demands for a universal "state pension account" for children were also published by the CSU at the end of December 2020 (and also included in the election programme in the summer of 2021). But it is not only internally that the traditional "camps" (which many observers already considered to be overcome) are positioning themselves; an open dispute about the direction of labour market and social policy also began between the parties in the run-up to the Bundestag election campaign.

At the beginning of January 2021, the Social Democratic Labour Minister Heil proposed to extend the simplified (low-condition) access to basic benefits to 2 years after the onset of long-term unemployment and also to extend the needs tests, which are more generous from the point of view of those entitled to benefits, with regard to housing costs and assets for another 2 years. There are perfectly good reasons for this. Even if one is sceptical about the efforts of individual jobseekers to look for new employment quickly, relief on existential issues such as housing is more likely to have a positive impact on search behaviour. But instead of focusing on a strategy based on empirical evidence, representatives of the CDU and FDP responded in moralistic jargon marked by clichés. It is implied that they are planning the introduction of an unconditional basic income by stealth (through the back door), while the Greens, at their last party conference, detached themselves from the model of unconditional property ownership (and the SPD has always rejected this concept anyway).

The era of harmony seems to be coming to an end and the *socio-political demarcations* as well as polarizations are likely to grow, which, however, also opens up learning opportunities. The Corona crisis has made the structural weaknesses of the classical Bismarckian social model visible in real terms – and not only debated at the meta-level of academic discourse and in social-philosophical salons. They are concretely tangible evidence of the erosion of the traditional social insurance state, which is increasingly interspersed with socio-political elements alien to the system (not defined by the equivalence principle), thus diminishing its discourse sovereignty. Using the policy streams approach, however, we will show that this by no means automatically implies fundamental change, for the German social security state, with its multitude of institutions and mixed bodies, is in itself also a bulwark against fundamental reform, if only because of its organisational interests. For this reason, opponents of basic income models, as has been repeatedly practised in the past, will once again rally round and insist on maintaining normality, or will try to discredit and ward off such models as neo-liberal ideas or "shutdown premiums". A look at the past decades does not bode well, as renowned welfare state researchers have noted: "In the expanded welfare states of the global North, social policy has largely become a matter of preserving the existence of state bureaucracies, the voter appeal of popular parties, the maintenance of the sinecures of interest groups and welfare organisations, and the judgments of a social jurisdiction that serves the socio-politically positively privileged as a means of safeguarding vested interests. Distributional conflicts now only take place within social policy. It is therefore anything but coincidental that path dependency has risen to become the dominant explanatory model of welfare state developments. Social policy is hardly seen as an instrument of a rational social policy that sets itself social goals, just as sociology would no longer see itself as a productive socio-political force. The contrast with the historical formation of sociology and social policy could hardly be greater" (Rieger 2019, p. 55).

In the following, we look – against the background of the convergence of several policy streams – for the *conditions of possibility* for an innovative transformation of the welfare state model, which aims at the inclusion of all members of society with increasing individual autonomy of action as well as responsibility for social cohesion. The next chapter describes the creeping and mostly not openly discussed transition to a transfer and investment state, which has an inherent acceleration dynamic that can form a new welfare state institutional system. However, it should not be forgotten what stability the welfare state system in Germany has shown despite comprehensive processes of social change. Perhaps the stability of the system can also be explained to some extent by the fact that conflicts have been regulated for decades at various "construction sites" and that dynamic processing has taken place as a result of this recurrence. Even if ad hoc solutions did not address the underlying design problems, the reforms had a cathartic effect or a therapeutic effect in that they repeatedly postponed the paradigm shift. While the need for welfare state regulation is likely to increase in the future, this does not mean that the development path will be strictly maintained in its existing organizational form. "Institutional change often and presumably mostly takes place as gradual change, which can be dismissed as marginal for a very long time, even if the marginal has thereby long since become the core of the matter, that it determines its developmental dynamics" (Streeck 2013, p. 14).

In the following, special attention will be paid to how and when policy change can occur in the social policy arena and which actor constellations are necessary for a stronger universalist orientation.

The Silent Transformation to the Transfer- and Investment State

3

3.1 Socio-economic Classification

In international comparison, the German welfare state is characterised not only by its close link to the employment system and formal gainful employment, but also by its *plural* (or rather fragmented) structure and a high degree of legalisation and bureaucratisation. In Esping-Andersen's famous typology of welfare state regimes it is classified as conservative-corporatist (cf. ders. 1990 as well as Kohl 2000 and Ullrich 2005). The historically conditioned institutional fragmentation, such as the division of labour between social insurance funds and municipalities, the separation into local and supra-local agencies, and the splitting up of various areas of responsibility within the social administration solidified in a path-dependent manner, became increasingly complicated, and not only from the outside more intransparent. The increased complexity is also expressed in the fact that instruments for potential beneficiaries of welfare state benefits are no longer used due to a lack of information or due to stigma effects. "Potential benefit claimants fear being perceived as less able or as 'free riders'. If claiming is visible to others, they will forgo a transfer payment that is beneficial to them because of this. The findings suggest that making the application and payment process as discreet as possible can help to reduce stigma and thus increase benefit claiming" (Friedrichsen and Schmacker 2019, p. 456).

On the one hand, this differentiation promoted an organizational stability of the German social administration, but on the other hand, it creates *consequential problems* that can be observed on a daily basis. "Every differentiation of administrative units ensures that they develop a life of their own and seal themselves off from

R. G. Heinze, J. Schupp, *Basic Income - From Vision to Creeping Transformation of the Welfare State*,
https://doi.org/10.1007/978-3-658-40269-3_3

other units. Thus, numerous interface problems arise, such as multiple case processing (each client who is cared for by several offices (has different contact persons, files, etc. there), information retention between offices, and so-called "shifting stations" (clients are referred from one office to another in order to save work and costs)" (Grohs 2020, p. 7; see also Bogumil and Seuberlich 2015; Brettschneider 2019; Stöbe-Blossey et al. 2020). The interface and coordination problems produced in this way increase in a dynamically growing social and health care sector with increasing specialisation and professionalisation, and even run the risk that the actual target groups of welfare state services are not (or no longer) reached. However, before the fragmentation is discussed, the main features of German welfare production, which is characterised by a variety of forms of providers and dynamic growth, should first be outlined.

Thus, at the local level, the majority of social services are provided by non-governmental agencies, especially the established non-profit welfare care. This specifically "German arrangement of welfare production" exhibits a striking "networked character" (Kaufmann 2003, p. 306; cf. also Dallinger 2016), which points to the close relations between welfare associations in particular and the state (sectoral corporatism). The partnership formula, which confirms both the self-governing right of the state and the municipalities and the self-design right of the "independent" providers, is the dominant and valid norm of cooperation between public and independent providers to this day. For some years now, a paradigmatic shift has been taking place in international comparative welfare state research, in which non-state actors and a revitalisation of self-help and public spirit are increasingly being taken into account. Conceptually, this involves welfare pluralism, welfare mix, new subsidiarity or nonprofit organizations and the third sector (see the contributions in Freise and Zimmer 2019; Heinze et al. 2018). This development is due to the fact that existing theories of *the* welfare state do not always reflect the *diversity of welfare production* in modern Western societies, however, the sometimes dazzling terms point to the heterogeneity of activities and forms of employment beyond the state and the market. The specifically German form of the welfare state with all its ramifications leads, on the one hand, to a certain lack of clarity, and on the other hand, quite definitely to a reduction in the burden on the state. "Most socio-political institutions are corporately independent and are therefore to a certain extent able to articulate and defend their interests vis-à-vis politicians. The high degree of association and the tradition of corporatist negotiation systems limits and relieves political decision-making processes of some steering tasks" (Kaufmann 2003, p. 306; cf. also Heinze 2020b).

The terms "social services" or "social services" (both terms are used synonymously here) are often only roughly outlined in the social sciences; the sector is determined by a great heterogeneity. Badura/Gross noted decades ago in their seminal book on social services that there is no sociologically binding definition of social services and speak of social services whenever they are socio-politically relevant person-related services (this. 1976). These have continuously expanded not exclusively in the tertiary sector of the economy and increasingly complement traditional monetary social services. But they are not only of great importance from a social point of view; they are also a steadily growing employment factor and provide dynamic impulses for the economy as a whole (social return on investment). The social investment character of early childhood education, for example, is also increasingly being recognised as a means of securing the demand for qualifications and implementing innovations. Investments in childcare and education have demonstrably positive economic effects that have been undisputed in research for many years and are also well documented empirically (cf. Heckman 2006; Spieß 2018).

But even beyond educational expenditure, there are monetisable effects of social and health-related services, which have been discussed in recent years in the discourse on a social and health economy. They can be seen, among other things, in the easily measurable positive employment effects, whereby even greater effects could be achieved here (for example, in the area of nursing), but which are not fully exploited on the one hand due to the often stressful working conditions – despite the systemic relevance often proclaimed especially at the beginning of the Corona pandemic – and on the other hand due to the still comparatively low remuneration for nursing and assistant professions, a shortage of labour prevails. At this point, the first report of the Council for Work in the Field of Nursing, appointed by the Minister of Labour and Social Affairs Heil in 2020 and presented in May 2021, also recommends that "staffing levels geared to the need for nursing care [are] the basic prerequisite for high-quality nursing care and good working conditions in nursing care. It is also the central adjusting screw when it comes to keeping nursing staff in the profession and attracting young people to the profession. For this reason, binding needs-based staffing levels must be introduced uniformly throughout Germany and anchored in law" (Rat für Arbeit 2021, p. 147).

In the presentation of his demands for self-determined care presented in the spring of 2021, Andreas Westerfellhaus, the Federal Government's representative for care, also supports the need for *future-oriented action concepts for* both the professional and the voluntary sectors. Thus it advocates also explicitly considerations for surface covering collective agreements in the care range as well as a complete refinancing by the respective cost bearers of the care achievements to be connected with it, so that "the price haggling" finds an end. At the same time, however, he is also in favour of limiting the cost sharing of those in need of nursing care themselves in future. For example, the additional costs for better working conditions for nursing staff "should be borne by society as a whole" (cf. Woratschka 2021/Tagespiegel). Such a path, in which above all the rising costs in the care sector can no longer be met within the social security system and at the same time the assets – and prospectively those of the heirs – of those receiving care would be protected, but instead the community of *all taxpayers* would be made responsible, would be a further step on the creeping path into the transfer state described in the book.

Since demand in these sectors will continue to grow in the future, not least for demographic reasons, the foreseeable labour bottlenecks must be sustainably reduced by a rapid reorientation of qualification policy as well as appreciation and gratification through an increase in collective bargaining coverage and better wages across the board in care for the elderly. If we take the health and social economy together, the economic and labour market significance and, above all, the dynamism of these sectors become obvious. Various studies speak of just under 15% of the workforce in Germany being employed here – with a growing trend (cf. the contributions in Dahlbeck and Hilbert 2017, 2020). In North Rhine-Westphalia, the largest federal state with a population of almost 18 million, the health economy accounted for around 1.4 million employed persons in 2015 (the same number of employed persons as in manufacturing). The share is around *15.7% of* all employed persons and has grown dynamically in recent years. There are variations between the federal states (Mecklenburg-Western Pomerania, for example, is ahead with a share of almost 20% of total employment), but there has been a steady increase everywhere, even in times of crisis. Seen in this light, social and health-related services have a dampening effect in times of economic crisis. Added to this is the strong regional embedding in the local economic structures; i.e. the income and investment impulses remain almost entirely in regional markets. This secures employment in other sectors (such as the skilled trades and retail trade). "The health sector in the broader sense is one of the largest industries in the German economy, with 4.2 million employees and approximately €240 billion in sales" (Ernst and Zühlke-Robine 2018, p. 140).

The health and social economy continues to grow and remains a central *employment driver* whose impact extends beyond socio-political boundaries. The health economy in Germany alone leaves an "economic footprint" of several 100 billion euros. "Every euro produced in the healthcare industry generates €0.81 of additional value added in the economy as a whole" (BMWi 2021, p. 6) – these are the official figures based on input-output model calculations from the Federal Ministry of Economics and Technology. These impressive monetised effects are hardly adequately perceived by the public. Due to the heterogeneous structure of the sector, it is only slowly being registered that the health and social economy has become the "hidden champions" on the labour market; the health economy alone "has created more than 1.6 million jobs since 2007" (BMWi 2021, p. 6).

With regard to the further development and realisation of a social investment welfare state, there are striking differences between national welfare states. For example, universalistic welfare states of the Northern European type are not only characterised by a tax-financed social security system and an inclusive education system, but have also invested heavily in social services and, moreover, their taxation system is strictly individualised. These social investments in comprehensive child and elder care are rooted in the higher labor force participation of women. At the same time, this service orientation supports the transformation from an industrial to a service society, which can also be seen in the extent of the social service sector. But also in Germany, during the main phase of welfare state expansion, which can be dated after the Second World War and until the mid-1970s, welfare state programmes and social insurances were extended to ever larger parts of the population (until long-term care insurance in the 1990s) (cf. Pabst and Rothgang 2000). At the same time, the social service sector grew significantly and steadily and continues to show growth dynamics at present, although the German model is very complex.

The complicated and to a large extent non-transparent architecture of the German welfare state is one of the reasons why the "employment giant" social and health economy is not sufficiently recognised by the public, especially since it is only unclearly identifiable as a consistent time series in the employment statistics with regard to the occupational delimitation of those working in this economic segment, as this sector is also characterised by many self-employed or freelance workers. "The German welfare state is a highly legalized, largely self-governing system of social security that spans payers, service providers, and clients in a triangular relationship. From a critical perspective, it is a problem that this system is highly fragmented, has many shifting stations between payers and focuses on compensation rather than prevention. The needs and interests of the clients are not necessarily in the foreground, but the refinancing by cost units. Experimental social policy pushes into the gaps that this system leaves" (Strünck 2017, p. 311; cf. also Cremer 2021).

The particular historical character of the nation-state security models also implies that they change only gradually. However, in recent decades, the Agenda reforms introduced during the Red-Green period of government and also maintained in principle by the subsequent government coalitions can certainly be seen as a rupture that has broken with the post-war social policy consensus (for example, by massively restricting the system of status protection). "Agenda 2010 undoubtedly stands for the most profound reform of the German welfare state model in recent history" (Manow 2018, p. 426). But it is not only in the field of labour market and basic security policy that corrections towards a *policy of social investment* – although less spectacular, they are nevertheless effective – are becoming apparent.

This places "education and (labour market-relevant) skills at the centre of welfare state activity and attempts to direct social policy towards this goal. Unlike compensatory social policy, which aims at a high degree of decommodification, i.e. enabling a solid standard of living even without labour market participation, the goal of the social investment state, which is characterised by activation, is thus rather (re)commodification, i.e. enabling labour market participation for all. Social policy is understood as a "productive factor" that is not per se directed against market forces ("politics against markets"), but uses them to promote social inclusion and economic performance" (Busemeyer and Garritzmann 2019, p. 793). Such a redirection clearly characterises the transformed labour market and social policy arena in Germany, which has undergone a multifaceted change of strategy and a multitude of reforms since the turn of the millennium. This can certainly be described as a creeping transformation of a contribution-financed standard-of-living security system into a basic security state: 'The social policy debates and – either following or preceding them – reforms in the field of benefits have shifted from the classical social insurance state towards the basic security state' (Nullmeier 2019a, b, c, p. 33).

3.2 The Expansion of the Public Sector and Welfare State Services

Processes of change with regard to the welfare state architecture can also be observed in other dimensions; for example, the development process towards a transfer and intervention state has also been underway for some time. While the social benefit ratio (the share of all social benefits in total economic output) was 6% at the end of the 1930s, after the Second World War it rose to a good 18% in the Federal Republic in the 1950s and then climbed to around 30% as early as the mid-1970s, fluctuating around this mark in recent decades. In 2020, the social benefit ratio was around 33%.

Today there are "150 different social benefits in Germany, which, if you include private, occupational and comparable insurance and pension benefits, amount to a total of around one trillion euros. To put that in perspective, that is as much as the national product of the Netherlands. The annual expenditure on pensions alone is slightly larger than the gross domestic product of Nigeria, a country with a population of 200 million. At least as interesting as the absolute magnitudes are the relative magnitudes: The federal budget for 2019 shows a whopping €145.3 billion for the Ministry of Labor and Social Affairs' budget, out of a projected total expenditure of €356.4 billion. 148.2 billion is the total budget of the European Union – a remarkable ratio. Almost as remarkable as the fact that the almost 150 billion euros that our federal budget earmarks for labour and social affairs is somewhat more than the total expenditure that we make available for defence, transport, infrastructure, education and research, home affairs, building, housing, health, family and senior citizens taken together. All the more so when one takes into account that, over and above the funds allocated in the budget of the Minister of Social Affairs, other ministries also incur not inconsiderable social expenditure, such as health and long-term care insurance – and not only in the form of pension payments. Taking these aspects into account, the share of social spending in the federal budget in the past year 2019 was 50.4% and, according to the plan for the current year 2020, it will be 51.3%. In other words, the welfare state is growing – and it is growing with an amazing continuity. But what is even more astonishing is that the public assumption is exactly the opposite" (Lammert 2020, p. 217; cf. also Bäcker et al. 2020, p. 64ff.).

The focus of social policy activities gradually shifted from exclusively monetary transfers to social services and the development of a publicly 'financed infrastructure offer. However, the institutional compartmentalisation remained, to be studied extensively in the field of social security for the elderly. German pension policy is a "monoinstitutional policy field" controlled by a few experts (a self-governing corporatism that has also been dubbed the relatively small "community of 'pension men'"), excludes social services, and is not linked to other policy fields (Nullmeier and Rüb 1993, p. 300 f.). These closure structures make it difficult at the local level to provide integrated appropriate care for older people, which is becoming increasingly significant for local social policy because of demographic change and falling levels of provision by family carers.

In the past decades, professional social services have been considerably expanded against the background of a growing need in the population as well as decreasing performance resources of individual self-help and family help. The number of *recipients of social benefits* in Germany already took a qualitative leap in the mid-1990s, because since then there have been more recipients of social benefits than producers. "The year 1996 marks a watershed in the German welfare state. Since then, there have been more pensioners, unemployed and welfare recipients in Germany than workers subject to social insurance contributions. The event marks a structural break in society. And at the same time it stands for a late and politically unintended triumph of the welfare state: with a growing number of benefit recipients, the social security systems become even more than before a state-supporting institution" (Czada 2008, p. 191 f.; cf. also Stelter 2021, p. 310ff.).

Despite the comprehensive and differentiated social statistics, however, it is extremely difficult to calculate the almost clandestine structural shift towards a society whose majority of members are provided for by the state in one way or another on the basis of the available statistical records, the respective tax-financed subsidy for the respective benefits and, above all, also on the respective number of beneficiaries. For this reason, the thesis of the "silent transformation" to a transfer state cannot be precisely substantiated with statistical figures at present. However, this trend can be emphatically demonstrated using the example of the federal government's contributions to the pension insurance scheme, which have grown in recent decades.

On the other hand, social services, which have gained even greater importance in social policy practice compared to monetary transfers, are discussed on the basis of the growing social and health sector. An important growth sector of the social economy is the aforementioned health care sector, which is now referred to in many discourses as the "health economy", although this definition is not based on the traditional distinction between prevention, curation and rehabilitation, but rather orders the institutions and enterprises of the health economy according to their position along the corresponding value chains. Social and health-related services have now emerged in Germany both as the foundation of the welfare state and as an important field of employment – with an upward trend. Seen in this light, they are the secret winners of structural change and represent a social trend towards a higher valuation of health and quality of life as well as a growing demand due to demographic change (in particular the ageing society, but also the growing employment of women) and individualisation tendencies. A whole series of the increased offers in the health sector are also no longer part of the statutory range of services of health or long-term care insurance, but have to be reimbursed by co-payment or completely privately. The *growth of* health-related and social professions will also continue to develop dynamically, making health and social care by far the largest employment sector, a point also made by the Federal Institute for Vocational Education and Training. "The ageing of the population ensures that the "health and social care" sector will provide by far the largest number of people in employment, with around seven million people in 2040. Between the years 2030 and 2040 alone, an increase in employment of around 0.5 million persons is to be expected" (Maier et al. 2020, p. 7).

However, this sector not only acts as a stable employment driver, but also as an innovation policy driver. The debate on digitalisation shows that health issues are one of the most important fields of application for high-tech solutions (from telemedicine and nanotechnology to robotics and biotechnologies or artificial intelligence in the field of diagnostics) and therefore also occupy a prominent position in the context of innovation policy debates (cf. Fleisch et al. 2021; Schulz 2018 and the contributions in Elmer/Matusiewicz 2019 and in Schroeder et al. 2020).

Despite the growing importance of social investment in the German welfare state and the structural shifts towards the growth sectors of the social and health economy, as well as the increase in investment infrastructure spending on education and training due to the corresponding financial expenditure in the budgets of the Länder and local authorities, it should not be ignored that most transfer payments still flow into the classic risk areas. First and foremost, the largest share of social policy expenditure goes to pension insurance (Fig. 3.1), and against the backdrop of demographic change, this ratio is unlikely to change much.

All available forecasts on further development assume a growing share of social and health-related services in total employment. This is why the upward trend in social services in Germany has not stopped, even in times of crisis. In addition to demographic change, impulses for the growth of the service sector come strongly

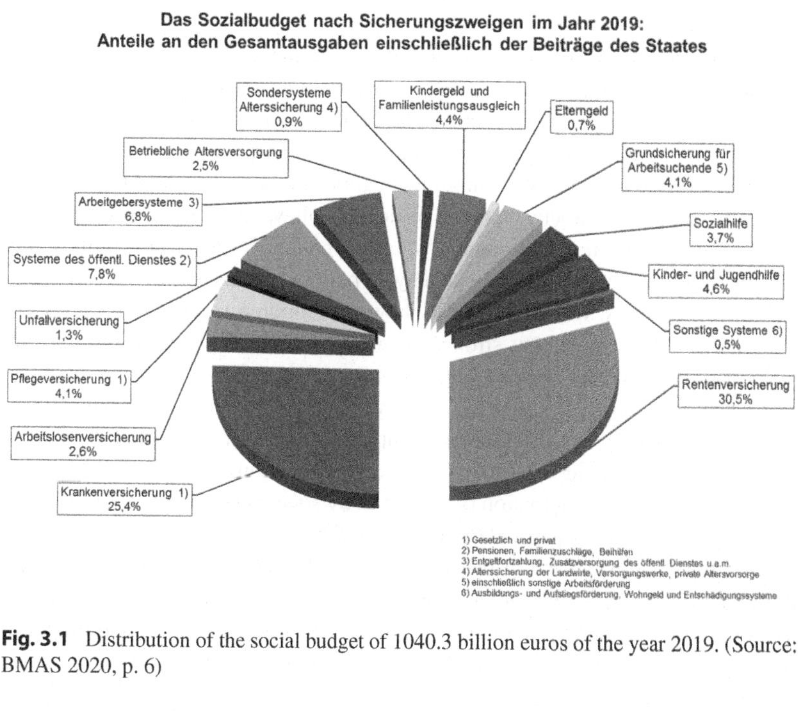

Fig. 3.1 Distribution of the social budget of 1040.3 billion euros of the year 2019. (Source: BMAS 2020, p. 6)

from the further increase in female employment. Assuming that the time frame for the work previously performed in the household is reduced when taking up gainful employment, an increase in the employment rate of women simultaneously means an increase in the demand for services. What was previously done in the household in terms of child rearing, care for the elderly, catering etc. and can no longer be done due to taking up employment could appear as growth in the corresponding service sectors, insofar as it does not remain statistically hidden in the field of undeclared work. In Scandinavian countries, this development pattern has been observed for decades and is partly responsible for the higher level of employment, which also has a *stabilising* effect on the social security systems. "Within a couple of decades, they erected an essentially universal childcare system based on – and this requires emphasis – extraordinarily high quality norms in all respects. In parallel fashion, they introduced very generous parental leaves and child allowances. The result was, of course, more gender equality in terms of career opportunities. And this has decisive second-order effects for inequality since maternal employment is a truly effective guarantee against child poverty. In my previous work, I have estimated that the risk of child poverty falls by a factor of 3–4 when the mother works" (Esping-Andersen 2015, p. 126; see also León 2017 and further contributions in Hemerijck 2017).

The importance of an expanded and also high-quality childcare infrastructure has also been recognized in Germany – albeit with a considerable time lag – and considerable funds have been spent on this relatively new field of social services despite strained public budgets. Child day care has grown considerably in recent years (with a dominance of welfare association providers). "Child (day) care is currently not only the focus of social or family policy, but is also a very good example of the economic reinterpretation of social policy. The expansion of the childcare infrastructure currently demanded by all political camps is economically justified in two respects: Research results show that children from families with low educational resources benefit strongly from early childcare insofar as disadvantages associated with social origin can be compensated. In addition, it is assumed that a well-developed childcare infrastructure outside the home contributes to enabling or accelerating mothers' re-entry into the labour market" (Schneiders 2020, p. 110). This is also evident in an international comparison: in countries with a high female labour force participation rate (such as Sweden, but also France), the formal social services sector is particularly extensive. The reference to Sweden illustrates how strongly the expansion of the service sector depends on political steering options and social values. Without a further expansion of care infrastructures, there is a risk of the consolidation of traditional gender structures or even a retraditionalisation of care work, which is already being discussed in the Corona crisis.

Similarly, a polarisation of employment opportunities in the service sector can be observed: In recent years, there has been an increase in both the number of skilled jobs (such as in education and health care) and the number of relatively unskilled and often insecure jobs. In addition, temporary employment relationships in this sector have also expanded in recent years; "around half of new hires in the social services sector in Germany are now temporary" (Schneiders 2020, p. 72; on the international classification of temporary employment, cf. among others Eichhorst et al. 2004, p. 179ff.).

In the coming years, the volume of employment is likely to increase even further due to demographic and socio-structural development trends that are already becoming apparent today. Even if the forecasts differ considerably in some cases with regard to the expected orders of magnitude, there is widespread agreement that increasing demand in the area of social services can be assumed in the future. "According to forecasts, social services will be the largest growth sector in the coming years: on the one hand, the baby boomers are approaching retirement age, which will foreseeably lead to an increasing need for employees in care services. On the other hand, working parents need care for their children. Already today, these professions (education, health, care) account for a labour market share of 18%. Forecasts predict an increase to up to one third of all employed persons. The share of women in this sector is very high: in 2015, 80% of employees in the education professions, 81% in health care, nursing, emergency services and midwifery, and 85% of employees in elderly care were women" (Jürgens et al. 2017, p. 63; see also Paul and Walter 2019).

However, the *quality of working conditions* has not kept pace everywhere with the quantitative expansion of social services. In the view of many employees and experts, the actual working conditions there have deteriorated in recent years. Deviations from the normal employment relationship have been noted and publicly criticised for some time (there is talk of "wage dumping" through outsourcing, for example). The improvement of work and qualification measures are thus central fields of action for an upgrading of social service work. The fact that low wages and stress at the workplace can be registered in various fields of the social economy is also due to the low degree of organisation on the employee side (e.g. in the care market), which has various reasons: "These include, among other things the late professionalisation of care for the elderly, alternative roles of predominantly female employees, high proportions of part-time workers, heterogeneous occupational structures, qualification profiles and employment biographies, as well as the increase in companies without collective bargaining agreements and works councils" (Evans 2018, p. 178; cf. also Schroeder 2018; Evans and Ludwig 2019; Bentele 2021, p. 20ff.).

Overall, *labour relations* in the third sector are fragmented and confusing; one can therefore certainly speak of institutional sclerosis (cf. Hilbert et al. 2013). Although health and elderly care services are among the systemically relevant employment sectors in the Corona pandemic, the remuneration and quality of work in these sectors has not yet been adequately perceived by large sections of the public. Only a minority of companies in the social economy offer collective agreements. Special agreements are widespread and special labour laws apply to denominational facilities. "The facilities of non-profit sponsors are considered tendentious enterprises, which means that the regulations of the Works Constitution Act apply to a limited extent – or in the case of facilities of church sponsors – not at all" (Bäcker et al. 2020, p. 1132). Here, the Corona crisis acts as a "magnifying glass for social inequalities" (Bentele 2021) and, in the best case scenario, can also act as an accelerator to improve the labour situation in these sectors, securing more employees through collective agreements and, with improved working and pay conditions, also leading to an alleviation of the current shortage of skilled workers. Whether the trend will be reversed and the virus will act as a wake-up call, however, remains a difficult undertaking because institutionally hardened power asymmetries can only be changed slowly.

The *shortage of skilled workers* in the field of nursing and in hospitals has become particularly pronounced as a result of the Corona crisis, because the high and permanent physical and psychological stresses are increasing the number of employees leaving this sector. Whether there will be a sustained push towards a fundamental improvement in working conditions in this sector remains to be seen. A consensus for action on this issue can be assumed in the meantime, but implementation is still patchy. Demographic change in particular, with an increasing number of very old people in need of assistance, will lead to further expansion and thus *demand* for workers in the health care and nursing sectors. In addition, there will be socio-structural changes (increased number of one- and no-child families, rising divorce figures and a further increase in female employment) which, coupled with increased mobility requirements on the labour markets, will tend to reduce the potential for family assistance. Nevertheless, familial intergenerational relationships continue to be of great importance, although the generations only very rarely live "under one roof", but are connected to each other in many ways and also provide mutual support (through financial transfers, help and care). Due to separations, the number of half-siblings can also increase in many cases and family relationships can also become more diverse and even increase in quantity. However, increased mobility, further occupational demands and demographic change (in particular the rising number of childless people and old age) increasingly point to a shrinking of this resource (cf. Hank and Steinbach 2020).

Rising needs are thus countered by *declining family assistance potential,* so that further growth in services for the elderly appears irreversible, which in turn raises the question of the future viability of social security systems and, in particular, the growing gaps in provision. However, the usual statistics in old-age care only record those activities and persons that are formally organised as gainful employment or registered as employees subject to social insurance contributions. If a certain activity, e.g. care for the elderly, which was previously carried out by the family itself, is now carried out either at home by an outpatient care service or in an old people's home, then the service sector can statistically record an increase. However, there is a hidden part of helpers (from the family or friend network, the neighbourhood or in "moonlighting") who are not recorded.

According to the Federal Statistical Office, at the end of 2019 around 4.13 million people were in need of long-term care as defined by the Long-Term Care Insurance Act, i.e. they received benefits from long-term care insurance (SGB XI). In comparison, the corresponding figure was still around 2 million in 1999 and rose to 2.34 million 10 years later in 2009. After a legal reform of long-term care also took place in 2017 and the definition of the need for long-term care was broadened, this led to an above-average increase. The majority (80%) of these are cared for at home, although a confusing growth in employment in forms of the shadow economy or "semi-legal" employment has also emerged here in recent years. According to the Federal Statistical Office, around 3.3 million elderly people are cared for at home. Due to the high costs of intensive care, more and more families resort – partly illegally or 'semi-legally' or tolerated – to (qualified and unqualified) care workers from Eastern Europe, for whom – even when using appropriate placement agencies – only a fraction of the costs for legal and minimum wage employees have to be paid. The exact number of caregivers in German households is unknown, estimates speak of several hundred thousand (especially Eastern European) women.

As 24 h care support is a "grey" market, no reliable data are available. "Rough estimates assume that up to 600,000 of them have aides living in their own homes" (Parnack et al. 2021, p. 19; see also the contributions in Städtler-Mach and Ignatzi 2020). In June 2021, the Federal Labour Court now formulated the requirement for this group that they would be entitled to the German minimum wage and appropriate on-call times. This ruling on the so-called "24 h care" caused considerable unrest, not only among the affected families or single elders, because the associated significant cost increases can not be absorbed in most cases. This means that there are considerable *design requirements for* politicians, particularly in the area of home care, and it will no longer be sufficient to ignore these undesirable developments, which have been known for decades ("non-decision-making"). "A pattern that has been rehearsed for years is being repeated: everyone knows about the immense problems in care. And everyone resigns themselves to fiddling around with them at best" (Parnack et al. 2021, p. 19).

In the multi-layered social sector, which has experienced impressive growth in recent years, the structural change of work and the new challenges for social security are reflected particularly vividly. In the so-called senior citizens economy, which is seen as a growth sector against the background of demographic developments, the collective ageing of the population and its greatly increased purchasing power, the economisation strategies can be observed, although they are now also shaping other areas of society. "Moreover, a change of strategy (or at least an expansion of strategy) in welfare production can currently also be stated: Alongside compensatory benefits, with which the welfare state secures the great perils of life (old age, illness, need for care and unemployment) through insurance systems and financial transfer payments, capacity-building measures are increasingly appearing, which aim to reduce future costs through investment in human capital: For example, investments in childcare are expected to generate higher tax revenues from mothers in the future. Lifelong learning and family care should prevent long-term unemployment and costly social indigence. The return on welfare state measures (the so-called social return on investment) is thus increasingly moving into the focus of politics and social sciences" (Freise and Zimmer 2019, p. 13 f.; cf. also Heinze et al. 2011; Schönert and Freise 2019).

In elderly care, for example, private outpatient care services already account for almost 60% of the providers. Similar trends are emerging in another area of the social and health care system that was strongly dominated by municipal and non-profit providers in the past, namely the hospital sector. For the future, too, experts predict a shift in the division of labour between public, semi-public and private providers in favour of the private sector, as well as hybrid forms of organisation located between the market, the state and the "independent providers". However, *no* dynamic privatization strategy is currently to be expected in the social and health sector (at most in selected segments). On the contrary, the value of public infrastructures and state-guaranteed services of general interest was emphatically emphasised in the Corona crisis, and it can therefore be virtually ruled out that a privatisation offensive in the health and social sector would find a political majority in the near future. Nevertheless, the immense problems, for example in home care, are far from being solved or are being dramatically intensified by the ruling of the Federal Labour Court on "24-hour care". Even the law on the further development of health care, which will come into force from 2022 and will be passed by the Bundestag in the summer of 2021, will not change much in the situation of home care, but will only lead to relief in the case of co-payments for inpatient care and higher wages for care workers through further tax funds provided by the federal government. Colin Couch has already drawn attention to another outlet in the field of caregiving: "When you impose obligations on employers, such as the minimum wage, you also give them an incentive to devise forms of employment that exempt them from fulfilling those obligations. For example, by claiming that those they employ are not workers (ibid. 2019, p. 97).

In some recent socio-political concepts, public services of general interest are conceived as a *counter-model* to the unconditional basic income (UBI) – in this book we refer to the German abbreviation BGE), "which could encourage further individualisation" (van Treeck 2021, p. 212). We do not agree with this view; public services of general interest (such as housing, childcare or healthcare) and a guaranteed and fundable basic income are not substitutive but complementary fields, and productive use of time is only possible if public infrastructures open up opportunities. Without reliable and stable infrastructures, the use of individual time preferences both for one's own further development (e.g. in the form of further education or qualification for new fields of activity) and for others (e.g. in the form of voluntary commitment in social networks, social organisations or associations, as well as to a self-determined extent for care activities) is not a viable service of general interest that also remains committed to the goal of creating equal living conditions in Germany and realising equal opportunities irrespective of the status of the parental home. Otherwise, there is a danger that the time gained will be passively "taken away" or even lead to increased consumption in the diverse digital world without being oriented towards social values such as social cohesion. A citizen's right acquired with a BGE can only represent a possible superior alternative to the existing contribution-financed system of social security if it is embedded and interlocked with a high level of public services of general interest as well as with a further development of a social and climate-friendly market economy. This will require continued solidarity-based support from civil society as well as state responsibility for those in particular need of protection and assistance.

A civil right that would empirically prove to stimulate contagion effects to mindless laziness, health-endangering addictive behaviour[1], as well as criminally sanctioned behaviour and thus ultimately also undermine the economic preconditions for the payment of a BGE, cannot be the goal of politics. The economist

[1] According to a survey by the Association of the German Games Industry, more than 34 million Germans play games regularly or occasionally – on mobile phones, tablets, computers (https://www.game.de/6-von-10-deutschen-spielen-games/) and in a survey by the German Children's Charity, 12% of children and young people stated that they had already recognised signs of media addiction in themselves. https://www.dkhw.de/schwerpunkte/kinderrechte/kinderreport-2021/

Birger Priddat expresses his scepticism in this regard as follows: "To only receive basic income without giving something back to society, in whatever form, appears to be parasitic. The neo-Romantic version of unconditional basic income, 'living into the day', is mentally unpalatable. Except in a version formulated in Herbert Marcuse: Freedom, Sensuality and Play. The civilizational aesthetic of play that Marcuse takes from Schiller takes on a consumer-cultural dimension in which the boundaries between work, leisure and pleasure merge. Marcuse's game takes on a completely different meaning in the digitalized world, for which the unconditional basic income recently seems to have become the appropriate complement: as a virtual amusement park of gaming. Ultimately, however, everything depends on the amount of unconditional payouts" (ibid. 2019, p. 138).

3.3 The Pendulum Swings Back or: The Market Model Fragments

In view of the profound disruption processes caused by the Corona pandemic, both public discourses and various scientific disciplines have called for a common good-oriented approach to the epidemic. In economics and in economic policy media, the topic of common property, for example in the form of commons, is also being addressed again, and not only with regard to the virus (cf. Banerjee and Duflo 2020 in detail). The current challenges posed by the Corona crisis as well as climate protection, digitalisation and demographic change all point to the contribution of services of general interest in securing the future viability and internal cohesion of society. It is therefore not surprising that various facets of the *common good economy* are once again on the political agenda. First, however, let us begin with a definition aimed at the welfare state framework of services of general interest, or collective infrastructures. "Daseinsvorsorge", which was initially located primarily in the municipal sphere, encompassed the entire public infrastructure of "provision", i.e. social services that could not be provided as cash transfers or personal services: it ranged from the supply of electricity and gas to transport services (railways, buses), from public baths and other facilities to road construction and sewage systems. In Germany, these public services of general interest can be understood as an external redistribution ring of the welfare state that has become a matter of course over the course of a century" (Leibfried 2001; cf. on current developments, among others, the contributions in Heinrich Böll Foundation 2020).

The Corona crisis has emphatically pointed out that public infrastructures (or more generally public goods) are of great importance and that a policy of services of general interest must be more offensive and also expand its radius of action (for example in the field of digitalisation through comprehensive broadband coverage that reaches all regions, but also public social and health-related services). Nevertheless, this does not mean that a "strong" state is now returning, even if this paradigm shift is gaining nourishment in view of the profound viral pandemic as well as the temporary restriction of civil liberties. In government practice, "there was and still is clearly more pragmatism in the interrelationship between state and market than in the ideological confrontations and juxtapositions between neoliberals and neo-Keynesians" (Böick 2021, p. 279; cf. also Korte 2021). Since many tasks (such as schools, hospitals, theatres, museums or swimming pools, not to mention social forms of care) can only be organised to a limited extent or not at all via the market alone, however, forms of organisation based on solidarity and non-profit are likely to gain further importance in the future. Already today, around three quarters of social services in Germany are offered by non-profit organisations such as the welfare associations. In recent years the structure of provision has become more pluralised and social entrepreneurship and other alternative projects have been added. All in all, there are probably around 3.7 million people currently employed in non-profit organisations in this country (and this figure continues to grow), which is a strong indication of the importance of this sector and should be included in the political debates on services of general interest and a new infrastructure policy (cf. Heinze 2020b).

In Germany, all these civil society initiatives function under the label "Daseinsvorsorge" and were elevated beyond expert circles to the political stage during the Corona crisis. "Daseinsvorsorge' is a German peculiarity, although similar concepts can be found in almost all industrialised countries. In the USA and Australia, publicly provided services such as energy or water supply and disposal are called 'universal service (obligations)', in Great Britain one speaks of 'public service' or 'services of general economic interest', while in France one speaks of 'service public' or 'service d'intérêt géneral'. At the level of the European Union, the term "services of general (economic) interest" is preferred to the concept of services of general interest. In Germany, the concept of Daseinsvorsorge was significantly shaped by the German constitutional and administrative lawyer Ernst Forsthoff from the late 1920s until the early 1970s. Forsthoff, however, did not formulate a legal framework for the design of public services, but always saw Daseinsvorsorge as a central legitimation component of state rule" (Neu 2009, p. 9; cf. also Kersten et al. 2015).

The term Daseinsvorsorge is often used in direct connection with *infrastructures* or even equated with them. The close connection is also real and Daseinsvorsorge can be understood as the "everyday processing of its infrastructural hardware" (Bode 2013, p. 17). In scientific disciplines such as economic geography or spatial and regional planning, infrastructures are referred to as basic social facilities. However, in the view of some authors, the digitisation processes are also rendering the classic demarcations between technical and social infrastructure obsolete. It is undisputed that infrastructure facilities are of great importance for the quality of life and the equivalence of living conditions. "The areas of social and technical services of general interest are central to people's participation in society, regardless of where they live. The comprehensive provision of these services and infrastructures forms the basis for ensuring spatial equity. Education, health, mobility and transport, digital infrastructure, but also more extensive areas such as housing, local supply for the purchase of daily needs and ATMs fall under this. Municipal finances should also be considered in order to illustrate municipal capacity to act, as municipalities are often responsible for the provision of services of general interest" (BBSR 2020, p. 66).

Even if the measurable elements of social infrastructure or services of general interest indicate a high density of supply, this does not mean that the quality of life in all regions is also high. The equivalence of living conditions has been the subject of debate in various places in recent years, and policymakers are trying out various projects, for example to strengthen social infrastructures in structurally weak regions. In its recommendations for action (BMI 2019), a commission on "Equivalent Living Conditions" set up in 2018 under the auspices of the Federal Ministry of the Interior, for Construction and Home Affairs (BMI) underlined the need for an active structural policy to reduce disparities between regions, as well as sustainable municipal funding. "Germany needs strong municipalities that are worth living in, so that local self-government and democracy can be experienced by the people and the necessary facilities for daily life remain available in their place of residence" (BMI 2019, p. 20). Under the heading "Social services of general interest", the Commission states: "Germany needs good and accessible services of general interest so that all people everywhere have good prospects for life and development. Reliable education, care, cultural or leisure services are of utmost relevance for the decision: 'Leave – or stay'" (BMI 2019, p. 23).

And it also takes an explicit stance on the topic of *commitment and cohesion* and announces corresponding programmes. "Germany needs a strong civil society commitment so that people can get involved in society and social cohesion is strengthened. Engagement and volunteering make a decisive contribution to finding solutions to current challenges and improving the quality of life on the ground (BMI 2019, p. 24). The Commission has identified the defined fields of action as a cross-cutting task that affects "all levels of government equally", even if, in budgetary terms, the areas initially fall under the responsibility of the Länder and local authorities. But with this report, the federal government has also acknowledged its – fiscal – responsibility to make additional funds available to the Länder from 2020 onwards, which can be used for municipal tasks. Thus, the municipalities are massively challenged to strengthen social cohesion and to improve the living situation especially of the "problem groups". On the whole, however, regional disparities in public infrastructure in Germany have tended to increase (above all, the south-north divide is widening). Analyses of the quality of infrastructure in Germany as a whole therefore come to critical conclusions: "In Germany, there has been far too little investment in public infrastructure in recent decades. This has led to a significant deterioration in the existing infrastructure, even if it is still relatively good by international standards. In some areas, particularly the expansion of electricity and gas grids and digital infrastructure, major investment efforts are needed to meet the challenges of the energy transition and the digital revolution and not lose touch with other industrialised countries" (Wiss. Beirat beim BMWE 2020, p. 51). Overall, public investment in Germany is below the EU average and has even declined in recent decades: in the early 1970s, it was still almost 5% of economic output (cf. Siller 2020).

Nevertheless, the seismographic function of the crisis stands out, which not only makes the tectonic picture of a society visible, but can also point to possible solutions for upcoming challenges. However, it is still too early to judge how these learning processes will turn out and provide a push towards a sustainable (resilient) and readjusted society design. If times of crisis are understood as tipping points, new entanglements of ordering principles and prioritizations can form here. These shifts in relevance are already emerging, as the fight against crises has given the state and civil society actors a new appreciation compared to a market ideology that had been proclaimed for years (cf. the contributions in Grande et al. 2021). However, society is still in a state of shock and political leadership is always needed in such situations, but this does not mean that this appreciation for a strong state will last for a long time. For the time being, there are no advocates of a free market agenda, because the rapid spread of the virus, with all its negative signaling effects on public life, has taught even Western countries, with an unpredictable rigor, how fragile global and digitalized capitalism is and that it cannot survive without state regulation and expanded public services.

However, there are different variants of welfare state development that must also be taken into account in the debates on basic income – if only to be able to assess the landscape of actors in this policy sector, but also to understand the basic architecture. The German (continental) welfare state, for example, is "on the whole more transfer-intensive than service-intensive, which at the same time shows it to be less suited to shaping the transition from an industrial to a service economy through public employment, above all because there are fiscal limits to an expansion of the public (social) service sector. If less is redistributed in real terms, inequality after taxes and transfers remains higher than in the Scandinavian (but lower than in the liberal) model" (Manow 2019, p. 301).

3.4 Specifics of the German Social, Health and Care Sector

It is therefore not without reason that researchers speak of the German welfare state's special path, which is characterised by the fact that in the provision of social services relatively autonomously operating non-profit welfare associations, to which public functions are attributed, dominate in many fields. In this respect, one can speak of a dual-structured welfare state, which is unique in Europe and provides organised civil society with opportunities for shaping policy (cf. Schmid 1996; Schroeder 2017; Heinze 2020b). In accordance with the *subsidiarity principle,* the welfare associations in Germany are the central social service providers and have a priority position under social law and in social policy practice. This distinguishes us, for example, from the Scandinavian path of welfare production, which not only has a high degree of social inclusion, but has also assigned a high degree of decision-making authority to municipalities. In the German system, welfare associations are privileged in comparison to state and municipal, but also profit-oriented, private institutions. Characteristic are the mutual interdependencies, which also show up in a milder form in other policy fields (sectoral corporatism) and are interpreted from a system-theoretical point of view as follows: "Numerous organizations of other functional systems (of education, social work, health care) hang on the hose of state funding and find their partners in the state administration in the responsible ministries. In the ministries of state administration, not least as a result of long-standing political patronage, there are networks between the authority and political parties which cushion the consequences of a political change at the top, but which can also be used by the new bosses to keep in touch with political opponents and, if necessary, to seek a resolution of political blockades" (Luhmann 2000, p. 408).

The activities of the *umbrella organisations of the non-statutory welfare sector* cover the whole of Germany and the entire field of social welfare. Although they are unspectacular in everyday life and primarily present through "meals on wheels", senior citizens' meetings or calls for blood donations, their *institutionalised position of power* in the German welfare state should not be underestimated. The social law expert Gerhard Igl (1988, p. 182) describes this peculiar situation as follows: "The reality of independent welfare work stands in stark contrast to what is known about it by the general public" and: "Who would suspect that independent welfare work is the largest employer in the Federal Republic after the state? And who is aware that wide areas of social activity would be inconceivable at all without free welfare work?" (ibid., 182). The actual basis of their social services lies at regional and municipal level, whereby the free welfare work does not offer the majority of its services on a free service market, but on a state-regulated "quasi-market". This is a triangular relationship with political consequences between public service providers and cost bearers, clients and non-profit service providers. The providers of non-profit welfare care are organised in the six umbrella organisations Arbeiterwohlfahrt, Deutscher Caritasverband, Diakonisches Werk, Deutsches Rotes Kreuz, Paritätische and Zentralwohlfahrtsstelle der Juden.

Compared to 1970, the number of full-time employees in their facilities and services has almost quadrupled to over 1.9 million. Overall, around three quarters of social services in Germany are provided by the welfare associations, and they thus represent the central framework of the social infrastructure in Germany. If we consider the non-statutory welfare sector as an economic sector, it is significantly larger (in terms of personnel costs) than, for example, building and civil engineering, the chemical industry, Deutsche Post or the railways. Social organisations employ almost 5% of the total workforce. "The employment and activity relationships in the Freie Wohlfahrtspflege range from full-time and part-time jobs to marginal employment; in addition, there are measures for integration into the labour market, internships and apprenticeships. This variety of different employment relationships is supplemented by activity relationships in voluntary, honorary and civic engagement, which take place in particular in the form of the Voluntary Social Year, the Voluntary Ecological Year and the Federal Volunteer Service, as well as in self-organised forms of engagement. According to rough estimates by the umbrella organisations, around 2.5–3 million citizens are currently still involved in the institutions and services of the Freie Wohlfahrtspflege" (Backhaus-Maul 2019, p. 84; cf. also the contributions in Hummel and Timm 2020).

For some time now, however, association research has been talking about the "extinction of the regular customer" and, in a weakened form, this also applies to welfare organisations. Their problems (e.g. recruiting volunteers) reflect weaker denominational and ideological ties. The reasons for this are manifold and can be found in particular in processes of change in society as a whole. First and foremost, the increasing individualization of society and the pluralization of social milieus must be mentioned here. This is accompanied not only by an increase in individualistic attitudes, but also by a decline in traditional organizational ties and obligations. Based on a representative survey, Allmendinger notes an increased social isolation and the withdrawal of people into small cocoons. "They often have few connections to people from other classes, no networks with them, there is no exchange beyond fixed circles of family and friends. Especially people with a low education are often only in these cocoons" (this. 2019, p. 70). Added to this are changing patterns of norms and values, in the course of which claims to self-actualization are gaining in importance both privately, professionally, and with regard to engagement. At the same time, the increase in spatial mobility, changed partnership and family arrangements, as well as changed employment biographies also play a central role, because often the (employment) working conditions and generally the living conditions simply do not (or no longer) allow the exercise of an organization-bound and long-term commitment.

The supply of unpaid services is not only shrinking in the family sector and in the context of informal primary networks. Volunteers, who are particularly important in the welfare sector, are also declining in some fields, while in other social fields their involvement has increased (e.g. refugee aid). Although new (often association-independent) potentials for commitment and help are emerging in social networks, there are, however, narrow limits to the instrumentalisation of unpaid social services by social policy, because self-help presupposes solidarity as a steering mechanism. Without a welfare state infrastructure, it cannot develop and therefore cannot be politically prescribed. The *structural change in commitment* can certainly lead to problems of legitimacy for the established welfare associations, because their priority position in the German welfare state, which is enshrined in social law, is also based on the fact that they draw on a reservoir of volunteers in the organisation of social services. Due to the socio-cultural and socio-economic processes of change, but also due to the spread of business forms of organisation and management concepts within the associations, this traditionally effective legitimation strategy is beginning to show cracks. "Abstract social insurance systems and established large welfare association organizations (with a certain bureaucratic-formalized character) stand in contrast to the greatly increased need for grassroots involvement. Moreover, individualisation and pluralisation are also changing the preferences and needs of clients and the appropriateness of large providers of social services. The "regular customer" is dying out – both as a member, as a volunteer and as a client" (Schmid 2018, p. 44 f.; cf. also Lünsmann-Schmidt 2021).

However, welfare associations are not self-contained organisations, but as a rule *network organisations* with more or less independent members. At the same time, the associations differ considerably among themselves in their organisational structure – both structurally and in their regional delimitations. They also differ from other providers in that, as institutionally secured umbrella organisations, they are not only providers of social services but also take on social advocacy tasks and, with their plural structures, shape a specific welfare culture. Some authors refer to this German special way of welfare production with powerful welfare associations as "a unique construct in Europe" (Wohlfahrt 2017, p. 211; cf. also the contributions in Heinze et al. 2018). Although in the following primarily the institutions and member organisations of the welfare associations are dealt with, private-commercial providers have increasingly spread with different emphases in various areas of social services (especially in the field of care for the elderly) in recent years, so that on the one hand non-profit welfare organisations still dominate, but private companies can also be found. In the literature on the role of welfare organisations and also in political statements, the terms social sector, social economy or social services in general are therefore not used in a clear-cut way. In our argumentation, too, there are overlaps that point to the hybrid core of social services, which often presents itself as a mixture of different organisational forms.

There is agreement on the growth dynamics: the social and health sector has become a *significant employment factor in* recent decades, but more precise quantifications are somewhat difficult in view of the unclear definitional situation. According to the indicators facilities, beds/places as well as employees, a continuous growth of the Freie Wohlfahrtspflege took place in the last decades – and this expansion is still going on. In 2016, there were 118,623 facilities with 4,166,276 beds/places as well as over 1.9 million full-time employees (BAGFW Gesamtstatistik 2018). For example, a good 650,000 people work professionally in the approximately 25,000 facilities and services of Caritas, making this welfare association also a key player in the German labour market. Overall, the welfare sector is an "engine" of the social economy, which has not only achieved considerable employment gains in recent decades, but also exhibits a constant growth dynamic, which will also continue in the future due to sustained demand. In this dynamic employment sector, the welfare associations have been able to almost "secretly" become not only central socio-political but also employment policy institutions. However, despite their prominent position in regional labour markets, they are hardly perceived by the public as employers. This is due to the control mechanisms of these organisations oriented towards the common good; they belong in the broad sense to the social economy and here hybrid forms of organisation have already spread in Germany as a result of historical influences. The social economy "is not only a collective term for certain economically relevant institutions and supporting structures. It is also a formula for the constantly new linking of different goals and logics – the logic of the social oriented to participation, equality of opportunity and demand of the individual on the one hand, and the economic idea of efficiency on the other" (Schulze-Böing 2021, p. 50; cf. also Schmale 2017; Zimmer and Paul 2018; Schneiders 2020).

Although in recent years the *economisation of* the social and health care sector is unmistakable, the specifically German triangular relationship under social law remains as a model of order for the independent providers of welfare production. Nevertheless, the market as a fourth actor is also entering this field: "Within this triangular relationship, however, the linearity of commissioning (from service provider to service provider) has changed significantly in recent years: The person entitled to assistance as a client is increasingly coming into focus. For example, the Federal Participation Act makes it very clear that the self-determination and freedom of choice of disabled people is to be substantially strengthened. Thus, it has become increasingly clear in recent years that the customer, and not the service provider, is in charge – for example, through the so-called personal budget. The customer chooses a provider with a service that suits him and pays" (Kubek and Weber 2020, p. 264). However, economisation does not automatically mean that it must be associated with an unleashed striving for profit on the part of the individual actors; it can also be a change towards more competition that results in a marketing culture. Although legal requirements (such as long-term care insurance) have opened up the market for private providers in some sectors and abolished the principle of cost recovery, the state does not usually act as a service provider itself, but concludes care contracts.

The *institutionalised power position of* non-profit welfare work is also consolidated by the fact that in recent decades there has been a shift in social policy at the instrumental level from monetary transfers to social services, which has given further impetus to providers and thus to the production of services by associations. The amalgamation of unemployment and social assistance has also given the welfare associations more control over labour market policy. Whereas in the past they were often a cooperation partner of the labour administration in job creation measures and in counselling the unemployed at the municipal level, the business areas have now expanded and questions of the effectiveness and efficiency of service provision are increasingly coming to the fore in the field of associations as well. In addition, there are the economisation strategies, which also affect the service sector. "The trend towards marketization may further increase the pluralization of the policy field. For example, welfare associations are currently in the process of functionally specialising their advocacy policies by organisationally separating their social service providers from the umbrella organisations. This restructuring has been triggered by the commercialisation of this sector. It means a differentiation of the welfare associations into a business association, which unites the providers and represents their economic interests, on the one hand, and a social association, which assumes social advocacy tasks, on the other. In this way, the welfare associations can professionalise themselves as lobbying interest organisations, because they relieve themselves internally of potential conflicts of interest between the sponsoring companies and their clients" (Trampusch 2009, p. 170; cf. also the contributions in Schroeder 2017).

The umbrella organisations of non-statutory welfare work continue to meet the characteristics of non-profit or third-sector organisations, although not all organisations affiliated to the umbrella organisations do. The operational units below the umbrella organisation level of the charitable organisations have an internal organisational and financing structure which in many cases does not differ significantly from that of private-sector companies. In terms of tax law, only some of these organisations operate within the non-profit framework; more and more welfare associations or their subdivisions are setting up "normal" limited liability companies in addition to non-profit limited liability companies. As a rule, however, the profits generated here flow back to the non-profit umbrella organisations. However, the new governance strategies are putting pressure on the associations, because they are increasingly seen as social economy agencies that have gained room for manoeuvre, but are also used as "gap fillers" due to their dependence on welfare state transfers, which in turn affects the normative model and the special position of non-profit organisations. However, the savings strategies in the different fields of action and municipalities are not uniform, so that the organisational units of the charitable organisations are also affected in different ways. Situational solutions are currently more likely to characterise the negotiation processes at local level, and the charitable organisations are less and less homogeneously acting organisations, but show a grown diversity. Overall, a *heterogenisation of* the association landscape has become *apparent* in recent years, which has also led to the growth of different organisational logics internally and has increased the complexity of the semi-sovereign structures in the German social and health sector. Parallel to the processes of differentiation between associations, new, specialized actors (such as social networks in refugee aid or "social entrepreneurs") have emerged, further reinforcing the hybrid character of the system (cf. Grohs et al. 2014).

However, the question arises as to whether *social entrepreneurship projects* are an originally new form of organisation and whether they develop new forms of social service production that have specific advantages over established providers (especially welfare associations). They can, but do not have to be, non-profit organisations in the sense of the "third sector", since they can have a profit orientation as well as a common good orientation and are conceivable as individual enterprises, foundations or non-profit associations. Within such a "new" social entrepreneurship sector, there are therefore also very different forms of organisation. The spectrum ranges from the powerful corporate foundation with a budget of several hundred million euros and the staff of a large company to the initiative of an individual who takes on a social problem that he or she feels is urgent and initially works on it as an individual entrepreneur without any other employees. Although no universally accepted definition of social entrepreneurship has yet been established and no separate legal form for social enterprises exists, there are some structural characteristics. First of all, like welfare institutions, they are non-profit, but explicitly point to their innovative character, which "can lie in the services offered as well as their creation and marketing, or precisely in the 'reconciliation' of economic and social goals. This criterion in particular seems to be partly responsible for the current 'hype' and hopes that can be gleaned from the discourse around social entrepreneurship. The third criterion refers to the importance of performance-based income, often as part of a hybrid financing structure. Social enterprises are mostly financed by a mix of public and private income, such as donations, government funding, performance fees but also membership fees" (Obuch and Grabbe 2019, p. 147; see also Grohs et al. 2017).

Michael Bohmeyer can be described as a "successful" social entrepreneur in the field of social policy and especially of the unconditional basic income, whom Ulf Porschardt created a public forum for in a full-page portrait entitled "Unternehmen Grundeinkommen" in the Welt on 19.8. 2020, which also met with a response in the international press. "Anyone who enters into conversation with Bohmeyer is amazed at the depth and differentiation of his reflections, which hardly fit (sometimes fitting) clichés of social entrepreneurs." By his own account, the former CEO of a start-up company got out of his business at the age of 29 and, as co-owner, continued to receive a share of the profits, which he described as "non-performing income" for himself and lived on for a year. As a result of his own positive experience, this served as the initial spark to test his own experience for transferability, and in 2014 he founded the Berlin-based non-profit My Basic Income. "I wanted to try running basic income like a modern start-up and started crowdfunding to raise €12,000 to give away. This has turned into more than €8 million over the years" (ibid 2020). The Transparency and Financial Report for 2019 not only shows a decidedly impressive track record of their high-profile BGE activities, but also documents the association's way of working: 'A basic income society must also rethink the world of work. Just as we bring the Unconditional Basic Income to life, we are also trying out the future of work in our team today. 2019 was particularly exciting for us: we decided together to work in a completely self-organized way, according to the principles of holocracy" (My Basic Income 2020a).

According to a study published in 2019 by Ashoka and McKinsey, there are now around 1700 particularly *innovative social enterprises* that see themselves as "hidden champions" and are certainly being heard in official politics (e.g. in the Bundestag). However, the well-orchestrated new link between social commitment and entrepreneurial action not only seems to market itself well, but there are now a large number of social projects behind it. "Social enterprises are particularly often found in the areas of labour market integration, social services, education and social inclusion. This then includes facilities and services such as kindergartens, hospitals, care services or workshops for the disabled. The newer generation of social enterprises is often active in areas that were previously not covered or only to a limited extent. Furthermore, the new generation of social enterprises increasingly relies on the use of new technologies to solve social problems" (Obuch and Grabbe 2019, p. 151; see also the contributions in Jansen et al. 2013). Spatially, social entrepreneurs are mainly concentrated in large cities such as Berlin, Hamburg, Frankfurt or Cologne.

Due to its (seemingly) visionary character, the concept of *social entrepreneurship* is highly attractive in the media and is also increasingly touching the political parties. For some political actors, this seems to be a way out of the dilemma of growing social tasks in the face of stagnating public finances, especially since there would also be a qualitative added value through the personal commitment of entrepreneurs in the field of social services. However, it is questionable whether the transfer of a model from the Anglo-Saxon area to the German welfare state reality, with privileged top-level associations possessing considerable performance potential, is so easily possible. Moreover, the personalization tendencies in the media lead to selected founding personalities being staged as social entrepreneurs and receiving attention from a sympathetic public that favors new events, while the day-to-day work of charities often does not achieve this transparency and media impact. *Diversity*, however, has already grown in the nonprofit sector for decades and has given rise to a scene of smaller self-organized projects at the local level in addition to the nationally organized welfare association service providers, most of which were also not represented in the corresponding local social and youth welfare committees, as these were reserved for the association representatives. "In the broad and often small-scale landscape of associations, forms of participation, support and self-help have gained in importance, which question traditional orientations, cultural patterns and attributions of responsibility (dealing with the environment, health, old age, old and new social institutions); state and municipal care systems are increasingly stabilised and de facto supported by complementary services provided by citizens (e.g. support associations). Post-traditional forms of engagement have in many cases taken shape and form outside the traditional integrating association system, but can also be observed as ferments of change in welfare organisations, churches, youth associations and trade unions" (Evers 2017, p. 239).

So far, social entrepreneurship projects still have relatively low capacities compared to the established players (in purely quantitative terms nationwide) and mainly serve socio-political *niches* (low-threshold care services, organisation of voluntary support services in the education and culture sector or refugee aid, etc.). However, they are highly innovative, especially in the areas of social marketing and the involvement of volunteers (cf. Grohs et al. 2014). For the most part, they correspond to the desire, often expressed by younger people in particular, for creative freedom and autonomy in the context of social engagement. Hierarchical top-down organisational structures and heteronomy are rejected by the majority, and this is the image that many charitable organisations have with their institutions. Against this background, it is not surprising that there are occasional tensions between the representatives of the social entrepreneurship scene and the established welfare associations. In the meantime, it is not only appealing to the media to make "entrepreneurial" solution proposals in the social sector a topic of discussion, but also politicians at the federal level see innovation potentials in this.

However, this focus does not take sufficient account of the special historical development path of welfare production in Germany, since social initiatives have always been formed or supported locally in the welfare sector, both historically and currently. In some fields of social services, the evolved landscape of associations has proven (sometimes with some delay) to be a "catch basin" and has integrated social innovations. Beyond the obvious hype for social enterprises, questions therefore arise as to what additional value these new forms of social activity bring to the existing structures of welfare production. One positive signal can be noted: due to the new organisational challenges, associations are forced to deal with their organisational logic and in particular with the question of how intrapreneurship can be actively promoted (cf. on this Steinke and Bibisidis 2018 as well as the contributions in Hummel and Timm 2020).

As a result, the well-rehearsed interaction between the state and welfare associations has also suffered a *loss of legitimacy in* some issues and regions in recent years, but it still shows a high degree of continuity or path dependency in the historical longitudinal section, which is also due to the fact that the associations are dependent on external financial resources. Without the welfare state transfers, the welfare associations could not survive; on the other hand, the welfare state institutions are dependent on the association services, because these cannot be replaced in the short term. This is why they also enjoy public status and are complementarily linked to the dynamically grown transfer state. If the associational social sector is included in the socio-political institutional system, it only becomes clear at a "second glance" how this system has grown and which bastion the welfare associations have conquered.

The *central pillars of* the welfare system are still in place, but they are becoming more differentiated – with the danger of fraying and, above all, new actors with non-traditional organisational ideas have come on board. Internationally, too, there is a reorientation towards welfare markets, competition between providers and a strengthening of private actors, which does not mean, however, that the marketisation of social services in Germany will intensify across the board, although business management criteria are gaining in importance in social institutions. This growing heterogenisation and operationalisation of the social services sector represents a multidimensional structural challenge for the established welfare care. "The welfare associations and the organisations associated with them represent an organisational model of social offers and services that seems outdated to many observers. New competition is emerging 'from below' through new initiatives and 'social entrepreneurs', 'from above' through large companies (especially in health and care) and franchise concepts: they are thus challenged by social innovation and scaling at the same time. Federated organisations stand between these two poles. Ideally, they can combine the innovation potential of small initiatives with the scaling potential of centralized competitors. To be sure, the reality is often quite different: The tenacious inertia of local institutions pairs with sluggish association structures that make decisions difficult and communication cumbersome" (Grohs 2018, 79 f.; cf. also Heinze 2020b).

However, the demand in the elderly as well as in the children's sector has so far only been taken up by politics to a limited extent. For example, an investment-oriented social policy should already begin in childhood, but this is only inadequately realised in Germany in an international comparison. This applies overall to public investment in Germany, which is below the EU average and has even declined in recent decades: In the early 1970s, they were still close to 5% of economic output. "An international comparison of government spending structures also confirms that Germany has fallen far behind in public investment. In addition to transport infrastructure, a particular need for investment is also seen in the area of education and research, where German spending is also low in an EU comparison. It is also striking that Germany occupies one of the top places in terms of monetary social transfers, while it is far behind in terms of personnel expenditure (including social services). This finding points to a heavy transfer burden and comparatively poor provision of social services. Government consumption expenditure is also below average. The same applies to the interest burden of debt service" (Rixen 2019, p. 349; see also Siller 2020).

However, this description of Germany's special situation with a low government deficit is a thing of the past. In the Corona crisis, the state took on enormous additional debt to finance programmes against the pandemic and its after-effects. The long-held principle (one can already speak of a reason of state) of incurring as little debt as possible and complying with the debt brake has now been postponed to the future. Thus, the current medium-term financial planning of the federal government provides that only "in the years from 2023 [...] the benchmarks will be planned to comply with the debt rule without making use of the exemption" (BMF 2021, p. 15). As justification for a current suspension of the debt brake, reference was made on the one hand to the experience of the last financial crisis in 2008/09 and the possible higher costs for the community in such a crisis situation to save: "For only with investments in social cohesion, in a strong public community and in a strong economy can Germany get through the crisis well. The planned measures are expensive, but doing nothing would be even more expensive in the end" (BMF 2021, p. 14).

Despite the restrictive fiscal policy course, the health and social sectors in Germany have proved to be engines of growth, in which civil society organisations (such as welfare associations) have expanded. Although this has not allowed a purely "different" social economy to develop as an autonomous sector beyond the logic of the market economy, civil society organisations have not only become quantitatively more important in some policy areas, but have also driven innovation; for example, in the field of labour and employment promotion. "The welfare associations, but also many small social entrepreneurial initiatives, were very early promoters, alongside the municipalities, of a social employment policy aimed specifically at disadvantaged groups in the labour market, such as the long-term unemployed, disadvantaged young people or the disabled. In the 1980s and 1990s, a large number of local employment initiatives emerged which made aggressive use of the instruments of job creation measures under the Employment Promotion Act and so-called "help for work" under the Federal Social Assistance Act to create additional employment opportunities for disadvantaged people. Such employment projects within the welfare associations have been successful in terms of labour market policy where they have built bridges between sheltered and publicly funded employment in a project and employment areas in the services of the providers, such as care facilities, and have opened the way for people from transitional employment to permanent employment in the "first labour market"" (Schulze-Böing 2021, p. 44).

Nevertheless, in recent decades they have made themselves increasingly dependent on public funds and thus *linked* their performance potential to the general economic situation and public financial flows: *if* tax revenues fall, then the scope for shaping the associations' priorities in social policy also falls automatically, because the income from donations is far lower by comparison. The claim of the welfare associations to convert their own profile also into own activity emphasis suffers from it. In a time, in which the donation income is distributed besides more strongly among many organizations and initiatives, one can lose thereby profile.

The size and bureaucratization of the welfare associations, but also the close links with state institutions, have in any case raised the question of whether this non-profit sector really represents an alternative to state control or whether it is not a publicly funded "cartel" that tends to eliminate internal competition between the associations by dividing up the market. This cartel hypothesis can be divided into a more left-alternative and a regulatory-market-liberal variety, depending on the state of discourse. From an alternative point of view, the exclusion of smaller citizens' initiatives, social movements and self-help groups is a particular issue. The regulatory-economic liberal critique (among others by the Monopolies Commission of the Federal Government) criticises competition-distorting aspects of the de facto oligopoly of the welfare associations (cf. among others Enste 2004).

Criticism of the established welfare associations has been further fuelled by the uncovering of non-transparent business relations and excessive salaries of the association's leadership circles in individual organisations and districts. Thus not only the district federation Hessen south of the workman welfare organization (AWO) stands under the suspicion of not always appropriate account of public funds, questionable appointments, interlacing of supervision and guidance and the self-enrichment of individual high-level personnel. Internal misconduct is also reported from other district associations of the AWO (in Mecklenburg-Western Pomerania and Thuringia) or from individual organisations of the church welfare organisations. In addition, in the opinion of the employees, the concrete working conditions have also deteriorated in many areas in non-profit social organisations. Deviations from the normal employment relationship have been noted and publicly criticised for some time (there is talk of "wage dumping" through outsourcing, work contracts etc.). As in other fields of the "third sector", low wages and atypical employment have spread as a result of the sharpened focus on efficiency aspects in service provision. "Non-profit organizations in particular seem to increasingly use atypical employment as a reaction to competition and planning uncertainty due to changes in funding modes (e.g. increase in – temporary – project funding), and even more so than state or private sector organizations" (Paul and Walter 2019, p. 184). The normative postulates of non-profit associations and empiricism seem to diverge more and more. However, precisely because established charities operate largely with public funds (partly with global allocations from the individual federal states), working conditions must be designed fairly and funding practices must be transparent.

Otherwise, in addition to the *damage to* their *image, there* is also a risk of loss of legitimacy and possibly the withdrawal of non-profit status and the associated tax advantages. The scarcity of resources, the need for public control and the growing number of private commercial providers, who can also act as competitors, have resulted in organisational control problems for many welfare associations. Developing greater efficiency and transparency is often difficult in traditional structures. "Under the pressure of private competition and the compulsion to modernise public administrations and their behaviour towards welfare associations (care rate policy), the policy, identity and position of welfare associations changed. The talk of service enterprises, at first still unfamiliar and understood as a possible but also problematic perspective name, today increasingly shapes the self-image of these tradition-rich institutions. Either the welfare associations are forced to use an entrepreneurial and managerial way of acting in order to keep themselves on the market, or the entrepreneurial option is so attractive in times of narrow financial room for manoeuvre that parts of the welfare associations choose it out of conviction. This happens, for example, through the spin-off of individual marketable and monetarily promising service areas into non-profit or even commercial limited liability companies. On the other hand, the internal organisation of the welfare associations themselves becomes a problem for them. If one wants to be able to act on the market, the old association structure and a functionaries in the association executive committees aiming at honorary inner-organizational commitment is obstructive. Since the 1990s, welfare associations have been adapting to operate entrepreneurially on welfare markets for social services" (Nullmeier 2002, p. 274; cf. also the contributions in Heinze et al. 2018).

However, the changed governance structures and the shift from status to contract should by no means be automatically interpreted as an indicator of a crisis of the subsidiarity principle or an erosion of the dominant position of the welfare associations in the German social services landscape. Various studies have pointed out that even in times of fiscal crisis, a pluralisation of the provider landscape is not necessarily to be expected, but rather a consolidation of corporatist structures. "The traditionally institutionalised partnership linkages continue to be the focus of the relationship. The welfare associations continue to regard themselves and are also regarded by the state as the most important contact in the welfare sector. Moreover, in practice, the political-administrative decision-makers interpret their discretionary powers with regard to the application of the new regulations mostly in favour of the welfare associations. The preferential treatment of and increased trust in welfare associations thus remain" (Reichenbachs 2018, p. 120 f.). Thus, in some municipalities, the freezing of tasks and agencies in the current state establishes a kind of "closed shop" that comes even closer than before to the corporatist ideal type of state-orchestrated representation monopoly.

One can therefore certainly speak of a *regulated welfare corporatism,* which can be seen, for example, in contract management, an essential component of new control models at the municipal level. Contract management has different effects on welfare work depending on the field of work. In municipalities where networks between local social policy, job centres and the welfare associations are maintained even in crisis situations (such as in youth welfare), they do not have a negative impact on the associations. In municipalities with more loose arrangements, competitive elements such as tenders for social services are more likely, although compliance with the general provisions of the Vergabe- und Vertragsbestimmungen für Leistungen (VOL/A) is now basically binding for almost all public contracting authorities. The downside of new governance models for associations, however, is that they are largely responsible for disagreements and financial adjustment pressures. Conflict resolution is thus shifted to the organisation and can lead to internal restructuring, but this can also unleash innovation. "An offensive approach to the demands of new governance models and social management can also open up scope for a pragmatic adaptation of instruments to professional requirements. In the future, social work and the social economy will have no choice but to account for their use of resources, the quality of their services and the effects achieved, whether this goes under the label of "management" or another" (Grohs 2018, p. 99).

However, not only the action strategies of the welfare associations, but of all actors in municipal social policy are affected by the interface problems that can lead to risks of exclusion for the addressees. The complexity of the German welfare state remains characterised by the institutional division of labour between social insurance funds and municipalities, the separation into local and supra-local agencies and the internal differentiation of various areas of responsibility. And as a result of this historical character and the legalisation that has been accelerated above all in recent years, a pillarisation can be stated that shows considerable deficits with regard to the active (and above all preventive) handling of social problems. The fragmentation of responsibilities promotes considerable interface problems and intransparencies, which appear as if in a magnifying glass, especially at the municipal level. "In Germany, the main competences for childcare, youth welfare and social services are the responsibility of the municipalities. Basic welfare services are often provided with the involvement of the employment agency. Schooling and vocational training are primarily located at the Länder level. The health sector is financed by various health insurance funds. The various preventive and curative services are provided in networks. The network consists of physicians in private practice and hospitals under different ownership. Medical associations and the Association of Statutory Health Insurance Physicians influence regulations that have concrete effects on the ground. Further actors are the health offices in the municipalities, although they have a rather limited portfolio. The coordination of the areas of child and youth welfare, general social services, basic security, education, health and employment is therefore highly complex" (Wieda et al. 2020, p. 23).

The heterogeneity of the structure of offers and providers in the field of social services is further supported by the different sources of funding and – with regard to prevention – the often only temporary funding of measures. This further increases the already considerable degree of non-transparency. Recent empirical studies confirm how the complicated structure of the German welfare state means that social risks are not adequately dealt with, let alone solved. "If one looks at social policy as a whole, it is already characterised in its fundamental structures by a constellation of diffusion – the implementation of the overarching objective of social justice and social security formulated in the SGBI takes place in different policy fields, each with specific governance structures, guiding principles and actor constellations. Here, with the formulation of a comprehensive participation objective, a cross-cutting task of social policy is formulated, the implementation of which is distributed among different policy fields and legal circles. The organisations each pursue specific goals and, as the evaluations show, are often more oriented in their implementation towards their respective organisational goals than towards their (potential) contribution to achieving the overarching goal. This diffusion of responsibility for the overarching participation goal represents a fundamental problem of social policy" (Stöbe-Blossey et al. 2019, p. 181).

While the number of laws supporting social problems has increased in recent decades and more actors are addressing social concerns, there is often a lack of strategic collaboration. "However, people have social problem situations that do not adhere to these responsibilities. In many places, the welfare state, which is well developed in itself, falls far short of its ability to prevent emergencies and make people strong. Awareness of the need to pool the forces of the welfare state has been growing for some time. Where cooperation succeeds under pandemic conditions, those responsible in the various institutions have practised cooperation over many years and used the legal scope for pragmatic solutions" (Cremer 2021).

At this point, the already ongoing process of digitalisation opens up both opportunities and risks in the social economy. "On the one hand, it offers previously unimagined potential for support and participation, but on the other hand it creates new forms of exclusion and discrimination" (Vilain 2020, p. 89). Digital offers, e.g. for information and communication, cannot be excluded by the organisations because they are often demanded by sovereign service recipients. With regard to social organisations, it is often emphasised in research that they find it difficult to initiate organisational restructuring, as they are not programmed for change. "Social economy organizations are often considered resistant to change. Structures and attitudes are often designed for longevity. However, increasingly more of these organisations are showing the flexibility and movement needed to meet current challenges. Effective planning, implementation and monitoring of change requires courage and the tools of effective leadership, in the self-organization approach to self-leadership. Such change does not necessarily have to be radical, but is often managed through soft channels" (Kaegi and Zängl 2019, p. 121).

However, contracts are no longer negotiated only in the responsible political bodies, but are decided in contract negotiations between the administration and associations or their member organisations. The traditional political links between individual welfare organisations and political parties are therefore also losing *their steering power* at the municipal level. Once the contract budgets are fixed, however, the associations can decide more autonomously than before on the use of funds. This creeping disempowerment of politics inevitably leads to a differentiation of the socio-political field of forces, which becomes pluralised. In times of growing competition for resources, this kind of operationalisation means for the welfare associations that their function of representing the interests of socially marginalised groups is neglected. The tolerability of some social markets disavows the idea that the providers of social services can always be the advocates of their potential customers at the same time. This in turn makes questions of justice virulent, which can bring the established welfare associations into new legitimation problems as well as role conflicts, especially if the classic rhetoric is not adapted to the new conditions and, on the contrary, even organisational policy scandals are widely publicised in the media.

In addition, contract management is not endowed with formal legal decision-making powers; it complements the democratically legitimised system and the traditional procedural channels of political decision-making, but does not replace them. This means that the state continues to play an important role in shaping the social sector. Thus, as a negotiating state, it can make *network governance* itself the subject of state policy by setting the procedural rules and influencing the composition of interests. In concrete terms in relation to social policy, this can be a way of strengthening welfare pluralism at the same time, in view of the pluralisation and individualisation of society and the strengthening of the rights of those receiving benefits.

Overall, the effects of new governance models are rather *contradictory:* On the one hand, the pressure to economise increases on the individual organisations of the welfare associations. On the other hand, this does not lead to an actual market regulation of the welfare state system. Economisation therefore does not automatically mean more competition, be it between private commercial and non-profit providers or large and small providers or between the individual providers themselves. Contrary to the labels, the corporatist system and the functional logics of the welfare associations are often stabilised at a low financial level, but at the same time many larger welfare associations are diversifying and becoming more operational. On the one hand, this provides them with greater autonomy and decision-making scope; on the other hand, this implies new questions regarding self-control capacity and legitimacy (cf. the contributions in Heinze et al. 2018 and in Grunwald and Langer 2018). Even if some critics (mainly from academia) have been warning for years of a loss of importance of the associations (for example, through emerging competition from private companies in subsectors such as care for the elderly), the associative services continue to expand within the framework of a general expansion of the social investment state and thus strengthen their prominent local positioning in regulated welfare corporatism.

3.5 Towards a Hybrid Welfare Mix

The social and health care sector is becoming more confusing as a result of new providers and changing demand structures, and the boundaries between organisational forms are becoming blurred, increasing complexity. New interweavings of welfare state, market-related and civil society elements in social institutions and services are making the already confusing architecture of the German welfare state even more complicated. This trend towards hybridisation and the multiple interdependencies it implies is likely to continue, especially since the compartmentalised problem-solving of traditional social corporatism with its tendency towards "closed shops" no longer corresponds to social diversity and the necessary problem-solving competencies. On the one hand, this differentiation can bring about social innovations, as the established support structures receive a wake-up call; on the other hand, it does not solve the interface problems that are so prominent in Germany. Integrative cooperation structures still need to be established. "Establishing successful cooperation is extremely demanding. In the German context, responsibilities and budgets are distributed across different institutions in different legal circles. Interdisciplinary and interinstitutional cooperation is little established. With regard to children in disadvantaged social areas, this fragmentation can have fatal consequences: Although each authority works administratively correct in its competence, it is not ensured that the social, health and educational needs of children are coordinated in such a way that thereby the way to an independent and self-reliant life is effectively supported. In political and administrative leadership, there is often still a lack of awareness of the strategic importance of community networks and prevention" (Wieda et al. 2020, p. 17).

The progressive ageing of society is also creating new challenges at local level in terms of ensuring and improving *medical and nursing care for* older people and thus further demand for social and nursing services. Against the background of an increasing singularisation of (especially) very old people, concepts are needed, as in the case of illness or need for care in old age, that can ensure participation in social processes as well as the highest possible degree of independence (cf. summarising Heinze 2020a). In local, neighbourhood-based projects, however, remaining in one's own home can in many cases only be made possible if both social care (professional social services as well as civic engagement) and technical assistance are used. Over 90% of older people over 65 live in private dwellings, just under 4% in old people's and nursing homes (beyond the age of 80 the figure rises to around 11%). According to the microcensus, 97% of those aged 60 and older live in a private household, i.e. alone or with a partner (cf. in summary BMFSFJ 2016; Generali-Altersstudie 2017 as well as the current data report 2021 from the Federal Statistical Office et al.).

Self-determined living at home continues to be the most popular form of housing for the vast majority of older people. The home and its immediate surroundings are increasingly becoming the focal point of life in old age, and often the sole place of residence in old age and when care is needed. Although the residential sector is gaining in importance, there is still a considerable need to catch up in the area of housing suitable for the elderly. This can be seen through the magnifying glass of the Corona pandemic, in which the elderly were sweepingly relegated to their own homes and the local environment as a risk group. "The reduced radius of life increases the importance of the home to the quality of life of the elderly many times over. The ability to move around the home appropriately is particularly significant for those with mobility impairments. In addition, other aspects of housing (such as access to a garden or a balcony) that are crucial for residential satisfaction are likely to gain in importance. These also include neighbourly relations and support structures. In addition to concrete assistance in everyday life, proximity to neighbours can also alleviate feelings of loneliness and social isolation, especially when contact with friends and family is limited" (Hoffmann et al. 2021, p. 90).

The development of a new supply infrastructure at local level, which is necessary for demographic reasons alone and independently of the specific crisis, must be viewed against the background of changed social structures. Households in Germany, for example, have not only become smaller and the proportion of older people in them has risen, there is also much to suggest that primary social networks have become somewhat more unstable, because traditional extended families are living together less and less frequently. Even if the signs of family erosion are unmistakable, this does not mean that there are no longer any ties between the generations. Although most adult family members do not live under the same roof, they are usually not far apart and can therefore experience a wide range of support services. Representative surveys of people over the age of 18 in Germany provide evidence of "settledness": people do not change "their" neighbourhood without further ado. 80% of all Germans and even 90% of the over-65 s have lived in their neighbourhood for more than 5 years. Taken together, over 90% of those surveyed say that they feel comfortable in their neighbourhood and expect politicians to provide public services in their community.

This attachment to the social environment also creates social cohesion, which is of great importance in an increasingly fragmented and singularised society. The neighbourhood can act as an anchor of identity, which is also reflected in the currently much discussed term "home". In view of a world that is becoming more complex and often more difficult for individuals to comprehend (globalisation, migration, climate change), many people are once again focusing more on their immediate social environment in order to meet their need for security there. It is therefore an important task of the municipalities, in addition to providing adequate basic material security in old age, to design the public space in the sense of providing for the public in such a way that encounters between the people living there are strengthened. In this understanding, they even have the special responsibility to network actors and institutions and to enable participation.

Despite this important role of municipal social policy, it has a shadowy existence in the social policy debate in Germany compared to state social policy. This is also due to the fact that the *municipalities,* despite the relief provided to the Länder by the federal government since 2020, still have the "short end of the stick" when it comes to putting forward their substantive and financial wishes. For example, there has long been a dispute about a reform of municipal finances and the realisation of the principle of connexity, which is constitutionally fixed, but which is often deviated from in reality. But it is not only in this respect that the financing structures in the German social system are (to put it mildly) extraordinarily complex and highly legalised. Due to the fragmented funding structures, it is "characterised by a mixture of different funding sources. This further increases the already considerable degree of non-transparency.

- When presenting the financing bases and structures, it is necessary – despite many similarities – to distinguish between the different provider groups for analytical reasons. Here, a general distinction can be made between public, independent and private commercial providers. A second systematisation asks about the respective origin of the funds. Public funds from tax and contribution revenues predominate. In addition, there are the (additional) payments of the users as well as – in the case of non-profit providers – own funds, in particular from membership fees, church taxes, donations and sponsoring. A third system relates to the different forms of financing. Here, a main distinction can be made between grants, service fees and service contracts. Finally, a fourth classification can be made according to the recipients of funding. Here, object funding, i.e. financial funding of the providers or the facilities and services, clearly dominates, while subject funding, which focuses on the direct allocation of money to the clients or customers themselves, is rather rare" (Bäcker et al. 2020, p. 1142).

These pillars and silos constitute an obstacle to the redirection and further development of social policy in the direction of a technically required focus on prevention, social spaces and individual preferences as well as the life courses of those entitled to benefits, because this requires an interdepartmental cross-sectional policy at the municipal level. One could also speak of a cross-actor and cross-sectoral "mission", which is called for not only in the field of social and health policy, but also in climate protection policy (cf. Mazzucato 2021; Leggewie 2021). However, such a *mission-oriented* strategy is difficult to implement in Germany, because a pronounced institutional segmentation with specific rules of the game and forms of discourse has shaped the German welfare state since its emergence, making it difficult to implement a consistent and cross-sectoral policy, as is increasingly required especially today. "Seen in this light, the Federal Republic appears, particularly in the field of social policy, as a collection of more or less loosely coupled policy communities, each of which is to be regarded as a negotiating system in its own right" (Czada 2000, p. 42).

Therefore, *intelligent interface management* is required, which must also actively counter the danger of "silo thinking" in order to both avoid duplicate structures and establish new forms of cooperation with actors from other fields of action. For example, in the area of care, the municipalities could take on an important moderation and coordination function with the central organisations in this field of action (medical and care facilities, the health and care insurance funds, if necessary self-help networks and the housing industry). Both the traditional neighbourhoods and the newly emerged forms of engagement should be included (a renewed "welfare mix"). In this context, a number of model programmes have been launched in recent years, but there are less deficits in knowledge than in implementation. What is needed, therefore, is a consistent policy approach that must be organised across ministries and policy fields and turn local politics into a laboratory for experimentally oriented social policy. The strengths of traditional welfare policy can be used, but the existing fragmentation, for example into payers and services or prevention, must be overcome in the direction of integrated care at the local level with more permeability between the forms of care.

This dual strategy of, on the one hand, observing the development paths with their well-rehearsed routines and, on the other hand, relying on new institutional arrangements, ties in with comparative welfare state research, in which it has been shown that the high hurdles – especially in the case of welfare state systems – to fundamental reforms can only be overcome by including these stabilising mechanisms. "Typically, a variety of organizations emerge in a society or policy area that take advantage of the opportunities offered by the prevailing institutions and are also highly interrelated and interdependent. Institutions, once established, have a self-reinforcing character and tend to be stable. The possible paths of development are neither predetermined nor immutable, but – and this is the core of the argument of path-dependent development – once institutions have been established, they severely limit the possibilities of future developments. A new start is no longer possible. If new ideas are to be implemented, the formal regulatory system must be adapted to this end. And, the more a new idea deviates from the existing routine and practice, the more difficult it is to accomplish. If reform ideas are to have a chance, they must therefore fit well with existing institutional arrangements" (Beyerler 2020, p. 289; see also Streeck and Thelen 2005). Examples from various countries show how reforms in the welfare state system have been realized via such modernization compromises. For our considerations on the restructuring and necessary further development of welfare state policy, we derive from this that the reforms and the implied institutional change processes must be incremental on the one hand and transformative on the other. The incremental change in individual fields of social policy, which often takes place invisibly and remains hidden from the general public, has already been pointed out. New models, such as the paradigm of a universalistic social policy, are anything but easy to implement and enforce in the institutional context of a social policy regime that has grown historically and functioned well for several decades. We know from organisational research that systems that no longer function so well and are threatened by inefficiency can survive for a long time.

With a view to reforms in the German welfare state structure, *lighthouse projects* for a better interlinked policy strategy focusing on prevention and sustainability have been considered and partly implemented in recent years. However, on the one hand, such cooperative reform strategies have only succeeded sporadically and temporarily in the fragmented German system; on the other hand, such strategic cooperations and resilient policies are currently in great demand at the local level – currently due to the Corona pandemic, but also due to long-term change processes (demographic change, new climate policy). For a networked policy of services of general interest, not only public infrastructure facilities but also enterprises in the service sector, retail trade or gastronomy play just as important a role as alternative forms of economy not geared to profit maximisation, such as cooperatives and welfare institutions. Local infrastructure has a significant influence on the quality of life and security of supply of the population and is thus also to be understood as a central component of a sustainable, socially investing social policy. "In this context, the (central) state primarily secures basic entitlements, while the actors in the local networks help to establish new integration and support services (voluntary work, association activities, employment opportunities, care networks) and thus offer options for action" (Beyerler 2020, p. 297).

However, new integrative care offers on site encounter numerous institutional hurdles (e.g. there is often no clear public funding responsibility for them), which can hardly be overcome without a change in the rules of formal structures. Against this background, it is not an easy task to establish small-scale networked care structures at the local level, which make it possible, for example, for older people to obtain necessary care and services, including nursing and care, within their neighbourhood at distances that are accessible to them, and thus to experience and maintain social contacts in the local area around their home. Such a restructuring of social services in the direction of socially integrated, networked care requires a strategic rethinking on the part of the central actors in this policy field. The focus on integrated, neighbourhood-based care structures thus implies a considerable need for political action, which must be taken at the various levels of the political system.

Against this background, the thesis of *resistance* to welfare state change put forward in comparative welfare state research is not surprising. "Mature welfare states are difficult to reform because of institutional entrenchment, numerous voter interests, and interest groups that the state itself has generated" (Dallinger 2016, p. 195). The pronounced institutional segmentation of policy fields with specific rules of the game has shaped the German welfare state in particular since its emergence and makes it difficult to manage tasks across sectors. Comparative welfare state analyses therefore speak with regard to Germany not without reason of a "frozen welfare state landscape" (Esping-Andersen 1999), which must first be "thawed out" in favour of integrative solutions. However, Esping-Andersen did not explicitly deal with the "Third Sector" or the potential of welfare associations in Germany in his highly regarded welfare state typology, which is based on the national welfare state accents of the 1980s and 1990s and would have to be recomposed today. In the socio-political publications of recent years (summarised, for example, in the Seventh Report on the Elderly by the Federal Government/cf. BMFSFJ 2016), emphasis is placed on the potential of civil society as a complementary contribution to social security. In addition to material security, "successful care" for people in need of support requires the intelligent and efficient interaction of relatives, friends, professional social services (i.e. primarily the welfare associations) and civically engaged people. Since the possibilities of living space decrease visibly with increasing age, there is a need for small-scale local care structures that enable older people to obtain the necessary care and services, including nursing and care, at distances that are within their reach and to experience and maintain social contacts in the local area.

For this reason, the municipalities are central addressees for a social policy reorientation and the municipal responsibility for a social coexistence of all generations is also often proclaimed in "celebratory speeches". However, its concrete implementation at local level remains a major challenge for all actors. "Despite the tendency to shift socio-political tasks to the central government level (e.g. through the introduction of long-term care insurance and through basic security for jobseekers, which is jointly financed with the federal government), the municipalities are still primarily responsible for the social infrastructure of society and for the provision of services of general interest. They are responsible for ensuring that social facilities and services are available to meet the needs of the local population. At the same time, they are the local providers of social welfare and youth welfare. The municipalities – independent cities, (rural) districts and cities belonging to districts) – regulate all matters of the local community in self-administration, insofar as the Federal Government or the Länder are not responsible. The most important tasks include social services, culture, health, sport and recreation, road construction and transport, energy and water supply, city cleaning, public order, construction and housing, and economic development" (Bäcker et al. 2020, p. 97).

However, the implementation of services of general interest should not only be regarded as a state task, but the coexistence of public services and non-profit organisations, which is regulated in Germany by the principle of subsidiarity, must also make an essential contribution to the provision of services of general interest at the local level. By virtue of their special legal status and structural principles, charities even have a duty to play an active role in shaping services of general interest, something that often does not register sufficiently in international discourses on fundamental economics (see, among others, Foundational Economy Collective 2019; Streeck 2019). The push for *integrated, local solutions* will succeed not only in this policy field only with the involvement of all actors concerned. For this, new forms of cooperation must be developed, especially between housing companies, social and health services and providers (including registered doctors and hospitals), the information and communications industry, local authorities, health insurance funds, as well as self-help associations and civic activists. Depending on the respective constellations of actors on site, drivers for new strategic partnerships in the field of integrated care are needed.

However, deficits can already be observed in the cooperation between municipalities and actors from the social and health economy. Some municipalities see themselves unable to actively pursue networking tasks due to the overload, especially since they often lack the financial resources to do so. "Municipal infrastructure and investment policy is always also financial and budgetary policy and therefore requires an integrated planning approach that is based on a discourse spanning all disciplines and periods. A prerequisite for this – especially in fiscally difficult times – is a city-wide claim to design, with which perspectives can be shown that point beyond the individual budget year and the period of medium-term financial planning. With new participation procedures and planning instruments, different actors and stakeholders (including citizens) can then also be involved in such processes" (Scheller 2017, p. 46).

Against this background, the state no longer possesses the required competencies and financial resources to guarantee comprehensive services of general interest at an equivalent level without the involvement of private actors and organisations. In the sense of a new management of social security, a paradigm shift from bureaucratic organisation and planning to a role as networking authority and coordinator is demanded of public institutions in order to overcome the fragmentation inherent in the German social security system. Networks in a socio-spatial context will gain in importance in the future and are currently also politically favoured. Here, open, plural cooperation structures can initially emerge in a niche field, but they no longer have the security of an orderly welfare system and must operate (often for a limited time) under turbulent conditions. What is needed, however, is not just temporary funding and lighthouse projects, but long-term cooperative solutions and new financing models. However, these also affect the network of relationships between the state and welfare organisations, whose governance structures have changed in recent years towards contract management.

Thus, for some years now, the state has been attempting to "steer Freie Wohlfahrtspflege more politically by introducing (operational) economic guidelines. Corporatism between the state and welfare associations persists in a modified form, but the balance of power between the state and welfare associations has shifted significantly in favour of the state" (Backhaus-Maul 2018a, p. 22). However, the self-governance of associations, which has been established in the German health and social sector over decades, continues to be a relevant power factor that plays a major role, especially in the health sector. As a result of the state's new demands for control, association leaders must mediate between member interests and state demands. Observers speak of an *intermediation dilemma*. "The intermediary position between members' interests and the state's mandate confronts association leaders with conflicting logics of action: As representatives of interests, they are obliged to their membership; as negotiating partners, they are required to be willing to compromise in the interest of the general public in exchanges with other associations and the state. The tension between representation and negotiation pushes them towards conflict moderation and compromise-building. This distinguishes association corporatism from pluralistic power struggles, which aim solely to assert interests" (Czada 2020, p. 313).

Despite the changes in governance structures, the landscape of social service providers in Germany will probably not change fundamentally, although more efficient interface management will be required. With regard to the growing tasks in the social and health sector, however, local authorities will only be able to fulfil these if they are given competences and, above all, financial resources. On the other hand, local social policy is increasingly expected to better network the interfaces of different care systems in the social space and to present its information offer transparently for potential service recipients. However, this is only possible if the federal government creates the necessary framework conditions and also provides financial resources for this purpose. In any case, social policy has developed in this direction in recent decades and the federal government has taken on more and more tasks, which "also means shifting the risks to the national budget and thus all taxpayers" (Eichhorst and Marx 2019, p. 422; cf. also Bahle 2019; Fux and Baumgartner 2019).

Despite these far-reaching but always selective real changes, it is unlikely that any political majorities will be found for the welfare state option of an unconditional basic income at present or in the legislative period from 2021. However, the breaks in continuity in labour market and social policy development implemented by the intensity of the Corona pandemic are (mostly unintentionally) bringing about a further step in the direction of an emerging *basic welfare state* with continuously growing autonomy claims on the part of (potential) benefit recipients. This creeping departure from the traditional development path of the German welfare state, which grants benefits according to principles of subordination, cannot be seen as a uniform strategy so far, but is happening almost invisibly in small doses, but the pandemic could lead to a new historical transformation phase. It is not unlikely that political parties, academia and, above all, public discourse will increasingly see more opportunities than risks for a conceptual reorientation as a result of the experience now gained.

In view of the Corona crisis, but also of globalisation processes, coupled with the spread of "shareholder value principles" in sectors traditionally protected in Germany, such as housing, education or health, more and more voices are being raised asking about the social responsibility and sustainability of such governance models. In general, the pendulum is swinging back from a rather radical market orientation towards a renaissance of state or "mixed economy" regulation. Here the focus is explicitly on the local area of the provision of public goods: it is a matter of actively shaping one's own associative social spaces. However, there is as yet no script for the restructuring process towards a better balance between the state, the market and "active" civil society, and the difficulty of structural restructuring is more than evident from the protracted and half-hearted reforms (e.g. in the field of care). In this sector, which will continue to grow in the coming years, it is clear how difficult it is to introduce structural reforms (e.g. in the form of generally binding sectoral collective agreements). For this reason, the dissatisfaction of many employees is likely to remain, which is already being expressed in individual protests and the exit option.

A readjustment of the architecture of the German welfare state would also herald a new phase of welfare state development, which some authors are already calling *post-industrialism,* because social security, which is ultimately tied to (socially insured) employment status, is qualitatively expanded and the real structural changes on the labour market are transformed into new socio-political models. "Post-industrial solidarity respects people globally rather than romanticizing a proletariat. Among other things, it means socially integrating service providers in a way that suits them, who from all their experiences, not just from a predominantly unprotected employment sector, have long been post-industrial; whose creativity, qualifications, mobility and flexibility have long been siphoned off by project capitalism without core workforce safeguards; and whose individualism, thus generated and reinforced, understandably responds poorly to the paternalistic imposition of snappy activation phrases that they might as well have penned themselves in one of their myriad commissioned works, since no one knows the long-worn vocabulary of project capitalism better than they do" (Albert 2019, p. 87). Here, the idea of solidarity does not stop with the (dependently) employed, but is conceived inclusively and universalistically for the whole of society. In this context, the concepts of basic income are also to be located, which start from the economic-social transformations as a fact and accordingly want to form new forms of autonomous self-determination as well as institutional solidarities as a modernization-theoretical variant.

This idea of modernisation has – as has already been shown – many predecessors and a great store of visionary power, which, however, often got stuck in *fundamental debates,* especially since even renowned social scientists are by no means convinced of the superiority of a BGE. Esping-Andersen, for example, was extremely sceptical and cautious about an unconditional basic income only 15 years ago: "The weakness of the proposal lies elsewhere, namely in its rather outdated diagnosis of the risks and needs of citizens. Social risks and needs are increasingly focused on care and on services that help citizens improve their life chances. The real problem, then, is that the inevitably huge cost of a basic income will crowd out the services that citizens really demand, namely access to affordable childcare, care for the elderly, lifelong education and training opportunities. No doubt we can reduce the financial cost of a basic income by taxing it again on those whose incomes are already high. But then why introduce it at all? Personally, I am not opposed to a guaranteed basic income and would readily support such a policy for families with children and for the elderly. But to advocate it for all citizens would, in my analysis, mean putting almost everything on a single card." (Esping-Andersen 2006, p. 73 [translation Heinze/Schupp]).

The following chapter therefore discusses the conditions for success that have often been neglected in the discourses on a BGE. For fundamental transformations, especially in a field such as social security, which has grown historically and is endowed with organisational diversity, it is not enough to outline inefficiencies and risks of the established systems and to formulate normatively appealing concepts; the forces of inertia must also be taken into account. However, constellations of power can also erode, especially when in reality there has long been a silent shift towards guaranteed basic security, which is also reflected conceptually in words such as basic pension or low-condition basic security in labour market policy.

4 From "Muddling through" to Policy Change: Obstacles and Success Factors

The previous chapters have shown how complex the architecture of the welfare state in Germany is and how these structural fragmentations are at odds with the real problems and needs of the people. Citizens are by no means guided in their actions exclusively by bureaucratic responsibilities, which is why the actually well-developed welfare state often falls far short of its ability to prevent and efficiently combat emergencies. The complexity is historically characterised by the division of labour between social insurance funds and local authorities, the separation into local and supra-local providers and the internal differentiation of various areas of responsibility. Added to this is the continuously growing degree of legalisation of social policy in the sense of a strong differentiation of legal bases or administrative orders with the consequence of considerable *enforcement problems* due to an ever increasing pillarisation. In addition, the strong division of labour and bureaucratisation leads to a diffusion of responsibility, changing contact persons of applicants, whereby the large number of new regulations even potentially increases this. A lack of coordination and dovetailing of the various assistance systems thus often contributes to the emergence of funding gaps, underprovision and misprovision, or leads to an increase in objections and a high level of recourse, up to and including increasing processing times for the social courts. This is not only currently evident in the processing of problems of refugees and migrants, but also in various social issues. "While the social problems to be dealt with are of a holistic nature, the responsible office structures, on the other hand, are fragmented: responsibility for social assistance lies with the Social Welfare Office, for youth welfare with the Youth Welfare Office, for rent subsidies with the Housing Office. These different offices are often located at different administrative levels (social and

R. G. Heinze, J. Schupp, *Basic Income - From Vision to Creeping Transformation of the Welfare State*,
https://doi.org/10.1007/978-3-658-40269-3_4

youth welfare at the district, housing assistance at the municipality). The result is a selectivity of assistance that is oriented towards the respective responsibilities determined by the legislator" (Grohs 2010, p. 29; cf. also Stöbe-Blossey et al. 2020).

Already in the case of classical risks, interface problems arose due to the pillarisation of benefits, and this applies all the more when combating the newly emerging social inequalities and risks (e.g. in a life course perspective, because interface problems arise in the case of risky biographical transitions). "It is true that a comparatively extensive social infrastructure exists at the municipal level, which is provided primarily by the non-profit welfare sector. But the associated services and offers only come into play when there is a tangible negative finding such as illness, unemployment, school failure or other specific experiences of exclusion. The fact that this is regarded as deficient – measured against the growing social challenges – is also evident from the debates that have been going on for about two decades about the concept of an investment, activating, preventive, precautionary, infrastructural or impact-oriented social policy. Even if the terminology varies, these different labels are linked to a similar understanding of social policy, which, with the help of personal services, networks, competent actors and social services, aims to activate individuals in order to prevent the occurrence of risks and to strengthen the potentials for a self-responsible way of life" (Schroeder et al. 2018, p. 1; cf. also Rieger 2019).

As before, the welfare state system in Germany is more *administered* than designed; there can be no talk of a fundamental paradigm shift, but rather of a lack of structural policy change. It can be assumed – despite the expansion through basic security benefits – that the German welfare state has a "fairly high capacity for self-stabilization" (Nullmeier 2021, p. 841). What is the reason for the insufficient reform capacity of the welfare state system? To answer this question, the following section will present a political theory approach that primarily describes process logics and claims to answer these phenomena. This is the *multiple streams approach* (MSA), which is based on the following basic assumptions: 'first, that political systems can be conceptualized as organized anarchies; second, that decision-making situations can be captured by thinking in terms of streams; and third, that agenda change depends on whether and how streams connect' (Herweg 2015, p. 326; see also Herweg et al. 2018). So far, this approach has hardly been taken up in socio-political research in Germany, although it could go some way to explaining the coordination deficits and the lack of integrity.

4.1 The Tenacious Transformation of the Traditional Welfare State

The basic pattern of German policy has so far been an obsession with detail and a lack of linkage between the various "streams", which would actually be urgently needed, especially with a view to dealing with the new social risks. Against this background, it is understandable that in recent decades there have only rarely been sustainable policy changes in Germany – and this applies explicitly to fundamental social policy issues. Academic diagnoses paint a picture of an exhausted and overburdened welfare state, which is also faced with problems of its democratic legitimacy, since large sections of the population perceive individual welfare state service areas as deficient: "However, our welfare state is also "getting on in years". In its current structure and institutional design, the welfare state in Germany is a result of the industrial modernity of the nineteenth and twentieth centuries. There are many reasons why the social sciences, as well as the media and the general public, are calling for a "general overhaul" of the welfare state. The technological revolution – keyword digitalisation – and the transformation of the economy are giving rise to new social risks and needs; the change in gender roles is calling into question the traditional division of labour and the differentiation between domestic and wage labour; demographic change is pushing the traditional financing models of welfare state services to their limits; the increasing pluralisation of society is calling for more individualised solutions and more differentiated services than have hitherto been provided by the welfare state's catalogue of services. In short, the welfare state as it has developed since the end of the nineteenth century is being put to the test. Its entrenched structures are no longer up to date and are increasingly being called into question" (Freise and Zimmer 2019, p. 5).

A positive example is repeatedly put forward as a counter-thesis. In order to claim the potential ability of government policy to reform, the *energy turnaround* is invoked, which led to a rapid policy change in the coalition government led by Angela Merkel after the external shock of the nuclear reactor disaster in Japan a decade ago. But there is another large-scale reform project, Agenda 2010 under Chancellor Gerhard Schröder, that also needs to be mentioned in this context. The multiple streams approach can be used to classify this paradigmatic change in the form of the Hartz IV legislation in German labour market policy and to explain its conditions of success. "The perception that unemployment would not fall at the expected rate until the next election shows that the problem stream was ripe. The policy stream was also ripe, as the main elements of the Hartz reforms had already been discussed at length in expert networks beforehand. However, the unfavourable conditions in the politics stream in the form of sectoral corporatism, the strong position of the pro-union Labour Ministry and the powerful traditionalist wing in the SPD initially prevented the adoption of structural labour market reforms. It was not until the policy entrepreneur Gerhard Schröder used the placement scandal at the Federal Labour Office to set up an independent commission of experts, thus playing around the Labour Ministry, that changes were made to the government's agenda. The MSA can thus explain the playing around of a multitude of veto players and party-political interests that could be observed in the adoption of the Hartz reforms" (Zohlnhöfer and Herweg 2014, p. 124 f.; cf. also Spohr 2015).

There was no exact blueprint for the rapid *policy change in* the fields of labour market and social policy, but the importance of political entrepreneurs and the right time to launch a fundamental reform initiative are clear. Without these favourable trigger conditions, the institutional restructuring would probably not have taken place. In "normal" times, reform is described as "going the way of the snail": "Not only do they take a long time, but they also deviate little from the status quo. To begin with, the institutional framework is characterized by a significant number of veto players. The most important institutional veto players include the Bundesrat, the independent Bundesbank, and the Federal Constitutional Court, which is strong compared to other high courts. These are complemented by party political veto players present in coalition governments at the federal and state levels. In each coalition government, the respective parties involved are veto players in the sense that their approval of a policy is necessary – just as in the case of institutional veto players" (Rüb 2014a, p. 12 f.). It is no coincidence that essential elements of bureaucratization and structural fragmentation in the administrative set-up have persisted in many basic features of the German welfare state to this day and are fostered by the inertia and vested interests of social policy actors. The primary organisational interest in preserving the status quo and continuity of responsibility lead to the path dependency stated in research as an explanatory model for the development of the welfare state in Germany.

Against this background, modernization efforts that sought to overcome traditional control and transfer, for example, modern concepts of *business management* to public administration and non-profit organizations must also be viewed with skepticism. This has certainly brought movement and unrest into the established welfare state institutions, but as a rule little has changed in the internal structures, because "administrative reforms fail not so much because of a lack of concepts, but above all because of strong inertial forces in the organizations. Without external pressure, the innovative capacity of the administration is not sufficient to bring about structural changes. The chances of success increase if there is a broad political consensus, if the most important decision-makers in politics and administration can be committed to common goals. If this is not achieved, or if it is inadequate, failure is likely. However, the reform process must also take place within the organization itself. Although it must be supported from outside, it can hardly be forced or controlled from outside. To this end, it is important to build a leadership coalition that guides and supports the change process" (Bogumil and Jann 2020, p. 368 f.).

Fundamental reforms are therefore extremely *demanding*, and this raises the question of the limits of the potential for policy transformation and reform, and how their success factors can be described. It becomes clear in the social and health sector how little politics can define its own scope for action; if one excludes the crisis mode as in the Corona pandemic, it is mostly driven by a multitude of very different actors with partly contradictory individual interests and thus loses further interpretative sovereignty and ultimately legitimacy. In addition, there is a deficit in policy control: apart from the German Council of Economic Experts (SVR), there is no (cross-departmental) advisory body of experts in Germany that independently analyses the challenges and weaknesses in a bundled manner and provides policymakers with reliable knowledge for recommendations for action. The Social Advisory Council, the advisory body that has been in existence since 1958 and whose office is located in the portfolio of the Federal Ministry of Labour and Social Affairs, also reflects the legislative bodies with its total of twelve members (four representatives of insured persons, four representatives of employers, three academics and one representative of the Deutsche Bundesbank). The Advisory Council's primary task is to comment on the Federal Government's annual pension insurance reports and to comment on current developments in old-age provision. A large number of reports of the federal government, which are either based on legal mandates or decisions of the federal government, are "produced in-house with scientific advice" (Tiemann and Wagner 2013, p. 7) and are the responsibility of the ministerial bureaucracy. "One of the central problems for the policy field of social policy is that no integrated social policy advice exists, and even research on policy advice only offers sectoral analyses of policy advice forms. The interaction of measures in the individual subfields of social policy as well as the long-term effects of highly fragmented policy action on social risk situations and state control options in the future are not made the subject of academic policy advice" (Nullmeier 2019a, b, c, p. 1).

At the level of social science, disillusionment and scepticism have set in with regard to the scope of state policy and political *control of society* (cf. Willke 2020; Heinze 2020b). Although "creeping paths" out of traditional path dependency have emerged in recent years, institutional reforms remain largely wedded to the classical model. Official policy still shies away from major institutional reforms and this also applies to the major social policy organizations whose success is closely linked to the classical welfare state model. The conclusion of the last few years of German social policy can be briefly summarized as follows: "Unpopular, comprehensive structural reforms failed to materialize overall, however, and their future financial viability can be questioned" (Voigt 2019, p. 415).

Rather, one can speak of a "reformless change" and a *creeping transformation of* the compensatory German welfare state model. The changes were driven by political factors, such as the assertion of actors' interests and the different power resources of the various social groups. The government's move to Berlin combined with the capital's representation of its countless lobbyist groups, as well as the media's constant scrutiny, are also likely to have played their part in this development. "Benefits do not go to those most in need qua functional suffering, but to the groups that can get their way. Social policy is not synonymous with vertical redistribution, but with the collectivisation of selected social risks at the expense and in favour of certain social groups. If anything, these distributional processes have become more complex in times of scarce resources because the needs of different groups are in greater rivalry. Therefore, one-dimensional left-right schemes are often no longer sufficient to represent the fronts of distribution policy" (Häusermann 2015, p. 608).

Ambitious redesigns of social security also face major problems because the *strategic capacity of* German politics is not rated too highly and states of exhaustion have also been observed in the socio-political structure for some time. For some time now, researchers have been asking the question: "Can politics (still) keep up with the momentum and time rhythms of social subsystems and the global world? This is the question of the (dys)synchronicity of politics and the environment, i.e. whether politics is able to coordinate with the developmental dynamics of the societal environment and to respond in a timely manner to given challenges with its decision-making production" (Rüb 2011, p. 72). Roughly speaking, the picture that emerges is more of a *policy* that tends to be *overburdened,* driven by various events, rather than solving problems rationally and as autonomously as possible. This observation is not entirely new, but has been shared in political science for some time. "Crisis management only ensures that time is saved. Politics in a crisis is reduced to bridging time; fighting the causes of the crisis is not seriously pursued. As a result, however, crisis-like tendencies remain present in the economy, while the political-administrative system "spends itself out" in rescuing the crisis, overstretches its resources, and has to contend with growing internal disorganization. In the long run, crisis management overtaxes the state. If, in addition, another economic crisis occurs not too far away, the already weakened state will no longer be able to muster the necessary capacity to act" (Klenk and Nullmeier 2010, p. 289; cf. also Streeck 2013).

Some observers therefore see a "slow-motion country", not only since recent times, which is oriented above all towards welfare state successes from the past and wants to defend the gained security and status attributions with all its might. The actors oriented towards maintaining the status quo do not necessarily need to take the offensive; rather, it is often sufficient to limit the discourse on models and organization to what they see as "safe" issues. In this context, political science research speaks of the "two faces of power" and "non-decision-making" processes. Specifically, this means: "the practice of limiting the scope of actual decision-making to "safe" issues by manipulating the dominant community values, myths, and political institutions and procedures. To pass over this is to neglect one whole "face" of power" (Bachrach and Baratz 1963, p. 632; cf. also this. 1962 and 1977, and Offe 1977).

By *not deciding* on fundamental questions, policy changes combined with institutional reorganizations are difficult to implement in such an environment; rather, a reform backlog is to be suspected. The mediation of stability and security is still regarded by the "middle-aged" Germans as the top priority of government policy; there is a lack of a culture of experimental and evidence-based politics. Therefore, it is not shaping society that is the order of the day, but rather a "muddling through" that is presented as the management of constraints. In recent decades, many people have therefore become alienated from politics, not least for this reason. However, this does not mean that the demands on politics have declined – on the contrary: "The fact that expectations of the ability of politics to act have continued to rise, instead of falling as the state's ability to steer has diminished, was and is – also – the consequence of a change in cognitive dispositions and moral mentalities, which can be summarised as a shift in the description of events and processes from misfortune to injustice. What used to be understood as the interplay of the unavailable and the contingent is increasingly deciphered as the result of human action or inaction, for which responsible parties can be named and changes made with the goal of greater justice. Political responsibility has taken the place of chance, fate or God, from diseases to natural disasters, from epidemics and famines to the consequences of earthquakes or floods" (Münkler 2010, p. 50 f.; cf. also Reckwitz 2019a, b).

In contrast to the ever-increasing demands for state control, there is a tendency for national politics to lose its power, both as a result of EU policy and the strong increase in *judicialisation in* recent years. The Federal Constitutional Court is having an increasingly direct effect on the legislature. On the one hand, the court ruled on 9 February 2010 that the provisions of SGB II concerning standard benefits for adults and children do not meet the constitutional requirement of guaranteeing a minimum subsistence level worthy of a human being (cf. BVerfG 2010 as well as Baer 2018). Secondly, the court ruled in November 2019 that the previous sanction practice in SGB II with a reduction of basic security benefits of more than 30% is also not in line with the Basic Law (BVerfG 2019 as well as in detail Sect. 1.3). In the increasing juridification of politics, observers see a fundamental change in corporatist labour and collective bargaining relations towards judicialisation: "With the erosion of traditionally corporatist network structures and a fragmentation of political arenas of action, the already important labour courts are gaining further importance" (Rehder 2015, p. 66). It is not only this political arena that has expanded, making political decision-making processes even more confusing, especially since the courts operate with a high degree of autonomy and are at the forefront of popular esteem – unlike the political parties.

4.2 Differentiated Policy Flows and Political-Organisational Silos

The constellations of actors and relationship structures have become even more confusing and intransparent, especially in the already complex social assistance systems, and not only from the perspective of politics itself. Overall, this makes it increasingly difficult to coordinate, formulate and implement a coherent policy from the partial interests. Consequently, policy changes are difficult to organize, because every "policy is composed of a total of three levels, which are hierarchically structured: The top level consists of fundamental belief systems or ideologies, the "deep core beliefs" of a policy, and concerns principles such as the state versus the market, individual responsibility versus solidarity, and the pros and cons of nuclear energy. The second, lower level concerns so-called "policy beliefs", relating to certain principles of a policy, which represent a concretisation and narrowing of the "deep core" in relation to a specific policy. In social policy, for example, this would be the social insurance principle, which favours contribution- and pay-as-you-go systems and guarantees politically defined needs, specifically wage- or status-oriented income replacement benefits. At the lowest level, so-called "secondary aspects" can be identified, such as a specific manifestation of the pension formula or adjustment techniques of benefits (Bafög, pensions, tax progression, etc.). Pure adjustment occurs when only the lowest and possibly the second level of a policy is covered. We speak of a policy change when a change takes place at the level of "policy beliefs" that also reaches into the realm of the "deep core" "(Rüb 2014a, p. 16).

There is no doubt that the fundamental restructuring of the welfare state architecture in the direction of a basic income concerns a centrepiece of the German welfare state. For this reason, attempts to tackle structural reforms also get caught up in the ramifications of socio-political regimes and prominent veto players. The differentiation patterns mentioned above are helpful in understanding this reform logjam. With the help of the MSA and organizational sociological studies, it can be explained relatively plausibly that policy decisions often proceed differently than classical political theories think, which assume a *rationality of political decision-making processes* with clear objectives and preferences. Explicit mention should also be made of the "garbage can theory" (Cohen et al. 1972), which refers to the complexity, susceptibility to disruption and randomness of political decision-making processes at the meso level, or the organizational sociological considerations of Weick (1995), who emphasizes the "disorder" and "unpredictability" inherent in organizations. Transformation processes, understood as cross-sectoral and consciously designed processes that differ from evolutionary social change, are therefore difficult to implement, especially in the German social system. This thesis is particularly valid against the background that the public sector has to overcome structural differences in innovation compared to the market sector anyway. "Innovation in the public sector is in many ways different in nature than corresponding activities within the private sector. It is easy to associate innovation with products, technology and business. In the public sector, innovation often involves new services or new ways of providing services, but it also involves developed organisational solutions that streamline how the public actors carry out their assignments. Unlike the business sector where the pursuit of competitive advantage is a driving force for innovation, public sector innovation pursues other more complex goals. It is about meeting the demands and needs of citizens through values such as democracy, efficiency and service, objectivity and legal certainty" (Vinnova and Engström 2020, p. 6).

In addition to the particular specifics in the public sector, the problem views and steering instruments also differ between the policy fields, e.g. energy and social policy. Both are characterized by a fragmentation of political influence structures, but while in energy policy there is a consensus on the direction to be taken with a view to an energy turnaround, this does not apply to the social policy arena, or only to partial issues. This implies a very low probability of structural transformation, because without a consensus on direction among the central actors, there will also be no consensus on action, which incidentally also applies to the transformation project of a post-fossil society. "The political system is finding it difficult to come to terms with the massive conflicts of distribution and interests. It is true that after the triple disaster of Fukushima there was a large parliamentary majority in favour of the energy transition. But this was only a general consensus on direction. The consensus on action necessary for the realisation of political programmes, on the other hand, did not materialise. Distributional conflicts between wind-rich, less industrialized regions and wind-poor federal states with traditional coal-fired power generation or high nuclear energy use hinder progress" (Czada 2020, p. 180).

Declarations of intent for interdepartmental policies that integrate all political levels can no longer solve the problems at hand – regardless of whether they concern climate issues, demographic upheaval, the challenges posed by extensive digitalization processes or the fight against pandemics; the *political strategy of* "business as usual" has been exhausted, but policy changes are difficult to stage because of the differentiated policy streams. So far, however, sustained learning processes have only occurred when external shocks hit. "The preconditions for rapid policy changes then include shock-like events that create opportunities for major changes of course. This, in the vocabulary of policy research, opens an "agenda window" or a "policy window." The reactor accident at the Fukushima nuclear power plant in Japan in 2011 was a shock that enabled a rapid change of course, as the nuclear phase-out by the black-yellow government of the 17th legislative period of the German Bundestag shows. The fact that this also provided the opportunity for a "change of conviction" and that the "change of conviction" also explains the change of policy should not be overlooked" (Schmidt 2014, p. 244).

From today's perspective, the political consensus on the direction of energy policy triggered by the external shock was temporary and cannot be transferred to other policy areas, let alone led to a comprehensive restructuring, because, as mentioned above, the consensus on action increasingly evaporated over time. Moreover, although the demographic challenges to social security have so far been used as a systemic reason for gradually raising the retirement age or introducing the Riester pension, there has not yet been any fundamental departure from the principle of contribution financing or the equivalence principle. The trigger conditions for policy change are situational and thus selective (see Rüb 2014b and Bandelow and Vogeler 2019). Since the organisations and public institutions involved in social policy largely (want to) stick to the status-quo, a paradigm shift does not get on the political agenda. Thus, there is no "one best way" to reform the welfare state; social configurations, time frames and the stubbornness of the actors involved have to be taken into account. A consensual strategy with a common view of and approach to the problem is *not* the norm, but must first be organised in many cases.

The multiple streams approach doubts both the rationality and the long-term nature of politics and instead points to relatively autonomously acting subsystems and different actor constellations and dynamics over time. Coincidences (such as the right moment: the "windows of opportunity" or certain political "entrepreneurs") nevertheless play a major role in political decision-making processes and can open horizons for a paradigm shift. "The addressed elements of the decision-making process (decision opportunities, problems, solutions and participants) are no longer in a fixed context, the decision-making process shows anarchic features. What is decisive is not the factual need to solve the problem, but the context of the decision-making process, i.e. which and how many decision-making opportunities present themselves, which problems the organization is currently dealing with, which solutions present themselves at the moment, how the participants divide their attention and time between different decisions and how much time is available. The coupling of the elements of the decision-making process can thus be described more as a random confluence of relatively independent streams. However, this does not imply a complete lack of rules; rather, these four flows are channelled in particular by organisational structures and the social structure of society" (Schmid 2011, p. 5; see also Kingdon 2003; Zahariadis 2007; Herweg 2015; Rüb 2014b).

The multiple streams approach assumes that there need not be a systematic link between a problem and a particular policy decision; policy is therefore *far less* rationally programmed and does not necessarily deliver problem-solving decisions. Different "streams" (multiple streams) can be distinguished, whereby the streams are characterized by the fact that they act relatively *autonomously* and have their own dynamics and driving forces. The following central streams can be distinguished:

- the problem stream with agenda setting (e.g. crises such as a nuclear reactor accident, the Corona pandemic)
- the policy stream, where ideas are tested, programmes formulated and discussed with stakeholders and experts
- Political Stream (Politics-Stream) with the implementation (here the "Zeitgeist" is added, national conflict cultures, power distribution of organized interests, ideology of the ruling party etc.: taken together: Bargaining Processes)

Due to these differentiated courses of development, controlled processes of change such as the restructuring of a historically successful welfare state project are extraordinarily difficult to implement, because the decision streams "exist largely independently of one another, their interactions are highly situation-dependent and therefore difficult to predict. Concrete decision-making processes therefore resemble the aforementioned dustbin in which the four streams meet more or less randomly. Obviously, there are different trash cans, and which solutions come together with which actors when depends, among other things, on which label the individual trash cans bear (hence the importance of organizational structures)" (Bogumil and Jann 2020, p. 223). A *paradigm shift* from bureaucratic organization and planning to a role as a networking instance is now required of public administration in the sense of a new management of social security. Organizations are now required to act as agents of change, and managers must become "change agents" or "social intrapreneurs" (cf. the contributions in Eurich et al. 2018). However, this new strategic option for managing social services is difficult to implement, as inclusive services face numerous institutional hurdles in the established landscape. The inertia and, above all, the vested interests of established political actors should not be underestimated, although research repeatedly points out that the scope for variations within a development pathway is relatively large and pathway combinations are also possible. However, these are not implemented as conscious transformation strategies because of the dominant vested interests and coordination deficits – for example, when gaps in security and inadequate provision become apparent and pressure from outside grows as a result. Rather, they are pressed into traditional organisational logics, because "rebuilding is more difficult than adding" (Czada 2020, p. 178).

4.3 Institutional Rigidities Instead of Sustainable Reorganisation: The Example of Demographic and Pension Policy

However, some challenges, such as climate change or demographic change, cannot be solved by partial additions – to remain in the image just mentioned: by renovating and rebuilding. This can be well illustrated by the example of demographic development processes, which have been showing a clear trend for decades despite all the minor changes. Whereas in Adenauer's time the rough formula "people always have children" still applied and pension policy therefore favoured a *pay-as-you-go system*, this construction principle is proving to be outdated and has been in need of fundamental change for some time now. Not only have birth rates halved since then, but the number of people paying contributions has also shrunk, while the number of pensioners has grown permanently and life expectancy has also risen considerably. For decades, however, government policy repeatedly communicated conciliatory formulas such as "the pension is secure", while the state subsidies in the form of the federal subsidy for the pension payments, which are actually financed on a pay-as-you-go and contribution basis, continued to creep up and currently already amount to over 25% of the federal budget.

For years, various experts have been making more or less well-founded contributions to *a reform of old-age provision,* but these have only hesitantly been taken up in the political decision-making arenas. Against this background, it is therefore surprising when forecasts presented in spring 2021 by the Scientific Advisory Council at the Federal Ministry of Economics and derived proposals for a reform of statutory pension insurance (cf. BMWi 2021) are dismissed by members of the Federal Government as "horror scenarios" (Finance Minister Scholz) and scaremongering. Similar to the recent ruling of the Federal Constitutional Court on climate change, the lead author of the report, the director of the Max Planck Institute for Social Law and Social Policy Axel Börsch-Supan, argues with the limitations of younger generations resulting from rising pension expenditures, which cannot be absorbed by shifting parts of it to taxpayers alone.

Irrespective of how the individual reform steps put forward are to be assessed, it would be the central task of politics to seriously examine the proposals and, in view of the structural overtaxing of the contribution-financed pay-as-you-go and equivalence system of social insurance, not to banish strategic considerations for restructuring from the political agenda or to declare them taboo. Otherwise, the state will manoeuvre itself further and further into a quandary and a credibility dilemma: both the challenges in social security are growing and the expectations are enormously high, especially with regard to the protection of elementary risks in old age. The options for action that have been tried so far (such as increasing federal subsidies to the pension insurance system) are limited against the background of the enormous debts of public budgets, and therefore the postponement tactic will be exhausted at some point. The report talks about strikingly rising funding problems in just the next few years. "This financing requirement is so large that the question arises as to whether the total burden can be financed at all, especially as important future expenditure (digitisation, climate change and energy transition, public infrastructure) is on the cards. The Council therefore advises against continuing to uphold the illusion of long-term secured stop-go lines. Instead, policymakers should immediately address possible alternatives" (BMWi 2021, p. 53).

Politicians have been ducking these fundamental decisions for years, and even the first official reactions do not point to a change in policy; instead, old arguments are put forward again and again, sometimes in a polcmical manner, against serious analyses and reform proposals. Even in the election programme of Bündnis 90/die GRÜNEN it says on the topic of financing pensions: "In order to limit the burdens on the insured and employers, tax subsidies should be increased if necessary." (Bündnis 90/Die Grünen 2021). Symbolically, politicians have discovered the demographic issue and are getting involved in individual questions, setting up commissions, etc., but the decisions taken so far are mere additions and facade decorations, without changing the architecture and, above all, without being able to credibly advertise the sustainability of the current system to the younger generation currently paying contributions. Fundamental questions, such as the reformulation of the pension formula with the degree of dynamisation of the pension level to income development or the extension of the working life, have so far been largely avoided or, as in the case of the increase in the pension insurance age limit to 67, tended to be softened again. Various pension commissions, such as the Federal Government Pension Commission set up by Federal Labour Minister Heil. "Reliable Intergenerational Contract", have to a certain extent *circumnavigated* the fundamental and pressing questions, above all of future financing, and recommended the establishment of a new body, "Alterssicherungsbeirat", for a binding determination.

Axel Börsch-Supan, who was also a scientific member of this Pension Commission, was unable to endorse the Commission's recommendation to "refrain from a further quantified recommendation for binding ceilings and thus also for the long-term quantification of the contribution rate and security level" (Kommission Verlässlicher Generationenvertrag 2020, p. 68). Furthermore, it also did not endorse the recommendation to postpone decisions until 2025 with regard to additional issues of old-age provision for working people. When sustainable proposals such as those made by the Scientific Advisory Council at the Federal Ministry of Economics and Technology come up, they are quickly dismissed as unserious by all parties in the governing coalition. From a scientific point of view, however, there is a noticeable increase in the number of voices saying "that the time is ripe for a comprehensive pension reform – especially since the last two federal governments have counteracted all previous efforts to increase the financial sustainability of the pension insurance system with their striking, primarily client-specific benefit expansions" (Rürup 2021, p. 1). The fact that both politicians and voters apparently denied the *facts for a* long time when it came to the issue of fundamental reforms of the statutory pension insurance system can also be explained by the political economy dilemma that there would practically always be losers in any possible solution proposals: "It is inevitable that either the younger people will have to be burdened more or that the older people will receive less or a mixture of both, possibly spiced up with other redistribution measures. This mixture is toxic in election campaigns. Sober facts do not win votes. But the strategy of denial and suppression costs us dearly as a society. The longer a reform, or even the debate about it, is delayed for obvious electoral reasons, the more difficult and expensive the solution to the problem will be" (Sunde 2021, p. 18).

This *suppression* is all the more serious because the consequences of the ageing of society had already been known since the mid-1970s. Nevertheless, the political actors initiated neither a discourse on the foreseeable consequences nor a strategic reorientation. Kaufmann (2002, p. 145ff.) speaks of "demographic blindness" with regard to the social benefit system in Germany. Even the proposals for a new social life course policy that have been available for some time (cf. the contributions in Naegele 2010) continue to be confronted with the problem of implementation and, although they often meet with great interest in politics, they remain based on a rather general consensus of direction. The rationality deficit of the political actors, which is then often lamented by scholars in particular, is thus understandable and is not only due to the veto players in these policy arenas who delay a restructuring of the systems, but also to institutional compartmentalization. The pronounced fragmentation of the German welfare state, coupled with the lack of political entrepreneurs who vehemently advocate restructuring and engage in agenda-setting, leads to *defensive tactics* that can be roughly described as "muddling through". The institutional segmentation and differentiation of policy fields with specific rules of the game and forms of discourse is characteristic of the German welfare state and makes "successful cross-sectoral consensus-building" (Lehmbruch 2000, p. 99), which would be necessary for a sustainable demographic policy, more difficult.

As already explained, demographic change and in particular the ageing of society were only perceived and dealt with at the political level relatively late, after a discourse on ageing had already been going on for some time at the cultural-media level. The changed influence of the media on political communication can be well illustrated by this thematization. The thesis of a grown mediatization of politics states that "what is of general interest in politics, is considered to have fulfilled an adequate function and has earned public attention, is increasingly determined by the media and no longer by parties, parliament or government. Politics is medialized to the extent that it has accepted the description of itself provided by the media, together with the resulting demands for action, as a valid orientation" (Marcinkowski 2015, p. 74).

With regard to demographic change, which has long been acknowledged by the scientific community, the Federal Government presented a demography report for the first time in 2011 (cf. BMI and Federal Government 2011), which emphasises how demographic change affects "all areas of people's lives" and how shaping these processes of change is one of the "major tasks for the future". In order to cope with the particular challenges in Germany, sustainable, "cross-level and cross-measure coordination" is also called for. Likewise, the role of the state is no longer seen as the sole, hierarchically ordering policy administrator, even though many of the tasks of shaping this "complex process" remain with it. Rather, reference is made to dialogue processes and exchange with other political actors and citizens.

Such programmatic statements on a coordinated and cross-sectoral policy strategy illustrate how a contemporary government policy would have to be set up, which can limit itself less and less to defending the status quo. Rather, in demographic policy, for example, it is called upon to bring together the various policy fields (education, social, labour market, old-age security and family policy) with a view to an "active old age". While the traditional welfare state organized a "transfer of risk from the individual to the state or society," according to Giddens, "it is now about much more: people must not only adapt to change in a dynamic environment, but must understand how to use change for their own purposes. [...]We should promote education and learning, prosperity, choice, active social and economic participation, and healthy lifestyles" (Ibid. 2007, p. 61). This change in strategy would lead to a dissolution of the boundaries of traditional senior citizens' policy and, overall, would amount to a *transformation of* compensatory statehood and make the hybrid structures of welfare production already mentioned more prominent. Due to the path dependency, especially in the field of welfare state security, these processes are, however, conflictual and require time as well as political entrepreneurs, without which a change of path cannot be realized. If one looks after 10 years at the follow-up effects of the first demography report of the Federal Government, one finds a recurring preoccupation with this topic at government level, various expert commissions delivered further reports, dialogue rounds met many times, but other conflict topics (such as the refugee flows) moved more into the centre and apart from publications and minor reform steps as well as funding initiatives, *no action-oriented restructuring strategy* can be discerned so far.

However, the hesitant attitude of government policy can also be explained by the fact that a change of control philosophy is subject to a particular risk, especially in the field of social security systems, because time delays are inherent in any reform policy: the expected "returns" lie in the future, while the disputes about status shifts and, above all, about losses and economic losers are conducted immediately. Consequently, a defense of the status-quo can be organized quickly, while establishing collective rationality becomes increasingly difficult for political actors. It is therefore not surprising that so far there has been no coupling of policy streams and that instead only reform semantics have dominated the political stage for years. Such "slogging through" seems to be possible for some time without the state running into problems of legitimacy, but it does give rise to new problems of control: "In fact, this can mean that the problem that has become apparent as pressure changes its character without losing any of its urgency. Financing problems of the pension insurance, for example, become increasing public debt. In social terms, problem shifting means that a problem is passed on to others, which in turn can lead to protest activities on their part. The rising national debt – to continue the example – affects the younger generation, not today's pensioners. In order to avoid the intergenerational distribution conflict today, intragenerational conflicts are conjured up in the future. In temporal terms, then, the problem is postponed, only to reappear sooner or later. This is also evident in the example. The more pressure potentials are merely postponed in this way, the more they pile up, which then again allows nothing but problem postponement, and so on – a vicious circle into which actors and constellations of actors can easily get caught and from which they then find it difficult to find their way out" (Schimank 2011, 24; cf. also ders. 2019).

The fact that the current welfare state model has already exceeded the limits of its carrying capacity has been emphasised among experts for years and is once again confirmed by the 2021 report of the Scientific Advisory Council at the Federal Ministry of Economics. For example, federal payments to the pension insurance scheme are now by far the *largest item in the federal budget;* they will rise to 106 billion euros in 2021 (BMI 2021), but the main burden of welfare state costs is borne by employees subject to social security contributions. The hitherto dominant normative principle of our contribution-financed welfare state model, namely an equivalence of benefits and counter-benefits (equivalence principle), is already no longer valid for quite a few groups. "In practice, this has long since ceased to be so clearly the case. Each of the 21 million pensioners mathematically receives on average about €400 per month from tax money. The equivalence principle has long been diluted" (Rürup 2019). Interesting in this context is also the recent proposal by the (former) "pension pope" Bert Rürup, instead of turning the three screws, contribution rate, pension amount and retirement age, to increase the tax portion to finance current pension payments. This would mean that the growing number of taxpaying pensioners, who already contribute "a considerable share of the tax revenue"[1], would be more involved in financing the pension system. We also interpret such a proposal as evidence of a creeping transformation of the welfare state. This fact, which is often not perceived by the public and in particular by the groups affected, the pensioners, has already been referred to in Sect. 2.4.

In addition, the calculation model of pension entitlements following the equivalence principle in the years of increased low-income earners has led to the fact that the current system of statutory pension insurance can only still safeguard against the problem of old-age poverty through a growing share of tax financing (cf. Niemeier 2020). "Currently, the dominant view in the major political parties is that what has been done so far has been 'successful'. The realization that the linchpin of Germany's new old-age security policy – dismantling the benefit level of the

[1] Cf. interview by Hendrik Munsberg with Bert Rürup in the Süddeutsche Zeitung of 26.8.2021.

GRV and replacing it with capital market-based old-age security – is not the solution to the problem of insufficient old-age incomes, but itself its cause, has not yet taken hold. The dismantling of the GRV is succeeding, but not the closing of the security gap. It would not be a disgrace if politicians were to admit that the effects of their decisions are different from those hoped for and propagated. But this would require courage, which would be necessary, because the path taken in German old-age security policy has the potential to become a socio-political time bomb" (Schmähl 2012, p. 313).

But cultural patterns of interpretation (such as the constantly flaring disaster scenarios of an "ageing" society) can also have an inhibiting effect on strategic policy changes. The procrastination of sustainable reforms not only affects the established fields of old-age policy such as pensions, but also applies to fields that cannot be assigned to the classic areas of old-age security. Examples include the social commitment of older people or the increasingly important area of "housing in old age" with all its challenges at the municipal level and its cross-sectional character. In order to allow the potentials of old age to unfold, an integrating policy for the elderly that transcends sectoral boundaries would be necessary. The collective ageing of society could then even become a "laboratory" instead of developing demographic horror scenarios. Generally speaking, the welfare state "needs constant reforms and adjustments to ensure social cohesion and not to degenerate into an ensemble of social vested interests or into a "nursing case". The latter is the case if the basic structure of the welfare state is not repeatedly adapted to the changing challenges at intervals of two to three decades. Politicians, however, shy away from such structural reforms because they inevitably lead to service cuts and cost votes" (Münkler and Münkler 2019, p. 331).

And it is not only the old-age pension systems that have been under pressure to act for years and would have to be restructured with a view to future capacity to act. The future of work, especially gainful employment, has also been discussed for a long time. One need only recall the debate on the "crisis of the labour society" in the 1980s (cf. the contributions in Matthes 1983). Attempts have subsequently been made to transform these social science diagnoses into political practice, and there have also been individual political reactions to this at the level of state governments (e.g. in the Future Commission of the states of Bavaria and Saxony) (cf. the contributions in Beck 2000). Reference has already been made to the various activities *outside* gainful employment, the informal side of welfare production (such as care and support in family networks, social commitment), without which today's welfare state could not function at all. Between gainful employment and non-gainful, individually used time, there continues to exist a sphere in which countless activities with social links can be found. Only those forms of work are subsumed under gainful employment in which employees earn an income in salaried or self-employed employment to secure their livelihood. However, this is the basis for social security and if the basis shrinks or fragments, this has serious consequences for the level of security of each individual (unless one is otherwise secured, but this is only relevant for a small minority in developed welfare states such as Germany).

If it is not possible to permanently integrate the vast majority of the population into social security systems through the eye of the needle of gainful employment, both tax-financed, universal security must be made available and the diverse forms of activities beyond the labour market must be addressed as complementary mechanisms for social integration. Ulrich Beck has described this in a pronounced way and against the defenders of the status quo at the time, who were and are to be found in all central political organisations as well as within social science, with the formula of "citizen work", which should be financed instead of unemployment. Its starting point, dwindling gainful employment, was certainly too globally formulated at the time; however, there were already clear indications of the effects of globalisation and digitalisation on employment structures, so that gainful employment-centred social security should have been examined more broadly in terms of its *future viability*, including a willingness to take fundamental alternative paths. This is in no way to deny that the subjective importance of traditional work would also erode or that women's labour market integration would not increase. "Keeping this paradox in mind – on the one hand, the volume of gainful employment is shrinking, on the other hand, it occupies a kind of monopoly of existence in our culturally prescribed sense of self-worth – the basic idea of the "citizen work" option can be introduced. Its aim is twofold: on the one hand, "work" outside the state and the market is to be socially upgraded, financially secured and cast in new roles within the voluntary sector oriented towards the common good. On the other hand, non-work in the form of free, political action is also introduced and exercised here in a flying transition" (Beck 2000a, b, p. 416 f.; cf. also Bonß 2000).

The current debates on impoverishment and social exclusion as well as on the various new lines of division in society continue and make public a discussion in sociology that already began in the 1980s with the debate on the victims of the labour market, the crisis of the labour society or the normalisation of the experience of unemployment. In an international comparison, the pronounced long-term unemployment in Germany is striking, leading to social exclusion. This does not imply a clear and unambiguous *dividing line* between the zones of social security and precarious life situations; rather, an overall flexibilisation and dissolution of boundaries in employment structures can be observed, which are accelerated by digitalisation processes. Likewise, in the discussions on the crisis of the labour society and driven by the women's movement, the need for a general revaluation of unpaid work (in the household, in care, etc.), which is performed predominantly by women, was already pointed out (cf. currently Ketterer 2019b; Winker 2020).

Despite an economic recovery in the years following the financial crisis, which also reduced unemployment, there is still an employment deficit explicitly for the long-term unemployed that should not be underestimated. Although this group reduced during the phase of job creation from 2010 onwards, it is now growing significantly again after the Corona crisis (over one million in spring 2021). Against the backdrop of rising unemployment once again, the "anachronism that developed welfare states pay for the involuntary inactivity of several million people and even tie payments to the promise of inactivity when persisting in it – while there are plenty of necessary and meaningful tasks in the social, cultural and environmental spheres that no one is tackling – is confirmed. But the model of civic work goes much further: the spectre of a working society without work is to be countered by a vision that understands and uses what appears in the unbroken paradigm of the full-employment society as a "crisis" and "catastrophe" as a historical opportunity, according to the motto: "Citizen engagement instead of financing unemployment!" (Beck 2000a, b, p. 417; cf. also ders. 2017 as well as Bregman 2020).

The protagonists of a citizen's work or a citizen's income were not concerned solely with securing a livelihood, but at the societal level with new forms of social integration and at the individual level with a fulfilling and satisfied life even beyond the orthodoxy of full employment. This should be understood as a response to the traditional "right to work" in the direction of a "civil right" that does not lead via the gainfully employed-centred classical system of social security. And that is why a tax-financed design was at the heart of such considerations. This could then also tend to break down the partitions and dividing lines between the zones of social security and precarious, insecure life situations. Today, this perspective does not appear to be utopian, as some critics have criticised in the debates on the crisis of the labour society, because the hopes of a return to the former secure employment relationships are fading more and more. Above all, the combination of various characteristics (low education and qualification, migration background, etc.) leads to an increased labour market risk, which was somewhat concealed by the positive employment development in the last few years before the Corona crisis, but not cancelled out.

If one considers these real processes on the labour market with an increase in socio-economic polarisation in recent decades and especially after the Corona pandemic, labour market policy can be attested to have acted quickly on this issue in the crisis mode of the Corona pandemic, but has so far only addressed the fundamental problems in isolated cases (e.g. with the minimum wage). The improvements for workers on the labour market that have emerged in recent years (such as the decline in low-wage employees and the increase in the wage share) owe more to demographic change and the shortages of skilled workers in expanding sectors (mostly from the service sector). A lack of political-organisational imagination, not only in the social and labour market policy fields of established politics, is unmistakable. The concept of citizen's work also failed *to counteract* the lack of organised imagination; the sociological debates petered out and continued at most in academic circles or in the environment of foundations and academies without broad resonance. Against the background of rising unemployment after the Corona crisis, the political actors are now once again left "empty-handed", despite some employment programmes (such as the social labour market) which are limited in volume. In this respect, this is also politically very short-term thinking, because there have been conceptual contributions not only from a sociological and socio-philosophical point of view, but also from established economists (such as Atkinson's "participation income" already mentioned in Sect. 1.4).

A first step in the current labour market policy situation with rising unemployment figures and a growing number of long-term unemployed would be a creative link to the international debates on overcoming and re-accentuating the classic compensatory social and labour market policy ("social investment turn") (cf. Busemeyer et al. 2018). With regard to specific labour market policy programmes, it is possible to link up with the discourses on the differentiation of the *concept of work* and greater consideration of the various forms of activity that are indispensable for the continued existence of a free and democratic community (such as civil society activities).

In our view, labour market policy has so far been too hesitant in pursuing this path, but it has also had only limited effect. It is therefore hardly surprising that the debates on basic income and civic work are flaring up again. "Citizen work is not paid, but it is rewarded, both materially and immaterially (through "citizen's money", qualifications, the recognition of pension rights and social periods, "Favour Credits", etc.). Materially, 'Citizen's Income' is given to those who are existentially dependent on it. The standards are the same as for the granting of social assistance; therefore, in the developed welfare states, the necessary resources can be taken from the budgets of social assistance and, where appropriate, unemployment assistance. However, the recipients of Citizen's Income are – all other things being equal – not recipients of social assistance or unemployment benefits, since they are engaged in non-profit activities in voluntary initiatives. Nor are they available to the labour market if they do not wish to be. They are not unemployed" ((Beck 2000a, b, p. 418).

So far, however, the traditional mainstream parties in Germany in particular have shied away from this fundamental debate. After the experience with the last "major" reform of this kind, the Agenda 2010, labour market policy insiders in particular are afraid of such a policy change. There seems to be an unspoken consensus among the political elites in Germany that it would be better not to tackle such structural reforms in concrete terms in future and also to abandon the expectation that the recommendations of a commission of experts will subsequently be implemented "one-to-one" in the parliamentary legislative process. Rather, *small steps* are preferred in silence which, although in principle already moving in the direction of universal social security, do not put targeted and sustainable restructuring on the agenda. In demographic matters, they range from attempts to redesign the world of work in such a way that older people can also contribute their skills there for longer and more productively, to efforts to adapt product and service offerings in such a way that the interests and needs of older people are given greater consideration. The health dimensions of old age are of central importance here, because it is of great importance both for the individual older person and for society that the years of life gained are as healthy as possible. The often unused and untapped potentials of old age beyond gainful employment are also of central importance. In order to cope with these increased demands for adaptation, however, there must also be a massive effort to change attitudes among the key players in society.

Any government policy must overcome the paradoxical situation that, on the one hand, political experimentation and strategic leadership are required to tackle the challenges productively, and on the other hand, the *basic trust* in government policy that is necessary for this is less and less present among the population. "The mental willingness to change course must be promoted" (Kocka 2006, p. 22). This sober diagnosis has not changed in 2021; perhaps the situation is even more difficult with regard to a public will to reform, because politicians have failed in recent legislative periods to get the electorate in the mood for fundamental transformation processes, even though expectations of politics have risen. Even the rather simple statement that what has been achieved can only be preserved if it is constantly renewed has been pushed back in favour of the "we can do it" thesis. A positive attitude to change and thus to reform has not been demanded by government policy, leading on the one hand to a certain lethargy among a large part of the population and on the other hand to open protests, as in the case of climate protection. Apparently, there is a lack of courageous entrepreneurs who do not just take up the societal challenges rhetorically, inform themselves comprehensively (evidence-based), point to fundamental processes of change and bring about a consensus for action, instead of suggesting to the population that everything can stay the same if the "gears" are serviced now and then.

Without the expertise and mediation skills of political entrepreneurs and their abilities in both interface management and self-management, fundamental socio-political reforms can hardly be implemented, as can be seen from the major social reforms. "It is plausible to assume that what was relevant to success was the ability of the key reform actors to condition themselves and their home organizations in the sense that they knew how to balance the perennial need for normative self-assurance with the ability to soberly perceive the world of action. For the task horizon of the more successful strategists consists not only of the external world of their counterparts and allies, but also extends to the internal world of the actor, be it the individual person, be it the group or organization" (Wiesenthal 2019a, p. 33).

4.4 Approaches to a Basic Income: On the Role of Scientific Policy Advice and Policy Management

With a view to a basic income, after the establishment and implementation of the Hartz IV laws, a group of academics and politicians from the CDU around the former Prime Minister of Thuringia, Dieter Althaus, presented a concept for a solidarity-based citizen's income (SBG) (cf. Althaus 2007). This can be interpreted as a departure from the Bismarckian welfare state and amounts to a variant of a partial unconditional basic income (UBI) – in this book we refer to the German abbreviation BGE). The multiple streams approach can be used to analyse which criteria would have to be met for such a BGE model to be successfully placed on the political agenda (cf. Rüppel 2020). Without dealing here with the various aspects regarding a placement of the model on the political stage (such as the apparent lack of acceptance among the population, lack of support in key organizations, influential veto players), Althaus arrives at the following assessment: "Accordingly, in order to place a concept on the government's decision-making agenda, it is necessary, in addition to a proposal that can be implemented in terms of content and is considered promising by experts in the policy community, to find either the necessary problem perception among the population and politicians or favorable political framework conditions – i.e., a mature problem or politics stream – that can be linked to the proposal developed in the policy stream. In addition, a window of opportunity must be open for the concept to become established, and a policy-entrepreneur must constantly support the project, link the streams, and ultimately place the policy at the relevant level. In the case of the SBG, it can be seen that neither can one speak of a sufficient maturity of the flows, nor could a policy-entrepreneur find and use windows of opportunity to place the topic accordingly" (ders. 2020, p. 60).

With the departure of the former prime minister in Thuringia, however, the topic was then not pursued further within the CDU after the presentation of a corresponding commission report – and this is still true today. It seems to be due to the lack of attention and political support, at least in the central bodies and persons. The promoter of such a basic income therefore sees only a "serious existential crisis in society" as a *driver* for such a project, "an integration of BGE models into existing systems, on the other hand, would be too costly to be implemented by politicians" (op. cit., 62). A possible "policy window" could be the Corona pandemic, but there is a lack of influential actors acting as drivers for the model and being heard in public discourses.

However, the circle of advocates for a comprehensive and at the same time holistic reform has become broader in recent years and also includes individual business personalities who do not express themselves in their criticism as representatives of employers' or industry associations. The consensus among all the different models is that the protagonists see the classical welfare state as having reached its limits and therefore argue for a radical simplification of the social benefit system by providing a tax-funded unconditional basic income (without means-testing or reciprocity) for all.

Reform policy efforts are nevertheless very likely to fail if they are oriented only to the bargaining processes between the established interests. What is needed is a new "opening up of the game" through an accentuated focus on reform, whereby it should be emphasised that it can no longer be the state alone that can guarantee responsible and sustainable governance. Answers should therefore be sought neither in market radicalism nor in a welfare state orthodoxy. Rather, what is called for are balanced links between the action logics of the state, the economy and society. Trend-setting reforms for institutional restructuring can no longer be expected from (corporatist) alliances between the state and organised interests. This means that politics is becoming *more volatile,* there is no "royal road" out of the crisis, and the door for a return to yesterday's solutions is also closed. Put negatively, this means the de facto recognition of diverse political-institutional segmentations, which makes evidence-based, interdepartmental policy, which is necessary from the point of view of ambition and principle, more difficult. All the experiences available so far indicate that the change of regulatory structures will probably only be possible at all through experimentally oriented, time-consuming and sometimes conflict-ridden planning and design processes. Cooperation is often impaired by this or does not come about at all because individual actors either have to fear being disadvantaged or others hope to be over-advantaged. Against this background, answering the future distribution question and aspects of a polarising or levelling degree of social inequality remains an important condition for the success of reform policy efforts, with horizontal aspects of intergenerational justice also becoming increasingly important in questions of social security.

However, a consistent social policy that transcends traditional fields of expertise must not only overcome "silos", but at the same time remains integrated into the institutional structures of public administration in Germany. Accordingly, municipalities primarily perform tasks in the sectors of internal administration and general government tasks, social welfare, education, health care, economic development, housing, transport and public facilities. In the near future, the demand for various forms of local services will grow strongly, especially in structurally weak, shrinking regions. At present, the care system in Germany is still inadequately prepared for these demographic shifts, which have been observed for some time now, and has not yet developed a comprehensive concept for life in an increasingly ageing society. The fragmented and in many cases over-bureaucratised social assistance system will hardly succeed in this; what is needed are both guarantee-based and cross-sectoral (interlinked) solutions. Although the fight against the Corona pandemic is considered to be the hour of the executive, this has "besides undeniable achievements also mercilessly brought to light the nerve-racking slowness and ponderousness of all levels of government" (Seibt 2021).

There is media hype about the *care issue,* which has also reached government policy – albeit years late. In addition, the "pension policy immobilism" (Ebert 2020) has not yet been overcome, which could ultimately affect the municipalities, which, although they have been relieved of the payment of minimum old-age security benefits by the federal government since 2014, nevertheless remain affected by the growing old-age poverty due to the assumption of the rising costs of accommodation. Innovation policy-oriented scenarios for a new map of positive welfare have so far only been marginally addressed in government policy, if at all. However, the foreseeable significant increase in the proportion of the elderly population in the coming decades makes the development of integrated forms of care and, associated with this, new age-appropriate products and services an urgent necessity that also offers economic opportunities. Since the vast majority of older people want to remain in their familiar living environment for as long as possible, innovative *integrated solutions* between social services and technical assistance systems are needed to help those in need of help to cope with everyday life in their familiar living environment. However, the pronounced institutional segmentation and differentiation of policy fields with specific rules of the game and forms of discourse make it difficult to build consensus across departments and sectors, as has already been pointed out. What is needed is smart political decision management and strategic leadership, which must coordinate three dimensions: "It must (a) take advantage of favourable times or procure them itself, it must (b) be courageous, i.e. take a risk despite uncertain circumstances and unforeseeable consequences, and (c) be able to take political responsibility for risky decisions" (Rüb 2014a, p. 26).

Without shocking events in the field of social security, these preconditions do not seem to have been met so far, although the inhibiting effect of the fragmentation of competences as well as waiting loops of competence checks have meanwhile also been taken note of in politics and administration. Programmatically, renewal processes are already evident at the various levels of the political-administrative system in the direction of a *cross-sector* and *cross-level* policy. So far, "talk" rather than "action" has dominated, especially at the central level of the federal government and the Länder. The expansion of policy advice in various formats also fits in with this: from the classic advisory councils at the ministries to ad hoc commissions and personal advisory processes with top politicians. It is already possible to speak of a *"commissonitis"*, yet consistent and cross-departmental solution strategies that link the various policy streams are still desiderata. The dynamic growth of academic policy advice is not only due to the increased complexity of challenges, but also to the expansion of state functions, exemplified in the social policy arena. "A deeper cause of the expansion of scientific policy advice, which can now be seen as an institutional level in its own right between politics and science, lies in the expansion of state functions that has been ongoing since the nineteenth century, culminating so far first in ever more expansive social legislation and most recently in comprehensive environmental protection and risk regulation that is in principle unrestricted. Scientific issues become important topics on the political agenda due to the state's duty of precaution" (Weingart 2019, p. 68; cf. also the contributions in Falk et al. 2019).

The fact that there is an increasing demand from political actors for social science orientation knowledge in the context of policy advice is due to the competence in describing social development trends and condensing them into sociological diagnoses of the times (cf. for example the debate on the "society of singularities" triggered by Reckwitz (2017)), which is particularly in demand in "uncertain" times. Social science consulting, however, has to keep an eye on the complex inherent logic and differentiation of policy production in order to generate efficient consulting services. Central guiding principles, especially of private sector-oriented or foundation-oriented as well as purely scientific policy advice, suffer from not recognizing the institutional stubbornness of the "policy-making system". "Any advice, whether of technocratic, decision-making or pragmatic provenance, has to be processed through the governmental apparatus. Here it proves significant that parliament and government constitute independent differentiated subsystems within the political system. For both possess their own rationalities of action, from which specific functions, tasks and organizational profiles follow. Above all, however, parliament and government have their own independent mechanisms of formal and informal decision-making and will-forming, as opposed to scientific advice. Given the stubbornness of parliament and government/administration, the transformation processes assumed in the Leitbilder prove to be unrealistic and therefore misleading" (Bröchler 2004, p. 23 f.; cf. also Blätte 2019; Bogumil and Jann 2020, p. 267ff.).

The growing importance of expert knowledge is a mosaic stone in the transformation of the political; external experts – be they scientific advisors, public affairs consultants or representatives of associations – are increasingly gaining influence on politics and administration. At the same time, policy management is becoming increasingly complex due to information overload, and informalization processes are spreading. "Alternative decision-making structures have been created in the immediate vicinity of the top actors by people with brokerage power. A shift of emphasis from the formalized to the informalized structures can be observed. The skills of top actors in dealing with this mix of formalized and informalized information channels are elementary for securing power and compelling in terms of democratic theory" (Korte 2019, p. 141). At the same time, these advisory formats are sometimes suspected of lacking transparency, and the advisory actors involved could be lobbying past democratic bodies. This accusation has been raised for a long time, but in the past it was primarily related to the influence of associations on political decisions.

The fact that selected interest groups "co-write" legislative projects is not doubted either in research or in politics, although structural shifts have also occurred here. In addition to *informalisation*, the direct influence of large companies should be noted, which increasingly act "alongside" and independently of the trade associations. In this respect, we are dealing with a pluralisation and new confusion of policy advice. And the observation of a tension between lobbyism and parliamentary democracy also historically accompanies the debate about the influence of differently organised interests on government policy. The reference to the intransparency of lobbying is undeniable, and this has not been changed by the official "lobby list" introduced in 1972, which in itself was intended to make the influence of associations on legislation more transparent and in which 2297 organisations are now entered (as of 1 June 2021). However, the entry says little about the real influence on legislation, so that for a long time there has been a struggle for more transparency. In 2021, after intensive discussions, it was also decided to introduce a lobby register in the Bundestag. The aim of the law is to create more transparency regarding the influence of lobbyists on decision-making processes in parliament and government. In future, professional interest representatives will be obliged to register publicly, together with details of their clients and financial expenditure.

Since an important position of power in policy formulation belongs to the ministries (see Baruth and Schnapp 2015 for a summary), meetings are to be recorded and documented down to the level of sub-department heads. At the same time, stakeholders will be required to agree to a code of conduct defining principles of advocacy with integrity, and violations will be punished as misdemeanours.

As comprehensible as these regulations are from the perspective of democratic theory, they can nevertheless only create partial transparency. Against the background of the different policy streams discussed in this chapter, they only apply *one lever* at a time and therefore remain limited in their effects. The processes of lobbying in politics have become more complex and professionalised. As already mentioned, informal policy management has become established among the top actors in government alongside administrative information and communication management, which is also rooted in the greater personalisation of government action in recent years. These developments generate a mix of formalized and informal information and decision-making channels that is difficult to see through from the outside, and such policy management is also susceptible to *commercial lobbying strategies*. This new scene of commercial lobbying has not yet been sufficiently explored academically, although observers assume that public affairs consultants have gained increasing power in the German political establishment. "Thus, media-effective campaigns are carried out by means of public affairs agencies that operate as commercial enterprises, and the mobilization of activists takes place on the net by means of the targeted lobbying work of an NGO that is financed by donations. This kind of interest representation – lobby work – no longer has much in common with the "good old days" of neo-corporatist interest representation, when the world was still in order and the representative of the farmers' association was a priori a member of the federal cabinet, and the welfare associations were largely responsible for the formulation of social laws" (Zimmer and Speth 2015, p. 13; cf. also Speth 2015). Overall, there has been both an intensification of corporate lobbying and, associated with this, a loss of importance of traditional lobbying by associations, as well as a trend towards an organisational differentiation of the influence of organised interests (which in recent years have increasingly included various self-organised networks and foundations etc.).

Combined with the increased number of advisory bodies and expert commissions, a confusing advisory landscape can be observed, which is already referred to as an "expertocracy", especially in times of crisis (as has been the case since 2020 in the Corona pandemic). "Accordingly, (expert) knowledge forms the highest decision-making authority in many political controversies" (Bogner 2021, p. 8). Political science observers already speak of a new "mode of consensus formation in pro-government summits and expert rounds. The approach emerged as the new standard of extra-parliamentary consensus mobilization" (Czada 2019, p. 405). In terms of policy change, delegating decisions to expert panels can, on the one hand, provide some relief for increasingly overburdened politicians and also help against populist manipulation; on the other hand, it risks undermining democratic bodies. Particularly when it comes to controversial issues such as the future of the social security system, policymakers should therefore certainly rely on expert commissions in the sense of rationalizing discourse, but should not transform the controversial issues that are most likely to arise into knowledge disputes, but should instead deal with them openly in the political arena.

In this context, one could speak of a dialogue-oriented, reflexive model of consultation. Here, the classic separation of roles between experts and laypersons, for example, is no longer maintained, and the classic relationship between the public, science and politics also tends to dissolve. "The rigid triangle between science, politics and experts dissolves, roles are changed, the focus is now on interactions and intersections, from which variable advisory publics emerge" (Leggewie 2007, p. 8; cf. also Nullmeier 2019a, b, c). Even if scientific policy advice cannot provide unambiguous forecasts, it can nevertheless expand the knowledge of policymakers and, with a view to multiple streams approaches, this enables a cohesive view of problems that is not so strongly dominated by the self-interests of the tangential actors. For this reason, policy-makers should also consider the proposal to implement *sustainable policy advice* in the field of social policy, which would have to meet the following requirements:

- Sustainable policy advice is understood to mean, first, policy advice that is permanent in nature, with an appropriate infrastructure, and which is also flexible enough to take up new, virulent issues without becoming an instrument of short-term political intervention.
- Secondly, sustainable policy advice is understood as an integrated, cross-cutting form of policy advice that takes into account the entire policy field of social policy and counteracts the fragmentation of social policy into sub-fields and sub-policy areas.
- Thirdly, sustainable policy advice is understood to be a form of policy advice geared towards the medium- and long-term further development of the policy field of social policy, which is not solely directed at current legislation. What is required is reflection also on the long-term consequences of policies as well as on the future response options of policy in the face of changing framework conditions of social development (Nullmeier 2019a, b, c, p. 3f; cf. also Strohschneider 2020).

Social policy can certainly be oriented towards other policy fields (such as energy policy) with regard to a sustainable and at the same time precautionary advisory strategy, but due to the high degree to which social policy changes affect individuals, these are sensitive issues that can easily lead to emotional agitation, especially when both trade unions and employers' associations are institutionalized actors in the field of social policy. "In a country where thousands of lobbying organizations scour every paragraph of a new law for their interests, there will be no social system that turns everything upside down" (Koch 2021). This can affect the scientific advisory scene, which has in any case fallen into the fairway of infotainment in recent years due to considerably increased mass media-structured communication (also through social media), which tangentially affects its classical role (especially its independence). On the one hand, advisors become a "resource of a new degree" in a mediatized society; on the other hand, they get caught up in the "unpredictable dynamics of media discourse" (Patzwaldt 2007, p. 226) and in communicative marketing strategies that altogether diminish the role of scientifically grounded knowledge. The media communication in the Corona crisis, which relies on personalization and intensification of conflict, is an example of how not only scientific soundness is undermined, but also losses of trust are induced in the population, so that the level of rationality of political decisions has not been significantly strengthened.

Despite the manifold expansion of scientific *policy advice, it* is therefore necessary to warn against excessive optimism with regard to the real steering of political processes. However, with the spread of the knowledge society and the associated belief in knowledge, as well as the ambitious claim of evidence-based impact research, these currents of influence cannot be stopped, even if there has been a worldwide spread of populist 'post-truths'. Scientific expertise has played a significant role in the political decision-making process for years, especially from the point of view of many scientists, yet scientists in particular are well advised to adopt a detached attitude and not to believe that scientific policy advice can always 'shed light on the darkness' or that it would necessarily be taken up and implemented by politicians even in the case of clear recommendations for action. "On the one hand, in the complicating mishmash of economic and social developments, scientific analyses and statements about causal interrelationships are also becoming increasingly difficult (if they exist at all). On the other hand, it cannot be assumed that the recommendations formulated by the scientific community actually influence policy decisions. Although politicians like to use the apparent objectivity of scientific expertise for external legitimation, it often remains unclear in the 'black box' of actual decision-making whether the facts presented by science were taken into account here or whether, for example, the mere fact of having commissioned an expert opinion on a topic is sufficient as legitimation" (Beckmann et al. 2017, p. 22; cf. also Streeck 2017).

Social science advice must have the complex *inherent logic of* policy production as well as the different rationalities of action of the actors in view and be informed about the different policy flows. Statements on the scope of scientific policy advice must therefore be grounded in the sociology of knowledge and organisation on the one hand, and must also be empirically substantiated on the other – especially since many policy advice models assume a relatively naive concept of knowledge and the rationality of organisational structures. This would then provide a far more complex picture of policy advice and could also explain the discrepancies between the self-descriptions of policy actors and the real inconsistencies and rationality gaps in policy organizations. In general, one should be wary – and this is again suggested by analyses of the MSA – of assuming a "best way" of reform policy. No matter how well-founded the scientific results of consultations may be, they are not reflected congruently in political decision-making processes, because these do not proceed according to the scientific logic of true and false, but must also always keep in mind the safeguarding of power in democratically constituted welfare states. "The typically scientific dream of rationalizing politics, however, amounts to exorcising from politics what is typically political, namely the negotiation of conflicts of interest and the laborious struggle to reach workable compromises" (Bogner 2021, p. 118 f., cf. also the contributions in Berlin-Brandenburg Academy of Sciences 2008). In this respect, the rationality potential of scientific policy advice is systematically limited.

Against this background, any form of policy advice is a difficult undertaking and, moreover, it must be acknowledged that most of the advice politicians receive does not stand up to the criteria of scientificity defined within the scientific system and that many politicians structure their policies not inconsiderably "from the gut" (cf. Bogumil 2017). For this reason alone, advising politicians through scientific expertise can also only be understood as a "saving straw" to approximate the complex and fragmented tasks at hand. Evidence-based policy through scientific policy advice is therefore an exception rather than the rule.

The agenda-setting and fine-tuning for a sustainable reform of social policy operating in overall contexts could be supported by a new body of scientists accompanying the reform process, such as a council of experts or a commission of enquiry, which is also regarded as a mediating body and form of organisation for carrying socially relevant discourses into parliamentary politics (cf. Altenhof 2002). However, this is not a sufficient condition for successful, fundamental change, because experience teaches that even many expert commissions are often primarily symbolic in character. Even if a topic enjoys high socio-political priority and is frequently played with in the media (such as basic income), the "structural "lateness" of "democratic" politics to problem situations brewing in the long term" (Offe 2015, p. 46) should not be underestimated. Redirection processes are endowed with many hurdles, which are not surprising from the perspective of organizational sociology and political theory. "Change that no longer reproduces the existing, but produces something new, only takes place in a few institutionalized situations in which negotiation processes are possible and long-practiced routines and policies lose their self-evidence" (Trampusch 2009, p. 225).

Germany's *reunification* shows that exogenous shocks do not quasi-automatically produce a fundamental change in policy, but that it is possible to react to them with traditional strategies of action out of aversion to further risks. Nor can it be completely ruled out that this option could also prove true in the phase following the acute Corona pandemic. It is therefore necessary to look for other factors that do not insist on the juxtaposition of constancy and dynamism, but rather aim at *incremental change*. Not only has the crisis management, which has lasted more than 18 months since the spring of 2020, brought politics to the brink of exhaustion, but the increased distribution problems as well as the social and cultural separatisms also make it difficult to formulate an integrative consensus of direction aimed at the overall context of social policy – not to mention an implementable strategy for action.

Nevertheless, dialogue-oriented and *reflexive policy advice*, but one that is explicitly aware of its own scope for action and limits, that develops design strategies in addition to addressing challenges, and that also reflects on scenarios of possible unintended side-effects, will remain an indispensable policy option in the future. However, such sociologically enlightened political and policy advice must not forget that there are no abstract guarantees of rationality or reform in the production of political decisions, and that the path from the actual state to the target state cannot therefore be straightforward and, moreover, rocky, and failure must always be taken into account. And this is not only due to the structural uncontrollability of consultancy processes (which is why neither doctors nor management consultants are paid according to success, but according to time), but rather to the specific logic of the political process in democratically constituted welfare states. Nevertheless, it is advisable not to hope for the big solutions, but rather to rely on temporary innovative experiments and their findings as well as a slow trickle-down/diffusion. Scientific advice cannot, for example, implement concrete organisational reforms, but it can provide strategic suggestions and orientations and collaborate in the creation of scripts, scripts as well as narratives for a strategic reorientation. "Political decisions, however, are moreover to be made on the basis of power and majority. The political rationality of decision makers to get re-elected has nothing in common with scientific rationality. Politicians like to hide behind scientists in times of dominant ignorance. But expert government would be a functional depoliticization of democracy; politics would be decoupled from party competition. Nevertheless, knowledge is an eminently resilience-enabling resource. How political management ultimately benefits from it, how it uses the resources, is part of a comprehensive and highly complex political advisory structure in Germany" (Korte 2021, p. 32; cf. also Busch 2021).

In academic discourses on the different reform capacities of the political-administrative levels, the municipalities have been accorded a certain pioneering role for some time now, since it is here, for example, that challenges accumulate with regard to social problems and solutions are expected directly from local politics. Although the municipalities in Germany are caught up in a multi-level interdependence and financial room for manoeuvre is centrally dependent on the federal and state governments, current examples demonstrate a certain scope for variation. However, municipal social administration already displays a high degree of complexity. Responsibilities are spread across many different authorities, offices and departments and between public and private agencies (such as welfare associations) and even private providers. This leads to considerable interface problems and therefore individual municipal actors are now striving to reduce unnecessary interfaces and avoid duplication of work, to strengthen cooperation and coordination where necessary and to speed up administrative procedures without any loss of quality.

The digitalisation of administrative processes also offers the opportunity here to provide citizens with increasing transparency and more easily accessible information and also to increase the speed of the process. With regard to the linking of the different policy streams, some Länder explicitly rely on cooperative, cross-sectoral arrangements for dealing with new social risks, which are based on the model of the social investment state (already mentioned in the second chapter). "The findings of our study indicate that change is taking place regarding the operational dimension of social policy. Much effort is being made to cooperate across the borders of organizations and policy fields to overcome compartmentalized problem-solving structures, which have proven to be ineffective for handling complex social problems. The results also suggest that politicians and public servants in charge of designing implementation arrangements for social investment programmes increasingly perceive themselves as metagovernors: they are aware of the typical pitfalls of local network governance, and they know that they can make a difference by using tools of metagovernance" (Berzel and Klenk 2021, p. 19; see also Sörensen and Torfing 2017 and Schroeder et al. 2018).

The fact that discourse-oriented deliberative processes achieve something politically can be demonstrated by labour market policy, where it has also been possible to achieve a certain autonomisation of policy vis-à-vis organised interests that are strongly oriented towards maintaining the status quo. It cannot be denied that the type of political governance has changed structurally since the 1980s; state actors are tying "more strongly than ever before to the self-regulatory potentials of social spheres and economic sectors, i.e. to the (self-)governance competencies of extra-state actors" (Wiesenthal 2006, p. 130; see also Heinze 2020b). Such an expansion of the corridor of action with a view to civil society potentials as well as expert knowledge is, however, dependent not only on the experimentation of an active political leadership but also on favourable time windows. Realistically speaking, it can be assumed that new transformation strategies that are not only related to the classic institutions will only slowly seep into the political decision-making processes. *Strong impulses* from outside will be needed to creatively address the multiple blockages and the separation of functional areas in politics and administrations. The Corona pandemic can highlight how external influences bring about curated governance. "Policy management combines the controllability of the political system with the controllability of key political actors. Governance as a form of policy management uses resilience to manage crises. [...] Institutional resilience relies on open (self-) learning processes: Fault tolerance, reversibility and openness are its hallmarks. Resilient learning is more than crisis management. Rather, it is the ability of actors in the system to continuously anticipate and proactively respond to change. The system remains in active learning mode of self-transformation" (Korte 2021, p. 28).

Such problem-solving learning, which is described and classified here as curated governance, has not (yet) been applied in the heterogeneous and confusing field of social security. Nor is this task conceivable via a master plan, but rather – and this is also demonstrated by the fundamental early social reforms – via experimental strategies. "The combination of autonomous initiatives and developmental conditions granted by the state would create a launching pad for the emergence of new social institutions – not unlike the pattern of "natural" evolution: favorable conditions for the generation of testable alternatives would correspond to the evolutionary mechanism of variation; the social attractiveness test of potentially reproducible forms would be equivalent to the evolutionary mechanism of selection; and the practical testing of socially accepted innovations would reflect the evolutionary mechanism of retention" (Wiesenthal 2019b, p. 380).

The basic income could be a narrative for implementing the changed communication about social policy, which has begun both in research and in individual federal states and municipalities and is reflected in various flagship projects, on a nationwide basis as well. It is now clear to many social policy actors that a preventive policy encompassing several policy fields (e.g. family, education and labour market policy) is necessary in order to actively meet the tasks of providing for the general interest as well as the increased social risks, in order to open up opportunities and perspectives for a self-determined life, and that the established bureaucratic structures often represent an obstacle to this. One building block for a social investment strategy of unbundling and de-bureaucratisation could be a guarantee-based basic security system which, complementing interdepartmental (cross-sectoral) problem-solving, simplifies state transfer payments, overcomes selective use and at the same time reduces stigmatisation effects and feelings of shame. Starting points for such a narrative have already been explicitly formulated in the debates on citizen work, for here – based on the softening of the wage-labour orientation of social insurance through the Care Insurance Act – the inclusion of citizen work in the socio-political security systems was demanded. "If, however, at the same time there is a justified demand to finance "noninsurance" – i.e. non-wage-labour-based – benefits by means of taxes, then once again the question arises of a tax-financed basic security system instead of increasing the federal subsidy in each case" (Beck 2000a, b, p. 440).

Obviously, however, this debate about alternative systems has not emerged as a trend-setting political current that has been taken up in government policy. After years of *repression* and *marginalisation,* however, these strategic considerations for the transformation of the "gainful employment-only society" into a mixed and sustainable activity society, which were dismissed as visionary ideas, are now being revitalised, and not only in the social media and some social experiments. Moreover, the younger birth cohorts now entering working life are increasingly losing faith that the equivalence principle of pay-as-you-go pension insurance will still apply when they retire in the distant future.

The positive effects of a significantly weakened basic security variant during the Corona pandemic are beginning to emerge in labour market policy with the low-condition basic security, which – according to initial empirical studies – has certainly proved its worth. It also became clear in one study that *digitalisation* has emerged as an enabling factor that can drive coordinated and tendentially preventive problem-solving. "Contrary to many fears at the beginning of the Corona pandemic, a large number of procedural processes can be easily handled digitally. This is especially true for the submission of documents and generally all highly standardized processes. The digitalisation of procedures and processes is not an end in itself: the aim must be to remove unnecessary bureaucratic hurdles and stumbling blocks in order to be able to transfer free resources to the mediation practice. The study also shows that such a digitalisation offensive must not be carried out at the expense of face-to-face interactions, which remain important, especially in those fields of activity that require a close, dialogue-oriented exchange between the administration and service recipients. What is needed, therefore, is a functional differentiation of digitization with the overriding goal of continuously improving the intensity and quality of advice" (Beckmann et al. 2021a, b, p. 19 f.).

Such experiences can act as necessary impulses – "nudging" – and help to stimulate further laboratories for a preventive, cooperatively organized welfare state in an over-bureaucratized social assistance system at the local level, which more specifically involve civil society resources and manage without bureaucratic coercive tools. Experiments with Universal Basic Income (UBI) in various countries show that even small changes in welfare and work logic have enormous effects, such as the removal of conditionalities and sanction regimes. "Other potential short-term measures towards implementing UBI as a long-term goal include the universalization of access to specific benefits, such as child allowance or disability benefits. Implementing such shifts on a large-scale basis would allow important pilot experiences to be generated, which may have a much stronger weight in future policy discussions than small, complex, short-term experiments. At the same time, it is evident that the scope and legitimacy of three-tier systems (involving lifelong, basic security, means-tested top-ups, and voluntary or compulsory contributions and voluntary savings elements) depend on the future of work and employment. UBI policies are only one measure in a policy basket to ensure sustainable and inclusive growth and development" (Haagh and Rohregger 2019, p. 23; see also Haagh 2019).

The experiences during the Corona crisis can act as a driver for the acceptance of basic income models based on guarantees, although these are anything but forms of an unconditional basic income in the sense just cited, but rather basic incomes that are accessible at a lower threshold, as well as graduated and verifiable basic incomes for selected groups. In the discourses on the consequences of Corona, however, there have also been calls for more far-reaching forms of a universal basic income as an existential safeguard for care work. "One way to realize this basic protection is the unconditional basic income, which has been discussed for a long time and could still have an effect during the pandemic. Since especially people with comprehensive care tasks need support in the areas of education and upbringing, of health and care, it is necessary to expand the public social infrastructure, to make it free of charge and to increase its quality" (Winker 2020, p. 401). Even if such proposals, which today seem rather visionary, unsurprisingly failed to find resonance on the political stage, they address a social problem area that is readily suppressed in official politics: The unpaid care work that flashes up in abbreviated form in the debates about a growing nursing emergency, making it clear that the real bottleneck in the health care system for successfully combating and containing the pandemic is not so much the number of available intensive care beds and their apparatus bottleneck, but rather the availability of sufficient nurses trained in intensive care medicine. Although such a "care revolution" is unlikely to appear on the political agenda in the near future – if only because of the fragmentation and entrenched structures in the German assistance system described above – the socio-political dimensions of the basic income debates become apparent here and can provide impetus for a reform debate that recognises both the relevance of public infrastructures and the recognition of personal care relationships.

Even though the socio-political institutional system has become fragile in several places, the actors interested in maintaining it and their "architects" have managed to preserve the foundation walls with the help of extensions and individual renovations. However, deviating from the historical and administrative ground plan, new *elements foreign to the system* have often been incorporated in a concealed manner, which in the medium term also amount to a new foundation in order to secure the building resiliently and securely against old and new natural hazards. Perhaps the discourse will then no longer be primarily determined by the major parties and the established socio-political institutions, but will be fed by influences outside the classic, channelled forms of political communication (including through digital social networks). Both new government constellations and new forms of political participation with differently defined political priorities can create enabling spaces, but presumably in a more polarized form than was usual in the consensus-oriented political debates.

This makes it even more difficult to assess the prospects of success, because the loss of function of the traditional mainstream parties can lead to the formation of coalitions that are difficult to calculate, making the formation of governments more difficult and more unstable in terms of time. On the other hand, it cannot be ruled out that precisely such diffusion processes could also bring new attention to controversial issues such as basic income, which have hitherto been neglected in the political institutions. "The domination of the issue agenda has diffused into the net, officially constituted politics is often merely reactive, it is now conversely "the great majorities beyond parliament" that spill over onto those of parliament, despite all the desperate attempts of established actors to regain something like discourse hegemony" (Manow 2020, p. 115). This largely digitally mediated political mobilization power, which enables "individualized collective action" (Tormey 2015, p. 84) via the Internet, is likely to keep the basic income issue on the political agenda, if only because of the widespread coverage of the experiments.

Nevertheless, the strong sense of security and the comparatively high risk aversion of the population in Germany must be taken into account, which are repeatedly invoked, especially in election campaigns, and which in the field of social security (according to the motto: "The pension is safe") already decades ago ensured a deceptive calm and ultimately delayed necessary reform steps. Security messages from the political leadership are important signals for fear reduction, especially in times of crisis such as the Corona pandemic, and can thus also have a stabilising effect on society. However, party and campaign strategists should only make temporary use of them to indicate a capacity to act. It is to be hoped that the experience of "curated" governance in a state of emergency will have increased the learning capacity of the political-administrative system as a whole and that the newly acquired political confidence in crisis mode will also have a productive effect on the handling of other systemic issues such as the future viability of social security. In terms of political strategy, the pandemic has brought the issue of a preventive social infrastructure and, more generally, the provision of services of general interest back to the fore and could also have a mobilising effect on the narrative of a basic income. With the gradual management of the pandemic, however, it is already clear that the undermining of established political practices functions primarily in a state of emergency. For the structural reconstruction of the welfare state architecture, this stress test nevertheless provides some indications of the fundamental ability of a transformation of the welfare state, since it is ultimately also a matter of managing risks here. "What is to be regulated wins out over what is market. Insofar as one gives direction to saving, there is an opportunity to shape the future as well. This applies to all aspects of a precautionary state, but certainly also to the great transformation towards a digital sustainability society. But change does not simply happen, it needs shaping" (Florack et al. 2021, p. 21).

In this context, global social science discourses today often speak of a new *social contract*, because times of crisis open windows for fundamental reforms (such as the development of the welfare state in Great Britain after the Second World War). However, the question is whether policy management still has the resources for such a transformation in the face of multiple challenges. The experienced academic policy advisor Minouche Shafik is optimistic and sees through the global pandemic "a moment of opportunity for change: I have learned after decades of conducting negotiations is that, sometimes, making the problem bigger makes it easier to solve" (this. 2021, p. 187).

But even when governments embark on this transformation path, resistance must be factored in from many organized interests who will scrutinize any change in the status-quo in terms of what it means for their patronage interests and build resistance accordingly, if necessary. Smart political management is then required to build broad coalitions to contain the established and mostly institutionalized interest groups. In addition, *political communication of* the restructuring processes is of elementary importance, which must not only be conducted through traditional channels, but must also include social media. The medialization of politics has become an important determinant for structural reform projects as well, which must be taken into account. Certainly, there is no "fixed menu" for a new social contract for all countries, because this depends on many framework conditions (both socio-economic and cultural factors) and there will also not be "the" national social contract, because historical experience teaches us that "most social contracts have been reformed in stages and over decades as a result of continuous pressure from society" (op. cit., 189).

Risks of Updating the Status Quo Without a Change in Strategy

5

5.1 Social Change: Individualisation, Singularisation

A number of development and social transformation processes collide with the construction principles of the current system of contribution-financed social security and lead us to expect that conflicts will continue to unfold in the future that can only be defused with difficulty or not at all within the existing system. In contrast, the gradual introduction of a UBI (– in this book we refer to the German abbreviation BGE) has – at least at first glance – partial advantages and can open up solution options for conflict reduction, which is why this concept appears again and again in a variety of discourses on the political stage.

The structural change of societies such as Germany was already characterised within the social sciences more than 30 years ago with the keywords of *increasing individualisation* and *a pluralisation of lifestyles*. Although the degree of social inequalities was by no means levelled out as a result of the sustained welfare increases of the last 40 years, an "elevator effect" (Beck 1986, p. 122) became effective to a certain extent – not least triggered by many years of net immigration from abroad – which also allowed lower income strata to participate in the growing income level. Real income increases could only be achieved in Germany within the market economy system with high competitive pressure due to the economy's high dependence on exports at the price of growing productivity. The economic and economic development was accompanied by an individualisation of social risks, at the end of which there is dependency as well as the granting of social transfers as a result of unemployment or low income. "There is an increasing split between a system of full employment and a system of flexible, plural, individualised

R. G. Heinze, J. Schupp, *Basic Income - From Vision to Creeping Transformation of the Welfare State*,
https://doi.org/10.1007/978-3-658-40269-3_5

underemployment. Worsening inequalities remain in the grey zone. The focus of life shifts from the workplace and business to the creation and experimentation of new life forms and lifestyles. The contrasts between men and women that arise in the break-up of the form of life come to the fore" (Beck 1986, p. 152).

Approaches to the individualization and pluralization of lifestyles assume that people's lifestyles are less and less ordered by class and status, but rather that new spaces for autonomy, but also for risk, are opening up in a liquefied social structure. Lifestyles are sorting themselves into new social milieus that are no longer defined primarily by occupation, education and income. Individualisation thus leads to the dissolution of boundaries, in that life options previously defined externally are increasingly being placed in the hands of the individual and people are thus becoming "choosers". On the one hand, this implies new scope for freedom; on the other, against the background of selective labour market integration, it can also exacerbate social security gaps. These observations from the 1980s were accentuated anew in the thesis of a "society of singularities", whereby singularisation goes beyond the thesis of individualisation: "Singularisation, however, means more than independence and self-optimisation. Central to it is the more complicated striving for uniqueness and exceptionality, which to achieve has admittedly become not only a subjective desire but a paradoxical social expectation" (Reckwitz 2017, p. 9). If this thesis is only partially confirmed, it will also have consequential effects on the steering capacity of politics and the shaping of society as a whole, because singularization means that self-selected collectives, which mostly have cultural patterns of justification (such as lifestyles), become the central form of socialization. "Singular collectives thus generally present themselves as socialities with intense affectivity, sharing not only practices but also narratives and imaginaries" (op. cit., p. 62).[1]

In the field of lifestyles, the US social researcher Elizabeth Currid-Halkett (2021) has also presented an investigation into the status symbols by which elites define themselves today and thus also mechanisms of social closure take place. She shows that above all consumption habits reproduce new elites and in doing so have reinforced the already existing divide between mobile, cosmopolitan and more highly qualified classes and low-skilled groups of society dependent on transfer payments. "Our consumption habits reveal who we are and who we want to be. Our choices around what we consume both connect us to and alienate us from different

[1] At this point, neither the empirically presented (Dietrich and Hess 2021) nor the sociological criticism of Reckwitz's studies will be addressed, but only the grown desynchronization of social change and welfare state security will be referred to; on the criticism, cf. among others Kumkar and Schimank (2021), Mau (2021) and Sachweh (2021).

groups within society" (this. 2021, p. 312). One result of these socio-cultural shifts and social fragmentation is growing gaps in security that cannot or cannot adequately be addressed through traditional welfare state mechanisms – including extensions such as the minimum wage that have been introduced in recent years.

Against the background of the economization of central social areas and especially the pressure on self-control and self-motivation, individual excessive demands are also produced. This is why subjective insecurities have increased in recent years. This is exacerbated by the concern that the socio-economic shocks triggered by the Corona pandemic are endangering Germany as a social location and that social security is becoming more fragile. Fears about maintaining status are therefore increasingly shaping the social atmosphere. Even if one can argue whether Germany is actually on the way to becoming a "descent society" (Nachtwey 2016) or whether images of a fragmented or granular society (Kucklick 2015) are not more suitable for reality, there is a consensus that the dream of a prosperous and protective welfare state has developed *cracks* and that it is becoming increasingly difficult for many groups to realise an autonomous way of life. There are thus signs of a crisis in a model of society that was successful for decades as an *upwardly mobile* affluent society with extensive social security. Now the pillars of this model seem to be increasingly crumbling. Moreover, the globalised markets that grew rapidly after the collapse of the Iron Curtain more than 30 years ago are becoming more and more unmanageable, as the financial crisis exemplarily demonstrated, and with the economic irritations the social-institutional arrangements of the welfare state security systems are also tottering. Consequently, phenomena of insecurity are also increasingly being addressed in social theories, with the focus on both socio-structural fragmentation and subjectively experienced insecurities; prominently outlined in the writings of Alain Ehrenberg on the "exhausted self" or on "unease in society": "The social bond is weakening, and as a consequence the individual must rely more and more on himself, on his personal abilities, his subjectivity, his 'inwardness'. Hence those mass psychological sufferings and the multiplication of psychological, medical, spiritual techniques or social support that take care of these "attachment pathologies." Concerns about subjectivity and the entrenchment of autonomy feed the notion that our societies are facing a triple process of de-institutionalization, psychologization, and privatization of human life" (Ehrenberg 2011, p. 19; see also Pörksen 2018; Grünewald 2019 as well as Mau 2019; Reckwitz 2019a, b).

The sixth Poverty and Wealth Report of the Federal Government, which will be presented in spring 2021, has now for the first time determined in an empirical expertise on social mobility to what extent the solidification and permeability of *living situations have become* pronounced over a period of 30 years. According to this report, the proportion of people who are in the lowest or highest social position has increased continuously since the 1980s. This development goes hand in hand with the continuing slight increase in the low-income ratio and gives an indication of one of the possible reasons for this development. There is also evidence of a consolidation and concentration of long-term unemployment over time (see Fig. 5.1). Moreover, the social mobility dynamics, especially in the lower segment designated as poverty, has decreased: "In the case of belonging to the situation designated as "poverty" in the research project, the probability of still belonging to it in the next five-year period has increased from 40% to 70% since the end of the 1980s" (BMAS 2021a, p. XVI).

In view of these risks of falling into poverty and having to claim financial assistance, which have increased in recent years, and also the growing fear among the middle class (cf. Lengfeld and Hirschle 2009 as well as Heinze 2011) of social decline, the current system of basic security still provides for an application and the associated means test. In contrast, an unconditional basic income – even if only in a partial amount – would initially be available to every citizen ex ante at the beginning of every month. An income check as well as possible offsetting of the paid basic income, on the other hand, would by logic only take place ex post, with the corresponding taxation and "offsetting" of a paid-out BGE against the tax allowance (after all, it amounts to €9744 in 2021 and for 2022 it rises to €9984). The

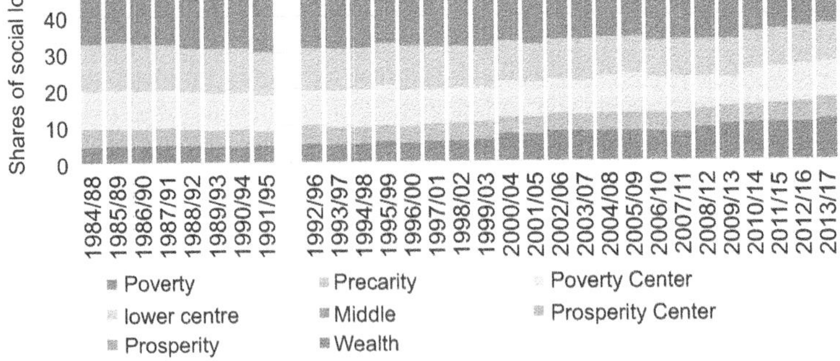

Fig. 5.1 Development of social situations, 1984–2017. (Source: BMAS 2021a, p. 142)

liberal sociologist Ralf Dahrendorf already pleaded in 1986 for such a basic income that can be guaranteed in the long term for all citizens: "Whoever, on the other hand, wants the guaranteed minimum income as a right of citizenship, must start with a moderate, but precisely guaranteed amount. This need not be significantly higher than the current social assistance rate. What is decisive is only its fundamental unassailability, i.e. its entitlement character" (ibid. 2019, p. 336). In doing so, he ties in with a model of state provision already developed in the so-called "Beveridge Report" during the Second World War, which was intended to cover all risks. The central principles included: "uniform, general and contributory insurance to secure to every man for himself and for his family at all times a minimum income of his own as a legal right; that is to say, without any form of means test or inquiry into what means are available to them" (Marshall 1992, p. 157 f.).

5.2 Changes in the World of Work and Digitalisation

A central strand of the debates on basic income relates to the supposed end of the gainful employment society as a result of digitalisation, the use of robots and, more recently, the use of artificial intelligence, which would bring about a progressive release of human labour. These debates about technological unemployment are not new either, but have been going on for decades with different emphases. What is new, however, are the particular manifestations of digitization and artificial intelligence that are changing the structure of production and the way society functions. "The prominence that basic income has gained recently owes much to the assessment of many observers that in the future, due to advances in automation and artificial intelligence, there will not be enough work to put everyone to work, not even under precarious conditions" (Crouch 2019, p. 97 f.) or in the words of Timo Daum, who researches online and the digital economy: "Digital capitalism is saying goodbye to the primacy of work and no longer imposes any compulsion to work. For those discarded by digitalisation, the BGE will then become the Hartz IV of the coming decades – sanction-free, because: There will then no longer be any work that anyone had to be forced to do" (ibid. 2017, p. 204).

The *term* digitalisation has had an astonishing career in recent years. In all studies on the central socio-economic trends, digitalisation is mentioned alongside globalisation, demographic change and individualisation. The upheavals in the world of work derived from the "digital revolution" are not only discussed in the abstract, but are already noticeable today, for example in that some professions are simply disappearing. Sociologists speak of a remeasurement of society, which is becoming increasingly granular and produces a "high-resolution" image of society for us through sensors and networks (cf. Mau 2017). However, the internet does not only serve as a communication medium, but also penetrates sensitive areas of life, for example when health diagnoses are obtained from the internet. The personalisation of security and health data shows how fundamental socio-economic and cultural *trends* – individualisation and digitalisation – meet and reinforce each other. In line with the zeitgeist, growing segments of the population are embracing health as a personally malleable variable and are increasingly taking care of a health-oriented lifestyle. Various health apps now offer digital solutions for this. Fitness and health apps are becoming increasingly popular. Self-measurement or self-optimization, which has so far been practiced primarily in the field of fitness, points to a social trend towards increasing individual resources through "self-work" that currently characterizes modern societies. "This leads to individuals having to invest more and more energy in maintaining their competitiveness and resource endowment in order to keep their place, in other words, to reproduce the status quo" (Rosa 2016, p. 219).

The spread of digitalisation is a *qualitative leap in* that many human activities can be replaced (from self-driving cars to telemedical procedures and 3D printing). To be sure, according to various studies on job development in Germany (cf. Arnold et al. 2016; Stettes 2020) digitalisation will not necessarily lead to significantly less gainful employment on balance. However, following a recent reassessment of the substitutability potential of occupational activities, the Institute for Employment Research calculated that around one third (11.3 million) of employees subject to social security contributions in 2019 were employed in occupations for which a high *substitutability potential was* calculated, implying that around eleven million jobs could be lost (cf. Dengler and Matthes 2021). In its latest Employment Outlook, the OECD stated that more jobs in Germany are exposed to a high risk of automation or change than the average of OECD countries (OECD 2019). Nevertheless, it has been shown for past automation processes that Germany has tended to experience employment growth in the middle-skill sector (OECD 2020). With regard to the new jobs, the question arises as to what kind of jobs these will be – will they be subject to social security contributions or will forms of self-employment expand in the future, for example through the platform economy, in which the employees are not integrated into the social security network that was previously sustainable.

This is the point of departure for Colin Crouch's comprehensive reform proposals to provide social security for precarious work in general in times of the *gig economy*. To this end, he proposes the creation of a special social security fund, which would be designed analogously to the current taxation system: "All adult residents of a country must pay into the social security system, regardless of whether they are in paid employment or not. The amount of contributions is not determined according to their status in the labour market (so non-workers and employed, self-employed and employees basically have to pay the same contributions), they vary according to income, regardless of the form in which it is told" (the same 2019, p. 118). Moreover, employers would also have to pay into this fund: 'All companies and other organisations using labour services above a certain threshold would have to pay social security contributions according to the number of hours they use services labour, regardless of whether their contract with labour providers is an employment contract and regardless of the duration of that contract' (ibid., 111). Such proposals aim at a comprehensive social security reform "that transforms it into a tax and is no longer based on the responsibility of an employer, but on the fact of the use of human labor" (ibid., 20). This reform – similar to the certainly less bureaucratic alternative of a BGE – would replace the historically grown system of German social insurance, which is also equipped with principles of self-administration, with a new central administrative and bureaucratic apparatus, albeit with a plethora of open questions of its concrete institutional anchoring and governance.

The most recent ILO report (2021) also looked at precisely these *new forms of employment* on digital labour platforms, which now make up a distinct part of the digital economy and will have a significant impact on the future of work. Those employed on internet platforms are referred to as "gig workers", "crowdworkers" or as "platform workers". The ILO study identified major gaps for these workers in terms of health insurance and occupational accident coverage, unemployment and disability insurance, and in terms of old-age security. In addition to regulating the working and employment conditions of those employed in the gig economy, there is also a need for political action to level the playing field between the various employment models and to ensure that Internet-based platforms are not able to develop monopoly power. The first report of the Council for the Working World, an advisory body of the Federal Ministry of Labour and Social Affairs, also recommends in the area of new forms of employment: "When considering better protection against income risks for the (solo) self-employed, care must be taken to ensure that the balance between entrepreneurial (personal) responsibility and socio-political risk provision is maintained and that the differences between dependent and self-employed work are not lost sight of. However, it should also be acknowledged that

- the increase in hybrid forms of employment and a potentially more frequent switch between both forms of employment in the future makes the separation of dependent and self-employed employment more problematic,

- there is a need for social security even in the case of self-employment
- and previous approaches offer only fragmented security" (Working World Council 2021, p. 90).

In this discourse, too, there are thus a number of arguments in favour of transforming our current social system in the long term – away from burdening the factor of labour towards greater financing from taxes.

Although the digitalisation processes are not spreading equally in all sectors of the economy, more and more young people are only familiar with the classic normal employment relationships from stories told by their parents and grandparents; they are primarily familiar with "atypical" forms of employment such as part-time work, contracts for work and services, etc. Based on their often negative experiences in the education system, young people from the lower social strata are often already so frustrated that they define themselves as "superfluous" who can no longer find a foothold in a society that has been penetrated by forced processes of economisation. The guarantees of dependent employment that have become a matter of course for the post-war generations are becoming increasingly selective for these groups. For all groups on the labour market, the compulsion to self-management is growing and some can hardly withstand this pressure for perfection. When security is lost, normative claims for a just world of work are not enough; a long-term policy must seek new forms of security. In his observation on the advancing social division, Heinz Bude noted: "The poor of tomorrow also include the group of those precarious individualists who have been driven out of the niches of their alimented survival by the mobilisation measures of the activating welfare state. They had settled down with an income mix of state transfers, small interest income from inherited reserves and periodic additional earnings in order to pursue their self-realisation projects on a low flame" (ders. 2008, p. 130).

As employment status continues to play the central role in Germany in terms of social risk protection, the flexible forms of employment driven by digitalisation are structurally disadvantaged in terms of social protection in the event of unemployment, illness or old age. Consequently, the question arises as to how they can be better protected institutionally and included in the systematics of social security. "The challenge lies in institutional support for coping practices of discontinuous employment that systematically reduces the risks of options for action in the context of household reference and biographical development, without limiting the design spectrum to the normative guiding concepts of the normality types of employee or entrepreneurship. The task lies in designing an institutional design perspective of gainful employment that encompasses the totality of forms of employment, is attuned to their respective particularities, and at the same time supports the possibility of their synchronous or diachronic combination" (Pongratz and Bührmann 2018, p. 72; cf. also the contributions in Haipeter et al. 2021).

These questions about the future of social security in an increasingly digital world of work will come increasingly into focus in the future, although they have not yet been adequately answered by concepts from the sociology of work and industry. Hopes of a return to more stable forms of employment or the options for "good work" and more state regulation, which are also repeatedly put forward by the trade unions, are understandable from the organisation's point of view[2], but will only have a limited effect. "We assume about 45% of jobs could be relocated. In fact, it's about 20% of employees who work in home offices during Corona. However, the fact that the large-scale trial of home office during Corona is working well is not only increasing the willingness of companies to offer home office as an option. There are also considerations to advertise a part of their workplaces only as home office employment relationships – not least with the intention of thus being able to save expensive office space" (Schroeder 2021).

There is no doubt that the Corona pandemic has also significantly accelerated these transformation processes of work and has also tended to dissolve the classic separation of employment, family and leisure roles, which is not only associated with gains in freedom for most workers, but can also create new burdens. Coupled with the digitisation options, the new flexible forms of employment (such as the platform economy) or the new hybrid links between dependent and self-employed work will continue to spread. Even if they are not yet a significant factor in the employment system, these hybrid forms create gaps in security, as they do not fit into the logic of the conventional system (cf. Beckmann and Spohr 2022).

What is needed are not only defensive measures to contain these rapidly increasing forms of employment, but also sustainable answers to a structurally changed world of work that can no longer be conceived within the regulatory framework of traditional welfare state protection. How a combination of collective protection rights and universalistic security concepts could be developed, however, is widely discussed by Colin Crouch, for example, and reference is also made to corresponding French and British studies (ibid., p. 91 f.) – nevertheless, such proposals have not yet been on the agenda of the labour policy actors. While the trade unions have so far shied away from fundamental innovations on this issue, the employers' organisations have kept a low profile and left it to individual business personalities to propagate far-reaching demands for an unconditional basic income.

---

[2] Cf. in this context also the topics of the 18th DGB Federal Congress on "Work of the Future and Social Security" in May 2018. https://www.dgb.de/themen/++co++76417c1e-5500-11e8-9aa6-52540088cada

The assumption often put forward by critics of a BGE that the rationalisation losers generated by digitalisation should be "pacified" with the help of a basic income (Butterwegge 2018, p. 211), and that this is therefore also in the interests of entrepreneurs, may be suitable above all for mobilising trade union forces against a basic income, but in doing so it paints the real exclusions and access thresholds of the current system in a mild light. More questionable is the speculation as to why many entrepreneurial personalities in Silicon Valley are so positively taken with the BGE as a "magic wand". It is to be suspected that with the help of a basic income, they like to forget to think about the critical social effects of the technologies they develop (such as the increase of an individualistic basic attitude and the withdrawal from public spaces).

The American historian Benavav, who conducts research at the Berlin Cluster of Excellence "Scripts", is rather sceptical about the change in the world of work towards more digitalisation and automation, as well as the potential solutions offered by an unconditional basic income, and refers to necessary preconditions: "If full automation can appear as both a dream and a nightmare, that is because it has no innate association with human dignity, and because it will not generate a post-scarcity world by itself. Nor will UBI. Perhaps if access to education and health-care were dramatically widened, communities revitalized through cooperation sharing of the work necessary to their reproduction, industries partially socialized, and massive investment made in the transition from fossil fuel to renewable sources of energy – then, a basic income could form one part of a larger project aiming at human freedom. Both the path to a post-scarcity world could also take some other form entirely. Without a clear vision of this coming world, it is easy to get lost along the way" (Benanav 2020, p. 97).

5.3 The Role of Minimum Wages

With the demand of their government programme: "Those who work all day must be able to live from their work without additional support. This, too, is a question of respect" (SPD 2021, p. 35), the SPD is pursuing the political goal in the Bundestag election campaign of raising the statutory minimum wage to €12, which would be equivalent to extending the increase proposed by the Minimum Wage Commission. The candidate for chancellor, Olaf Scholz, also sees a higher minimum wage as the alternative to an unconditional basic income[3]. However, it is

[3] SPD candidate for chancellor: Scholz thinks unconditional basic income is "neoliberalism" | Politik (fr.de)

doubtful whether an increased minimum wage can be a superior alternative to a living wage at all. This is because the minimum wage in Germany is an hourly wage. But even for childless single people, a minimum wage of €12 is not enough to independently secure their existence in larger cities. This implies that if even singles are on the poverty line with the current minimum wage, such a minimum wage is not enough for multi-person households with children to secure an adequate existence. Thus, Buttel also summed up the repercussions of the introduction of the minimum wage and its poverty-reducing effect: "Overall, the minimum wage appears to be a poorly targeted instrument for reducing benefit receipt and the risk of poverty" (Bruttel 2020, p. 9). However, even at a level of €12, the minimum wage is currently not very suitable as a means of combating poverty in old age. Such a minimum wage level is currently not sufficient to achieve a pension level above the current level of basic security in old age for 39 h per week and 45 years of employment[4].

Nevertheless, a minimum wage will remain necessary in the future, especially in those economic sectors and employment relationships where the lack of collective agreements and low levels of unionisation among employees have led to an increase in low pay. This also applies to employment relationships that are deemed reasonable by job centres. Nevertheless, it must be stated that despite the application of the minimum wage, in many cases the hourly wage actually paid is still below the statutory minimum wage. As part of the evaluation of the Minimum Wage Commission, with regard to the quantification of the number of employment relationships with hourly wages lower than the legally applicable hourly wages for 2018, it was stated that "Thus, 2.4 million employees earned less than the minimum wage. Based on the direct survey of hourly wages in the SOEP, on the other hand, the calculated value is 2.1% and 745,000 employment relationships. Regardless of the data source selected, however, similar patterns emerge with regard to the types of employment: "Wages below the minimum wage threshold are found significantly more frequently among marginally employed persons than among employees subject to social security contributions" (BMAS 2020, p. 50).

Proponents of a BGE therefore argue that the freedom to "say no" to employment relationships below the minimum wage would increase the negotiating position of precisely this group of employees vis-à-vis their employers, as they would be less susceptible to financial blackmail in the future for performing such activities. However, there is also the possibility that, with the introduction of a BGE, those employees in particular who are predominantly intrinsically motivated to

[4]Microsoft Word – 2105Auswertung-schrFrage Mindestlohn-Birkwald.docx (linksfraktion.de)

work could be more willing to do extra work voluntarily and without pay. This form of undermining minimum wages would only be likely if done voluntarily by the employee and could nonetheless result in a creeping undermining of minimum wage agreements to the point of adherence to collectively agreed wages. "Many more employees than today would therefore probably be prepared to work for a minimum wage. Any wage would then have the character of an additional income to the BGE, and even the statutory minimum wage would be hard to maintain. Its central justification, that the wage in full-time employment must at least be living wage, could no longer be asserted with a BGE" (Krämer 2018, p. 333).

5.4 Breaks in the Socio-political Model of the Community of Need

The push towards individualisation described in Sect. 5.1. has led in particular to women catching up with men in terms of educational qualifications, and they have now surpassed men in terms of educational success. With regard to their participation in the labour market and their careers in working life, they have made considerable progress in their increased integration into the labour market, despite continuing disadvantages. Nevertheless, an assessment of the increased employment rate of women must take into account the still different working time preferences compared to men: "Measured in terms of hours worked, however, women participate significantly less than men, because women's employment is predominantly part-time. Nearly 60% of employed women worked in part-time jobs in 2019, meaning they held three-quarters of all part-time jobs, compared to only one-third of all full-time jobs. Thus, while women accounted for almost 48% of all employed persons in 2019, they contributed only 40% to the overall volume of work in the economy" (Wanger 2020, p. 83).

A recently published study by RWI investigated the question of whether the gender-specific difference in labor force participation rates and hours worked is mainly due to personal preferences or also partly to policy-induced disincentives. Using microsimulation studies, the study was able to determine that "a switch to individual taxation would significantly increase labour supply in Germany. This increase would amount to 389,000 FTEs if a switch to individual taxation took place without any additional adjustment of the tax rate. If the increased tax revenues were returned to taxpayers via an increase in the basic allowance, the increase in hours worked would be 581,000 FTEs" (Bachmann et al. 2021, p. 23). From this, the authors conclude that abolishing the marital splitting and switching to individual taxation would, on the one hand, reduce gender inequalities in the labour market and, on the other hand, lead to economic gains: "Given the large positive labour supply effects, the aggregate gains are larger than the aggregate losses. A switch to individual taxation is clearly desirable from an efficiency perspective. Nevertheless, such a reform produces winners and losers, and value judgment is required to decide whether the gains for some outweigh the losses for others. Specific measures targeting the losers of a switch to individual taxation could accompany such a reform" (ibid., p. 23).

The previous political attempts to overcome the marital splitting failed so far to CDU/CSU and it has all appearances that this is likely to be so also in the future: "The marital splitting is the most modern form of taxation of women and men and also of same-sex partners in a gainful employment and maintenance community, and quite independent of who goes to work and who decides for the family or for a reduced professional activity outside the family. This creates freedom and can only be realized in this way "said the CDU politician Friedrich Merz in an interview with FAZ in June 2021[5].

Sociologist Jutta Allmendinger, on the other hand, makes a clear plea for the abolition or restructuring of marital splitting: "The goal of independent security for women is not compatible with marital splitting, which rewards unequal incomes in partnerships. In the short term this leads to financial relief, but in the medium and long term it is mostly at the expense of women. Marital splitting must be restructured, for example in the direction of family splitting" (Allmendinger 2021, p. 100).

Gösta Esping-Andersen refers to the process of "de-familialisation, including of care responsibilities" that has taken place above all in the Nordic countries in recent years, whereby the "familialism" he refers to is a characteristic feature of the conservative welfare state model that also characterises the German welfare state: "Familialism was probably practicable as long as the male breadwinner could guarantee an adequate level of security and women devoted themselves mainly to domestic production. Today it is counterproductive, both for women's striving for autonomy and, paradoxically, for family formation" (Esping-Andersen 2006, p. 77).

This development also has manifold consequences for social policy: "Demographic problems of social security result from growing life expectancy, declining birth rates and cross-border migration. The family household form of life is practiced (in cross-section) by a decreasing part of the resident population and extends (in biographical longitudinal section) over decreasing parts of the life course; for both reasons – and for the further reason of a changed gender role understanding of many women – the family as a micro-network of social security

[5] *Friedrich Merz defends the Union's expensive plans in an interview (faz.net).*

experiences a loss of function, which had to be taken into account, among others, in the introduction of a social long-term care insurance" (Offe 2019b[1995] p. 144 f.).

It remains questionable whether the trend towards the individualisation of female life plans and their desire to participate in working life can be permanently slowed down or even reversed: "As a result, the power of the family, especially of the man, is further limited. Women are no longer, as most women of the previous generations were, relegated to marriage for the sake of securing their economic existence and social status. They can decide – perhaps not freely, but more freely than in the past – whether to marry or to remain single; whether, if the marriage does not meet their hopes, they will seek divorce if necessary rather than endure constant conflict. This means that even in the normal female biography the logic of individual life plans is gradually asserting itself, the compulsion to solidarity is being further broken" (Beck-Gernsheim 1994, p. 123).

At this point, the idea of a basic income would secure an independent existence for women, even in partnerships and marriage, and would strengthen women's individual autonomy and meet the equality policy demand for individuality and independence. "It makes men and women financially independent of each other. Marital status is no longer a reference point. It makes men and women financially independent of each other. Marital status is no longer a reference point. There is no forced communalization as in the so-called community of need under the Social Code. The individualised payment corresponds to the modern way of life, the cross-gender individualised life plans in their growing plurality. It recognises that earlier "normal biographies" can no longer be a realistic reference point for social policy measures. If the scheme of permanent full-time work in its generality applied primarily to men anyway, the basic income opens up the possibility of boldly daring to take self-determined life paths, to try out new things, and to leave gender stereotypes behind in the process" (Fischer 2018, p. 99).

However, whether in a world of an unconditional basic income between men and women there would also automatically be a change in the gender-specific division of labour and a stronger assumption of care activities by men remains open at present: "How women and men will engage in the areas of society on the basis of the basic income and whether the gender-specific division of labour will change cannot be predicted. In any case, the conditions for negotiating a distribution of tasks appropriate to one's own needs and desires will become more favourable because women, like men, will be freed from the compulsion to engage in gainful employment, and this may also change collective patterns of interpretation of areas of life that are to be valued" (ibid., p. 112).

6 Conclusion and Outlook: Universalist Welfare State as an Emancipatory Guiding Model

"There has never been so much knowledge about our not knowing and about the compulsion to act and live under uncertainty". Jürgen Habermas, Frankfurter Rundschau, 10.4.2020.

In our outlook, we would like to take up an insight expressed by Jürgen Habermas at the beginning of the Corona pandemic, which we also interpret as an appeal to us social scientists to humbly concede that, despite all our disciplinary knowledge, we should not be too sure about our predictive power. We simply do not know what developments and future challenges, as well as possible welfare state transformations and further developments of our civil society and social cohesion, we will be confronted with in the short, medium and long term. Reflecting on the topic of this book, we can on the one hand conclude that the pace of welfare state transformations should not be overestimated, especially in Germany with its differentiated institutional structure that has grown over many decades, even if a wealth of good reasons for fundamental restructuring can be cited and a younger generation of political actors will also assume responsibility. In view of the global challenges ahead of us, such as climate change, pandemics, inequalities and scarcities of resources, the current system of social security will, however, be faced with major new burdens and who wants to rule out at present that, for example, a sudden in-

R. G. Heinze, J. Schupp, *Basic Income - From Vision to Creeping Transformation of the Welfare State*,
https://doi.org/10.1007/978-3-658-40269-3_6

crease in unemployment might not also lead to "tipping points" in our contribution-financed welfare state model, which could also lead to a political change of direction towards a basic income model.

6.1 Systematic Expansion of the Basic Income Discourse

The previous chapters have pointed out that fundamental policy changes are the exception rather than the rule in German politics. Several "currents" have to come together in order to overcome the institutionally anchored tendencies towards inertia in the system of welfare state security. A central argument is the *question of financing,* which has often not been given sufficient attention (at least from the point of view of the majority of the population) in many of the conceptual and, in particular, strategic considerations of the actors who are backing an unconditional basic income. In addition, the conceptual link between basic income and the promotion of social activities through a public policy of provision of general interest or infrastructure has been too little discussed. On the contrary: in socio-political discourses, public services of general interest have even been presented as a counter-model to unconditional basic income (UBI) – in this book we refer to the German abbreviation BGE). In contrast to these polarising debates, which ultimately amount to a preservation of the status quo with minor, rather cosmetic changes, the argumentation presented here amounts to a complementary strategy of restructuring and further development of the welfare state.

It is not just a matter of providing security and reducing bureaucratic overregulation and stigmatisation among certain social groups, the social integration effects of which should not be underestimated, especially in view of the current accumulation of crises. Rather, we want to combine basic material security with the creation of options for a productive use of time, for which incentives must be created. Some new participation formats have already been promoted at local level in recent years (e.g. voluntary work agencies and other contact points for social commitment), but their radius of action remains limited and tends to appeal more to the social centre. This does not succeed in reducing social inequalities, but they are nevertheless necessary in order to constructively counteract the structural change in involvement, because traditional clubs and associations are finding it difficult to organise their potential for involvement and to open up new fields of activity against the background of an individualised and singularised society. In addition to the stronger participation of even "weak" interest groups, the *timing of participation is* significant for political decision-making, which is also explicitly pointed out by the multiple streams approaches. "Second, simultaneity is important in such citizen participation. Gladly, deliberative citizen forums take place very early in the policy development process. The results are then fed into the further political process, which involves not only parliamentarians, but also experts and bureaucrats. In the end, the original proposals are then barely recognisable. This has the potential for further frustration. If experts, bureaucrats and citizens are involved at the same time, the will of those involved can be reconciled with factual necessities; ideally, understanding of legal and technical limitations grows at the same time" (Schäfer and Zürn 2021, p. 210 f.).

Although voluntary social engagement has grown in recent decades, the public infrastructure – despite all the political assurances of how important social engagement is – is not yet sufficiently attuned to these fluid potentials of civil society. In many cases, there is a lack of social infrastructures and communal locations for the relatively high willingness to get involved, which has been empirically proven time and again. Digital networks, as they have spread en masse, represent a new socio-technological option that can also be used to coordinate engagement, although they are also subject to the trend towards the *granularisation of* social relationships (cf. Kucklick 2015). They must therefore also be classified as limited in terms of social integration power. Digitalisation reinforces tendencies towards a "fractured" society (Mau 2019), thus ensuring spontaneous, not always resilient social contacts among individual groups, but can also only make limited productive use of the undoubtedly existing civil society potentials to date, although the Stifterverband certainly recognises digitalisation as a potential for development in the field of voluntary engagement (cf. Gilroy et al. 2018).

Our assumption is that a basic income would enable a real revival of the many forms of social engagement to unfold – both within and outside the family (e.g. in neighbourhood networks, hobby groups and associations, self-help groups and digital networks). A basic income in the form of a citizen's income for all would then not support the retreat into the "hammock" that many critics have been invoking again and again for decades, but could promote different models of a time use oriented towards the common good and thus provide at least optionally meaningful forms of activity also for those groups that find no or too little recognition on the flexibilised and dynamised labour markets. Social networks and commitments, which have so far been limited to selective participation, could thus be strengthened by basic security. In addition, they can also act as a springboard for business start-ups and social innovations in general, as they alleviate the problems of security that arise in the start-up phase.

In general, measures aimed at a *participatory society* are likely to gain in importance insofar as in the future in Western countries the era of steadily increasing prosperity coupled with the expansion of "normal" gainful employment will not come to an end completely, but will become significantly less important simply because of the challenges of climate change and the ecological restructuring of our society, and for this reason alone new forms of social control will have to be sought and tested. Development dynamics have been moving in this direction for some time now; the transfer state has expanded further and further, albeit largely in the shadow of official politics and social administrations as well as socio-political associations, which remain committed to and defend the status quo in a path-dependent manner.

The Corona crisis shook up these rigidities and put topics such as basic security and basic infrastructures on the political agenda. There was already a *need for action* in almost all fields of the welfare state, and the question of how civil society's performance potential can be better used is not new. However, while the last major social challenge (the refugee immigration in autumn 2015) led civil society to mobilise enormously, its radius of action remained limited or was even scaled back due to the necessary contact restrictions in the Corona pandemic. Government action currently seems to be programmed to act only when structural breaks are unmistakable or when political protest constellations form that call the ability to govern into question (for example, as a result of the growth of right-wing populist movements). Seen in this light, the virus that is rampant worldwide can act as an accelerator for development processes that were already *quietly* taking place and have now become visible. In this control context, universal basic security coupled with an infrastructure that provides for the general good can be understood as a framework for stimulating social transformation processes and in this way also opening up perspectives for a welfare state model that is still utopian at present.

6.2 Growing Time, Individual Gains in Freedom and New Communitisation

In the following, the focus of the debate on basic income, which is dominated in particular by economists, is to be corrected to the extent that the one-sided fixation on the financing perspective is overcome in the direction of a discourse on a re-foundation of social security that relies on collective, public infrastructures and a re-qualification of time. Thus, it is not only about a basic income to be received by all members of society, which would certainly help to reduce the fears currently spreading in many strata of the population against the background of the Corona pandemic, but also about the currently empirically open question of how the (free) time potentials that have become larger can be used productively and also in a resource-saving way in times of the implementation of climate goals. Even if someone does not share the view of human beings that with an unconditional basic income many will passively withdraw into the social safety net, about which doubts are raised at least on the basis of anecdotal evidence (Bohmeyer and Cornelsen 2019), the question of the *requalification of time* and inclusive infrastructures to be guaranteed by the state is of great importance not only from a sociological perspective. Claus Offe arrives at a similar assumption regarding a considerable overestimation of negative motivational effects of a BGE: "That people who could earn a sufficient income even without working will stop working to a dramatic extent because of this is almost as daring a hypothesis as the assumption that the entitlement to free health services would have the consequence that people would now visit their doctor all the time. Both cases fail to take into account the intrinsic value of gainful employment and its social environment, or the intrinsic unvalue of patient status." (ibid. 2019[1990], p. 141).

This implies a debate about an expanded concept of work, which aims at activities in the family, neighbourhood, among friends, etc., which are socially meaningful and considered essential for the functioning of a community and which extend to political-social engagement. And also the traditional work-centeredness will undergo changes in the future and more "income mixes" will spread. "In the new working society, gainful employment will continue to play a considerable role, but progressive shortening of working hours and increasing life expectancy could make the other forms of work, self-employment, exchange work, voluntary work in the non-profit sector, come more to the fore" (Strasser 1999, p. 62 f.; cf. also Vobruba 2019).

This then also addresses the core issues of an economic order that is primarily profit-oriented and, in particular, undermines the logic of increase that is inherent in the system, which causes quasi-natural resistance among a large part of the economic and political elites, who also regard such a paradigm shift as a threat to their privileged situation as well as to the model of action they have practised up to now. On the other hand, the option of a basic living income could bring about new securities, especially among population groups, with positive effects both on the quality of work and on society's general capacity for innovation. "What makes the idea of an Unconditional Basic Income so attractive at present are recent developments in social policy, which evaluate welfare state benefits solely in terms of their market adequacy and push for a corresponding restructuring of benefit systems. Transfers should not impair incentives to invest in one's own human capital and to engage in labour markets, or even eliminate them altogether, but rather stabilise and strengthen them. This is the common denominator of the education and social policy reforms of recent decades, with 'Hartz IV' and 'Bologna' as landmark examples. It is therefore important to see that an Unconditional Minimum Income aims at the heart of the capitalist transport and competition economy, in which the pursuit of market income is supposed to be the sole and inevitable driving force of all economic activity. This is ensured by the risk of unprovision, i.e. the danger of simply not being able to exist as a person without a regular and sufficiently high income from work" (Rieger 2019, p. 64 f.; cf. also further contributions on this in Baumgartner and Fux 2019).

Irrespective of the question of financing, however, it must also be critically asked whether a basic income will lead to quasi-automatic structural social inclusion and whether social, cultural as well as political activities and informal activities outside the household will spread on a large scale. To answer such questions, the pilot projects presented in the first section can provide valuable empirical findings. In this context, the argumentation of the two Nobel Laureates in Economics of 2019 is interesting. Although Banerjee and Duflo consider an unconditional basic income to be more effective in combating poverty in developing countries than the previous form of development aid and are therefore to be counted among the advocates of a basic income, they have great doubts as to whether it also represents an effective means, for example, in the event of job losses in developed economies (cf. Banerjee and Duflo 2020, p. 440ff.). To justify this, the two economists draw on results from time-use surveys in the USA, on the basis of which they show that the leisure time that has increased in recent decades is on balance spent more on passive activities such as TV consumption and video games than on an increase in voluntary or neighbourly activities. This is because in developed welfare states, unlike in the past, the "two variables – work and leisure – have an "inverse relationship" to each other: production and the work required to produce these new forms of high-value production have an impact on free time. Today it is no longer a sign of higher social status to have a lot of free time" (Currid-Halkett 2021, p. 28 f.).

The particularly sociologically exciting question of how the growing amount of available time (at least for a large number of individuals) could be converted into welfare values without this time first having to be converted into monetary income as paid working time or as self-employed economic activity was dealt with some time ago (cf. for theoretical elaboration and an international comparison Offe/Heinze 1990 and the contributions in Heinze/Offe 1990). Against the background of the wave of digitalisation and currently of the Corona pandemic, there is currently again a discussion about a re-cutting of the distribution pattern between formal gainful employment and informal activity, i.e. activity which is not allocated and remunerated by market mechanisms. As an alternative model – similar to the visionary ideas on basic income – cooperation or exchange rings have historically already been conceptually developed for some time, aiming at establishing a supra-household collectivisation of self-sufficiency institutions. According to this model, they are organized neither communally nor administratively, but market-like, "however, with the two special features that (a) the exchange of services does not run via the general medium of money, but via service vouchers as a parallel currency, which are valid only within the circle of participants and only for the purpose of the exchange of services between a locally delimited number of households, and that (b) the emergence and existence of such a market, which is excluded by a non-convertible proper currency, is publicly subsidized by the provision of spaces, equipment, in-kind services, and human capital" (Offe and Heinze 2018, p. 208 [1986]).

The cooperation or exchange networks were not about designing a completely different economic order, but rather about limited supplements and compensation mechanisms that are clearly within the scope of reform policy. So far, under the social and economic structural conditions as they exist in Germany and other comparable countries, the possibilities of a "productive" use of time past the medium of money are severely limited, even if they are not completely absent. In addition, there is a growing "competition" of "productive use of time" in the form of the enormous growth of the leisure industry, especially in the last decades, in which leisure consumption has been increasingly linked with services of communication and entertainment electronics. "The relationship between work and leisure in saturated Western societies does not merely result from the law of minimizing leisure to the limit of the efficiency of work performance, but must at the same time also take leisure into account as a variable of increasing sales. The wage-earner does not merely need enough leisure time to be able to sell his wages on the market. Consumption here becomes a second complementarity of work alongside recreation, which constitutes the addictive structure mentioned above" (Gimmel 2017, p. 58 f.). On the one hand, these restrictions lead to the economically irrational, at least suboptimal, fallowing of factors of social welfare and consequently to a lower level of provision. On the other hand, they lead to the hardly acceptable finding that precisely those population groups for whom unused time resources are available and who, due to their general supply situation, would most urgently need to convert this available time into "use values", are least able to do so (e.g. the unemployed). A functioning institutional system of non-monetary social use of time could therefore, in addition to the proposals for monetary redistribution of income, open up a perspective for a fairer distribution structure of life chances, which could at the same time also strengthen social cohesion, despite or precisely because of the preservation of voluntary personal commitment, which can be terminated at any time. An unconditional basic income, which refers to the fact of a productivity free of (labour) constraints, contains a momentum of *time sovereignty,* in order to be able to redefine the relationship between laziness, leisure, productive and consumptive use of time.

From today's perspective, a basic income appears to be a pragmatic attempt beyond nostalgic retrospectives on "ideal" communities or comprehensive welfare state planning or a different economic order. In this respect, such strategic considerations certainly fit into a heterogeneous, singularised society: "Late modern society is not a community, not a homogeneous collective, and never will be. It is pluralized in lifestyles, stratified in classes, and multiethnic. Rather, the challenge lies in the constitution of a social general that is able to assert itself in the midst of social differences and cultural heterogeneities. In contrast to the "community", in late modern "society" there is no binding form of life shared by all, and individuals are each irreducibly special – nevertheless, or precisely because of this, it is dependent on rules and their enforcement, and requires forms of recognition that carry the individuals in their, ab er also in spite of their, difference" (Reckwitz 2019, p. 290). Since participation in a voluntarily entered community – and these are cooperation networks, but also the self-organized civil society initiatives that have blossomed in recent years – and each individual transaction in it is based on voluntary decision, it is an interactional relationship that can be terminated at any time and has a high solidarity potential. In a certain contrast to traditional lifelong obligations (for example, in welfare associations or church congregations), they appear attractive not only to younger people precisely because traditional forms of community building and obligatory commitment can hardly be relied upon under highly individualized conditions of life and society. Moreover, they also represent a superior alternative to the recently renewed discussion of compulsory service for young adults.

Although experts estimate that around 800,000 civil society organisations (with around 3.7 million employees) are now active in Germany, and that there are over 600,000 registered associations alone (cf. Alscher et al. 2021 and Alter et al. 2021, p. 124), it cannot be assumed that such networks will spontaneously form and maintain themselves on a broad social basis and develop reliable organisational structures. This is especially true for those population groups where a significant welfare-enhancing and egalitarian effect could be expected from such non-monetary household-based communities. It follows that civil society organisations can only develop and spread as a result of supportive, facilitative policy initiatives: they need to be staged and developed into the social norm, and supported by a public infrastructure. A basic income could provide an impulse for this, since as a result of the "unconditional" payment by all taxpayers, an expectation of reciprocity could be triggered in the sense of a leap of faith in the citizens.

Although there have been attempts in recent decades to establish such civil society initiatives in various communities (mainly in the urban-alternative sector), German society has so far shown little imagination in inventing such experimental social arrangements, for which there is sufficient historical and international experience. In times of crisis, however, such collaborative activities beyond the market and the state have flourished (for example, in the refugee crisis), and they also play an important role in the Corona phase. The aforementioned cooperation rings or exchange networks have not developed beyond certain subcultures in Germany (in urban-alternative and student milieus), but the experiences from these socially innovative experiments have been taken up and successfully commercialised by companies of the platform economy (e.g. Airbnb with the original idea of accommodation and apartment exchange rings). Digital capitalism with all its new facets seems to be able to take up ideas and concepts from the non-profit sector and feed them into its logic of exploitation.

The still relatively high standard of living for broad sections of the population and the ingrained (if not already encrusted) political-institutional procedures for dealing with social problems limit the potential creativity of self-organised initiatives. In addition, there is the gender issue and the dominance of the male breadwinner model, which, despite signs of erosion, is still often found in the everyday lives of couples, and issues of reproduction and especially "care work" tend to be regarded as marginal. "Even if the basic income can be seen as a symbolic recognition of the contribution of all activities to social wealth, in practice it is at least questionable to what extent actors in a society still shaped by the creation of meaning within the framework of gainful employment would be prepared to completely forego social recognition in gainful employment. The question arises in particular with regard to the gender issue: a basic income can in principle be regarded as a prerequisite for Fraser's "universal caregiver model", according to which women and men could divide the roles of gainful worker and caregiver between themselves on an equal footing. Nevertheless, greater male engagement in social reproduction cannot be expected without additional policy measures and societal change" (Ketterer 2019b, p. 339).

As a result of the Corona pandemic and, in particular, the closure of public institutions (schools, kindergartens, etc.) combined with the marked expansion of home office work, the *private household* has suddenly returned to the centre of welfare state care structures. This will also provide insights into current distribution patterns (e.g. according to gender, but also social status), which can empirically stimulate the debate on "care work". The first data available to date often emphasise a retraditionalisation of gender relations (cf. Allmendinger 2021, Hipp and Bünning 2020), but premature generalisations should be warned against, as fathers also became more involved in childcare activities during the Corona pandemic (cf. Zinn et al. 2020 and Jessen et al. 2021).

In contrast, there is consensus on the relevance of public infrastructures for everyday life and especially with regard to care services (be it children or elderly people in need of help). Here, the pandemic could even give a push ("nudging") and bring the issue onto the political stage. Strategic considerations on the renewal of the economy of everyday life or a new *infrastructure policy are* also aimed in this direction. What is needed for this are "hybrid organizations and fundamental economy alliances in which either local/regional administrations or intermediary institutions take the lead in order to move politics towards a renewal of the fundamental economy" (Foundational Economy Collective 2019, p. 233; cf. also Streeck 2019; Heinze 2020b). However, the complementary interconnectedness of local infrastructure policy and a time policy oriented towards collective needs is still in its infancy in Germany, although sociological and socio-political discourses have been pointing to this for decades. So far, self-organised forms of care (be they exchange rings, childcare facilities, housing projects for the elderly, or intergenerational neighbourhood initiatives, etc.) have primarily emerged in a specific economic and socio-cultural environment, which is clearly less recruited from the socially disadvantaged groups. The withdrawal of many individuals from collective contexts (be it from the party system, trade unions, welfare associations and churches as well as clubs) also makes it difficult for cooperative networks to flourish at the local level. However, in questions of counter-movements to established politics and self-organised, non-market networks in the social and health sectors, a new dynamic has emerged in recent years. Empirical studies show a broad radius of voluntary organisations, which have also spread into disadvantaged urban neighbourhoods and focus on a policy of social integration and ecological sustainability. The organisational fields, content-related reference points and manifestations of such social innovations and specifically innovative social services are very diverse in this context (cf. Kopf et al. 2015, Roth 2020 and the contributions in Becher and Hastedt 2019).

In this context, public services of general interest would also have to be reorganized and could productively tap the hitherto unexploited potential of the nonprofit sector. The added value of civil society organizations lies not only in the provision of social services, but these can also have a socially innovative effect and stimulate public debates on the future of the social system. In this context, Collier speaks of a moral pragmatism "that could inspire a change of political course: away from polarized failure towards cooperative efforts to overcome the divisions in our societies" (Ibid. 2018, p. 291). A very far-reaching claim of a necessary future public welfare of existence with the aim of cementing such divisions would result in an "infrastructural socialism": "Economic citizenship rights, however, must also regulate the lives of working people outside the sphere of acquisition. They should establish a moratorium on rent increases and guaranteed access to electricity, water and the Internet. Health care should also be taken out of the market, and large companies should be obliged to orient their economic activities towards the common good. All these would be elements of an infrastructural socialism that could create much better conditions for working people in general – and especially for the unrecognised high achievers among them – to work and live in dignity without existential fear. This would not yet overcome class society, but it would be an important step in this direction" (Mayer-Ahuja and Nachtwey 2021, p. 120).

One dilemma regarding the *dissolution of boundaries* between gainful employment and non-work-related, socially meaningful activities must not be forgotten. It lies in the fact that, under the given framework conditions, this dissolution of boundaries offers an attractive perspective above all for those who can "afford" to employ qualified people. However, large parts of the working population currently do not have the economic leeway at all to be able to forego part of their gainful employment and thus their income, especially since it is also primarily higher income groups that benefit from subsidies in the form of tax write-offs for household-related services. Empirical studies made the problem clear as early as the 1980s: extended informal work or involvement in networks is mostly attractive to those who receive regular income from normal employment and are integrated into work- and business-related networks. When people lose their jobs, the level and scope of informal activities also decline, as evidenced by various time-budget studies (see Banerjee and Duflo 2020). In addition, there is another phenomenon. While flexible working hours and part-time work are becoming more attractive among large groups of employees, full-time employment is regaining importance at the two poles of labour demand: both for highly skilled and demanding tasks and out of necessity, especially among those who can only earn a low income anyway, even in the best case.

By adhering to traditional security institutions, the reality remains that gainful employment is the docking point to a system that promises security and maintenance of living standards. With this mechanism, the work society counterproductively places premiums and status on the worker's way of life. But not all useful activities of which man is capable have to be threaded through the eye of the needle of gainful employment. This is particularly true of the household sector and the care and provision economy: 'Around €825 billion a year is worth the unpaid work of women in Germany, according to the latest survey from 2012. This figure makes it clear: women's contribution to our standard of living in the form of unpaid work is of enormous economic importance" (Peter and Rudolf 2021). Measured in terms of the total "volume of work" (i.e. both paid and unpaid work), it can even be shown that "the share of the care and supply economy accounts for 64% of the total volume of work in Germany ... and is thus the largest sector of the economy" (ibid.) and thus also shapes our current standard of living. Given the high volume in terms of time and at the same time low visibility in economic policy debates, this raises a number of questions also regarding a social revaluation of these activities. "In the course of automation, many jobs will be lost. What is clear, on the other hand, is that care work, whether unpaid or paid, will not become less. We therefore see an urgent need to give this work the significance and value it deserves and to include it in considerations of sustainable care economies" (ibid.).

Consequently, it is interesting to consider the repertoire of institutional *alternatives* to gainful employment that is still available in modern societies or that could be staged and newly created. If work in the common sense remains reduced to paid time – or at least time that can be organized in a marketable way – how can a use of time be imagined and, if necessary, institutionalized that on the one hand provides individual as well as social and overall societal benefits, and on the other hand is not only valued and appreciated in monetary terms?

However, there is a very fundamental asymmetry between the media 'time' and 'money'. Money can be used to buy time, i.e. to procure time-saving goods and services, thus freeing up time quotas for consumption. In our social system, however, it is not always possible (at least not under the present economic and socio-structural conditions), and not for everyone, to procure money for time, i.e. to cover money requirements by an individually selectable way of using time (gainful employment). This asymmetrical exchange relationship between time and money privileges money and discriminates against time. Another advantage of money over time is based on the fact that time in itself is often not worth very much. The mere "having of time" is not an immediate source of enjoyment and quality of life, even though it holds such potentials of its transformation. For the most part, time only becomes valuable in combination with money (keyword leisure consumption) or in interaction with people. In contrast to money, saving or accumulating time itself is only possible within narrow limits. Individual time quotas cannot be pooled like many individual deposits into a savings account and then spent in arbitrary quotas. On the other hand, regardless of income and wealth position, lifetime is a "scarce commodity", which Keynes already succinctly summed up with the words "in the long run we are all dead". However, where the available time contingents coincide with high incomes, the quality of life certainly increases. Where this is not the case, however, symptoms of an institutionally induced devaluation of those portions of time that cannot be organised in a useful and socially recognised manner are apparent.

Therefore, any form of *re-qualification* of time needs an infrastructural basis. This could be a basic income at the national level, but it would also have to be supplemented by a collectively usable public service at the local level, without which time contingents potentially available for the community could easily evaporate in an increasingly individualistic consumer behaviour. In the coming years, therefore, there will be no getting around the need to start promoting and supporting collective forms of general interest provision, self-organised activities and the development of new basic social security elements to complement the traditional welfare state system (cf. Heinze 2020b). Some of the current projects aiming in this direction are still in the shadows, but they nevertheless have a potential for innovation and experience that can blossom especially in times of crisis. However, it is not only in the "hip" grassroots movements for energy transition and climate policy as well as the municipal aid networks for refugees that social cohesion is strengthened and diverse social services are organised, but also in the "normal" forms of civil society organisation – from sports clubs and senior citizens' groups to cultural initiatives, neighbourhood offices, social cooperatives and village shops. Fields of action for such socially innovative networks exist in the provision of public services in various areas, whereby the *social innovations* mostly come "from below". "Impulses for social innovations usually come from non-state actors. In addition to charities, these are numerous initiatives, foundations and projects, but also companies and social enterprises and, of course, communities such as neighbourhoods and the family. Social services are usually embedded in a kind of "welfare mix". State social services supplement family help and care, welfare organisations contribute professional services, and neighbourhood networks are a kind of early detection and aftercare system" (Strünck 2017, p. 318 f.; cf. also the contributions in Heinze 2019a).

According to the fifth German Volunteer Survey published in spring 2021, around 28.8 million people volunteered in 2019, which is almost 40% of the German population aged 14 and over. If we look at the areas in which people volunteer, "sport and exercise" is at the top, followed by "culture and music" as well as "social sector" and "school and kindergarten". Although the rates of involvement have remained stable, there has been a structural change in involvement, which is also reflected in the data. While traditional volunteering with its relatively fixed ties to organizations is shrinking, a "new" type of volunteering is growing that is more situational and flexible. The temporal scope must "fit" biographically and is accordingly smaller or more irregular. "In 2019, about seventeen percent of the engaged spend a lot of time on their voluntary activity with six or more hours. This shows a continuing trend towards less time-intensive volunteering since 1999: between 1999 and 2019, the proportion of engaged people spending a lot of time on their volunteering at six or more hours per week fell by 5.9 percentage points. In the same period, the proportion of those who invest significantly less time in their voluntary activity with up to two hours per week increased (1999: p. 50.8%, 2019: 60.0%)" (BMFSFJ 2021, p. 5).

As a result, the *engagement landscape* in Germany has become more diverse, but also more confusing, which has already been addressed with reference to the structural change in engagement, which particularly affects traditional organizations such as charities. Since 1985, the Socio-Economic Panel (SOEP) has been collecting data on the current voluntary commitment of the population aged 17 and over living in Germany (this is voluntary, non-remunerated activity within the framework of clubs, associations or social services). Whereas in 1990 around 27% of those surveyed were active as volunteers, in 2017 this figure had already risen to 32% (which extrapolates to a total of 22 million people involved in voluntary work). Here, it is important to point out the different findings on the quantitative extent of engagement due to slightly different question wording (cf. Kelle et al. 2021), because in the Volunteer Survey it is 44% instead of 32% as in the SOEP, and thus 30.9 million people instead of 22 million. The data for the different generations are revealing, because apparently engagement varies according to life stage. "The middle ages of 30–59 show the highest engagement rates overall. One striking thing is the rising trend among young adults. Among 17–29 year-olds, the proportion of those involved in volunteering increased from 26% in 1990 to one-third now. The main increases in this age group occurred as early as 2009 – well before the suspension of compulsory military service in 2011. Secondly, the increases in the oldest age groups are striking. The engagement rate of 60–76 year-olds, i.e. those who are about to retire or have just passed the statutory retirement age, increased by more than ten percentage points to 33% during the period under review. Even for the – due to increasing life expectancy – growing group of persons who are 77 years or older and have already long since reached retirement age, the share has increased by 14% points since 2009 to now 23%. Overall, it can be seen that people over 65 in particular are more involved today than they were 20–30 years ago" (Burkhardt and Schupp 2019, p. 769; cf. also Generali Altersstudie 2017 and Erlinghagen and Hank 2019).

The willingness to volunteer therefore continues to be strong and is even more likely to be promoted by demographic change, because older people are now in good health for longer and are increasingly getting involved in various areas of civil society. However, these potentials must also be promoted; i.e. the most flexible and low-threshold offers possible must be provided and links to existing social organisations should be established in order to avoid duplicate structures and to generate a welfare mix that should include forms of digital time commitment. But according to the SOEP data, the younger generation (those born between 1983 and 1999) is also more committed than previous generations of the same age, thus putting into perspective some skeptical statements about the allegedly more self-centered young people who hardly care about the common good. In contrast, they are more committed than average and are thus likely to increase the overall potential for charitable activities alongside the older generation, which will grow considerably in the coming years.

With regard to the *change in motivation*, an increase in intrinsically motivated engagement can be observed. Empirical studies suggest a double subjectification of engagement in some areas (cf. Heinze et al. 2017). At the individual level of those involved, it is apparent that claims to self-actualisation are widespread, especially in dynamic fields such as refugee aid. This corresponds with a tendency to reject hierarchical organisational structures, as is still the case in many traditional social organisations. The change in motivation is therefore flanked by a change in organization. Established (large) civil society organisations are increasingly being replaced by bottom-up initiatives and self-organised networks and projects. These processes of change emerged in exemplary fashion in the refugee crisis, and the Corona pandemic also revealed the various forms of social engagement in social networks, in the neighbourhood and the family, and special and successful sponsorship models of the local population with refugees developed (cf. Jursch et al. 2020).

In the first phase of the Corona crisis, they were even celebrated as systemically relevant actors from the perspective of social cohesion and gave a boost to all these social organizations by showing how important social cohesion is as the "cement" of a society and that various forms of organization participate in it that are primarily not organized through market as well as profit-oriented relationships. In the Corona pandemic, organised civil society as well as neighbourhood and family social networks were now seen as systemically relevant actors from the perspective of social cohesion. "In the last major crises in Europe – the euro crisis and the refugee crisis – the great importance of social capital and the strength of civil society were particularly evident. Commitment and action in solidarity increased then, as did various forms of political protest. The autumn of 2015 is rightly considered the 'finest hour' of civil society in Germany. At that time, millions of citizens got involved, many of them for the first time, countless initiatives to help refugees were founded, and established associations and charities also got involved" (Grande and Hutter 2020, p. 27; cf. also the contributions in Grande et al. 2021).

However, this public esteem has not been sustained, nor have the conditions for social cohesion improved – on the contrary. After more than a year of pandemic experience, the situation is now different: there is hardly any talk of a lasting return of a state with the power to act after the mishaps in the area of virus control measures, and public debates discuss government policy failures and an *exhausted country*. Disappointments with politics and dysfunctionalities of state regulations (such as the diffusion of responsibility) characterize the image of society in the spring of 2021, although the achievements of individuals and civil society organizations continue to be evaluated positively.

However, the required social distance as well as the exit restrictions have negatively affected many civil society organisations and networks (from senior citizens' groups and choirs to sports clubs and self-help groups) because they ultimately cannot function permanently without close distance. For example, sports clubs, which have more than 24 million members in Germany, have not only been temporarily hit by the lockdowns, but have seen a significant drop in membership (especially among children and young people). It is therefore not surprising that 52% of them expect an "existence-threatening situation" in the coming months (cf. Bidder et al. 2020). With the motto "stay at home", it is difficult to maintain social networks and also to practice solidarity if social contacts and community building are to be limited to the bare minimum in order to minimise the risk of contagion. The deceleration associated with the abrupt and unprecedented disruptions of public life has referred many people back to their immediate living environment and triggered a *withdrawal* from public space. Forms of community spirit, as seen in the management of the refugee crisis, were also evident at the onset of the Corona pandemic, but the restrictions on contact have caused these to shrink with the duration of the pandemic. Interviews on the ground point to the limits of solidarity-based aid potentials and the need for public infrastructures. "What remains questionable in our interviews, however, is how resilient village-level support services are in the long term. It is possible that the great willingness to help only exists and functions in the case of minor everyday challenges and as long as only a few are affected by the epidemic. For the stability of social structures, it therefore remains important that local public institutions are able to act – from local government to Caritas" (Simmank and Vogel 2020, p. 2; cf. also Klein 2021).

In the meantime, social cohesion is no longer growing, but is being put to the test, and unlike companies, which in most cases can restart their "business" after the pandemic, this is difficult for many civil society organisations. Some of them are threatened with collapse (as many sports clubs report) because social engagement just does not re-establish itself "at the push of a button", if one disregards the high spontaneous readiness in the neighbourhood as well as civil society after the heavy rainfalls in mid-July 2021 in Rhineland-Palatinate and areas in North Rhine-Westphalia. Without public funding, some of these social infrastructures, which are centrally the "social glue" of society, will very likely not survive. Civil society would then not be the winner of the Corona crisis, which many social diagnosticians hoped for, but would have to be understood as a victim (cf. the contributions in Grande et al. 2021.).

6.3 Services of General Interest and Collective Infrastructure as a Public Task

In federal policy, too, a shift towards services of general interest as a task of the state can be seen in various pronouncements by the governing parties CDU/CSU and SPD. In particular, the leading municipal associations (the German Association of Cities and Towns, the German Association of Towns and Municipalities and the Association of Municipal Enterprises) emphasise the importance of municipal infrastructures, which create quality of life and social cohesion locally. It was not only in Germany that strategic considerations on a new infrastructure policy at the local level were already rampant before the spread of the Corona pandemic. Mariana Mazzucato, director of the London-based Institute for Innovation and Public Purpose, is also critical of the long-held assumption of a "lean state" within the social sciences and advocates the expansion of state infrastructure programmes: "Recent research on the effect of the size of the state on economic growth is almost unanimous that little state is bad. Then, for example, it is unable to maintain basic infrastructure, the rule of law (in the form of funding for the police and the educational needs of the population. On the other hand, the same research concludes that too much government might be "bad" if it is the result of policies that crowd out (that is, reduce) the private sector[1] or interfere incisively with private sector activities and interfere in too many people's lives (Bergh and Henrekson 2002). Within these obvious parameters, however, the ideal size of the state is difficult to quantify – not least because it depends to a large extent on what the state is supposed to do and what value one attaches to the state's activities" (Mazzucato 2019, p. 308).

It is interesting to note the broad political spectrum in Germany, which is in favour of opening up to *solidarity-based economic strategies* and encompasses almost all political currents. At the EU level, the revitalisation of the idea of solidarity and also explicitly of the idea of cooperatives is also being sought in the context of the debate on social innovations. In the meantime, government policy also sees the limits of its own ability to act and in many issues relies on the co-production and self-responsible contribution of individual and collective social actors. Nevertheless, the ultimate responsibility lies with the guaranteeing state, although

---

[1] "Crowding out usually refers to the negative effects that government spending can have or government investment can have on private investment, mainly because government borrowing drives up interest rates (making it harder for private businesses to borrow or because the government moves into areas previously reserved for the private sector). Analyses of this crowding out do not shape up easily because of the lack of analysis of what the private sector is willing to do" (Mazzucato 2019, p. 308)

the implementation and provision of services in the various fields of services of general interest can be carried out by public, non-profit or private institutions. Even if there is a certain consensus in public discourse as well as among political actors that market radicalism as a system of governance has run its course, new mixed-economy (subsidiary) solutions continue to be difficult to implement in an unsettled environment with a great deal of mistrust. Although the state, overcoming its regulatory barriers, has learned its lesson from the historical crises and has launched large-scale economic stimulus programmes, this has placed an enormous burden on public budgets and the effects in terms of overcoming the Corona pandemic cannot yet be clearly predicted. Above all, the enormous mountains of debt and their at least gradual reduction will drastically restrict the state's further options for action in the future, although there is hope that new management models will be implemented.

Since the conventional methods of risk hedging have themselves become risky, neither a strategy of nationalisation nor one of marketisation is appropriate, but rather a new complementarity between politics, the economy, communal capacity for action (an "active" civil society) and also individual responsibility are increasingly in demand. Even if the negative excesses of an "unleashed" digital capitalism have recently become persistently apparent, the market still has a central importance for the governance of society, which is also emphasised by authors who call for the domestication of market-liberal trends: "A society without a market would be a large community, that is, a type of social organisation of which the older and more recent past teaches us that it was commonly based on ruthless structures of domination or on degrading paternalistic relations of dependency. To abolish the market is a thoroughly reactionary utopia, a kind of backward-looking utopia that Marx already derided. Modernity is inconceivable without the market" (Castel 2005, p. 134; cf. on this already Polanyi 1978, esp. p. 297ff.).

So, at present, politics is about the realisation of a new *mix* of state, civil society and market, although in recent years the risk management of the market has failed and destroyed a lot of trust. Therefore, a new balance between the often ideologically occupied positions must now be sought, and if one looks at the welfare state discourses, then there is less and less talk of competing welfare state worlds (á la Esping-Andersen), rather a certain *convergence* towards socially investing and activating elements is emerging, which have also quietly transformed the German welfare state to some extent. But even these gradual steps are already difficult in an organised society in normal times of government policy, and it is even more difficult to break out of selective crisis management in favour of a formative and forward-looking perspective. What is required is a *resilient policy,* but not just in the aftermath of the immediate pandemic. "Promoting resilience means leaving the familiar comfort zone of gradual adaptation and post-crisis crisis management. In fact, resilience requires a strategic approach to building governance systems that have an impact beyond the mere correction of disruptions and failures" (Willke 2014, p. 71; cf. also ders. 2020 as well as Korte 2021). This will only succeed if the political governance repertoire is enriched through interplay with the organizations that play a decisive role in the respective functional systems and if new forms of cooperation with civil society are also established at eye level. There is no doubt that the factual power relations in the form of institutional obstacles and traditional models stand in the way of these new formative coalitions, but the Corona crisis also made it clear how fragile some power constellations are and how blockades can also be overcome. However, several factors must come together in order to reorganise the established structures in a field as sensitive as social security, especially in Germany – and this in the direction of both universalistic security and greater participation by civil society actors.

In the political-administrative system, the municipalities, in accordance with Article 28 (2) of the Basic Law, perform a large number of service and security functions within the framework of their self-administration in socio-political matters, but must be provided with the necessary financial resources for this, which obviously did not happen in the past in a comprehensive and sustainable enough manner. This applies in particular to the currently indebted municipalities, which urgently need financial support or debt relief perspectives from the federal and state governments in order to ensure the social and infrastructural services of general interest for their citizens in cooperation with independent and private providers and to be able to enforce the principle of equal living conditions in Germany enshrined in the Basic Law. For some years now, a change in the welfare state has also been observed in the field of services of general interest policy, which has been described as a development towards a welfare society, making it clear that *public services of general interest* are increasingly being implemented in the mode of co-production by the state, the economy and civil society (i.e. primarily organised civil society). Accordingly, in line with the control concepts outlined above, the discourses on services of general interest in Germany are concerned with the development of an appropriate "welfare mix" at local level, which relies on a readjustment of the various forms of control. However, services of general interest cannot be understood merely as the provision of goods and services with which people are supplied as passive recipients. In a modern understanding, services of general interest are aimed at promoting and strengthening people's autonomy of action and enabling them to lead a good life independently, to participate in social life and to help shape it.

In this context, the pronounced fragmentations in the German care model must be overcome, which, against the background of diverse challenges (expanded problem situations and needs, cost pressure, problems of legitimacy and control, declining mobilisation capacity of the established social organisations), are meanwhile also perceived by the actors themselves as restrictions to action. "Only with integrated concepts and an intensification of knowledge flows between the various actors can these challenges be mastered. Since both social innovations and economically useful innovations increasingly result from the linking of different subject areas, interactive learning processes of systemically networked actors must therefore be initiated. From the perspective of many local socio-political actors, the main problem is not unresolved problems but a lack of coordination in dealing with them" (Grohs 2018, p. 97 f.).

If one considers the complexity of the social policy institutional system at the municipal level, including the entanglements with civil society organizations such as the welfare associations, then it is not surprising that recent policy research theories and organizational sociological studies speak of a "bounded rationality". From the perspective of micropolitical approaches, the *veto positions* still dominant in most political organizations, which want to leave everything "as it was" or prefer a strategy of problem postponement, become more understandable (cf. Bogumil and Schmid 2001). However, a classic "business-as-usual" strategy can no longer provide the necessary regulatory services of politics and, moreover, such a slogging through creates new problems of control.

As initiators and moderators of control processes, local authorities have a decisive role to play, particularly with regard to hybrid forms of care. Care should be provided where it is needed, irrespective of sectoral boundaries. With a view to the care and provision of elderly people who are increasingly dependent on support services, the task of enabling and securing the availability and networking of professional services in the neighbourhood is particularly important for the municipalities. In addition, an infrastructure must be provided that supports the independent organisation of everyday life, opens up access to shops, authorities and offices, public transport, specialist medical care, but also to leisure, cultural and educational opportunities that is as barrier-free as possible and thus enables people to remain in their familiar living environment even with increasing restrictions. This view is explicitly expressed in the Federal Government's Eighth Report on the Elderly, which was presented in August 2020. There, with regard to the *potential uses of digitalisation* for improving local public infrastructure, it states. "Basic infrastructures of municipal services of general interest (energy and transport networks) form the basis for neighbourhood platforms that network and make visible a wide range of local actors (municipal institutions, companies, civic activists) and their offerings. Offers can be accessed via one's own internet access (e.g. via smartphones), and some neighbourhoods also use digital displays in public spaces (as a "digital bulletin board") to make information flows visible" (BMFSFJ 2020, p. 50 f.; cf. also the contributions in Heinze et al. 2019).

However, it is increasingly expected from politics that the interfaces of different care systems as well as actor structures in the social space are better networked. Both municipalities and non-profit social organizations are challenged in this matter, especially since the challenges to public services have increased considerably in recent years and will continue to grow due to demographic change alone. Some sociologists already saw the Corona crisis as a fundamental transformation and a concrete turning point for a reorientation of society: "Part of this analysis is to point out that the dominant paradigm of society has entered a deep crisis, so that the operative normal mode is suspended in many areas – which is why the opportunity for a change of path now exists. That an effective instrument for this is available in the form of the state capable of acting has been impressively demonstrated by the crisis reaction" (Rosa 2020, p. 211).

However, this focus on the spirit of solidarity at the beginning of the pandemic turned out to be a temporally and objectively limited care for one another, because social selectivities became massively apparent after only a few months of experiencing the crisis. For this reason, restraint should be exercised with pathetic formulations on the breakthrough of solidarity as a special resource (Promberger 2020) or social design maxim; rather, the different degrees to which the health effects are affected, depending on socioeconomic position, are becoming increasingly apparent (Wachtler et al. 2020), and the socially disintegrating effects of the pandemic also need to be addressed. These can be seen in the intensification of socio-economic polarisation as well as in an increase in conflicts (for example, demonstrations against the Corona requirements by numerically small but widely perceived circles in the media, often in conjunction with politically right-wing groups). "The longer the crisis lasts, the more clearly the respective economic and social interests become apparent. Already existing fault lines within and between societies are now becoming clearly visible. From a sociological point of view, there is nothing to suggest that the virus and the pandemic crisis are levellers or cohesion boosters. On the contrary, the pandemic is a relentless accelerator of division. Covid-19 attacks social cohesion" (Vogel 2020, p. 468). Dörre is similarly gloomy about the socio-economic and ecological consequences triggered by the Corona pandemic and specifically sees "the danger that harsh distributional struggles, increasing inequality and desolidarization will further complicate a sustainability turnaround" (Dörre 2020, p. 165; cf. also Rehder 2021). Moreover, the Corona pandemic also leads to new experiences regarding the use of time in a phase of deceleration due to output constraints as well as a grown budget of freely available time. "The time is there, but the leisure is missing. This restlessness we feel doesn't just come from the outside, as we thought. It also comes from within, which can be seen precisely in the fact that instead of listening to a Wagner opera or reading Thomas Mann, we surf through social media or fire up Netflix. So we do things that deliver short-cycled high stimulation density at low resonance value" (Rosa 2021).

Following the various waves of the Corona pandemic, this tendency to spend time passively could also be supported by the fact that a thoroughly considerable number of shops and gastronomic establishments will not survive at local level, which can already be seen in many cities after a good year and a half of the virus. What is needed, therefore, are *strategic alliances* that revitalize the inner cities and town centers and turn them into attractive public spaces. One could orientate oneself on the following guiding ideas, which could also provide starting points for a re-vitalisation of voluntary engagement forms:

- more (public) offers in the fields of culture, education, health, green and water areas;
- more (social/cooperative) housing in the immediate inner city context;
- more areas for environmental transport, more public transport services, sustainable design of delivery and CEP transport (CEP: courier, express and parcel services);
- more initiatives in public space, more attractive public space;
- more social infrastructure facilities;
- more small shops, craft businesses, start-ups;
- more involvement, consultation and ownership of the local business community;
- more consideration of climate protection;
- more participation of the population. (Hatzfeld and Weis 2021, p. 3).

The list makes it clear that there are many opportunities to promote and strengthen civil society at the municipal level, if the willingness of citizens to get involved is accompanied by suitable opportunities and freedom for participation. "In recent years, municipalities have developed into exciting fields of experimentation for new forms of democratic participation. In view of the increasing divisions in our society, building bridges between different social groups and improving the ability and willingness to engage in dialogue should play a central role in promoting citizens' willingness to get involved. I think it is particularly important to have projects that are not just about 'having a say' and that focus on *doing things together*, as is the case in neighbourhood self-help, citizen cooperatives, village shops, etc." (Grande 2021, p. 179). However, ideas and projects of this kind also require support, whether through public funding or through the diverse foundation culture in Germany.

If the consideration is followed that a vibrant civil society is not without preconditions, but rather is more necessary than ever, especially in the wake of the Corona pandemic, through an *active engagement policy* for the targeted promotion of sustainable civic engagement, one can follow up on proposals by Edgar Grande (2021), who identified fields of action and places for engagement learning: on the one hand, through greater promotion of learning civic engagement as part of school activities. "In this way, on the one hand, engagement can be learned in cooperation between schools and local civic organizations, and on the other hand, bridges can be built to local associations and initiatives, and thus organized civil society can be better networked and strengthened" (loc. Cit., p. 177) Another field for promotion is the expansion of voluntary services for young people into a more binding – and at the same time better materially compensated – form of engagement. Whether the introduction of a compulsory social year, which has recently been the subject of increasing public debate, would really be the superior alternative to the principle of voluntarism with improved incentives is open to doubt. Here, too, Edgar Grande's proposal seems to be the most effective way forward: "What is important here is that society formulates a clear expectation of young people: We want you to do something for society! You may decide for yourself what you do and how you do it, but doing nothing is not an acceptable option" (op. cit., p. 177). Another important point is aimed at the hinge as well as the interlocking between civic activities and gainful employment and the question of how the permeability between the wage-centered world of work and volunteer engagement can be improved. One proposed solution is the introduction of paid "engagement leave." "Incidentally, it is not only civil society that would benefit from this; the experience gained by employees in the course of their social and cultural activities could also benefit companies... The promotion of civic engagement is not just a task for the state; companies are also called upon to do this" (loc. Cit., p. 179).

6.4 Implementation Options (Basic Child Allowance)

With the child benefit, an unconditional cash benefit is already granted by the state today, since no expectations regarding the respective use are connected with it. With a one-time simple application at the beginning of life, a fixed amount – depending on the number as well as age-related order of the siblings – is then regularly transferred up to a certain age. Currently, the monthly amount is 219 for the first and second child, 225 € for the third as well as 250 € for the fourth as well as further children. It is usually paid to the parents, who are also responsible for the child's living expenses. Child benefit is a tax concession (negative tax) with the aim of exempting the minimum subsistence level of the child from income tax. For parents with a (very) high income, this payment is offset against the child allowance (currently €8388/year). So also the millionaire receives a tax bonus/exempt amount in this way for himself as well as for his possibly already very wealthy children.

Child benefit can thus be regarded as a partial basic income for a certain age group of a society, since it is paid unconditionally. Various authors, such as the physician and psychotherapist Baukje Dobberstein[2], also call for the general conversion of the basic tax allowance into a partial basic income against this background. In terms of financing, the conversion of the basic personal income tax allowance into a partial basic income paid out monthly would be a largely cost-neutral reform – apart from the bureaucratic administrative implementation costs. "In the process, further experience with unconditional payments can be gained and an important contribution made to a more positive understanding of the state. It could also be implemented initially as a model project in one region for all those living there" (Dobberstein 2021). The argumentation is that it makes a difference, especially psychologically, to receive money as opposed to not having to pay money, and that it cannot be ruled out that the relationship between the state and its citizens will change if one receives a cash payment every month instead of having something deducted from one's tax obligations at the end of the month.

With regard to the implementation of a basic child benefit, the Bündnis 90/DIE GRÜNEN party has provided for a fixed guaranteed amount for children in its election manifesto for the Bundestag elections. "Our proposal: to combine child benefit, child supplement, social benefit for children and the needs for education and participation into a new independent benefit. With a basic child benefit, every child receives a fixed guaranteed amount, and children in families with low or no income also receive a GarantiePlus amount" (Bündnis 90/ Die Grünen 2021, p. 53). In doing so, their plans take up a motion already tabled in parliament in 2019 to introduce a basic child allowance (Deutscher Bundestag 2019). The underlying reform concept builds on a concept paper presented by Becker and Hauser (2012) some time ago. The aim is to hereby contribute to reducing hidden child poverty and also to change the current situation in which parents with high incomes receive higher tax-financed support from the state through tax allowances for their children than parents with small or medium incomes who receive child benefit payments. One of

[2] *Child benefit for all – unconditional basic income (baukje.de)*

the core elements of such a *basic child allowance* is the principle that a basic child allowance is a child's benefit in its own right, which is no longer counted as income by parents (or the community of need) when they receive means-tested benefits from the social security system. Thus, as much as possible, the multitude of child-related benefits would need to be consolidated into one integrated benefit. As the parents' income increases, the basic child benefit could be reduced to a minimum amount that corresponds to the current maximum relief provided by the tax allowances for children.

A motion submitted by the party "Die Linke" (German Bundestag 2020) aims in the same direction to introduce a basic child allowance. This too aims to re-determine the subsistence minimum for children and young people and to change the empirical basis of calculation. Both proposals were discussed in a public session of the Committee for Family Affairs, Senior Citizens, Women and Youth of the German Bundestag in spring 2020 and the majority of the invited experts were sympathetic to both proposals. Nevertheless, an expert report (Bonin 2020) pointed out that the proposals made by the Greens and the Left for a basic child allowance would involve a high financial outlay. For example, simulations of a generously funded basic child security model (like that of the Left Party) have shown that this would lead to *net costs* for the public purse of more than €40 billion per year. The Greens' model would also result in costs of between €20 and €25 billion.

With regard to a basic security for children, the SPD's concept is currently still comparatively far removed from the position of the Greens. "We have therefore developed a concept of basic child security consisting of two central areas. Firstly, an infrastructure that enables fair education and participation for all children. It includes good and non-contributory day-care centres, all-day provision for school children, a social infrastructure for young people and free travel for children and young people on local bus and rail services. On the other hand, the basic child allowance consists of a new child allowance that is automatically paid out to secure the family's existence and is graduated according to the family's income – the higher the need for support, the higher the child allowance" (SPD 2021, p. 49). So far, the SPD refuses to engage in a debate within the Grand Coalition on the adequacy of the level of basic welfare benefits. Although it is clear that the SPD is obviously initially focusing on improving the infrastructure for children's education and participation – such as the introduction of a statutory right to all-day care for primary school children – it remains unclear at present whether the SPD would also go along with an increase in the tax minimum subsistence level and an increase in child benefit.

The CDU/CSU, on the other hand, are primarily aiming for a full basic tax-free allowance for children in their election manifesto in order to introduce "child splitting" in taxation (CDU/CSU 2021).

The Free Democrats advocate a so-called child opportunity allowance, which consists of a basic amount, a flexible amount and a non-material opportunity package (FDP 2021).

One month before the election day for the German Bundestag, a broad alliance of different organizations presented – as already mentioned – the demand for a basic child security: "We call on all parties to give the highest priority to the fight against child poverty and to introduce a basic child security. The basic child allowance belongs in the next coalition agreement and must be implemented as a priority project in the coming legislative period."[3]

6.5 Basic Guaranteed Income in the Election Programmes of the Parties Represented in the Bundestag

In Sect. 1.6, the topic has already been classified for all parties represented in the Bundestag[4] . Within the CDU/CSU parliamentary group there is a clear rejection of an unconditional basic income. This is most recently documented in the CDU/CSU's rejection of the draft bill by the Federal Minister of Labour and Social Affairs, Hubertus Heil, to introduce means-testing, at least for a limited period of time, for people drawing Social Code Book II. The proposal did not make it into the cabinet, but was rejected in advance by the CDU/CSU parliamentary group. "However, we continue to stand by the principle of 'promote and demand' and also reject a deferral of these special regulations." A "creeping introduction" of an unconditional basic income would be out of the question. "Because this devalues work and makes placement in work largely less attractive."[5] In the election manifesto of the CDU/CSU presented in June 2021, the BGE is also given a public stage for the first time by an explicit rejection: "But there will not be an unconditional basic income with us".[6]

[3] https://www.dgb.de/presse/++co++845a0f6e-00f6-11ec-a312-001a4a160123

[4] With regard to the AfD's position on this, cf. Section 1.6.

[5] ZEIT-Online of 10 January 2021. *dispute over Hartz IV: CDU rejects plans of SPD Minister Heil on social benefits | ZEIT ONLINE*

[6] P. 61 *Government programme.pdf (csu.de)*

The term "basic income" does not appear at all in the current SPD party programme. The previous basic income (Hartz IV) is to be further developed and "renamed" as a citizen's income in the "future programme" and is to be seen as an introduction to a new "understanding of a welfare state that provides support and is close to the people" (SPD 2021, p. 41). Nevertheless, in the meantime, even within the SPD – at least within various working groups – individual papers and proposal concepts are fermenting which no longer have any fundamental reservations about elements of a basic income. For example, within the working group for the self-employed in North Rhine-Westphalia, a welfare state paper has been drawn up which also outlines in detail an institutional transition of our present system of social security into a fundamentally reformed concept "Welfare State 2030" extended by unconditional and guarantee elements of basic security. This would entail a paradigm shift in all social security systems as well as in the tax system; elements of a gradual introduction would be included[7]:

- All employed, unemployed and disabled citizens would receive a tax-financed basic income of €1200 per month. The payment would be made by the federal government and the entitlement to a basic income would only arise after a certain waiting period.
- Child benefit would be replaced by an education allowance for all parents amounting to €600 per month.
- In old age, a third tax-free stage of the basic pension of 1200 € for 40 years of work would be introduced. Likewise, by transferring young civil servants and politicians into the pension and simultaneously abolishing the income threshold, a pension level beyond 55% should be due after 45 years of work and there should be a compulsory minimum company pension financed by employers.[8]

Although such a comprehensive reform concept as well as the paradigm shift still show strongly employment-centred elements of the granting, the proposal of the working group proves that in the meantime also within the SPD innovative ideas of a comprehensive restructuring of the social, income and tax systems are maturing, in which the minimum safeguarding of a social participation would in future primarily be taken over by the welfare state.

[7] https://www.agsnrw.net/wp-content/uploads/sites/1216/2020/10/Waru_wir_einen_neuen_Sozialstaat_ben__tigen_.pdf, P. 4

[8] https://www.agsnrw.net/wp-content/uploads/sites/1216/2020/10/Waru_wir_einen_neuen_Sozialstaat_ben__tigen_.pdf

In its election manifesto for the 2021 Bundestag elections, the FDP relies on a so-called "liberal citizen's income". In it, the means-tested system of social basic security benefits is to be maintained, but all tax-financed social benefits such as unemployment benefit II, basic security in old age, assistance with living costs or also housing benefit are to be combined in one benefit and also one state agency. "Basic security must become less bureaucratic, more dignity-preserving, more performance-based, more digital and above all more opportunity-oriented" (FDP 2021, p. 72). In addition, the FDP wants to improve the opportunities for SGB II benefit recipients to earn additional income in the sense that the transfer withdrawal rate would be reduced. To this end, the Friedrich Naumann Foundation of the FDP has already commissioned a microsimulation study to estimate the additional costs associated with improved incentive structures in the low-income sector (cf. Blömer and Peichl 2019). The reform scenarios conclude that employment would increase without causing additional costs for the state budget and could even lead to additional revenues. A reform of the supplementary income rules in the transfer sector advocated by the FDP could increase the efficiency of the tax and transfer system and at the same time lead to higher disposable incomes for the households concerned.

In its election manifesto, the Bündnis 90/Die Grüne party is also committed to the basic principles of a means-tested minimum income scheme. Nevertheless, the party also wants to overcome Hartz IV and replace it with a "guaranteed security". The concept of their guaranteed security includes the following elements. On the one hand with the immediate increase of the rule set around 50? as well as in the future fundamentally renewed computation methodology for the determination of an appropriate height of the soziocultural subsistence level. Further the past sanction practice is to be stopped and the bureaucratic personnel resources necessary for this into the job switching to be steered. The imputation of income is to be made more attractive in the sense that the transfer withdrawal rate is to be lowered so that additional gainful employment leads to a noticeably higher income. Young people in benefit-receiving families should be allowed to earn money without offsetting. The current means test is to be made less bureaucratic and in future will be checked solely with the help of a self-disclosure. In addition, the benefits of the guarantee scheme are to be gradually individualised. In organisational terms, subsistence benefits are to be merged in future and their payment integrated into the tax system. Model projects to evaluate the effect of an unconditional basic income are explicitly welcomed and should be supported (Bündnis 90/ Die Grünen 2021, p. 46).

In this context, the election programme of Bündnis 90/Die Grünen (Alliance 90/ The Greens) for the elections to the Berlin House of Representatives, which will also take place in September 2021, goes one step further and is more concrete with regard to the implementation of model projects: "In the long term, we must take into account the diversification of the world of work, which is particularly noticeable in Berlin, and look for new ways to be able to provide people in the most diverse life situations with secure support and assistance when needed. Based on the experiences with the Corona emergency aid, the Participation Opportunities Act as well as the pilot project of a "solidary" basic income, we therefore want to develop a pilot project for an unconditional basic income in Berlin in cooperation with Berlin research institutions... The pilot project is intended to change this by examining the possible effects of a basic income, among other things, on opportunities in employment and on the social situation in Berlin. The pilot project is intended to change this by researching the possible effects of a basic income on, among other things, job search opportunities, entrepreneurial activities, civic engagement, physical and mental health, integration and social participation"[9] (paragraph 311–329).

In its election manifesto, the Left Party intends to create a "new welfare state". The party wants to ensure "that no one has less than 1200 € at their disposal per month. That is our limit for a fair minimum income. We want an insurance against unemployment that also covers the self-employed. The time for Hartz IV is over. We are introducing a minimum income that is free of sanctions, i.e. cannot be reduced.[10]

6.6 Consumption Tax or Money Transaction Taxation

Oswald Sigg was one of the initiators of the 2016 referendum in Switzerland on an unconditional basic income, which failed with 23%. The former vice-chancellor and speaker of the Swiss Federal Council announced in April 2021 that he currently intended to make a second attempt for a basic income in Switzerland. Under the motto "For an affordable basic income", the initiative text has now been published (Fig. 6.1) and the initiative intends to collect signatures for a second attempt at a new referendum as early as summer 2021.

Corona and the growing economic existential hardship of many households had been the reason for him to launch a second initiative with the aim of achieving "social crisis resistance through a secure livelihood for all". In contrast to the first referendum, however, the central unresolved issue of financing a basic income is

[9] Chapter 4: Creating the Future – Innovations and Opportunities (Election Programme-LDK 2021, Antragsgruen) (antragsgruen.de)

[10] https://www.die-linke.de/wahlen/wahlprogrammdebatte-2021/wahlprogrammentwurf-2021/

The Federal Constitution is amended as follows:

Art. 110a Unconditional basic income

1. The Confederation guarantees people resident in Switzerland an unconditional basic income. This is intended to enable a dignified existence in family and society, participation in public life and commitment to the common good.
2. The basic income should be designed in such a way that it contributes to the maintenance and further development of social security.
3. The law regulates the amount and the receipt of the basic income.
4. It also regulates the financing of the basic income. All sectors of the economy contribute to the financing on a solidarity basis, based on their earnings. In particular, the financial sector and technology companies are taxed appropriately and the burden on gainful employment is reduced.

Art. 197 No. 13

13. transitional provisions on Art. 110a (unconditional basic income)

1. The Federal Assembly shall issue the implementing provisions for Article 110a no later than five years after its adoption by the people and the cantons.
2. The law regulates the coordination of the unconditional basic income with the benefits of the existing social insurance schemes as well as any adjustments to these benefits.
3. It determines the extent to which an unconditional basic income can be paid to people who are not resident in Switzerland.
4. In order to ensure financing through revenues from all sectors of the national economy, the Confederation shall tax appropriately in particular:
   a. the transactions of the financial sector;
   b. the sales of technology companies; and
   c. the capital income.
5. For this purpose, the Confederation shall disclose the total sum of the income of natural persons and the total sum of the profits of legal persons.
6. The Swiss National Bank publishes data on all cashless payment transactions, including giro transfers, interbank payments, intrabank payments and payments via new technologies.

Fig. 6.1 Initiative text of the federal popular initiative "Living in dignity" – for an affordable unconditional basic income. (Source: https://grundeinkommenschweiz.ch//)

the focus of the popular initiative this time. To this end, on the one hand, all transactions in the financial sector should be taxed in Switzerland in future, i.e. the introduction of a *micro-tax,* which Sigg has been advocating for years. Furthermore, appropriate taxation of the turnover of technology companies as well as of capital income is to be financed. With regard to compatibility with the system of social security in force in Switzerland, the text of the initiative also argues for the "preservation and further development of social insurance" and not for a mere substitution by a BGE. However, as in the first referendum, the initiative again makes no precise statements regarding the specific amount of a BGE.

If it should indeed be possible to concretise the financing of a BGE and not to solve a taxation of the labour factor with the help of a corresponding increase in income tax, but to successfully establish a corresponding tax in times of the advancing digitalisation of all monetary transactions, it is by no means impossible that the scepticism towards the BGE will decrease significantly.

A money transaction tax would also have the advantage, compared to a consumption tax propagated by DM founder Götz Werner (2018), that low-income households would not currently be disproportionately affected by price increases and could therefore easily find themselves worse off than under the current system.

The model of an Automated Payment Transaction (APT) Tax, on which the new Swiss initiative is based, has been discussed in financial science for some time (cf. Feige 2000). For Switzerland, Bollinger (2017) calculated that with a tax rate of 1 per mille (0.5 per mille for debits as well as 0.5 for credits) as well as the current payment transaction amount, an annual additional tax revenue of 200 billion Swiss francs. The renowned financial scientist Marc Chesney of the University of Zurich is also discussing the introduction of a micro-tax on all electronic financial transactions and is a co-initiator of a corresponding Swiss popular initiative. His initiative promotes such a tax not for purposes of a BGE, but to replace Switzerland's existing value-added tax and direct federal taxes and their bureaucracy through this new tax (the same, 2019). Overall, the experience with the discourse on a basic income in Switzerland shows that this has gradually introduced the political system and the public to the topic, and that the increase in attention has also led to a rise in *approval ratings*. Nevertheless, there remains a lot of "socio-political work in which the most suitable interfaces between the existing and a guaranteeist welfare state are identified, appreciated and used" (Albert 2019, p. 97).

In 2019, the Scientific Service of the German Bundestag determined the volume of all annual financial transactions[11] in Germany (Wissenschaftlicher Dienst 2019). The estimate amounts to more than 300,000 billion euros. All financial transactions would in principle be usable for a micro tax such as an APT tax and could generate additional tax revenues of more than 300 billion euros per year with a tax rate of 1 per mille in total as well. With such perspectives of possible tax revenues, it becomes clear that a society that is fundamentally ready for a basic income and the politicians would also have found a political majority for corresponding changes in the law, then the financing question could also be politically implemented by levying new taxes that would also not burden the labour factor.

6.7 Linking Climate and Social Policy (CO_2 Tax)

On April 30, 2021, the Federal Constitutional Court (Bundesverfassungsgericht, BVerfG) in Karlsruhe published its decision on a constitutional complaint against the Climate Protection Act of 2019, finding that the national climate protection targets and the annual emission levels allowed until 2030 are incompatible with

[11] This included financial transactions by all private individuals, all legal entities, all companies and all persons acting within the scope of German federal law.

fundamental rights of our constitution because "sufficient measures for further emission reductions from 2031 onwards are lacking."[12] The judges in Karlsruhe gave the legislature until the end of 2022 to reform the Climate Protection Act. The core of the ruling is above all that for the path to the goal of greenhouse gas neutrality by the year 2050, transparency must be established for drastic steps to reduce emissions, so that after the year 2030 the burden on the younger generation in particular is not disproportionate. Thus, one generation should not be allowed "to consume large parts of the CO_2 budget under a comparatively mild reduction burden, if this would at the same time leave the following generations with a radical reduction burden – described by the complainants as a "full brake" – and expose their lives to serious losses of freedom" (BVerfG 2021, para. 192).

In its ruling, the court addressed the *freedoms* protected under the Basic Law as well as *intergenerational justice,* which could possibly also raise the question of the intergenerational justice of the current principle of contribution equivalence in the further debate, which was elaborated as no longer given in Chap. 2. In the judgment, the judges ultimately call on policymakers to determine, through democratic competition, the best way of legally mandating climate protection in harmony with as many associated freedoms as possible. As a possible way to meet climate targets, however, it is not ruled out that this could end up being implementable only with less freedom for all. "In practical terms, the protection of future freedom here requires us to initiate the transition to climate neutrality in good time. In all areas of life – such as production, services, infrastructure, administration, culture and consumption, ultimately with regard to all processes that are still CO_2 relevant today – developments must begin that make it possible to make meaningful use of fundamental freedom even later, then on the basis of CO_2 free behavioural alternatives" (BVerfG 2021, para. 248).

The ruling could have the consequence that it becomes the starting point for a *general reorientation in* the entire party landscape, in which the reality of the climate crisis and the reduction of emissions that cannot be postponed is widely accepted. This is because, for the first time, it is stated that "Article 20a of the Basic Law is a justiciable legal norm intended to bind the political process in favour of ecological concerns, also with a view to future generations that are particularly affected" (BVerfG 2021, p. 197). Thus, it cannot be ruled out that, as a result of the

[12] Decision of 24 March 2021–1 BvR 2656/18.

BVerfG's ruling, climate protection "will finally become a culture war issue"[13] in which political actors – as, incidentally, was observed in the USA under the last President Donald Trump – quite deliberately resist insight, and invoke people's freedom to continue to want to live with the help of fossil energy and accuse eco-lobby groups of wanting to prevent free living. On the other hand, it cannot be ruled out that the long-practiced *repression on the part* of politicians and voters alike on the subject of climate change will now also spill over into the subject of the demographic challenges facing the social security system. "In this context, experience from the climate change debate should have shown by now that prolonged denial and suppression does not solve the problem but makes it worse. Perhaps climate policy will gain momentum more quickly and more effectively than the debate on pensions, because ageing is more difficult to grasp and to present in the media than the consequences of recent extreme weather events" (Sunde 2021, p. 18).

It remains to be seen how a more ambitious climate package for Germany will be designed and whether a reduction of CO_2 emissions by 2030 from 55% will be increased to a rate of rather 62 or even 68%, as recommended by the climate expert councils. But one consequence seems to be indisputable or almost "without alternative" for a market-based solution; namely that the estimated CO_2 consumption taxation[14] must be raised *significantly in order* to be able to achieve substantial behavioural changes in the direction of a CO_2 consumption reduction in the medium and long term. A strategy of this kind would not be very effective if pursued by the individual countries alone, and it is imperative that it be flanked by international coordination of CO_2 pricing. In its most recent report, the German Council of Economic Experts (SVR) also recommended reducing distorting incentives through energy price reform while at the same time strengthening CO_2 pricing in order to strengthen the market's coordination function. According to calculations for the SVR, the price necessary to achieve the national climate targets in 2030 would be between €70 per tonne of CO_2 in the most favourable scenario and €350 per tonne of CO_2 in the least favourable scenario (SVR 2020, para. 380).

Based on the current price of fossil fuels of around €25, it should become clear that this will result in enormous *price increases*. In its last report, the SVR pointed out that distributional effects from a rising CO_2 price would have to be addressed with appropriate measures. "A CO_2 price that would ensure target achievement in

[13] See the commentary by Jonas Schaible „Jetzt bloß kein Kulturkampf"on SPIEGEL Online from 29.4.2021

https://www.spiegel.de/politik/deutschland/erfolgreiche-klimaklage-jetzt-bloss-kein--kulturkampf-a-504b72f8-9951-44b2-bde8-f46f249fd3c9

[14] https://www.bmu.de/themen/klima-energie/klimaschutz/nationale-klimapolitik/co2-preis/

2030 therefore has distributional relevance" (SVR 2020, para. 381). Also the DIW Berlin has already brought up the model of a so-called climate premium, which could also be classified as a partial BGE, in the context of an expert opinion for the Federal Ministry for the Environment, Nature Conservation and Nuclear Safety (BMU) regarding possible distributional effects of a growing CO_2 price. "The additional revenue from the energy tax, which falls to private households, should initially be returned to them in the form of a "climate premium", which is designed as a uniform per capita transfer in the amount of €100 per year (adjusted by the general price development). The climate premium is to be paid out as an equal amount to every inhabitant, from the newborn to the elderly, from the homeless to the billionaire" (Bach et al. 2019, p. 66).

In the context of the BVerfG ruling and the structural changes called for by politicians, sociologist Sighard Neckel observes: "Without social differentiation, it is precisely those broad sections of the population that contribute significantly less to greenhouse gases and have saved significantly more CO_2 in recent decades that are taken into custody in the demands for ecological renunciation. Thus, even in countries such as Germany, climate change is becoming a justice problem on which social conflicts about the fair distribution of burdens are igniting" (Neckel 2021, p. 18). In the meantime, it seems indisputable that an increasing CO_2 price requires not only an economic policy but also, and above all, a *socio-political flanking, for* which various measures are proposed and publicly debated (cf. Petersen and Rausch 2021). In addition to means-tested transfer payments to low-income households, proposals that would be more compatible with basic income models are discussed in particular. "The payment of a lump sum to all citizens* (i.e. a capitation payment) and all businesses." (ibid. 2021, p. 3). The reason given is that "higher CO_2 prices threaten to increase existing social inequalities because they will hit poor and small households particularly hard" (ibid. 2021, p. 7).

These future scenarios are also the starting point for Brüne Schloen's considerations, which seek to link the CO_2 price necessary to achieve the Paris climate targets with the introduction and financing of a substantial basic income. The initial consideration: "without a substantial basic income, an environmentally effective CO_2 tax cannot be socially legitimised; there is thus a mutual dependency relationship between the two. One can also call this a synergetic relationship" (Schloen 2020, p. 46). Against this background, it becomes clear that the management of major societal challenges that are already noticeable today must be organised on a *cross-sectoral* basis, and that this can also give rise to a new conjuncture for a basic income. Irrespective of whether a BGE in combination with a CO_2 price fulfils the expected steering function towards climate-friendly behaviour, this contribution to the discussion points to a broadening of the discourse on climate change and basic income in terms of content and political strategy. It should not be underestimated that the various civil society NGOs are striving for horizontal networking activities, and their effects on the agenda-setting of politics should be undisputed after the experiences of recent years. For example, climate activist Luisa Neubauer has been actively campaigning for the introduction of a basic income for some time now: "That's why people are promising billions to obsolete industries instead of considering whether artificial job security shouldn't come to an end now at the latest, in order to open the doors for an unconditional basic income. As far as I am concerned, we can also call this a life innovation premium".[15] One of the first to concretize the idea of financing a BGE with eco-taxes was Ulrich Schachtschneider, who at the same time also made the reference to the post-growth society: "No lifestyle will be banned, but resource-heavy ones will become heavier and resource-light ones lighter. And not only because the security of a basic income creates space for experimentation and the search for meaning beyond consumerism, but also because the increase in the cost of environmental consumption supports not only 'different' but also 'less' consumption: The serenity we need for a post-growth economy" (ibid. 2014, p. 11).

6.8 Last but Not Least: Constructive Forms for Overcoming Blockades in Thinking and Discussion

Obviously, there is a strong interest among the population, which has been further increased by the Corona pandemic, in considering and testing fundamental alternatives to the existing social security system. If this system is expanded in the future to include elements of individualized as well as low-condition or even unconditional entitlements, this holds the potential of a superior alternative to our previous conservative welfare state model. This is because the latter requires an enormous amount of bureaucracy, which has grown in recent decades and is therefore too high, with many applications and the consequence that – as a number of empirical studies show – it is also characterised by a very high proportion of non-utilisation despite fulfilment of the eligibility requirements. In this context, progressive *digitalisation* – with a similarly personalised and secure ID as, for example, the current ELSTER portal at the tax authorities – offers new possibilities for granting tax-financed benefit entitlements of a welfare state to all citizens in the form of a

[15] *taz FUTURZWEI N°16 of 10 March 2021.* https://taz.de/Luisa-Neubauer-in-taz-FUTURZWEI/!

"negative income tax". The future institutions of the welfare state would then be left with the task of being able to concentrate on factual advice, mediation and integration and therapy services.

An objectification and constructive further development of the debate on a BGE, which has been animated by civil society for a long time anyway, could be substantially further developed in the next few years by a *strategy package* comprising the following five points:

1. When the newly elected German Bundestag is constituted in autumn 2021, the parliamentary groups could jointly decide to set up an Enquete Commission on the Welfare State 2030. This body, consisting of a balanced mix of academics and politicians, could discuss the advantages and disadvantages of fundamental welfare state models by the end of the legislative period and, in the best case, also agree on a possible common reform path or transformation path by 2030. The degree of practicality of the BGE for pending welfare state reforms as well as a better coordination of taxes, transfers and levies, especially in the lower income segment, can be assessed here[16] . Different financing models can be weighed up and a timetable and phased plan for a possible implementation phase can be developed. Through media coverage, such a commission of enquiry also offers sufficient opportunity to clarify comprehensive reform measures in public debates. At the same time, expectations of such a commission should not be too high. "Enquiry commissions are therefore able to reinforce an already existing trend, but they do not initiate one" (Altenhof 2002, p. 341).
2. In order to flank a factual, open-ended debate of an Enquete Commission, the federal government newly formed in 2021 should initiate and implement three to five-year scientifically accompanied model projects for evidence-based further development and testing of the current welfare state model under the leadership of the competent ministries of the BMAS, BMFSFJ and BMF, in order to conduct socio-political reform debates in the future with a stronger evidence base and less traditional adherence to principles. In terms of content, the model projects should be oriented towards the provision of a basic income with or without conditions, and should be designed in such a way that both generalisable impact analyses are possible and comparability between the individual

[16] The urgent need for reform of the tax and transfer system for those capable of working has also been identified by the German Council of Economic Experts (Sachverständigenrat zur Begutachtung der gesamtwirtschaftlichen Entwicklung, SVR) in the chapter "Securing opportunities for advancement, strengthening incentives to work" (paragraphs 648–723) in its Annual Report 2020.

models is sought. In this way, the following possible transformation steps could be tested in concrete terms in model projects, accompanied scientifically and the basis for discussion for future debates on the welfare state could be broadened on the basis of evidence:

- The effects of an increased standard need or even lower-condition conditions for receiving minimum income benefits could be tested.
- Furthermore, the existing transfer withdrawal rates could be reduced by up to 50% in several model variants when taking up employment.
- The amount of untouchable assets and financial reserves (Schonvermögen) could be increased.
- The effects of a complete abolition of sanctions could be part of a trial.
- Strict individualisation of eligibility conditions for married and non-married persons in joint households, combined with reforms of maintenance obligations.
- Simplified payment procedures by tax authorities in the sense of a negative income tax model.
- What difference does it make to people to receive a basic monthly payment ex ante rather than pay correspondingly lower taxes/levies ex post?

3. In addition to scientifically independent evaluation research, the competent ministries should initiate an open dialogue with a "Reform Alliance Welfare State 2030", in which, in addition to the trade unions and employers' associations as central actors of the contribution-financed welfare state, welfare associations, churches, representatives of the solo self-employed and cultural workers should also be involved for participation. In such a body, which complements the work of parliament, government and civil society organisations, *institutional transformation processes* for a welfare state model 2030 should also be concretised.
4. In parallel to these activities, a "Welfare State 2030 Monitor" could be established in 2022, also jointly coordinated by the BMAS, BMFSFJ and BMF, in which comparative empirical studies on short-, medium- and long-term changes in social sentiment in the area of social policy and state welfare could be conducted. The aim is to take a *representative stock of* the assessments and the mood regarding reform options currently being debated.
5. In order to also duly involve civil society in such a debate and to overcome the level of populist and polarisingly fuelled yes-no citizens' petitions as a direct

democratic involvement, the topic "Welfare State 2030" could be taken up by *citizens' councils* within the newly created forum. This could offer the chance to pacify the current controversial debate to some extent. After all, a fundamental restructuring of our welfare state would potentially affect all citizens, which is why the appropriate participation of people in the discussion process would also be of central importance. This form (in addition to a welfare state monitor) would take account of the population's need for participation – as is also the case at grassroots level in parties and organisations alike. Citizens' councils are a negotiating format of discourse at eye level, in which arguments would be weighted back and forth. Conflicting debates seem to be particularly suitable as topics for citizens' councils. In the end, responsibility would remain with the respective political leaders.

This bundle of measures for a *change management process* would give politicians, associations, researchers, the media and the general public the opportunity to develop an informed factual basis and a basis of opinion on a politically and factually difficult and complex issue and to transform the current vision of a basic income into a realistic reform option. This functional linking of incremental reforms with a sustainable socio-politically focussed transformation strategy would be a constructive way of achieving sustainable social security and could help to overcome the blockades that have existed to date. We expect that in the *long-term transformation path of* a gradual replacement of the primarily contribution-financed system of social security with a tax-financed individual basic income, means-tested elements of social security will continue to be on hand. It will be just as important – in accordance with the principle of equality of the Basic Law – to provide all citizens with an appropriate range of public goods of general interest by investing in central areas of infrastructure and, in doing so, to include and expand the potential of civil society in a targeted manner.

After a "cash check" by the newly formed federal government in autumn 2021, however, it cannot be completely ruled out that there could be a renaissance of the debate on the scope and level of the welfare state, as it was already very widely conducted in Germany at the beginning of the 2000s. For, as explained in the book, the primarily contribution-financed system of social security, as well as the balance sheets of the social security funds, is in an increasingly *deficit state,* with the consequence of necessary increasing tax-financed compensation payments. Against this background – also in the light of coming to terms with the learning processes caused by the Corona pandemic – a broad dialogue will be necessary in society as to what *level of welfare state as well* as the availability of public goods and infrastructures the population in Germany will at all be prepared to afford and by whom and to what extent these social benefits can be financed in the future, also in the sense of a generationally just solution. In this context, it will also play a role whether the future burdens will be allocated to the federal budget alone and which ones can be assumed additionally by the Länder and the municipalities. For the pressure to justify the pure expansion of the welfare state will certainly increase in the comparatively short time remaining until the ambitious climate targets are achieved, as will the demographically induced pressure on the social security systems.

Against this background, social policy will probably also have to answer the question of whose needs should be prioritized and at what *pace* reforms and transformations should take place. Fundamental reform proposals could easily be associated with overly high hopes which, when tested in practice, could be linked to major unintended side-effects. In our view, the future social system should therefore be closely interlinked with an investing and coordinating state in the area of municipal infrastructure and livelihood provision, and should be committed to the principles of citizen-friendliness, sustainable and inclusive socio-cultural livelihood provision. A less bureaucratic granting and claiming of basic security benefits must also include improved incentive effects for all forms of *work*, taking into account the sense of justice of a broad majority of the population. The time should therefore be used to place the future of our welfare state at the centre of a broad, empirically substantive and open-ended debate, including the vision of an unconditional basic income as a reform option.

References

Abgeordnetenhaus Berlin, 2021: Wortprotokoll der 67. Sitzung des Ausschuss für Integration, Arbeit und Soziales vom 27. Mai 2021, Berlin

Adriaans, J./Liebig, S./Schupp, J., 2019: In Germany, younger, better educated persons, and lower income groups are more likely to be in favor of unconditional basic income. DIW-Weekly Report, 9(15), 128-134

Agersnap, O./Jensen, A.S./Kleven, H., 2020: The Welfare Magnet Hypothesis: Evidence from an Immigrant Welfare Scheme in Denmark. NBER Working Paper 26454

Albert, E., 2019: Ein neues Modell in der Experimentierphase: Das Grundeinkommen als Instrument sozialstaatlicher Modernisierung, in: Baumgartner, A. D./Fux, B. (Ed.), Sozialstaat unter Zugzwang, Wiesbaden: Springer VS, 75–100

Allmendinger, J., 2019: „Eine Art Lügendetektor". Interview mit J. Allmendinger, in: Die Zeit v. 9.5. 2019, 70

Allmendinger, J., 2021: Es geht nur gemeinsam! Wie wir endlich Geschlechtergerechtigkeit erreichen, Berlin: Ullstein

Altenhof, R., 2002: Die Enquete-Kommissionen des Deutschen Bundestages. Wiesbaden: Westdeutscher Verlag.

Alter, R./Schrade, M./Graf Strachwitz, R., 2021: Zivilgesellschaft in der Corona-Bewährungsprobe, in: Klein, A., Sprengel, R., Neuling, J., (Ed.), Zivilgesellschaft in der Corona-Krise und ihre Gestaltungsaufgaben (Jahrbuch Engagementpolitik 2021), Frankfurt: Wochenschau Verlag, 121–127

Althaus, D., 2006: Für ein solidarisches Bürgergeld, in: Stimmen der Zeit, 224 (11), 723–728

Althaus, D., 2007: Das Solidarische Bürgergeld. Sicherheit und Freiheit ermöglichen Marktwirtschaft, in: Borchard, M. (Ed.), Das Solidarische Bürgergeld – Analysen einer Reformidee, Stuttgart: Lucius & Lucius, 1–12

R. G. Heinze, J. Schupp, *Basic Income - From Vision to Creeping Transformation of the Welfare State*,
https://doi.org/10.1007/978-3-658-40269-3

Alscher, M./Priller, E./Burkhardt, L., 2021: Zivilgesellschaftliches Engagement, in: Statistisches Bundesamt et al., Datenreport 2021. Ein Sozialbericht für die Bundesrepublik Deutschland, a. a. O., 399–407

Andreß, H.-J./Kronauer, M., 2006: Arm – Reich, in: Lessenich, S./Nullmeier, F. (Ed.): Deutschland – eine gespaltene Gesellschaft, Frankfurt: Campus, 28–52

Arnold, D./Arntz, M./Gregory, T./Steffes, S./Zierahn, U., 2016: Herausforderungen der Digitalisierung für die Zukunft der Arbeitswelt, in: ZEW policy brief, No. 8/2016, Mannheim

Ash, T.G., 2021: Neue Lösungen für neue Probleme: warum (und wie) sich der Liberalismus im 21. Jahrhundert neu erfinden muss, in: Neue Zürcher Zeitung vom 19.1.2021. https://www.nzz.ch/feuilleton/timothy-garton-ash-so-gelingt-die-zukunft-des-liberalismus-ld.1596438

Atkinson, A.B., 1996: The Case for a Participation Income, in: The Political Quarterly 67(1), S. 67–70

Atkinson, A.B., 2015: Inequality. What Can Be Done? Cambridge, MA/London: Harvard University Press

Bach, S./Schupp, J., 2018: Solidarisches Grundeinkommen: alternatives Instrument für mehr Teilhabe, DIW aktuell, No. 8, Berlin: DIW

Bach, S./Isaak, N./Kemfert, C./Kunert, U./Schill, W.-P./Schmalz, S./Wägner, N./Zakla, A., 2019: CO_2-Bepreisung im Wärme- und Verkehrssektor: Diskussion von Wirkungen und alternativen Entlastungsoptionen, Politikberatung kompakt No. 140, Berlin: DIW

Bachrach, P./Baratz, M. S., 1962: Two Faces of Power, in: The American Political Science Review, 56(4), 947–952

Bachrach, P./Baratz, M. S., 1963: Decisions and Nondecisions: An Analytical Framework, in: The American Political Science Review, 57(3), 632–642

Bachrach, P./Baratz, M. S., 1977: Macht und Armut. Eine theoretisch-empirische Untersuchung, Frankfurt am Main: Suhrkamp

Bachmann, R./Jäger, P./Jessen, R. 2021: A Split Decision: Welche Auswirkungen hätte die Abschaffung des Ehegattensplittings auf das Arbeitsangebot und die Einkommensverteilung? RWI-Materialen Heft 144, Essen: RWI

Bäcker, G./Naegele, G./Bispinck, R., 2020: Sozialpolitik und soziale Lage in Deutschland, 6. Auflage (2 Bände), Wiesbaden: Springer VS

Backhaus-Maul, H., 2018a: Unergründete Tiefen. Zum Stand der immer noch jungen Wohlfahrtsverbändeforschung, in: Heinze, R.G./Lange, J./Sesselmeier, W., (Ed.), Neue Governancestrukturen in der Wohlfahrtspflege, a. a. O., 17–37

Backhaus-Maul, H., 2018b: Sozialpolitische Entwicklungslinien in Deutschland, in: Grunwald, K., Langer, A. (Ed.), Sozialwirtschaft. Handbuch für Wissenschaft und Praxis, Baden-Baden: Nomos, 118 ff

Backhaus-Maul, H., 2019: Zentrifugalkräfte in der Freien Wohlfahrtspflege: Wohlfahrtsverbände als traditionsreiche und ressourcenstarke Akteure, in: Freise, M., Zimmer, A., (Ed.), Zivilgesellschaft und Wohlfahrtsstaat im Wandel, a. a. O., 83–100

Badura, B./Gross, P., 1976: Sozialpolitische Perspektiven, München: Piper

Baer, S. 2018: Kein Glücksversprechen: Deutsches Verfassungsrecht und „Das Gute Leben", in: Mayer, K.U. (Ed.), Gutes Leben oder gute Gesellschaft?, Stuttgart: Wissenschaftliche Verlagsgesellschaft, 179–192

Bahle, T., 2019: Soziale Mindestsicherung, in: Obinger, H./Schmidt, M. G. (Ed.), Handbuch Sozialpolitik, Wiesbaden: Springer VS, S. 761–782

Bandelow, N.C./Vogeler, C.S., 2019: Koalitionsverhandlungen als Entscheidungsfenster im deutschen politischen System? Das Beispiel PKW-Maut, in: Zohlnhöfer, R./Saalfeld, T. (Ed.), Zwischen Stillstand, Politikwandel und Krisenmanagement. Eine Bilanz der Regierung Merkel 2013–2017, Wiesbaden: Springer VS, 533 ff

Banerjee, A.V./Duflo, E., 2020: Gute Ökonomie für harte Zeiten, München: Penguin

Bartsch, M./Beyer, S./Fichtner, U./Garbe, S./Gathmann, F./Knobbe, M./Kosanke, L./Medick, V./Schaible, J./Schrader, H./Traufetter, G., 2021: Das Märchen von den wechselwilligen Deutschen, in: Der Spiegel Nr. 24 vom 11.06.2021

Bauer, F./Bennett, J./Dietz, M./Fuchs, P./Gellermann, J./Globisch, C./Gottwald, M./Kupka, P./Nivorozhkin, A./Promberger, M./Lobato, R./Wolff, J./Zabel, C., 2021: Evaluation des Teilhabechancengesetzes: Erste Antworten, aber noch viele offene Fragen, IAB-Forum 16. März 2021

Baumgartner, A.D./Fux, B. (Ed.), 2019: Sozialstaat unter Zugzwang? Zwischen Reform und radikaler Neuorientierung, Wiesbaden: Springer VS

Baruth, S./Schnapp, K. U., 2015: Ministerialbürokratien als Lobbyadressaten, in: Zimmer, A./Speth, R. (Ed.), Lobby Work. Interessenvertretung als Politikgestaltung, Wiesbaden: Springer VS, 245 ff

BBSR (Bundesinstitut für Bau, Stadt- und Raumforschung), 2020: Regionale Lebensverhältnisse – Ein Messkonzept zur Bewertung ungleicher Lebensverhältnisse in den Teilräumen Deutschlands, BSR-Online-Publikation Nr. 06/2020

Becher, B./Hastedt, I. (Ed.), 2019: Innovative Unternehmen der Sozial- und Gesundheitswirtschaft, Wiesbaden: Springer VS

Beck, U., 1986: Risikogesellschaft. Auf dem Weg in eine andere Moderne, Frankfurt am Main: Suhrkamp

Beck, U., 2000a: Die Zukunft von Arbeit und Demokratie, Frankfurt am Main: Suhrkamp

Beck, U., 2000b: Die Seele der Demokratie: Bezahlte Bürgerarbeit, in: Beck, U. (Ed.), Die Zukunft von Arbeit und Demokratie, Frankfurt am Main: Suhrkamp, 416–447

Beck, U., 2017: Die Metamorphose der Welt, Berlin: Suhrkamp

Beck-Gernsheim, E., 1994: Auf dem Weg in die postfamiliale Familie – Von der Notgemeinschaft zur Wahlverwandtschaft, in: Beck, U./Beck-Gernsheim, E. (Ed.), Riskante Freiheiten, Frankfurt am Main: Suhrkamp, 115–138

Becker, I./Hauser, R., 2012: Kindergrundsicherung, Kindergeld und Kinderzuschlag: Eine vergleichende Analyse aktueller Reformvorschläge, in: WSI Diskussionspapier 180, Düsseldorf.

Becker, I./Hauser, R., 2009: Soziale Gerechtigkeit – Ein magisches Viereck, Berlin: Edition Sigma.

Beckert, J., 2010: Die Finanzkrise ist auch eine Vertrauenskrise. Jahresbericht 2009 der Max-Planck-Gesellschaft zur Förderung der Wissenschaften e. V., München, 14–23

Beckmann, F., 2019: Minijobs in Deutschland, Wiesbaden: Springer VS

Beckmann, F., 2020: Die soziale Sicherung geringfügig Beschäftigter: Zur Bedeutung individueller Erwerbspräferenzen in Zeiten flexibilisierter Arbeit, in: Zeitschrift für Sozialreform 66(2), 99–127

Beckmann, F./Hoose, F./Schönauer/A.-L., 2017: Alles bleibt, wie es nicht war. Wirtschaftliche und gesellschaftliche Entwicklungen im Spannungsverhältnis von Kontinuität und Wandel, in: Hoose, F./Beckmann, F./Schönauer, A.-L. (Ed.), Fortsetzung folgt. Kontinuität und Wandel von Wirtschaft und Gesellschaft, Wiesbaden: Springer VS, 3–32

Beckmann, F./Heinze, R. G./Schad, D./Schupp, J., 2021a: Hartz-IV-Reformvorschlag: Weder sozialpolitischer Meilenstein noch schleichende Einführung eines bedingungslosen Grundeinkommens, Berlin: DIW Aktuell Nr. 58 vom 12.2. 2021

Beckmann, F./Heinze, R. G./Schad, D./Schupp, J., 2021b: Erzwungene Modernisierung? Arbeitsverwaltung und Grundsicherung in der Corona-Pandemie, Politikberatung kompakt 161, Berlin: DIW Berlin

Beckmann, F./Schad, D., 2021. Der soziale Arbeitsmarkt in Zeiten der Corona-Krise: Auslauf- oder Zukunftsmodell?, in: Sozialer Fortschritt 70(1), 3–18.

Beckmann, F./Spohr, F., 2022: Arbeitsmarkt und Arbeitsmarktpolitik: Grundlagen, Wandel, Zukunftsperspektiven, Konstanz: UVK/utb.

Bentele, V., 2021: Wir denken neu. Damit Deutschland sich nicht weiter spaltet, München: Europa Verlag

Bergh, A./Henrekson, M., 2002: Government size and growth. A survey and interpretation in the evidence, in: Journal of Economic Surveys, 25(1), 91–110

Berlin-Brandenburgische Akademie der Wissenschaften (Ed.), 2008: Leitlinien Politikberatung, Berlin

Bernau, P., 2021: Amtsmüde, in: Frankfurter Allgemeine Sonntagszeitung vom 27.6.2021, 21

Berzel, A./Klenk, T., 2021: Metagovernance in the Social Investment State – Lessons from the German Case, MS, in: Pinheiro, R./Trondal, J. (Ed.), Organizing and Governing Local Government Institutions (i. E.)

Beyeler, M., 2020: Gemeinschaft und Sozialstaat? Transformationschancen in unterschiedlichen Wohlfahrtsregimen, in: Baumgartner, A. D. /Fux, B. (Ed.), Sozialstaat unter Zugzwang?, a. a. O., 281–302

Benanav, A., 2020: Automation and the Future of Work, London/New York: Verso.

Beznoska, M./Hentze, T./Hüther, M., 2021: Zum Umgang mit den Coronaschulden. Simulationsrechnungen zur Schuldenstandquote, IW-Policy Paper 7/21

Bidder, B. et al, 2021: So geht es uns, in: Der Spiegel Nr. 9 vom 27.02.2021, 8–16

Blätte, A., 2019. Politikberatung aus sozialwissenschaftlicher Perspektive, in: Falk, S. et al. (Ed.), Handbuch Politikberatung, a. a. O., 25–38

Bledow, N./Busemeyer, M. R., 2021: Lukewarm or enthusiastic supporters? Exploring union member attitudes towards social investment and compensatory policy, in: Journal of European Social Policy, Vol. 31(3), 267–281

Blömer, M./Peichl, A., 2019: Anreize für Erwerbstätige. Zum Austritt aus dem Arbeitslosengeld-II-System und ihre Wechselwirkungen mit dem Steuer- und Sozialversicherungssystem, Studie Im Auftrag der Friedrich-Naumann-Stiftung, Ifo Forschungsberichte 98/2019

Blömer, M./Peichl, A., 2021: Mikrosimulation verschiedener Varianten eines Bedingungslosen Grundeinkommens in Deutschland. ifo Forschungsberichte 121/2021, München

BMAS (Bundesministerium für Arbeit und Soziales) (Ed.), 2020: Gesamtbericht zur Evaluation des allgemeinen gesetzlichen Mindestlohns nach § 23 Mindestlohngesetz, Forschungsbericht 558, Berlin

BMAS (Bundesministerium für Arbeit und Soziales) (Ed.), 2021a: Lebenslagen in Deutschland, Der Sechste Armuts- und Reichtumsbericht der Bundesregierung, Berlin

BMAS (Bundesministerium für Arbeit und Soziales) (Ed.), 2021b: Sozialbericht 2021, Berlin

BMF (Bundesministerium für Finanzen) (Ed.), 2021: BMF Monatsbericht April 2021, Berlin

BMFSFJ (Bundesministerium für Familie, Senioren, Frauen und Jugend) (Ed.), 2016: Siebter Altenbericht. Sorge und Mitverantwortung in der Kommune – Aufbau und Sicherung zukunftsfähiger Gemeinschaften, Berlin

BMFSFJ (Bundesministerium für Familie, Senioren, Frauen und Jugend) (Ed.), 2020: Achter Altenbericht. Ältere Menschen und Digitalisierung, BT-Drucksache 19/21650 vom 13.08.2020, Berlin

BMFSFJ (Ed.), 2020: Dritter Engagementbericht der Bundesregierung: Zukunft Zivilgesellschaft: Junges Engagement im digitalen Zeitalter, Bonn: Deutscher Bundestag/Drucksache 19/19320 vom 14.05.2020

BMFSFJ (Bundesministerium für Familie, Senioren, Frauen und Jugend) (Ed.)/Simonson, J. et al/DZA, 2021: Freiwilliges Engagement in Deutschland. Zentrale Ergebnisse des Fünften Deutschen Freiwilligensurveys, Berlin

BMF (Bundesministerium für Finanzen), 2020: Finanzbericht 2021. Stand und voraussichtliche Entwicklung der Finanzwirtschaft im gesamtwirtschaftlichen Zusammenhang, Berlin

BMI (Bundesministerium des Inneren/Bundesregierung), 2021: Demografiebericht. Bericht der Bundesregierung zur demografischen Lage und künftigen Entwicklung des Landes, Berlin

BMI (Bundesministerium des Inneren), 2019: Unser Plan für Deutschland. Gleichwertige Lebensverhältnisse überall, Berlin

BMR (Business Metropole Ruhr), 2020: Wirtschafts-Bericht Ruhr 2020, Essen

BMWE (Bundesministerium für Wirtschaft und Energie) (Ed.), 2020: Gutachten des Wissenschaftlichen Beirats beim Bundesministerium für Wirtschaft und Energie: Öffentliche Infrastruktur in Deutschland: Probleme und Reformbedarf, Berlin

BMWi (Bundesministerium für Wirtschaft und Energie), 2021: Vorschläge für eine Reform der gesetzlichen Rentenversicherung. Gutachten des Wissenschaftlichen Beirats beim BMWi, Berlin

Bode, I., 2013: Die Infrastruktur des postindustriellen Wohlfahrtsstaats, Wiesbaden: VS

Bogner, A., 2021: Die Epistemisierung des Politischen, Stuttgart: Reclam

Bogumil, J., 2017: Die verschlungenen Wege der Politikberatung. Erfahrungen aus dem Bereich der Verwaltungspolitik der Bundesländer, in: Hoose, F./Beckmann, F./Schönauer, A.-L. (Ed.), Fortsetzung folgt. Kontinuität und Wandel von Wirtschaft und Gesellschaft, a. a. O., 431–445

Bogumil, J./Schmid, J., 2001: Politik in Organisationen. Organisationstheoretische Ansätze und praxisbezogene Anwendungsbeispiele, Wiesbaden: VS

Bogumil, J./Seuberlich, M., 2015: Gestalten statt Verwalten. Ressortübergreifende Präventionspolitik. Erfolgsfaktoren und Hindernisse in den KeKiz-Kommunen, Schriftenreihe Arbeitspapiere wissenschaftliche Begleitforschung »Kein Kind zurücklassen!«, Band 4, Gütersloh

Bogumil, J./Jann, W., 2020: Verwaltung und Verwaltungswissenschaft in Deutschland. Eine Einführung, Wiesbaden: Springer VS (3., vollständig überarbeitete Auflage)

Bohmeyer, M./Cornelsen, C., 2019: Was würdest Du tun? Wie uns das Bedingungslose Grundeinkommen verändert, Berlin: Econ

Böick, M., 2021: Vom Markt zurück zum Staat: Was den Umbruch von 1990 mit der Krise von 2020 verbindet, in: Florack, M./Korte, K.-R./Schwanholz, J. (Ed.), Coronakratie. Demokratisches Regieren in Ausnahmezeiten, Frankfurt/M., 269–281

Bollinger, F., 2017: Reinvent the System. Mikrosteuer auf dem Zahlungsverkehr (automatische Mikrosteuer). Working Paper (mimeo), Zürich

Bonin, H., 2020: Stellungnahme im Ausschuss für Familie, Senioren, Frauen und Jugend, Ausschussdrucksache 19(13)84, Berlin

Bonß, W., 2000: Was wird aus der Erwerbsarbeitsgesellschaft?, in: Beck, U. (Ed.), Die Zukunft von Arbeit und Demokratie, a. a. O., 327–415

Bourdieu, P., 1982: Die feinen Unterschiede. Kritik der gesellschaftlichen Urteilskraft, Frankfurt/Main: Suhrkamp; zuerst 1979: La distinction. Critique sociale du jugement, Paris: Les Éditions de Minuit

Bregman, R., 2020: Utopien für Realisten. Die Zeit ist reif für die 15-Stunden-Woche, offene Grenzen und das Bedingungslose Grundeinkommen, Reinbek: Rowohlt (13. Auflage)

Brettschneider, A., 2019: Editorial: Fragmentierung und Integration – Schnittstellenprobleme und Schnittstellenmanagement im deutschen Sozialstaat. in: Sozialer Fortschritt 68 JEd., 741 ff

Bröchler, S., 2004: Kalliope im Wunderland. Orientierungen, Bedarfe und Institutionalisierung von wissenschaftlicher Politikberatung im bundesdeutschen Regierungssystem, in: R. Schützeichel/T. Brüsemeister (Ed.), Die beratene Gesellschaft, Wiesbaden: VS, 19ff

Bruckmeier, K./Hohmeyer, K., 2018: Arbeitsaufnahmen von Arbeitslosengeld-II-Empfängern: Nachhaltige Integration bleibt schwierig, IAB-Kurzbericht No. 2/2018

Bruttel, O., 2020: Die Auswirkungen des gesetzlichen Mindestlohns – Eine Bilanz. Ifo Schnelldienst 73(4), 7–9

Bude, H., 2008: Die Ausgeschlossenen. Das Ende vom Traum einer gerechten Gesellschaft. München: Hanser

Bude, H., 2010: Einübung in Bürgerlichkeit, in: Bude, H./Kaiser, P./Kauffmann, B. (Ed.), Bürgerlichkeit ohne Bürgertum. In welchem Land leben wir?, München, 189 ff

Bude, H., 2021: Pandemie und Gesellschaft. Ein Gespräch über eine Zeitenwende (Ed. Von T. Hartmann/J. Dahm/C. Krell), Bonn: Dietz, 12–58

Bundesarbeitsgemeinschaft der Freien Wohlfahrtspflege e. V. (BAGFW) (Ed.) 2018: Gesamtstatistik 2016, Berlin

Bundesministerium für Wirtschaft und Energie (BMWi) (Ed.), 2019: Gesundheitswirtschaft – Fakten und Zahlen, Ausgabe 2018, Ergebnisse der Gesundheitswirtschaftlichen Gesamtrechnung, Berlin

Bundesverfassungsgericht (BVerfG), 2010: Urteil des Ersten Senats vom 09. Februar 2010 – 1 BvL 1/09 – Rn. 1–220 (Regelleistungen nach SGB II), Karlsruhe

Bundesverfassungsgericht (BVerfG), 2019: Urteil des Ersten Senats vom 05. November 2019 – 1 BvL 7/16 – Rn. 1–225 (Sanktionen im Sozialrecht), Karlsruhe

Bundesverfassungsgericht (BVerfG), 2021: Beschluss des Ersten Senats vom 24. März 2021- 1 BvR 2656/18 -, Rn. 1–270 (Verfassungsbeschwerden gegen das Klimaschutzgesetz teilweise erfolgreich), Karlsruhe (http://www.bverfg.de/e/rs20210324_1bvr265618.html)

Bündnis 90/Die Grünen 2021: Deutschland. Alles ist drin. Bundestagswahlprogramm 2021, Berlin

Burkhardt, L./Schupp, J., 2019: Wachsendes ehrenamtliches Engagement: Generation der 68er häufiger auch nach dem Renteneintritt aktiv, in: DIW Wochenbericht, 86(42), 765–883

Busemeyer, M. R./de la Porte, C./Garritzmanna, J. L./Pavolini, E., 2018: The future of the social investment state: politics, policies, and outcomes, in: Journal of European Public Policy 25, 801–809

Busemeyer, M. R./Garritzmann, J. L., 2019: Bildungspolitik und der Sozialinvestitionsstaat, in: Obinger, H./Schmidt, M. G. (Ed.), Handbuch Sozialpolitik, Wiesbaden: Springer VS, 783–806

Busemeyer, M. R./Neimanns, E., 2019: Öffentliche Meinung und Policy Feedback, in: Obinger, H./Schmidt, M. G. (Ed.), Handbuch Sozialpolitik, Wiesbaden: Springer VS, 275–293

Buslei, H./Geyer, J./Haan, P./Harnisch, M., 2019: Starke Nichtinanspruchnahme von Grundsicherung deutet auf hohe verdeckte Altersarmut, in: DIW Wochenbericht, 86(49), 909–917

Busch, A., 2021: Wissen allein genügt nicht: Die Nutzung von politikberatenden Institutionen während der Corona-Pandemie im Vergleich, in: Florack, M./Korte, K.-R./Schwanholz, J. (Ed.), Coronakratie. Demokratisches Regieren in Ausnahmezeiten, Frankfurt/New York: Campus, 282–293

Butterwegge, C./Rinke, K. (Ed.), 2018: Grundeinkommen kontrovers, Weinheim/Basel: Beltz Juventa

Butterwegge, C., 2018: Weder gerecht noch sozial, in: Butterwegge, C./Rinke, K. (Ed.), Grundeinkommen kontrovers, a. a. O., 189–213

Castel, R., 2005: Die Stärkung des Sozialen. Leben im neuen Wohlfahrtsstaat, Hamburg: Hamburger Edition

CDU/CSU 2021: Das Programm für Stabilität und Erneuerung für ein modernes Deutschland, (https://www.csu.de/common/download/Regierungsprogramm.pdf)

Chesney, M. 2019: Eine Mikrosteuer brächte der Schweiz Konkurrenzvorteile, Interview mit U.P. Gasche vom 3.10.2019 „Eine Mikrosteuer brächte der Schweiz Konkurrenzvorteile" – infosperber

Choi, H./Varian, H., 2012: Predicting the Present with Google Trends. in: The Economic Record 88 (Special Issue) 2–9

Cohen, M.D./March, J.G./Olsen, J.P., 1972: A garbage can model of organizational choice, in: Administrative Science Quarterly (17), 1 ff.

Collier, P., 2018: Sozialer Kapitalismus! Mein Manifest gegen den Zerfall unserer Gesellschaft, München: Siedler

Cremer, G 2019a: Das bedingungslose Grundeinkommen: Kein Weg in das Reich der Freiheit. In: Roman-Herzog Institut (Ed.), Das bedingungslose Grundeinkommen. Zum für und wider eines gesellschaftlichen Reformkonzepts, Diskussionen 32, München: Roman Herzog Institut e. V., 17–27.

Cremer, G., 2019b: Für ein bedingungsloses Grundeinkommen den Sozialstaat aufgeben?, in: ORDO – Jahrbuch für die Ordnung von Wirtschaft und Gesellschaft 70(1), 215–238

Cremer, G., 2021: Ein Jahr Corona: Der Sozialstaat im Stresstest, in: Frankfurter Allgemeine Zeitung vom 15.3. 2021

Crouch, C., 2019: Gig Economy. Prekäre Arbeit im Zeitalter von Uber, Minijobs & Co.. Berlin: Suhrkamp

Currid-Halkett, E., 2021: Fair Gehandelt? Wie unser Konsumverhalten die Gesellschaft spaltet, München: btb

Czada, R., 2000: Konkordanz, Korporatismus und Politikverflechtung: Dimensionen der Verhandlungsdemokratie, in: Holtmann, E./Voelzkow, H., (Ed.), Zwischen Wettbewerbs- und Verhandlungsdemokratie: Analysen zum Regierungssystem der Bundesrepublik Deutschland, Wiesbaden: Westdeutscher Verlag, 23 ff

Czada, R., 2008: Irrwege und Umwege in die neue Wohlfahrtswelt, in: Evers, A./Heinze, R. G. (Ed.), Sozialpolitik: Ökonomisierung und Entgrenzung, Wiesbaden: VS, 186–207

Czada, R., 2019: Politikwenden und transformative Politik in Deutschland, in: Der moderne Staat-, H. 2/2019, 400–417

Czada, R., 2020: Governance-Transformation durch Richterrecht? Juristische Diskurse zur Selbstverwaltung im Gesundheitswesen, in: dms H. 2/2020, 300–321

Dahlbeck, E./Hilbert, J. (Ed.), 2017: Gesundheitswirtschaft als Motor der Regionalentwicklung, Wiesbaden: Springer VS

Dahlbeck, E./Hilbert, J., 2020: Mehr Gesundheit wagen: Eine regionale Gestaltungschance für mehr Lebensqualität und wirtschaftliche Entwicklung vor Ort, in: Lange, J. (Ed.), Mehr Gesundheit wagen. Gesundheitsregionen als Zukunftstreiber für Lebensqualität, gute Arbeit und nachhaltiges Wachstum, Loccumer Protokolle, Ev. Akademie Loccum, 9–28

Dahrendorf, R., 2019 [1986]: Ein garantiertes Mindesteinkommen als konstitutionelles Anrecht, in: Kovce, P./Priddat, B. P. (Ed.), Bedingungsloses Grundeinkommen, 331–336, Berlin: Suhrkamp

DAK Gesundheit, 2019: Regionale Pflegekompetenzzentren. Innovationsstrategie für die Langzeitpflege vor Ort. Online verfügbar unter: https://rekopflege.de/wp-content/uploads/2019/02/Handout_ReKo.pdf

Dallinger, U., 2016: Sozialpolitik im internationalen Vergleich, Konstanz: utb

Daum, T., 2017: Das Kapital sind wir. Zur Kritik der digitalen Ökonomie. Hamburg: Edition Nautillus.

Decker, O./Weißmann, M./Kiess, J./Brähler, E., 2010: Die Mitte in der Krise. Rechtsextreme Einstellungen in Deutschland 2010, Berlin: FES

Dengler, K./Matthes, B., 2021: Auch komplexere Tätigkeiten könnten zunehmend automatisiert werden. IAB-Kurzbericht Nr. 13/2021.

Deutscher Bundestag 2019a: Faire Chancen für jedes Kind – Kindergrundsicherung einführen. Bundestagsdrucksache 19/14326 vom 22.10.2019

Deutscher Bundestag, 2019b: Volumen der jährlichen Finanztransaktionen in Deutschland, Wissenschaftliche Dienste, Sachstand WD 4 – 3000 – 008/19

Deutscher Bundestag 2020a: Kinderarmut überwinden, Kindergrundsicherung einführen. Bundestagsdrucksache 19/17768 vom 11.03.2020

Deutscher Bundestag, 2020b: Petition 108191, Einführung eines Bedingungslosen Grundeinkommens vom 14.03.2020 (https://epetitionen.bundestag.de/petitionen/_2020/_03/_14/Petition_108191.nc.html)

Deutscher Städtetag, 2019: Städtetag, Gemeindebund und VKU: Daseinsvorsorge für zukunftsfeste und lebenswerte Städte und Kommunen!, Pressemitteilung vom 22.06.2019, (https://www.staedtetag.de/presse/pressemeldungen/staedtetag-gemeindebund-und-vku-daseinsvorsorge-fuer-zukunftsfeste-und-lebenswerte-staedte-und-kommunen)

Dietrich, H./Hess, D., 2021: Neue Mittelklasse? Ein empirischer Beitrag zur Reckwitz-Debatte. Infas Lagemaß, Ausgabe 11, 10–13.

Dobberstein, B., 2021: „Kindergeld für alle". Post beim Netzwerk Grundeinkommen vom 22.4.2021, (https://www.grundeinkommen.de/22/04/2021/kindergeld-fuer-alle.html)

Dörre, K., 2020: Die Corona-Pandemie – eine Katastrophe mit Sprengkraft, in: Berliner Journal für Soziologie, 30 (2), 165–190

Dörre, K./Rosa, H./Becker, K./Bose, S./Seyd, B., (Ed.), 2019: Große Transformation? Zur Zukunft moderner Gesellschaften. Sonderband des Berliner Journals für Soziologie. Wiesbaden: Springer VS

Ebert, T., 2020: Das Dilemma der Alterssicherung. Plädoyer für eine umfassende Systemreform. WISO-Diskurs No. 12/2020, Bonn: Friedrich-Ebert-Stiftung

Ehrenberg, A., 2011: Das Unbehagen in der Gesellschaft, Berlin: Suhrkamp

Eichhorst, W. et al., 2001: Benchmarking Deutschland: Arbeitsmarkt und Beschäftigung. Bericht der Arbeitsgruppe Benchmarking, Berlin/Heidelberg: Springer

Eichhorst, W./Thode, E./Winter, F., 2004: Benchmarking Deutschland 2004. Arbeitsmarkt und Beschäftigung, Berlin/Heidelberg: Springer

Eichhorst, W./Marx, P., 2019: Der Wandel der Arbeitswelt als Herausforderung für die Sozialpolitik, in: Obinger, H./Schmidt, M. G. (Ed.), Handbuch Sozialpolitik, Wiesbaden: Springer VS, 409–430

Eichhorst, W./Schroeder, W., 2019: Soziale Innovationen in der Arbeitsmarktpolitik, in: Zivilgesellschaft und Wohlfahrtsstaat im Wandel, Wiesbaden: Springer VS, 205–226

Elmer, A./Matusiewicz, D. (Ed.), 2019: Die digitale Transformation der Pflege: Wandel. Innovation. Smart Services, MWV

Enste, D. H., 2004: Die Wohlfahrtsverbände in Deutschland. Eine ordnungspolitische Analyse und Reformagenda, Köln (IW)

Ernst, G./Zühlke-Robine, K., 2018: Dienstleistungen – Wissenschaft und Forschung. Arbeit und Innovation, Baden-Baden: Nomos

Esping-Andersen, G., 1990: The Three Worlds of Welfare Capitalism, Cambridge: Polity Press

Esping-Andersen, G., 1999: Social Foundations of Postindustrial Economies, Oxford: Oxford University Press

Esping-Andersen, G., 2006: Warum brauchen wir eine Reform des Sozialstaats?, in: Leviathan 34 (1), 61–81

Esping-Andersen, G., 2015: Welfare Regimes and Social Stratification, in: Journal of European Social Policy 25(1), 124–134

Eurich, J./Glatz-Schmallegger, M./Parpan-Blaser, A. (Ed.), 2018: Gestaltung von Innovationen in Organisationen des Sozialwesens, Wiesbaden: Springer VS

Evans, M., 2018: Der „Faktor Arbeit" macht den Unterschied: Die Governance sozialer Dienstleistungsarbeit und die Institutionalisierung von Arbeitgeberverbänden im deutschen Pflegemarkt, in: Heinze, R.G./Lange, J./Sesselmeier, J., (Ed.), Neue Governancestrukturen in der Wohlfahrtspflege, a. a. O., 155–194

Evans, M./Ludwig, C., 2019: Zwischen Aufwertung, Abwertung und Polarisierung. Chancen der Tarif- und Lohnpolitik für eine arbeitspolitische „High-Road-Strategie" in der Altenpflege, Hans Böckler Stiftung: Working Paper Nr. 128, Düsseldorf

Evers, A., 2017: Lokale Governance. Engagement und die Rolle der Wohlfahrtsverbände, in: Hoose, F./Beckmann, F./Schönauer, A.-L. (Ed.), Fortsetzung folgt. Kontinuität und Wandel von Wirtschaft und Gesellschaft, a. a. O., 231–250
Falk, S./Glaab, M./Römmele, A./Schober, H./Thunert, M. (Ed.), 2019: Handbuch Politikberatung, 2., völlig neu bearbeitete Auflage, Wiesbaden: Springer VS
Freie Demokratische Partei (FDP), 2021: Nie gab es mehr zu tun. Wahlprogramm der Freien Demokratischen Partei zur Bundestagswahl 2021, (programmentwurf-nie-gab-es-mehr-zu-tun-2.pdf (fdp.de))
Feige, E.L., 2000: Taxation for the 21st Century: The Automated Payment Transaction (Apt) Tax, in: Economic Policy 15(31), 475–511
Fischer, U., 2018: Eine feministische Utopie? Grundeinkommen und Geschlechtergerechtigkeit, in: Butterwegge, C./Rinke, K. (Ed.), Grundeinkommen kontrovers, Weinheim/Basel: Beltz Juventa, 93–112
Flassbeck, H./Spiecker, F./Meinhardt, V./Vesper, D., 2012: Irrweg Grundeinkommen. Die große Umverteilung von unten nach oben muss beendet werden, Frankfurt am Main: Westend Verlag
Florack, M./Korte, K.-R./Schwanholz, J., 2021: »Coronakratie«: Konturen einer neuen demokratischen Normalität, in: Florack, M./Korte, K.-R./Schwanholz, J. (Ed.), Coronakratie. Demokratisches Regieren in Ausnahmezeiten, a. a. O., 11–22
Foundational Economy Collective, 2019: Die Ökonomie des Alltagslebens. Für eine neue Infrastrukturpolitik, Berlin: Suhrkamp
Fleisch, E./Franz, C./Herrmann, A./Mönninghoff, A., 2021: Die digitale Pille. Eine Reise in die Zukunft unseres Gesundheitssystems, Frankfurt/M.: Campus
Freise, M./Zimmer, A. (Ed.), 2019: Zivilgesellschaft und Wohlfahrtsstaat im Wandel, Wiesbaden: Springer VS
Friedrichsen, J./Schmacker, R., 2019: Die Angst vor Stigmatisierung hindert Menschen daran, Transferleistungen in Anspruch zu nehmen, DIW Wochenbericht 86(26), 456–461
Fux, B./Albert, E., 2019: Individualisierender oder kollektivierender Sozialstaat – Pfadwechsel als Option?, in: Baumgartner, A.D./Fux, B., (Ed.), Sozialstaat unter Zugzwang?, Wiesbaden: Springer VS, 325–357
Fux, B./Baumgartner, A.D., 2019: Demokratische Sozialintegration: Über Chancen und Grenzen wohlfahrtsstaatlicher Reformen, in: Baumgartner, A.D./Fux, B. (Ed.), Sozialstaat unter Zugzwang?, Wiesbaden: Springer VS, 411–431
Generali Deutschland AG, 2017: Generali Altersstudie 2017. Wie ältere Menschen in Deutschland denken und leben, Berlin/Heidelberg
Gentilini, U./Grosh, M./Rigolini, J./Yemtsov, R., (Eds.) 2020: Exploring Universal Basic Income a Guide to Navigating Concepts, Evidence, and Practices, Washington, DC: World Bank Group.
Giddens, A., 2005: „Durchwachsene Bilanz", Interview, in: Mitbestimmung H. 3/2005, 48 ff
Giddens, A., 2007: Vom negativen zum positiven Sozialstaat, in: perspektive 21, H. 33, 53 ff
Gilroy, P./Krimmer, H./Dufft, N./Kreutter, P./Olfe, P., 2018: Denkanstöße Zur Digitalisierung Der Zivilgesellschaft. Ein Mutmacherpapier. Berlin: ZiviZ
Gimmel, J. 2017: Mußevolle Arbeit oder ruheloser Müßiggang, in: Dobler, G./Riedl, P.P., (Ed.), Muße und Gesellschaft, 47–59, Tübingen: Mohr Siebeck

Glotz, P. 1986: Freiwillige Arbeitslosigkeit. Zur neueren Diskussion um das „garantierte Grundeinkommen“, in: Opielka, M./Vobruba, G. (Ed.), Das garantierte Grundeinkommen, a. a. O., 135–148

Grabka, M.M./Braband, C./Goebler, K., 2020: Beschäftigte in Minijobs sind VerliererInnen der coronabedingten Rezession, in: DIW Wochenbericht 87(45): 842–847

Grande, E., 2021: Entwicklungen und Herausforderungen der Zivilgesellschaft in Deutschland, in: Grande, B./Grande, E./Hahn, U., (Ed.), Zivilgesellschaft in der Bundesrepublik Deutschland, a. a. O., 165–181

Grande, B./Grande, E./Hahn, U. (Ed.), 2021: Zivilgesellschaft in der Bundesrepublik Deutschland., Bielefeld: transcript

Grande, E./Hutter, S., 2020: Wer hilft den Helfern? Die Zivilgesellschaft in der Corona-Krise, in: WZB Mitteilungen H. 168, 27–29

Gretschmann, K./Heinze, R. G./Hilbert, J./Schulz, E./Voelzkow, H., 1989: Neue Technologien und Soziale Sicherung. Antworten auf die Herausforderungen des Wohlfahrtsstaates, Opladen: Westdeutscher Verlag

Grözinger, G./Maschke, M./Offe, C., 2006: Die Teilhabegesellschaft – Modell Eines Wohlfahrtsstaates, Frankfurt am Main: Campus

Groh-Samberg, O./Büchler, T./Gerlitz, J-Y., 2020: Soziale Lagen in multidimensionaler Längsschnittbetrachtung. Begleitforschung zum Sechsten Armuts- und Reichtumsbericht der Bundesregierung, Berlin

Grohs, S., 2010: Modernisierung kommunaler Sozialpolitik. Anpassungsstrategien im Wohlfahrtskorporatismus, Wiesbaden: VS

Grohs, S., 2018: Wohlfahrtsverbände als föderale Organisationen. Die Rolle der Mitgliedschaftslogik im Governancewandel?, in: Heinze, R.G./Lange, J./Sesselmeier, W. (Ed.), Neue Governancestrukturen in der Wohlfahrtspflege, a. a. O., 79–102

Grohs, S., 2020: Historische und theoretische Bezüge zum (Selbst-)Verständnis von öffentlicher Verwaltung, in: P. Gromann (Ed.), Soziale Arbeit in der öffentlichen Sozialverwaltung, BASA-online-Modul 0–8.7 (Version v. 9/2020)

Grohs, S./Schneiders, K./Heinze, R. G., 2014: Mission Wohlfahrtsmarkt. Institutionelle Rahmenbedingungen, Strukturen und Verbreitung von Social Entrepreneurship in Deutschland, Baden-Baden: Nomos

Grohs, S./Schneiders, K./Heinze, R. G., 2017: Outsiders and Intrapreneurs: The Institutional Embeddedness of Social Entrepreneurship in Germany, in: Voluntas 28, 2569–2591

Grünewald, S., 2019: Wie tickt Deutschland? Psychologie einer aufgewühlten Gesellschaft, Köln: Kiepenheuer und Witsch

Grunwald, K./Langer, A. (Ed.), 2018: Sozialwirtschaft. Handbuch für Wissenschaft und Praxis, Baden-Baden: Nomos

Haagh, L., 2019: Review Article: The Political Economy of Governance Capacity and Institutional Change: The Case of Basic Income Security Reform in European Welfare States, in: Social Policy & Society, 18(2), 243–263

Haagh, L./Rohregger, B., 2019: Universal basic income policies and their potential for addressing health inequities, Copenhagen (WHO Regional Office for Europe)

Haipeter, T./Hoose, F./Rosenbohm, S. (Ed.), 2021: Arbeitspolitik in digitalen Zeiten. Entwicklungslinien einer nachhaltigen Regulierung und Gestaltung von Arbeit, Baden-Baden: Nomos

Häusermann, S., 2015: Sozialpolitik, in: Wenzelburger, G./Zohlnhöfer, R. (Ed.), Handbuch Policy-Forschung, Wiesbaden: Springer VS, 591–613
Habermacher, F./Kirchgässner, G., 2013: Das bedingungslose Grundeinkommen: Vielleicht wünschenswert, aber nicht bezahlbar, in: Wirtschaftsdienst 93(9), 593–595
Hank, K./Steinbach, A., 2020: Familiale Generationen-Beziehungen, in: Aus Politik und Zeitgeschichte (APuZ), 70 (H. 52–53), 18–24
Hassel, A., 2018: Unconditional basic income is a dead end, in: Downes, A./Lansley, S. (Ed.), It'a Basic Income, 113–117, Bristol: Polity Press
Hatzfeld, U./Weis, P., 2021: Die „neuen Innenstädte": zwischen Multifunktionalität und Gemeingut, Friedrich-Ebert-Stiftung WISO-Direkt 14/2021, Bonn
Hauser, R. 2007: Alternativen einer Grundsicherung – soziale und ökonomische Aspekte, in: Heinrich Böll Stiftung (Ed.), Die Zukunft sozialer Sicherheit, Band 2, Berlin: Böll Stiftung, 62–78,
Heckman, J.J., 2006. Skill Formation and the Economics of Investing in Disadvantaged Children, in: Science 312, 1900–1902
Heilmann, T./Schön, N. (Ed.), 2020: NEUSTAAT. Politik und Staat müssen sich verändern, München: Finanzbuch Verlag
Heinrich-Böll-Stiftung (Ed.), 2020: Öffentlicher Raum. Politik der gesellschaftlichen Teilhabe und Zusammenkunft, Frankfurt/M.: Campus
Heinze, R. G., 2011: Die erschöpfte Mitte, Weinheim/Basel: Beltz-Juventa
Heinze, R. G., 2020a: Wohnen und Teilhabe im Alter: Innovation durch Vernetzung, in: Gesellschaft • Wirtschaft •Politik (GWP) 69(2), 182–193
Heinze, R. G., 2020b: Gesellschaftsgestaltung durch Neujustierung von Zivilgesellschaft, Staat und Markt, Wiesbaden: Springer VS
Heinze, R. G./Offe, C. (Ed.), 1990: Formen der Eigenarbeit: Theorie, Empirie, Vorschläge, Opladen: Westdeutscher Verlag
Heinze, R. G./Streeck, W., 2000: Institutionelle Modernisierung und Öffnung des Arbeitsmarktes: Für eine neue Beschäftigungspolitik, in: Kocka, J./Offe, C., (Ed.), Geschichte und Zukunft der Arbeit, Frankfurt/New York: Campus, 234–261
Heinze, R. G./Streeck, W., 2003: Optionen für den Einstieg in den Arbeitsmarkt oder: Ein Lehrstück für einen gescheiterten Politikwechsel, in: Vierteljahreshefte für Wirtschaftsforschung H. 1, 25–35
Heinze, R. G./Olk, T./Hilbert, J., 1988: Der neue Sozialstaat: Analyse u. Reformperspektiven, Lambertus
Heinze, R. G./Naegele, G./Schneiders, K., 2011: Wirtschaftliche Potentiale des Alters, Stuttgart: Kohlhammer
Heinze, R. G./Beckmann, F./Hoose, F./Schönauer, A.-L., 2017: „Ich mach' mein Ding" – Wie Subjektivierung und Digitalisierung das soziale Engagement verändern, in: Bonner Akademie für Forschung und Lehre praktischer Politik (BAPP) (Ed.), Integration vor Ort. Praxiserfahrungen aus dem Ruhrgebiet, Bonn, 20–27
Heinze, R. G./Lange, J./Sesselmeier, W. (Ed.), 2018: Neue Governancestrukturen in der Wohlfahrtspflege, Baden-Baden: Nomos
Heinze, R. G./Kurtenbach, S./Üblacker, J. (Ed.), 2019: Digitalisierung und Nachbarschaft, Baden-Baden: Nomos
Heinze, R. G./Paetzel, U./Bölting, T. (Ed.), 2019a: Wasser, Wohnen, Werte. Genossenschaften schaffen Mehrwert, Essen: InWIS/Emschergenossenschaft

Hemerijck, A. (Ed.), 2017: The Uses of Social Investment, Oxford: Oxford University Press

Hensche, D., 2009: Befreiung von der Arbeit oder in der Arbeit, in: Neuendorff, H./Peter, G./ Wolf, F.O., (Ed.), Arbeit und Freiheit im Widerspruch? Bedingungsloses Grundeinkommen – ein Modell im Meinungsstreit, Hamburg: VSA-Verlag, 210–213

Herweg, N., 2015: Multiple Streams Ansatz, in: Wenzelburger, G./Zohlnhöfer, R. (Ed.), Handbuch Policy-Forschung, a. a. O., 325–353

Herweg, N./Zahariadis, N./Zohlnhöfer, R., 2018: The Multiple Streams Framework: Foundations, Refinemens, and Empirical Applications, in: Weible, C.M./Sabatier, P.A. (Ed.), Theories of the Policy Process, New York, 17–53

Hilbert, J., Bienzeisler, B., Becka, D., 2013: Gesellschaftlich notwendige Dienstleistungen – gestalten und finanzieren, Bonn (FES).

Hipp, L./Bünning, M., 2020: Parenthood as a Driver of Increased Gender Inequality During Covid-10? Exploratory Evidence from Germany, in: European Societies 23(sup1), 658–673

Hoffmann, E./Lozano Alcántara, A./Gordo, L. R., 2021: „My home is my castle“: Verbundenheit mit der eigenen Wohnung im Alter, in: Statistisches Bundesamt et al (Ed.), Datenreport 2021, 88–92

Hoynes, H./Rothstein, J., 2019: Universal Basic Income in the United States and Advanced Countries, in: Annual Review of Economics 11, 929–958

Hummel, K./Timm, G., (Ed.), 2020: Demokratie und Wohlfahrtspflege, Baden-Baden: Nomos

IAB (Ed.), 2020: Befunde der IAB-Forschung zur Corona-Krise – Zwischenbilanz und Ausblick, Nürnberg/26.08.2020 (http://doku.iab.de/grauepap/2020/IAB_Befunde_COVID-19.pdf)

Igl, G., 1988: Die Freien Wohlfahrtsverbände, in: v. Maydell, B./Kannengießer, W., (Ed.), Handbuch Sozialpolitik, Pfullingen, 182–189

ILO, 2021: The Report World Employment and Social Outlook 2021: The Role of Digital Labour Platforms in Transforming the World of Work, Genf: ILO

Institut der Deutschen Wirtschaft (IW): Corona kostet 300 Milliarden Euro BIP, IW-Nachricht vom 24.05.2021

Jain Family Institute 2021: Guaranteed Income in the U.S.A Toolkit of Best Practices, Resources, and Existing Models of Planned and Ongoing Research in the U.S. New York (mimeo), (https://www.jainfamilyinstitute.org/news/overview-toolkit-on-guaranteed-income-in-the-u.s./)

Jansen, S. A./Heinze, R. G./Beckmann, M. (Ed.), 2013: Sozialunternehmen in Deutschland: Analysen, Trends und Handlungsempfehlungen, VS Springer

Jessen, J./Spiess, C.K./Waights, S./Wrohlich, K., 2021: Sharing the Caring? The Gender Division of Care Work During the Covid-19 Pandemic in Germany, IZA Discussion Paper No. 14457

Jürgens, K./Hoffmann, R./Schildmann, C. 2017: Arbeit transformieren!, Bielefeld: transcript-Verlag.

Jursch, B./Kroh, M./Krieger, M./Legewie, N./Löbel, L.M., 2020: Patenschaften zwischen Geflüchteten und Einheimischen: Determinanten von Zufriedenheit in der Tandembeziehung, in: Gesemann F./Nentwig-Gesemann I./Seidel A./Walther B. (Ed.), Engagement für Integration und Teilhabe in der Einwanderungsgesellschaft, Wiesbaden: Springer VS, 307–326

Kaegie, U./Zängl, P., 2019: Was ist Management?, in: Wöhrle, A. et al. (Ed.), Organisationsentwicklung – Change Management, Baden-Baden: Nomos, 77–127

Kalina, T./Weinkopf, C., 2021: Niedriglohnbeschäftigung 2019 – deutlicher Rückgang vor allem in Ostdeutschland, IAQ-Report 06 (https://doi.org/10.17185/duepublico/74521)

Kaufmann, F.X., 2002: Sozialpolitik und Sozialstaat: Soziologische Analysen, Wiesbaden: VS Verlag für Sozialwissenschaften

Kaufmann, F.X., 2003: Varianten des Wohlfahrtsstaats, Frankfurt am Main: Suhrkamp

Kaufmann, F.-X., 2015: Christentum und Sozialstaat, in: Wegner, G. (Ed.), Die Legitimität des Sozialstaates. Religion–Gender–Neoliberalismus, Leipzig, 63–74

Kelle, N./Burkhardt, L./Kausmann, C./Simonson, J./Schupp, J./Tesch-Römer, C. 2021: Auswirkungen von Referenzzeiträumen auf die Selbstangaben zum freiwilligen Engagement: Ergebnisse einer experimentellen Studie, SOEPpapers on Multidisciplinary Panel Data Research 1125, DIW Berlin

Kersten, J./Neu, C./Vogel, B., 2015: Der Wert gleicher Lebensverhältnisse, Bonn: FES

Ketterer, H., 2019a: Bedingungsloses Grundeinkommen und Postwachstum, in. Petersen, D.J. et al. (Ed.), Perspektiven einer pluralen Ökonomik, Wiesbaden: Springer VS, 395–428

Ketterer, H., 2019b: Bedingungsloses Grundeinkommen als materielle und symbolische Ermöglichungsstruktur von Praktiken für die gesellschaftliche Transformation, in: Dörre, K. et al. (Ed.), Große Transformation? (Sonderband des Berliner Journals für Soziologie) Wiesbaden: Springer VS, 333–348

Kingdon, J.W., 2003: Agendas, Alternatives, and Public Policies, 2nd Edition, Boston/Toronto

Klein, A., 2021: Zivilgesellschaft im Ausnahmezustand: Corona und die Folgen, in: Klein, A./Sprengel, R./Neuling, J. (Ed.), Zivilgesellschaft in der Corona-Krise und ihre Gestaltungsaufgaben, a. a. O., 113–120

Klenk, T./Nullmeier, F., 2010: Politische Krisentheorien und die Renaissance von Konjunkturprogrammen, in: dms – der moderne staat (2), 273 ff

Klös, H.P./Schäfer, H., 2021: Der deutsche Arbeitsmarkt in der zweiten Welle der Pandemie. IW-Kurzbericht 7/2021

Knuth, M., 2018: Sozialer Arbeitsmarkt – ein Ansatz zur Erfüllung des Teilhabeauftrags des SGB II, in: Zeitschrift für Wirtschaftspolitik, 67(2), 174–188

Koch, H., 2021: Pilotprojekt Grundeinkommen: Nur eine schöne Idee, in: TAZ vom 02.06.2021

Kocka, J., 2006: Arbeiten an der Zukunft, in: Kocka, J. (Ed.), Zukunftsfähigkeit Deutschlands, Sozialwissenschaftliche Essays, Berlin (WZB-Jahrbuch), 9 ff

Kocka, J., 2020: Der Sozialstaat, ein Langzeitprojekt. Wie Bismarck sich nicht durchsetzen konnte und doch Bleibendes schuf, in: WZB-Mitteilungen H. 160, 6ff

Kohl, J., 2000: Der Sozialstaat: die deutsche Version des Wohlfahrtsstaates – Überlegungen zu seiner typologischen Verortung, in: Leibfried, S./Wagschal, U., (Ed.), Der deutsche Sozialstaat. Bilanzen – Reformen – Perspektiven, Frankfurt/New York: Campus, 115–152

Kommission Verlässlicher Generationenvertrag, 2020: Bericht der Kommission Verlässlicher Generationenvertrag Band I – Empfehlungen, Bundesministerium für Arbeit und Soziales (BMAS)

Kopf, H./Müller, S./Rüede, D./Lurtz, K./Russo, P., (Ed.), 2015: Soziale Innovationen in Deutschland. Von der Idee zur gesellschaftlichen Wirkung, Wiesbaden: Springer VS

Köppe, S./Nullmeier, F./Wiesner, A., 2007: Legitimationswandel des bundesdeutschen Sozialstaats, in: Sozialer Fortschritt 56 (9–10), 227–236

Korte, K.-R., 2019: Politikberatung von innen, in: Falk, S. et al. (Ed.), Handbuch Politikberatung, a. a. O., 129 ff

Korte, K.-R., 2021: Kuratiertes Regieren: Bausteine der Resilienz, in: Florack, M./Korte, K.-R./Schwanholz, J., (Ed.), Coronakratie. Demokratisches Regieren in Ausnahmezeiten, a. a. O., 25–42

Kovce, P., 2020: Bedingungsloses Grundeinkommen als Grundrecht?, in: Aus Politik und Zeitgeschichte (APuZ), H. 39–40, 39 ff

Kovce, P./Priddat, B.P. (Ed.), 2019: Bedingungsloses Grundeinkommen. Grundlagentexte, Berlin: Suhrkamp

Krämer, R., 2018: Grundeinkommen – Ökonomisch und finanziell nie bedingungslos, in: WSI-Mitteilungen 71(4), 331–333

Krebs, T./Scheffel, M., 2021: Raus aus der Minijobfalle. Reformen zur Entlastung geringer Einkommen und ihre Auswirkungen auf Beschäftigung, Wachstum und Verteilung sowie die öffentlichen Finanzen, in: Bertelsmann Stiftung (Ed.), Gutachten, Berlin: Bertelsmann Stiftung

Krockow, C. v., 1976: Reform als politisches Prinzip, München: Piper

Kronauer, M., 2020: Bedingungsloses Grundeinkommen oder besser ein Recht auf Arbeit?, in: WSI Mitteilungen 73(2), 143–145

Krupp, H.-J., 2007: Bürgerversicherung für das Alter – Gesetzliche Rentenversicherung als Bürgerversicherung, in: Wirtschaftsdienst 87 (1), 23–30

Kubek, V./Weber, H., 2020: Arbeit in der Sozialwirtschaft, in: Ernst, G., et al. (Ed.), Digitale Transformation. Arbeit in Dienstleistungssystemen, Baden-Baden: Nomos, 263–274

Kubis, A./Rebien, M. 2019: Langzeitarbeitslosigkeit in Zeiten von Fachkräfteengpässen, in: Wirtschaftspolitische Blätter, Jg. 66, 39–57

Kucklick, C., 2015: Die granulare Gesellschaft. Wie das Digitale unsere Wirklichkeit auflöst (2. Aufl.), Berlin: Ullstein

Kumkar, N./Schimank, U., 2021: Drei-Klassen-Gesellschaft? Bruch? Konfrontation? Eine Auseinandersetzung mit Andreas Reckwitz' Diagnose der »Spätmoderne«, in: Leviathan H. 1/2021, 7–32

Lammert, N., 2020: Die Zukunft des Sozialstaats, in: Roters, W./Gräf, H./Wollmann, H., (Ed.), Zukunft denken und verantworten. Herausforderungen für Politik, Wissenschaft und Gesellschaft im 21. Jahrhundert, Wiesbaden, 215–222

Lee, K.-F., 2019: AI Superpowers. China, Silicon Valley und die neue Weltordnung, Frankfurt/M.: Campus, zuerst: Lee, K.-F., 2018: AI Superpowers. China, Silicon Valley, and the New World Order Boston New York: Houghton Mifflin Harcourt

Lee, S., 2018: Attitudes Toward Universal Basic Income and Welfare State in Europe: A Research Note, in: Basic Income Studies, 13 (1), 1–9

Leibfried, S., 2001: Über die Hinfälligkeit des Staates der Daseinsvorsorge, Beitrag Schader Stiftung (https://www.schader-stiftung.de/themen/gemeinwohl-und-verantwortung/fokus/oeffentliche-daseinsvorsorge/artikel/ueber-die-hinfaelligkeit-des-staates-der-daseinsvorsorge/)

Lengfeld, H./Hirschle, J., 2009: Die Angst der Mittelschicht vor dem sozialen Abstieg. Eine Längsschnittanalyse 1984–2007, in: Zeitschrift für Soziologie 38(5), 379 –399

León, M., 2017: Social Investment and Childcare Expansion: A Perfect Match?, in: A. Hemerijck (Ed.), The Uses of Social Investment, a. a. O., 118–127

Leggewie, C., 2007: Das Ohr der Macht und die Kunst der Konsultation: Zur Einleitung, in: Leggewie, C. (Ed.), Von der Politik- zur Gesellschaftssteuerung. Neue Wege öffentlicher Konsultation, 7 ff, Frankfurt/New York: Campus

Leggewie, C., 2021: Neues vom Grand Hotel Abgrund. Der Paradigmenwechsel vom Kosmopolitismus zur Kosmo-Politik, in: Zeitschrift für Vergleichende Politikwissenschaft, 15(1), 119–136

Lehmbruch, G., 2000: Institutionelle Schranken einer ausgehandelten Reform des Wohlfahrtsstaates. Das Bündnis für Arbeit und seine Erfolgsbedingungen., in: Czada, R./Wollmann, H., (Ed.), Von der Bonner zur Berliner Republik, Wiesbaden: Springer VS, 89ff

Lessenich, S., 2003: Dynamischer Immobilismus: Kontinuität und Wandel im deutschen Sozialmodell, Frankfurt am Main: Campus Verlag

Lessenich, S., 2009: Das Grundeinkommen in der gesellschaftspolitischen Debatte. Expertise im Auftrag der Friedrich-Ebert-Stiftung. WISO-Diskurs – Expertisen und Dokumentationen zur Wirtschafts- und Sozialpolitik, Bonn

Liebermann, S., 2015: Aus dem Geist der Demokratie: Bedingungsloses Grundeinkommen. Frankfurt am Main: Humanities Online.

Lindemann, K., 2018: Das Grundeinkommen – oder: Die heimliche Abkehr von kollektivrechtlicher Gestaltung, in: WSI-Mitteilungen 71 (4), 334–336

Lüders, K./Schroeder W., 2020: Die Legitimität des Sozialstaats, in: Kneip, S./Merkel, W./Weßels, B., (Ed.), Legitimitätsprobleme. Zur Lage der Demokratie in Deutschland, Wiesbaden: Springer VS, 341–364

Lünsmann-Schmidt, S., 2021: Lauter gute Leute. Das Ehrenamt in den Sozialen Diensten zwischen Legitimationsnutzen und Transaktionskostenregulierung, Wiesbaden: Springer VS

Luhmann, N., 2000: Die Politik der Gesellschaft. Frankfurt/M.: Suhrkamp

Lutz, B., 1984: Der kurze Traum immerwährender Prosperität: Eine Neuinterpretation der industriell-kapitalistischen Entwicklung im Europa des 20. Jahrhunderts, Frankfurt am Main: Campus

Maier, T./Zika, G./Kalinowski, M./Steeg, S./Mönnig, A./Wolter, M.I./Hummel, M./Schneemann, C., 2020: COVID-19-Krise: Die Arbeit geht weiter, der Wohlstand macht Pause, bibb report 4/2020 (Bundesinstitut für Berufsbildung)

Maaß, V., 2001: Experimentierklauseln für die Verwaltung und ihre verfassungsrechtlichen Grenzen, Berlin: Duncker und Humblot

McGrane, S., 2020: A Guaranteed Monthly Check Changed His Life. Now He Sends Out 650, in: The New York Times am 06.11.2020

Manow, P., 2018: Die politische Ökonomie des Populismus, Berlin: Suhrkamp

Manow, P., 2019: Wohlfahrtsstaatsregime, in: Obinger, H./Schmidt, M.G., (Ed.), Handbuch Sozialpolitik, a. a. O., 297–313

Manow, P., 2020: (Ent-)Demokratisierung der Demokratie, Berlin: Suhrkamp

Marcinkowski, F., 2015: Die „Medialisierung“ der Politik. Veränderte Bedingungen politischer Interessenvermittlung, in: A. Zimmer/R. Speth (Ed.), Lobby Work. Interessenvertretung als Politikgestaltung, a. a. O., 71 ff

Marshall, T. H., 1992: Bürgerrechte und soziale Klassen. Zur Soziologie des Wohlfahrtsstaates, Frankfurt/New York: Campus
Mason, P., 2016: Postkapitalismus: Grundrisse einer kommenden Ökonomie, Berlin: Suhrkamp
Mason, P., 2019: Klare, lichte Zukunft. Eine radikale Verteidigung des Humanismus, Berlin: Suhrkamp
Matthes, J. (Ed.), 1983: Krise der Arbeitsgesellschaft? Verhandlungen des 21. Deutschen Soziologentages in Bamberg 1982, Frankfurt/New York: Campus
Mau, S., 2017: Das metrische Wir. Über die Quantifizierung des Sozialen, Berlin: Suhrkamp
Mau, S., 2019: Lütten Klein. Leben in der ostdeutschen Transformationsgesellschaft, Berlin: Suhrkamp
Mau, S., 2021: Konturen einer neuen Klassengesellschaft? Einige Anmerkungen zur Konzeption der Mittelklasse bei Andreas Reckwitz, in: Leviathan H. 2/2021, 164–173
Mazzucato, M., 2019: Wie kommt der Wert in die Welt? Von Schöpfern und Abschöpfern, Frankfurt/New York: Campus
Mazzucato, M., 2021: Mission. Auf dem Weg zu einer neuen Wirtschaft, Frankfurt/New York: Campus
Mein Grundeinkommen e.V. 2020a: Unser Jahr 2019. Transparenz- und Finanzbericht. Mein.Grundeinkommen E.V., Berlin. unser-jahr-2019.pdf (mein-grundeinkommen.de)
Mein Grundeinkommen e. V., 2020b: Pilotprojekt Grundeinkommen. Wie verändert ein Grundeinkommen unsere Gesellschaft? Wir wollen es wissen (Projektmagazin), Berlin. https://images.meinbge.de/image/upload/v1/pilot/projektmappe/Pilotprojekt_Grundeinkommen_Magazin.pdf
Meinhardt, V./Zwiener, R., 1997: Steuerfinanzierung von versicherungsfremden Leistungen in der Sozialversicherung, in: Vierteljahreshefte zur Wirtschaftsforschung, 66(3–4), 352–361
Milanovic, B., 2020: Kapitalismus global. Über die Zukunft des Systems, das die Welt beherrscht. Berlin: Suhrkamp
Mitschke, J., 1985: Steuer- und Transferordnung aus einem Guß, Baden-Baden: Nomos
Münkler, H., 2010: Regierungsversagen, Staatsversagen und die Krise der Demokratie, in: Berliner Republik (5), 48 ff
Münkler, H./Münkler, M., 2019: Abschied vom Abstieg. Eine Agenda für Deutschland, Berlin: Rowohlt
Nachtwey, O., 2016: Die Abstiegsgesellschaft: über das Aufbegehren in der regressiven Moderne, Berlin: Suhrkamp
Naegele, G. (Ed.), 2010: Soziale Lebenslaufpolitik, Wiesbaden: VS
Neckel, S., 2021. Keine Einstellungsfrage – Infrastrukturen als kollektive Bedingungen nachhaltigen Lebens, in: agora 42, Ausgabe 3, 14–18
Neu, C. (Ed.), 2009: Daseinsvorsorge. Eine gesellschaftswissenschaftliche Annäherung, Wiesbaden: VS
Niemeier, E., 2020: Politische Ursachen für Rentenprobleme und Altersarmut erfordern grundlegende Reformen, in: Wirtschaftsdienst, 100(8), 597–599
Nullmeier, F., 2002: Auf dem Weg zu Wohlfahrtsmärkten?, in: Süß, W. (Ed.), Deutschland in den neunziger Jahren, Opladen, 269 ff
Nullmeier, F., 2016: Politische Theorie des Komparativs, in: Mittelweg 36 – Zeitschrift des Hamburger Instituts für Sozialforschung, Heft 2, 56–73

Nullmeier, F., 2019a: Begründungen des Wohlfahrtsstaates, in: Obinger, H./Schmidt, M.G. (Ed.), Handbuch Sozialpolitik, Wiesbaden: Springer VS, 57–76

Nullmeier, F., 2019b: Die Sozialstaatsentwicklung im vereinten Deutschland. Sozialpolitik der Jahre 1990 bis 2013, in: Schroeder, W./Schulze, M. (Ed.), Wohlfahrtsstaat und Interessen-organisationen im Wandel, Baden-Baden: Nomos, 19–40

Nullmeier, F., 2019c: Nachhaltige Gestaltung sozialpolitischer Politikberatung, Düsseldorf: FGW

Nullmeier, F., 2021: Sozialstaat, in: Andersen, U./Bogumil, J./Marschall S./Woyke, W. (Ed.), Handwörterbuch des politischen Systems der Bundesrepublik Deutschland, Wiesbaden: Springer VS (8. überarbeitete und erweiterte Auflage), 836–842

Nullmeier, F./Rüb, F., 1993: Die Transformation der Sozialpolitik. Vom Sozialstaat zum Sicherungsstaat, Frankfurt/M./New York: Campus

Nussbaum, M. C., 2014: Politische Emotionen, Berlin: Suhrkamp

Obinger, H./Schmidt, M. G. (Ed.), 2019a: Handbuch Sozialpolitik, Wiesbaden: Springer VS

Obinger, H./Schmidt, M. G., 2019b: Einleitung, in: Obinger, H./Schmidt, M. (Ed.), Handbuch Sozialpolitik, Wiesbaden: Springer VS, 1–8

Obinger, H./Petersen, K., 2019: Die historische Entwicklung des Wohlfahrtsstaates: Von den Anfängen bis zum Ende des Goldenen Zeitalters, in: Obinger, H./Schmidt, M. G. (Ed.), Handbuch Sozialpolitik, Wiesbaden: Springer VS, 9–31

Obuch, K./Grabbe, C., 2019: Sozialunternehmertum und Social Entrepreneurship in Deutschland: Change Maker im Kommen?, in: Freise, M./Zimmer, A. (Ed.), Zivilgesellschaft und Wohlfahrtsstaat im Wandel, a. a. O., 143–168

OECD, 2019: Employment Outlook (2019) – The Future of Work, Paris: OECD

OECD, 2020: Employment Outlook (2020) – Worker Security and the Covid-19 Crisis, Paris: OECD

Offe, C., 1977: Einleitung, in: P. Bachrach/M. S. Baratz, Macht und Armut, a. a. O., 7–34

Offe, C., 1984: Contradictions of the Welfare State, London: Hutchinson

Offe, C., 1994: Vollbeschäftigung. Zur Kritik einer falsch gestellten Frage, in: Gewerkschaftliche Monatshefte (45), 796–806

Offe, C., 2015: Temporalstrukturen sozialer Macht, in: H. Straßheim/T. Ulbricht (Ed.), Zeit der Politik. Demokratisches Regieren in einer beschleunigten Welt, Baden-Baden: Nomos, Leviathan-Sonderband 30, 29–51

Offe, C., 2019a[1990]: Akzeptanz und Legitimität strategischer Optionen in der Sozialpolitik, in: Offe, C. (Ed.), Der Wohlfahrtsstaat und seine Bürger, Ausgewählte Schriften, Wiesbaden: Springer VS, 123–142

Offe, C., 2019b[1995]: Schock, Fehlkonstrukt oder Droge? Über drei Lesarten der Sozialstaatskrise, in: Offe, C. (Ed.), Der Wohlfahrtsstaat und seine Bürger, Ausgewählte Schriften, Wiesbaden: Springer VS, 143–156

Offe, C./Heinze R.G., 1990: Organisierte Eigenarbeit: Das Modell Kooperationsring, Frankfurt/New York: Campus

Oostendorp, A./Paulus, A., 2021: Grundeinkommen – Was Wäre Wenn? Warum unsere Vorhersagen verzerrt sind und wie Experimente sie verbessern können. Impuls#01 der Stiftung Grundeinkommen, München

Opielka, M. 2008: Chancen eines Grundeinkommens in Deutschland. Internationale Revue für Soziale Sicherheit 61 (3), 81-102.

Opielka, M., 2004: Sozialpolitik. Grundlagen und vergleichende Perspektiven, Reinbek: Rowohlt

Opielka, M., 2019 [1984]: Das garantierte Einkommen – ein sozialstaatliches Paradoxon? Warum ein garantiertes Einkommen den Sozialstaat zerstören, retten oder aufheben kann, in: Kovce, P./Priddat, B.P. (Ed.), Bedingungsloses Grundeinkommen, Berlin: Suhrkamp, 300–321

Opielka, M./Ostner, I. (Ed.), 1987: Umbau des Sozialstaates, Essen: Klartext

Opielka, M./Vobruba, G. (Ed.), 1986: Das garantierte Grundeinkommen. Entwicklung und Perspektiven einer Forderung, Frankfurt/M.: Fischer

Opielka, M./Müller, M./Bendixen, T./Kreft, J., 2010: Dilemmata und ihre Lösung in der Idee des Grundeinkommens?, in: Opielka, M./Müller, M./Bendixen, T./Kreft, J. (Ed.), Grundeinkommen und Werteorientierungen, Wiesbaden: VS, 147–149

Osterkamp R., 2015: Ist ein bedingungsloses Grundeinkommen in Deutschland finanzierbar?, in: Osterkamp R. (Hg), Auf dem Prüfstand: Ein bedingungsloses Grundeinkommen für Deutschland, Baden-Baden: Nomos, 225–245

Ott, E./Landsberg, G., 2018: Vorwort, in: Deutscher Städte- und Gemeindebund/Deutscher Genossenschafts- und Raiffeisenverband (Ed.), Genossenschaften und Kommunen, a. a. O., 3

Paine, T., 2019 [1797]: Agrarische Gerechtigkeit, in: Kovce, P./Priddat, B. P. (Ed.), Bedingungsloses Grundeinkommen, a. a. O., 78–98

Pabst, S./Rothgang, H., 2000: Reformfähigkeit und Reformblockaden: Kontinuität und Wandel bei Einführung der Pflegeversicherung, in: Leibfried, S./Wagschal, U. (Ed.), Der deutsche Sozialstaat. Bilanzen–Reformen–Perspektiven, Frankfurt: Campus, 340–377

Parnack, C./Rebmann, S./Rudzio, K., 2021: Wird Pflege zu Hause unbezahlbar?, in: Die Zeit, Nr. 27 v. 1.7. 2021, 19

Patzwaldt, K., 2007: Was leistete Politikberatung in den rot-grünen Arbeitsmarktreformen?, in: Wolf, K. D. (Ed.), Staat und Gesellschaft – fähig zur Reform?, Baden-Baden: Nomos, 211 ff

Paul, F./Walter, A., 2019: Frauen in sozialen Dienstleistungsberufen: Verliererinnen der neuen Wohlfahrtsstaatlichkeit?, in: Freise, M./Zimmer, A., (Ed.), Zivilgesellschaft und Wohlfahrtsstaat im Wandel, a. a. O., 169–193

Peter, A./Rudolf, C., 2021: Ein feministischer Blick auf eine zukunftsfähige Versorgungsökonomie, in: Makronom, Economists for Future (https://makronom.de/ein-feministischer-blick-auf-eine-zukunftsfaehige-versorgungsoekonomie-39582)

Petersen, T./Rausch, T., 2021. CO2 braucht einen Preis – Mit einer wirtschaftspolitische Flankierung. Policy Brief #2021/02 der Bertelsmann Stiftung.

Plumpe, W., 2012: Ohne Krisen keine Harmonie: Eine kleine Geschichte der Gleichgewichtsstörungen in der Wirtschaft, in: Kursbuch 170 („Krisen lieben"), Hamburg: Murmann Verlag, 64–83

Pörksen, B., 2018: Die Große Gereiztheit, München: Hanser

Polanyi, K., 1978 [1944]: The Great Transformation. Politische und ökonomische Ursprünge von Gesellschaften und Wirtschaftssystemen, Frankfurt/M.: Suhrkamp

Pongratz, H.J./Bührmann, A.D., 2018: Diskontinuität und Diversität beruflicher Selbstständigkeit, in: Bührmann, A.D./Fachinger, U./Welskop-Deffaa, E.-M. (Ed.), Hybride Erwerbsformen. Digitalisierung, Diversität und sozialpolitische Gestaltungsoptionen, Wiesbaden: Springer VS, 51ff

Priddat, B.P., 2019: Arbeit und Muße. Über die europäische Hoffnung der Verwandlung von Arbeit in höhere Tätigkeit, Marburg: Metropolis
Promberger, M., 2020: Resilienz: Was Organisationen und Regierungen aus der Corona-Krise lernen können, in: WSI-Mitteilungen, 73(6), 462–467
Rat für Arbeitswelt, 2021: Vielfältige Ressourcen stärken – Zukunft gestalten. Impulse für eine nachhaltige Arbeitswelt zwischen Pandemie und Wandel, Berlin
Reckwitz, A., 2017: Die Gesellschaft der Singularitäten, Berlin: Suhrkamp
Reckwitz, A., 2019a: Das Ende der Illusionen. Politik, Ökonomie und Kultur in der Spätmoderne, Berlin: Suhrkamp
Reckwitz, A., 2019b: Ein kurzes Gespräch mit Andreas Reckwitz, in: Soziologie – Forum der Deutschen Gesellschaft für Soziologie 48(2), 236–240
Reckwitz, A., 2020: Verblendet vom Augenblick, in: Die Zeit v. 10.6. 2020, 45
Rehder, B., 2015: Justizialisierung statt Korporatismus? Verrechtlichung der Interessenvermittlung in den Arbeitsbeziehungen, in: Zimmer, A./Speth, R. (Ed.), Lobby Work. Interessenvertretung als Politikgestaltung, a. a. O., 53 ff
Rehder, B., 2021: „Unorganisierte" Interessen: Zivilgesellschaft unter Druck von Basis, Politik und Medien, in: Florack, M./Korte, K.-R./Schwanholz, J., (Ed.), Coronakratie. a. a. O., 223–235
Reichenbachs, M., 2018: Der Korporatismus ist tot, lang lebe der Korporatismus! Über die Klassifizierung von Staat-Verbändebeziehungen und wieso sich Deutschland in der Ära des regulierten Wohlfahrtskorporatismus befindet, in: Heinze, R.G./Lange, J./Sesselmeier, W. (Ed.), Neue Governancestrukturen in der Wohlfahrtspflege, a. a. O., 103–127
Reuter, T., 2016: Das bedingungslose Grundeinkommen als liberaler Entwurf. Philosophische Argumente für mehr Gerechtigkeit. Wiesbaden: Springer VS.
Rieger, E., 2019: „Gesetzgebung der Zukunft". Ideen in der Sozialpolitik und der Soziologie, in: Baumgartner, A.D./Fux, B., (Ed.), Sozialstaat unter Zugzwang?, Wiesbaden: Springer VS, 43–72
Ritter, G. A., 2006: Der Preis der deutschen Einheit. Die Wiedervereinigung und die Krise des Sozialstaats, München: C.H. Beck
Rixen, T., 2019: Die Verwaltung des Überschusses, in: R. Zohlnhöfer, T. /Saalfeld (Ed.), Zwischen Stillstand, Politikwandel und Krisenmanagement. Eine Bilanz der Regierung Merkel 2013–2017, Wiesbaden: Springer VS
RKI, 2021: Faktenblatt: Soziale Unterschiede in der COVID-19-Sterblichkeit während der zweiten Infektionswelle in Deutschland (16.03.2021)
Roman Herzog Institut (Ed.), 2019: Das bedingungslose Grundeinkommen: zum Für und Wider eines gesellschaftspolitischen Reformkonzepts, München
Rosa, H., 2016: Resonanz. Eine Soziologie der Weltbeziehung, Berlin: Suhrkamp
Rosa, H., 2020: Pfadabhängigkeit, Bifurkationspunkte und die Rolle der Soziologie. Ein soziologischer Deutungsversuch der Corona-Krise, in: Berliner Journal für Soziologie (30. JEd.), 191–213
Rosa, H., 2021: „Die Umwege fehlen jetzt". Interview in der TAZ vom 24.4.2021 (https://taz.de/Soziologe-Hartmut-Rosa-im-Gespraech/!5763329/)
Rosanvallon, P., 1982: Nach der Sozialdemokratie. Die Kosten der Solidarität oder Die Gesellschaft auf der Suche nach sich selbst, in: Freibeuter H. 11, 63–75
Roth, R., 2020: Zukunftsfähigkeit: Impulse der Zivilgesellschaft, in: Roters, W./Gräf, H./Wollmann, H. (Ed.), Zukunft denken und verantworten, a. a. O., 329–351

Rüb, F. W./Alnor, K./Spohr, F. 2009: Die Kunst des Reformierens. Konzeptionelle Überlegungen zu einer erfolgreichen Regierungsstrategie, in: Schriftenreihe: Zukunft Regieren. Beiträge für eine gestaltungsfähige Politik, Gütersloh: Bertelsmann Stiftung

Rüb, F.W., 2011: Inkompatible Welten? Politik und die Grenzen wissenschaftlicher Politikberatung, in: Lamping, W./Schridde, H. (Ed.), Der konsultative Staat, Opladen/Farmington Hills, 63ff

Rüb, F. W., 2014a: Rapide Politikwechsel in der Bundesrepublik. Eine konzeptionelle Annäherung an ein unerforschtes Phänomen, in: Rüb, F.W. (Ed.), Rapide Politikwechsel in der Bundesrepublik. Theoretischer Rahmen und empirische Befunde, Baden-Baden: Nomos (Sonderband 6 der „Zeitschrift für Politik"), 9–45

Rüb, F. W., 2014b: Bausteine für ein Modell rapider Politikwechsel, in: Rüb, F.W. (Ed.), Rapide Politikwechsel in der Bundesrepublik. Theoretischer Rahmen und empirische Befunde, a. a. O., 251–270

Rüppel, M., 2020: Bedingungsloses Grundeinkommen in der Politikfeldanalyse – Welche Kriterien müssen Grundeinkommensmodelle für eine erfolgreiche Agendaplatzierung erfüllen? Analyse anhand des Solidarischen Bürgergeldes von Dieter Althaus, Masterarbeit an der Universität Potsdam (Politikwissenschaft)

Rürup, B., 2019: Interview, in: ZEIT-Online, 15.11.2019 (https://www.zeit.de/2019/47/grundrente-bert-ruerup-rentensystem-altersarmut-einkommen)

Rürup, B., 2021: Rentenpolitik ist mehr als Mathematik, Handelsblatt Research Institute (Der Chefökonom vom 11.6. 2021)

Sachverständigenrat zur Begutachtung der gesamtwirtschaftlichen Entwicklung (SVR), 2007: Das Erreichte Nicht Verspielen. Jahresgutachten 2007/08, Stuttgart: Metzler-Poeschel

Sachverständigenrat zur Begutachtung der gesamtwirtschaftlichen Entwicklung (SVR), 2019: Den Strukturwandel meistern. Jahresgutachten 2019/20, Stuttgart: Metzler-Poeschel

Sachverständigenrat zur Begutachtung der gesamtwirtschaftlichen Entwicklung (SVR), 2020: Corona-Krise gemeinsam bewältigen, Resilienz und Wachstum stärken. Jahresgutachten 2020/21, Stuttgart: Metzler-Poeschel

Sachweh, P., 2021: Klassen und Klassenkonflikte in der postindustriellen Gesellschaft. Soziale Spaltungen und soziokulturelle Polarisierung in den Mittelklassen, in: Leviathan H. 2/2021, 181–188

Schachtschneider, U., 2014: Freiheit, Gleichheit, Gelassenheit. Mit einem Ökologischen Grundeinkommen aus der Wachstumsfalle. München: oekonom

Schäfer, A./Zürn, M., 2021: Die demokratische Regression. Die politischen Ursachen des autoritären Populismus, Berlin: Suhrkamp

Scharpf, F.W., 1993: Von der Finanzierung der Arbeitslosigkeit. Zur Subventionierung niedriger Erwerbseinkommen, in: Gewerkschaftliche Monatshefte 44(7), 433–443

Scheller, H., 2017: Kommunale Infrastrukturpolitik. Zwischen Konsolidierung und aktiver Gestaltung, in: APuZ H. 16–17, 39–46

Schimank, U., 2011: Wohlfahrtsgesellschaften als funktionaler Antagonismus von Kapitalismus und Demokratie. MPIfG Working Paper (11/2), Köln

Schimank, U., 2019: Politische Gesellschaftsgestaltung heute – sozial- und gesellschaftstheoretische Erwägungen angesichts von Transformationsvorhaben wie der „Energiewende", in: dms. der moderne Staat H. 2/2019, 251–265

Schloen, B., 2020: Grundeinkommen und seine Finanzierung. Klimasolidarisch und menschenwürdig, 2., überarb. Auflage, Wiesbaden: Springer Gabler

Schmähl, W., 2012: Von der Rente als Zuschuss zum Lebensunterhalt zur ‚Zuschuss-Rente', in: Wirtschaftsdienst, 92(5), 304–313

Schmale, I., 2017: Sozialgenossenschaften: eine wieder entdeckte Rechts- und Wirtschaftsform in der Sozialwirtschaft, in: Schmale, I./Blome-Drees, J., (Ed.), Genossenschaft innovativ, Genossenschaften als neue Organisationsform in der Sozialwirtschaft, Wiesbaden: Springer VS, 11 ff,

Schmid, G./Schroeder, W., 2020: Die Krise nutzen: Es ist Zeit für eine Arbeitsversicherung, in: WZB Mitteilungen H. 168, 56–59

Schmid, J., 1996: Wohlfahrtsstaaten im Vergleich. Wiesbaden: VS Verlag für Sozialwissenschaften

Schmid, J., 2011: Mikropolitik – Pluralismus mit harten Bandagen?, in: Bandelow, N. C./ Hegelich, S., (Ed.) Pluralismus – Strategien – Entscheidungen, 324 ff, Wiesbaden: Westdeutscher Verlag

Schmid, J., 2018: Schwankende Riesen? Riesige Schwankungen? Die unklare Stellung der Wohlfahrtsverbände im deutschen Modell, in: Heinze, R.G./Lange, J./Sesselmeier, W. (Ed.), Neue Governancestrukturen in der Wohlfahrtspflege, a. a. O., 39–53

Schmid, T. (Ed.), 1984: Befreiung von falscher Arbeit. Thesen zum garantierten Mindesteinkommen, Berlin: Wagenbach.

Schmidt, M. G., 2003: Rot-grüne Sozialpolitik (1998–2002), in: Egle, C./Ostheim, T./Zohlnhöfer, R. (Ed.), Das rot-grüne Projekt. Eine Bilanz der Regierung Schröder 1998–2002, Wiesbaden: Westdeutscher Verlag, 239–258

Schmidt, M. G., 2007: Die Sozialpolitik der zweiten rot-grünen Koalition (2002–2005), in: Egle, C./Zohlnhöfer, R. (Ed.), Ende des rot-grünen Projektes. Eine Bilanz der Regierung Schröder 2002–2005, Wiesbaden: VS Verlag, 295–312

Schmidt, M. G., 2014: Rapide Politikwechsel – Kommentar, in: Rüb, F. W. (Ed.), Rapide Politikwechsel in der Bundesrepublik. Theoretischer Rahmen und empirische Befunde, a. a. O., 239–249

Schmidt, M.G., 2021: Geschichte der Zivilgesellschaft in der Bundesrepublik Deutschland, in: Grande, B./Grande, E./Hahn, U. (Ed.), Zivilgesellschaft in der Bundesrepublik Deutschland, a. a. O., 21–33

Schneider, H., 2017: Das Bedingungslose Grundeinkommen: Der Löchrige Traum vom Schlaraffenland, Bonn: IZA-Standpunkte Nr. 88

Schneiders, K., 2020: Sozialwirtschaft und soziale Arbeit, Stuttgart: Kohlhammer

Schöb, R., 2020: Der starke Sozialstaat: Weniger ist mehr. Campus

Schönert, C./Freise, M., 2019: Soziale Investitionen als Strategie im deutschen Wohlfahrtsstaat, in: Freise, M./Zimmer, A., (Ed.), Zivilgesellschaft und Wohlfahrtsstaat im Wandel, a. a. O., 55–80

Schroeder, W., 2018: Interessenvertretung in der Altenpflege. Zwischen Staatszentrierung und Selbstorganisation, Wiesbaden: VS Springer

Schroeder, W., 2019: Interessenvermittlung: Die IG Metall als sozialpolitischer Akteur, in: Schroeder, W./Schulze, M., (Ed.), Wohlfahrtsstaat und Interessenorganisationen im Wandel, Baden-Baden: Nomos, 219–238

Schroeder, W., 2021: „Arbeit, Familie und Freizeit finden fast gleichzeitig statt". Interview, in: Frankfurter Rundschau vom 25.6. 2021 (https://www.fr.de/rhein-main/arbeit-familie-und-freizeit-finden-fast-gleichzeitig-statt-90825535.html)

Schroeder, W. (Ed.), 2017: Konfessionelle Wohlfahrtsverbände im Umbruch, Wiesbaden: VS Springer

Schroeder, W./Weinert, R., 2006: Teilhabegesellschaft via investiven und infrastrukturellen Sozialstaat, in: Grözinger, G./Maschke, M./Offe, C. (Ed.), Die Teilhabegesellschaft. Modell eines neuen Wohlfahrtsstaates, Frankfurt: Campus, 194–206

Schroeder, W./Klenk, T./Berzel, A./Stöber, M./Akel, A., 2018: Vorbeugende Sozialpolitik als Antwort auf soziale Ungleichheiten und neue soziale Risiken. Kommunikation und Steuerung vorbeugender Sozialpolitik in den Bundesländern, Düsseldorf: FGW

Schroeder, W./Bitzegeio, U./Fischer, S. (Ed.), 2020: Digitale Industrie. Algorithmische Arbeit. Gesellschaftliche Transformation, Bonn: Dietz

Schulz, T., 2018: Zukunfts-Medizin. Wie das Silicon Valley Krankheiten besiegen und unser Leben verlängern will, München: DVA

Schulze-Böing, M., 2021: Sozialwirtschaft – Chance für den sozialen Arbeitsmarkt? Neue Perspektiven durch das neue Förderinstrument im SGB II, in: Sozialer Fortschritt, 70(1), 41 ff

Schulze Buschoff, K./Hassel, A., 2019: Beschäftigungsrekorde bei zunehmender Ungleichheit auf dem Arbeitsmarkt. Arbeitsmarktentwicklung und -politik in der dritten Regierung Merkel (2013 bis 2017), in: R. Zohlnhöfer, T. /Saalfeld (Ed.), Zwischen Stillstand, Politikwandel und Krisenmanagement. Eine Bilanz der Regierung Merkel 2013–2017, Wiesbaden: Springer VS, 397 ff.

Schupp, J./Volz, J./Wagner, G./Zwiener, R., 1999: Zuschüsse zu den Sozialversicherungsbeiträgen im Niedriglohnbereich: Wenig zielgerichtet und teuer, in: Wochenbericht des DIW Berlin 66(27), 499–509

Schupp, J., 2020a: Was das BGE-Pilotprojekt leisten kann – und was nicht. Beitrag im Makronom vom 31.8.2020 (https://makronom.de/was-das-bge-pilotprojekt-leisten-kann-und-was-nicht-36874)

Schupp, J., 2020b: Bedingungsarme Grundsicherung statt bedingungslosem Grundeinkommen jetzt! (Kommentar), in: DIW Wochenbericht,87(15–16), 296

Schupp, J., 2020c: Bedingungsloses Grundeinkommen: Viel Zustimmung, aber auch große Ablehnung, in: Wirtschaftsdienst, 100(2), 112–116.

Schupp, J., 2020d: Keine Forschung zum Grundeinkommen könnte das höhere Risiko darstellen, Kommentar in: DIW Wochenbericht 87(36), 632–632

SEED (Stockton Economic Empowerment Demonstration), 2018. Our vision for Seed: A Discussion Paper (mimeo) (https://www.stocktondemonstration.org/)

Seibt, G., 2021: Nimm das, FDP. Identitätsstreit, Verwaltungselend, Staatsphlegma: Wird der Liberalismus seine Chance nutzen?, in: Süddeutsche Zeitung vom 19.3. 2021

Shafik, M., 2021: What We Owe Each Other. A New Social Contract, London: The Bodly Head

Shiller, R.J., 2020: Narrative Wirtschaft. Wie Geschichten die Wirtschaft beeinflussen – ein revolutionärer Erklärungsansatz, Kulmbach: Plassen

Siller, P., 2020: Politik der öffentlichen Räume und Netze? Anforderungen an eine neue Infrastrukturpolitik, in: Heinrich-Böll-Stiftung (Ed.), Öffentliche Räume, a. a. O., 11–95

Simmank, M./Vogel, B., 2020: Städte halten den Atem an, Dörfer atmen tief durch – Corona auf dem Land: Soziologische Momentaufnahmen, SOFI Göttingen (April 2020) (http://www.sofi-goettingen.de/fileadmin/Maike_Simmank/SOFI_Corona_auf_dem_Land.pdf)

Sirovátka, T./Guzi, M./Saxonberg, S. 2019: Satisfaction with Democracy and Perceived Performance of the Welfare State in Europe, in: Journal of European Social Policy 29(2), 241–256

Soomi, L., 2018: Attitudes Toward Universal Basic Income and Welfare State in Europe *Basic Income Studies* 13 (1), 1-9

Sörensen, E./Torfing, J., 2017: Metagoverning Collaborative Innovation in Governance Networks, in: American Review of Public Administration, Vol. 47(7) 826–839

SPD (Sozialdemokratische Partei Deutschlands), 2021: Das Zukunftsprogramm. (https://www.spd.de/fileadmin/Dokumente/Beschluesse/Parteispitze/20210321_Zukunftsprogramm_Leitantrag.pdf)

Spermann, A., 2017: Basic Income in Germany: Proposals for Randomised Controlled Trials using Nudges, in: Basic Income Studies 12 (2), 1–9

Speth, R., 2015: Public Affairs Agenturen, in: Zimmer, A./Speth, R., (Ed.), Lobby Work. Interessenvertretung als Politikgestaltung, a. a. O., 155ff

SPIEGEL 2020: „Das 1.200 € – Experiment". Interview von Florian Diekmann mit Jürgen Schupp, SPIEGEL-Online vom 18.8.2020

Spieß, C.K., 2018: Die Ökonomie frühkindlicher Bildung und Betreuung: Ist sie in Deutschland angekommen?, in: Erlinghagen, M./Hank, K./Kreyenfeld, M. (Ed.), Innovation und Wissenstransfer in der empirischen Sozial- und Verhaltensforschung, Frankfurt am Main – New York: Campus, 267–29

Spohr, F., 2015: Pfadwechsel in der Arbeitsmarktpolitik. Eine Analyse aktivierender Reformen in Großbritannien, Deutschland und Schweden anhand des Multiple Streams Ansatz, Baden-Baden: Nomos

Staab, P., 2019: Digitaler Kapitalismus, Berlin: Suhrkamp

Städtler-Mach, B./Ignatzi, H. (Ed.), 2020: Grauer Pflegemarkt. 24-Stunden-Unterstützung durch osteuropäische Betreuungskräfte, Göttingen: Vandenhoeck & Ruprecht

Statistisches Bundesamt (Destatis), Wissenschaftszentrum Berlin für Sozialforschung (WZB), Bundesinstitut für Bevölkerungsforschung (BiB), 2021: Datenreport 2021. Ein Sozialbericht für die Bundesrepublik Deutschland, Bonn (bpb)

Steinke, J./Bibisidis, T., 2018: Die Sicherung und Weiterentwicklung des Sozialstaates ist nichts für Sprinter. Oder: Worum es bei Debatten um die Zukunft der Freien Wohlfahrtspflege gehen sollte, in: Heinze, R.G./Lange, J./Sesselmeier, W. (Ed.), Neue Governancestrukturen in der Wohlfahrtspflege, a. a. O., 265–280

Stelter, D., 2021: Ein Traum von einem Land. Deutschland 2040, Frankfurt/M.: Campus

Stern, A., 2016: Raising the Floor. How a Universal Basic Income Can Renew Our Economy and Rebuild The American Dream: New York: Public Affairs

Stettes, O., 2020: (Keine) Angst vor Robotern? Aktualisierte Befunde zu potenziellen Beschäftigungseffekten der Digitalisierung, IW-Trends 47(4)

Stöbe-Blossey, S./Köhling, K./Hackstein, P./Ruth, M., 2019: Integration durch Bildung als Kooperationsaufgabe: Potenziale vorbeugender Sozialpolitik, Wiesbaden: Springer VS

Stöbe-Blossey, S./Brussig, M./Ruth, M./Drescher, S./Alfuss, C., 2020: Schnittstellen in der Sozialpolitik: Differenzierung und Integration in der Absicherung sozialer Risiken, Universität Duisburg-Essen (IAQ)

Strasser, J., 1999: Wenn der Arbeitsgesellschaft die Arbeit ausgeht, Zürich: Pendo
Straubhaar, T., 2008: Warum das „bedingungslose Grundeinkommen" mehr ist als ein sozialutopisches Konzept, in: Roman Herzog Institut (Ed.), Bedingungsloses Grundeinkommen. Eine Perspektive für die Soziale Marktwirtschaft?, München, 6–9
Straubhaar, T. 2017: Radikal Gerecht. Wie das bedingungslose Grundeinkommen den Sozialstaat revolutioniert, Hamburg: Edition Körber-Stiftung
Straubhaar, T., 2018: Was ist ein Grundeinkommen und wie funktioniert es? In: Butterwegge, C./Rinken, K., (Ed.), Grundeinkommen kontrovers, Weinheim-Basel: Beltz Juventa, 10–31
Straubhaar, T., 2021: Grundeinkommen jetzt! Nur so ist die Marktwirtschaft zu retten. Basel: NZZ Libro
Streeck, W., 2013: Gekaufte Zeit. Die vertagte Krise des demokratischen Kapitalismus, Berlin: Suhrkamp
Streeck, W., 2017: Wissenschaftliche Politikberatung. Was wird verlangt, was kann sie bieten?, in: Hoose, F./Beckmann, F./Schönauer, A.-L. (Ed.), Fortsetzung folgt. Kontinuität und Wandel von Wirtschaft und Gesellschaft, a. a. O., 489–506
Streeck, W., 2019: Vorwort, in: Foundational Economy Collective, Die Ökonomie des Alltagslebens, a. a. O., 7–31
Streeck, W./Heinze, R. G., 1999: An Arbeit fehlt es nicht, in: Der Spiegel Nr. 19, 38–45
Streeck, W./Thelen, K., 2005: Introduction: Institutional change in advanced political economies, in: dies (ED.) Beyond Continuity, Oxford: Oxford University Press, 1–39
Strohschneider, P., 2020: Zumutungen. Wissenschaft in Zeiten von Populismus, Moralisierung und Szientokratie, Hamburg: kursbuch.edition
Strünck, C., 2017: Experimentelle Sozialpolitik. Ein Kampf gegen Kostenträgerlogik und Fragmentierung im deutschen Wohlfahrtsstaat, in: Hoose, F./Beckmann, F./Schönauer, A.-L. (Ed.), Fortsetzung folgt. a. a. O., 309–325
Sunde, U., 2021: Land der Verdränger, in: Frankfurter Allgemeine Zeitung vom 2.8.2021, 18
Tennstedt, F./Leibfried, S., 1985: Politik der Armut und Die Spaltung des Sozialstaats, Frankfurt am Main: Suhrkamp
Tiemann, H./Wagner, G.G., 2013: Die Wissenschaftliche Politikberatung der Bundesregierung neu organisieren, RatSWD Working Paper No. 220, Berlin
Tormey, S., 2015: Vom Ende der repräsentativen Politik, Hamburg: Hamburger Edition
Trampusch, C., 2009: Der erschöpfte Sozialstaat. Transformation eines Politikfeldes, Frankfurt/New York: Campus
van Treeck, T., 2021: Resilienz: Für ein neues Leitbild der Wirtschaftspolitik in Zeiten der allgemeinen Verunsicherung, in: Florack, M./Korte, K.-R./Schwanholz, J., (Ed.), Coronakratie, a. a. O., 205–213
Ullrich, C. G., 2005: Soziologie des Wohlfahrtsstaates, Frankfurt/New York: Campus
Vahland, K., 2020: Ende der Monokultur, in: Süddeutsche Zeitung vom 4.8. 2020, 4
Van Parijs, P., 2019 [1991]: Warum Surfer durchgefüttert werden sollten, in: Kovce, P./Priddat, B. P. (Ed.), Bedingungsloses Grundeinkommen, Berlin: Suhrkamp, 373–411
Van Parijs, P., Vanderborght, Y., 2017: Basic income. A Radical Proposal for a Free Society and a Sane Economy, Cambridge/London: Harvard University Press
Vatter, A./Milic, T./Rousselot, B., 2020: Beteiligung an Direktdemokratischen Verfahren, in: Faas, T./Gabriel, O.W./Maier, J., (Ed.), Politikwissenschaftliche Einstellungs- Und Verhaltensforschung, Baden-Baden: Nomos, 348–375

Vesper, D., 2020: 30 Jahre Deutsche Einheit. Ein finanzpolitischer Blick auf Länder und Gemeinden in Ost und West. Berlin, WISO DISKURS 08/2020 der Friedrich-Ebert-Stiftung, (http://library.fes.de/pdf-files/wiso/16397.pdf)

Vilain, M., 2020: Sozialwirtschaft vor der digitalen Herausforderung, in: Ernst, G. et al. (Ed.), Digitale Transformation. Arbeit in Dienstleistungssystemen, Baden-Baden: Nomos, 89–104

Vinnova-Engström, R., 2020: Public Sector Innovation – The case of Sweden (Vinnova-Rapport-VR 2020:02), Stockholm

Vobruba, G., 2019: Entkopplung von Arbeit und Einkommen (3. Auflage), Wiesbaden: Springer VS

Vogel, B., 2020: Covid-19 als Weckruf? Plädoyer für eine neue Politik öffentlicher Güter, in: WSI Mitteilungen H. 6/2020, 468–471

Voigt, L., 2019: Let the good times roll. Eine Bilanz der Sozialpolitik der dritten Großen Koalition 2013–2017, in: Zohlnhöfer, R./Saalfeld, T. (Ed.), Zwischen Stillstand, Politikwandel und Krisenmanagement. Eine Bilanz der Regierung Merkel 2013–2017, a. a. O., 415 ff

Wachtler, B./Michalski, N./Nowossadeck, E./Diercke, M./Wahrendorf, M. et al. 2020: Socioeconomic inequalities in the risk of SARS-CoV-2 infection – First results from an analysis of surveillance data from Germany. Journal of Health Monitoring 5(S7), 18–29, DOI https://doi.org/10.25646/7057

Wagschal, U., 2019: Steuerpolitik als Sozialpolitik, in: Obinger, H./Schmidt, M.G., (Ed.), Handbuch Sozialpolitik, Wiesbaden: Springer VS, 807–832

Wanger, S., 2020: Entwicklung von Erwerbstätigkeit, Arbeitszeit und Arbeitsvolumen nach Geschlecht, IAB -Forschungsbericht 16–2020, Nürnberg

Weick, K. E., 1995: Der Prozess des Organisierens, Frankfurt: Suhrkamp

Weingart, P., 2019: Wissensgesellschaft und wissenschaftliche Politikberatung, in: Falk, S. et al (Ed.), Handbuch Politikberatung, a. a. O., 68 ff

Welzer, H. 2019: Alles könnte anders sein. Eine Gesellschaftsutopie für freie Menschen. Frankfurt am Main: Fischer

Werding, M., 2009: Der Arbeitsmarkt als Motor für eine dynamische gesellschaftliche Mitte, Bad Homburg

Werding, M./Läpple, B. 2019: Wie variabel ist der demografische Alterungsprozess? Effekte von Geburten und Zuwanderung – Folgen für die soziale Sicherung, Kurzstudie, Bertelsmann Stiftung Gütersloh

Werding, M., 2020: Rentenfinanzen und fiskalische Tragfähigkeit: Aktueller Rechtsstand und Effekte verschiedener Reformen (No. 06/2020), Arbeitspapier

Werner, G., 2017: Ist der Mensch Mittel oder Zweck?, in: Kovce, P. (Ed.), Das bedingungslose Grundeinkommen. Die Debatte, Stuttgart: Verlag Freies Geistesleben, 210–223,

Werner, G., 2018 [2007]: Einkommen für alle. (Überarb. und akt. Neuausgabe), Köln: Kiepenheuer & Witsch

Werner, G.W./Eichhorn, W./Friedrich, L., 2013: Bedingungsloses Grundeinkommen, Soziale Marktwirtschaft, Finanzierungsfrage: Begriffserklärungen und Ergebnisse, in: Wirtschaftsdienst 93 (9), 588–592

Widerquist, K. 2013: Independence, Propertylessness, and Basic Income: A Theory of Freedom as the Power to Say No, New York: Palgrave Macmillan

Wieda, C./Grohs, S./Beinborn, N., 2020: Kommunale Prävention für Kinder und Familien. Erfahrungen aus Europa, Gütersloh: Bertelsmann Stiftung

Wiesenthal, H., 2006: Gesellschaftssteuerung und gesellschaftliche Selbststeuerung, Wiesbaden: Westdeutscher Verlag

Wiesenthal, H., 2019b: Institutionelle Transformationen gestern – und morgen?, in: Dörre, K. et al. (Ed.), Große Transformation?, a. a. O., 367–382

Wiesenthal, H., 2019a: Einleitung, in: Wiesenthal, H., Rationalität und Organisation 2, Transformationspfade, Wiesbaden: Springer VS, 1 ff

Willke, H., 2014: Regieren. Politische Steuerung komplexer Gesellschaften, Wiesbaden: Westdeutscher Verlag

Willke, H., 2020: Die Krise der politischen Steuerung (Gespräch mit Josef Oberneder), in: Reinbacher, P./Oberneder, J./Wesenauer, A., (Ed.), Warum Komplexität nützlich ist. Auf der Suche nach Antworten mit Helmut Willke, Wiesbaden: Springer VS, 215 ff.

Winker, G., 2020: Aufbau einer solidarischen und nachhaltigen Care-Ökonomie. Ein Plädoyer in Zeiten von Corona, in: Volkmer, M./Werner, K. (Ed.), Die Corona-Gesellschaft. Analysen zur Lage und Perspektiven für die Zukunft, Bielefeld: transcript, 395–404

Wissenschaftlicher Beirat beim Bundesministerium der Finanzen, 2021: Bedingungsloses Grundeinkommen (Gutachten). Berlin

Wissenschaftlicher Beirat beim Bundesministerium für Wirtschaft und Energie, 2020: Öffentliche Infrastruktur in Deutschland: Probleme und Reformbedarf (Gutachten), Berlin

Wissenschaftlicher Dienst, 2019: Volumen der jährlichen Finanztransaktionen in Deutschland. WD 4 – 3000 – 008/19, Berlin

Wohlfahrt, N., 2017: Strategische Neuausrichtung der Freien Wohlfahrtspflege in Folge von Ökonomisierung, in: Ceylan, R./Kiefer, M., (Ed.), Ökonomisierung und Säkularisierung. Neue Herausforderungen der konfessionellen Wohlfahrtspflege in Deutschland, a. a. O., 211 ff

Wolf, M., 2021: Schneller ist nicht immer besser: Sanktionen können sich längerfristig auf die Beschäftigungsqualität auswirken. (https://www.iab-forum.de/schneller-ist-nicht-immer-besser-sanktionen-koennen-sich-laengerfristig-auf-die-beschaeftigungsqualitaet-auswirken/)

Woratschka, R., 2021: Reformideen des Pflegebevollmächtigten „Es braucht mutige Konzepte", in: Tagesspiegel am 18.05.2021. (https://www.tagesspiegel.de/politik/reformideen-des-pflegebevollmaechtigten-es-braucht-mutige-konzepte/27201934.html)

Younes, N./Reips, U.-D., 2017: The changing psychology of culture in German-speaking countries: A Google Ngram study, in: International Journal of Psychology 53(S1), 53–62

Zahariadis, N., 2007: The Multiple Stream Framework: Structure, Limitations, Prospects, in: Sabatier, P.A., (Ed.), Theories of the Policy-Process, Boulder (2. Aufl.), 65 ff

Zimmer, A./Paul, F., 2018: Zur volkswirtschaftlichen Bedeutung der Sozialwirtschaft, in: Grunwald, K./Langer, A., (Ed.): Sozialwirtschaft, a. a. O., 103 ff

Zimmer, A./Speth, R., 2015: Einleitung. Von Interessenvertretung zu „Lobby Work", in: Zimmer, A./Speth, R. (Ed.), Lobby Work. Interessenvertretung als Politikgestaltung, a. a. O., 9 ff

Zinn, S./Kreyenfeld, M./Bayer, M. 2020: Kinderbetreuung in Corona-Zeiten: Mütter tragen die Hauptlast, aber Väter holen auf, DIW aktuell 51 vom 28. Juli 2020, Berlin: DIW

Zohlnhöfer, R. (2019). Zwischen Stagnation, Reform und Krisenreaktion, in: Zwischen Stillstand, Politikwandel und Krisenmanagement, 645–664, Wiesbaden: Springer VS

Zohnlhöfer, R./Herweg, N., 2014: Paradigmatischer Wandel in der deutschen Arbeitsmarktpolitik: Die Hartz-Gesetze, in: Rüb, F. W. (Ed.), Rapide Politikwechsel in der Bundesrepublik. Theoretischer Rahmen und empirische Befunde, a. a. O., 93–125

The manufacturer's authorised representative in the EU is Springer Nature Customer Service Centre GmbH, Europaplatz 3, 69115 Heidelberg, Germany. If you have any concerns regarding our products, please contact ProductSafety@springernature.com

Printed and bound by CPI Group (UK) Ltd, Croydon, CR0 4YY
28/09/2026
02224076-0002